Turning the Legislative Thumbscrew

Turning the Legislative Thumbscrew

Minority Rights and Procedural Change in Legislative Politics

Douglas Dion

Ann Arbor

THE UNIVERSITY OF MICHIGAN PRESS

First paperback edition 2001
Copyright © by The University of Michigan 1997
All rights reserved
Published in the United States of America by
The University of Michigan Press
Printed and bound by CPI Group (UK) Ltd, Croydon, CR0 4YY

2004   2003   2002   2001   5   4   3   2

A CIP catalog record for this book is available from the British Library.

Library of Congress Cataloging-in-Publication Data

Dion, Douglas, 1961–
    Turning the legislative thumbscrew : minority rights and
procedural change in legislative politics / Douglas Dion.
        p.   cm.
    Includes bibliographical references and index.
    ISBN 0-472-10820-4 (cloth)
    1. United States. Congress—Rules and practice.   2. Parliamentary
practice—United States.   3. Legislative bodies—United States.
    I. Title.
    KF4937.D56   1997
    342.73'05—dc21   97-22819
                                                                       CIP

ISBN 0-472-08826-2 (pbk. : alk. paper)

ISBN13 978-0-472-10820-6 (cloth)
ISBN13 978-0-472-08826-3 (paper)
ISBN13 978-0-472-02269-4 (electronic)

For Mary

yet behold, always as you turn your legislative thumbscrew, and will press and even crush till Refractories give way . . .
—Thomas Carlyle, *The French Revolution*

Contents

Contents

Preface

In this book, I try to understand why majorities within legislatures take away minority rights at particular times rather than others. The main context for studying this problem is the nineteenth-century House of Representatives, an institution that over roughly six decades enacted a number of procedural reforms that relieved the minority of its most effective tools for obstruction. The explanation for the particular timing of these changes, I argue, can be found in the strategic interaction of majorities and minorities, and in the realized fortunes of electoral contest. When majorities are small, they are more cohesive. A cohesive majority forces the minority to forgo hopes of "dividing and conquering" the majority party. As a result, minorities will utilize obstruction, attempting to stop the majority from implementing its policy program. Majorities, recognizing the problem of obstruction, enact procedural changes that deprive the minority of the tools of obstruction.

In making this argument, I have two basic aims. The first is to focus attention on legislatures as interesting sites for the study of issues of majority rule and minority rights. It would, of course, be ludicrous to say that legislative scholars haven't been concerned with these issues, but for the most part they have been concerned with the majoritarian or nonmajoritarian *effects* of legislative arrangements. Does the committee system undermine the majoritarian possibilities of the American political system? How does legislation alter the structure of minority rights within society? These and other questions are extremely important. At the same time, however, the ability of many legislatures to determine for themselves the rules under which they will be governed suggests that we look at the institutional structure of legislatures as an instrument for the *construction* of a regime of minority rights within a majoritarian institution. We know exceptionally little about minority rights within legislatures. This book attempts a contribution, with hopes that others will follow.

The second aim is more thoroughly methodological. The study of American political development has, in my view, made a stunning contribution to the literature on American politics. Most importantly, this literature has eroded the aura of American exceptionalism that falsely justifies the continued disjuncture between the study of American politics and the study of comparative politics. A key argument in that transformation has been the recognition that structural–functional models are radically incomplete. In many ways, the literature on legislative organization has yet to come to grips with this finding. Thus we often find the ghost of some dead sociologist lurking in the dreary garden of American legislatures: legislatures change in response to their environment. One of the purposes of this book, which is one I believe I share with the literature on American political development, is the desire if not to exorcise this pernicious apparition, then at least to force it to see reason. The response to environmental changes is always strategic, a result of the interplay of state officials within an institutional context.

I also follow the literature on American political development in using comparative evidence to check accounts about American politics. With notable exceptions, the study of legislative politics in the United States is primarily centered on the study of the U.S. Congress and in particular the House of Representatives. While more studies of the Senate are being produced, we are still far from equal representation of the two houses in the field of legislative studies. And, again with exceptions, our understanding of the House vastly exceeds our understanding of state legislatures, or even non–U.S. national legislatures. The solution is not to have other people do the checking for theories of the U.S. House, but for those who look at the House to begin thinking comparatively.

But where I depart from much of the literature on American political development is my insistence that institutional transformation be explained as a result of strategic calculation. I mean only that I insist that *my* explanations be formally modeled, not that anyone else's should. My motivation for doing formal modeling is a bit perverse, and in these times when imperialist motives are always suspected, let me be clear about them. Reading American political history with an eye toward theoretical explanation reveals either that those theoretical explanations occupy perhaps a scant paragraph or line here and there (the average historian), or that the theoretical explanations are so rich and multifaceted that one could not imagine what pattern of historical occurrences they would not fit (the average political scientist). Let me state here that I am well aware of the pitfalls of an obnoxious concern with falsification and that I am also aware that we should see the world in all its delicious variety. Call it the malaise of modernity or what have you, but I do not find those sorts of approaches ultimately satisfying. My preference is for a theory that can easily be shown to be incorrect. Exploring the reasons for its failure is much more interesting than a too-easy incorporation of every new fact that comes along.

At the same time, however, I recognize that the formal literature has treated Clio as cordially as the Wicked Witch treated Dorothy. Consequently, my aim in this work has been to try hard to take the historical side of the enterprise as seriously as the formal side. No one is more aware than I how the historical record eludes the grasp of the formal theory at many places. My modest claim is that no one *would have noticed* (well, maybe a few of you eagle-eyes out there) had I simply placed an ambiguous theoretical structure at the front of the historical enterprise or had I placed an ambiguous historical account at the end of the formal enterprise. It is precisely the desire to have readers notice the flaws (and thus to work harder to avoid them) that I think motivates the best theoretical work, formal or otherwise. Perhaps the biggest flaw that will be noticed is how far short the work falls from this ideal.

It is through no naive wish to appease critics (can they ever be appeased?) that I admit that in the pages to follow, I fully expect democratic theorists to be disappointed with the democratic theory, formal theorists to be disappointed with the formal theory, historians to be disappointed with the history, and curmudgeons to be disappointed with the whole. But my hope is that each will find partial contentment. Like a relative's smile at a piano recital, historians and democratic theorists may exhibit pleasant surprise that deductive work is willing to take history and democratic thought at least somewhat seriously. Historians and formal theorists may be happy to see their banners advanced in the field of democratic theory. One can work through all the permutations: if even one of them holds true, this work will have some value.

A brief preview for the impatient. In the first chapter, I set out the argument for seeing obstruction as a minority right. Once obstruction is seen as a minority right, then, I argue, the House of Representatives during the partisan era (for my purposes, 1837–95) becomes a critically useful case. Chapter 2 contains the theory of the conditions under which majorities will limit minority rights. Much of the presentation in this chapter is mathematical. I have tried to make the chapter as self-contained as possible (so that those who are willing to do some unfamiliar thinking might get through it), but I have also presented the basic argument as clearly as I can for nonmathematical readers. These first two chapters constitute part 1 of the book, and taken together set out the conditions under which majorities will limit minority obstruction.

Part 2 of the book presents the evidence from the record of procedural changes that took place in the House of Representatives over the partisan era. It is worth noting that just 10 years ago it was still considered a rarity to have a formal theory tested against empirical evidence. Those days are fading, gone I suppose the way of skinny ties, beta tapes, and undergraduate memories of the Reagan presidency. Chapter 3 begins the empirical section of the book with a discussion of some initial empirical tests. Formal theories often have a number of moving parts and assumptions, and it is often the case that these foundational claims are left unassessed: this chapter constitutes my attempt to right the balance. Chapters 4 and 5 are dedicated to exploring in detail the major rules changes that took place in the partisan era, with the Civil War as the dividing line between the two chapters. I show that in all four major rules-change years identified in the literature, rules changes regarding obstruction were adopted, and that the votes (but more importantly the *rhetoric*) regarding these rules changes divided along party lines. Rational choice is often criticized for being stunningly unconcerned with the self-understandings of historical agents. I hope through this intensive study of the congressional debates to show that concerns over majority rule and minority rights (and in particular, rights to obstruct) were central to what was going on. Chapter 6 takes up (and hopefully quiets) concerns about the problem of "selecting on the dependent variable." The cumulative outcome of these chapters, I believe, is to establish the plausibility of the account I am sketching here for the historical pattern of rules changes in the partisan era House.

There is, of course, nothing in the formal theory that specifically states that the results "do not apply outside the lower House of the American legislature in the nineteenth century." This is an important objection to formal models of the legislative process, which tend almost invariably to be (modern) House-centered. I thus turn in the third part of the book to other institutions. Chapter 7 considers the steps taken to limit obstruction in the U.S. Senate. The Senate's tradition of free debate might make it seem to be a relatively unlikely place for the partisan calculations I have suggested to obtain, but I think the reader will find that they do. The chapter also contains what I believe to be the first statistical treatments of cloture in the Senate, shedding light on among other things the relationship between cloture reform and the civil rights era.

While a comparison of the House and the Senate is more comparative than American legislative studies often gets, it is still quite narrow. If my claims regarding American political development and comparative analysis are to have even the false ring of sincerity, I need to do a little more than look at American institutions. Chapter 8 therefore applies the theory to two non-American legislatures, the House of Commons and the Austrian Parliament. While there is certainly a great deal more work to be done, I hope that in these pages the reader will find convincing evidence that it may be likely that the processes discussed here are not simply a fluke of the nineteenth-century House or of American exceptionalism.

The final portion of this work (chapter 9) offers a conclusion and some suggestions for future work. In that chapter, I compare the theory presented here with more general accounts of minority rights. I explicitly disclaim in the text and I also disclaim here any pretension to having formulated a general account of minority rights. Nonetheless, by thinking through the implications of the results presented here, we may get a better handle on the possible limits of these "general" theories.

Charles Baudelaire wrote that he had no political convictions, as those of his century understood them, because he had no ambition. In that sense, this book too is apolitical. Such a disclaimer becomes necessary given the intensely partisan context in which this book was written. Republican members have for many years complained about the lack of respect for minority rights, an argument wrapped up quite tightly with concerns about House Republicans as a "permanent minority." It appears that permanence, like nostalgia, is not what it used to be: now that the Republicans have captured the majority, Democrats seem to have found a new respect for the rights of the opposition (few signs of which could have been more fascinating than the debate on the adoption of the rules for the 104th Congress, which witnessed—mirabile dictu—Democrats impugning Republicans for the use of restrictive procedures). I have tried in this book to maintain an exacting balance in my treatment of majority rule and minority rights. Where I seem to defend the right of the minority to obstruct on the one hand or the actions of the majority to eliminate obstruction on the other, I hope the reader will be gracious enough to infer no partisan subtext.

Acknowledgments

I doubt if I would have been an academic had it not been for C. Ford Runge, whose undergraduate course on democratic theory at the University of North Carolina–Chapel Hill introduced me to the issues of institutional change, democratic theory, and strategic interdependence. William Keech kindly took me under his wing when Ford departed, directing my honors thesis and providing my first real glimpse into what positive political theory was all about. Thanks also to John Aldrich, who helped convince me that political science might be more appropriate for me than agricultural economics. Aldrich's work on parties in legislatures has had a deep impact on my thinking and I shall be eternally grateful for his generosity in allowing me to read his work in prepublication form.

This book had its start as a Ph.D. dissertation in the Department of Political Science at the University of Michigan. I would like to thank the members of that committee—Bob Axelrod, John Chamberlin, Allan Gibbard, Rick Hall, and especially John Kingdon—for their continuing support and advice. I would also like to thank Chris Achen, Nancy Burns, Don Herzog, John Huber, and Bob Pahre for offering the kind of comments that those familiar with their high scholarly standards would expect. They all appear to be motivated by an irrational personal affection which is warmly reciprocated. Pradeep Chhibber listened too long and too patiently. A note of appreciation as well to Kenneth Organski for saying the right thing at the right time.

Much of what follows has benefited from the generous comments of those who have heard me give talks based on this work or who have corresponded with me about it. I would in particular like to thank James Alt, Stephen Ansolabehere, Sarah Binder, Henry Brady, David Canon, Jim Fearon, Gary King, and George Tsebelis. They have probably forgotten what they said, but I haven't. The work presented in the third part of this book would have been impossible without a grant of release time from the Department of Political Science, and the University of Michigan's junior leave policy. I am grateful as well to David Crampton and Ravi Bhavnani for providing research assistance at crucial stages. A tip of the hat as well to Kevin M. Rennells of the University of Michigan Press for saving me from numerous editorial howlers.

I would also like to record here my deep personal thanks to Juan Lopez and especially to Dan Brzozowski. In a very real sense, I could not have completed this book without them.

George Dion taught me the value of integrity. Carole Dion made me a social scientist by continually asking in as many contexts as you can imagine "Why do people do that?" It is easier letting this work go out knowing their love is not contingent on its fortunes.

There are two people left to thank. While Katrina may (with luck) get her own book someday, this one belongs to Mary Knudson. I hope its pages repay her faith in me.

PART 1

Minority Rights in Legislatures

That the forms of proceeding, as instituted by our ancestors, operated as a check and controul on the actions of Ministers; and that they were, in many instances, a shelter and protection to the minority, against the attempts of power.

—Arthur Onslow, Speaker of the House of Commons

The right of the minority is to draw its pay, and its function is to make a quorum.

—Thomas Brackett Reed,
Speaker of the House of Representatives

CHAPTER 1

Introduction

"Lucius Catilina, scion of a noble family, had great vigour both of mind and body, but an evil and depraved nature. From youth up he revelled in civil wars, murder, pillage, and political dissension . . . " With these words the Roman historian Sallust in *Bellum Catilinae* introduced the dark figure whose name would become synonymous with conspiracy and the sad decline of the Roman Republic. Catiline was a member of that class one often sees in historical accounts: old money without the money, a family whose name has become its most valuable possession. Like other aristocratic Romans in similar straits, he took to politics (the line between authority and extortion being profitably unclear), but his hopes for prosperity were dashed as he lost election after election to candidates who were, in his opinion, clearly inferior.

Catiline did not see the frustration of his personal ambitions as the sign of a vigorous republic (as we teach the losers of elementary school races and presidential elections to do) but instead as the final confirmation of the need for radical political change. To effect that change, Catiline assembled a circle of conspirators, revealing his plans for armed revolt (with the subsequent abolition of debts) only after having those assembled first swear an oath sealed with the drinking of human blood. The purpose of this ghoulish ritual, Sallust relates, was "that they might be more faithful to one another because they shared the guilty knowledge of so dreadful a deed" (Sallust, *Cat.* 22).

Social scientists will of course find much to admire in this clever commitment mechanism. Unfortunately the admiration of social scientists has never been a guarantee of success, and news of the plot leaked out through the indiscretion of one Quintus Curius, a coconspirator. Expelled from the Senate for his immorality, Curius is portrayed by Sallust as so thoroughly corrupt as to be witless (he "could neither keep secret what he had heard nor conceal even his own misdeeds"). In what reads as a standard trope of aristocratic decadence, Curius recounted the details to his increasingly distant mistress, the nobly born Fulvia. Fulvia, however, appears not to have been as taken by the tale as Curius had anticipated, for she passed along the revelations to Marcus Tullius Cicero, consul and target of the conspiracy. With this prior warning, Cicero escaped assassination, the insurrection was suppressed, and five of the conspirators were arrested to face trial before the Senate. (Catiline himself escaped, dying in the bloody battle that concluded the revolt, "his body pierced through and through" (Sallust *Cat.* 60).)

Pronouncing sentence on such blatant traitors would seem to be a simple matter, but there were weighty issues to consider. Roman law forbade the lashing of a Roman citizen and also prohibited the Senate from acting as a judicial body. Both considerations made a sentence of death (arguably harsher than lashing) problematic. But to allow the conspirators to escape with their lives might well fuel the fires of future revolt, and postponing the decision could only signal irresolution. The danger of delay outweighing the rest, the Senate chose to act, on the Nones of December (Dec. 5), 63 B.C., ironically (or therapeutically, as one prefers) at the Temple of Concord.

Suetonius has provided us with a glimpse of the proceedings of the Roman Senate on that day. The Senate, with but one exception, appeared to favor the death penalty. That exception was praetor-elect Julius Caesar, who advocated imprisonment and the confiscation of the rebels' estates. The soon-to-be-divine Julius, having come and seen, decided to conquer by delivering a speech suggesting to the Senate that the approval of a death penalty could result in retaliation by the commons. The specter of class warfare appears to have roused close to a majority to Caesar's position, for Suetonius notes,

> Caesar would have prevailed too, for a number had already gone over to him, including Cicero, the consul's brother, had not the address of Marcus Cato kept the wavering senate in line. (*Div. Jul.* 14)

Cato was a leader of the Optimates, the faction opposed by Caesar and the Populares. While classicists never tire of warning potential raiding social scientists that the Optimates and the Populares were not in any sense modern political parties, there was clearly a political cleavage in the Senate, and one that was activated by Caesar's willingness to advocate leniency.

Judging from Suetonius, then, Cato appeared to command a quite fragile majority. Did Caesar recognize that Cato would apparently win this contest, and sit down? It appears not, as Suetonius again makes clear.

> Yet not even then did he cease to delay the proceedings, but only when an armed troop of Roman knights that stood on guard about the place threatened him with death as he persisted in his headstrong opposition. They even drew their swords and made such passes at him that his friends who sat next him forsook him, while a few had much ado to shield him in their embrace or with their robes. (14)

We are accustomed to a Caesar of action, crossing the Rubicon, conquering Gaul, and so forth. But a filibustering Caesar? It would appear so, and one not only willing to engage in obstruction but dissuaded from that course only by the threat of death. Swords apparently do make for effective cloture: Suetonius notes that Caesar kept away from the Senate for the rest of the year.[1]

This may be one of the earliest references to parliamentary obstruction, but it is hardly the last. Judex (a self-described "Democratic Leader") in the *North American Review* of 1890 noted that "the filibustering tactics by which, in recent years, the minorities of legislative bodies have sought to prevent the majorities from exercising control over parliamentary business have awakened in many minds serious doubts as to the future of parliamentary governments" (237). Judex was no mere fin-de-siècle paranoid: his concerns were echoed over a decade later, when Georg Jellinek, after a survey of many of the world's legislatures, wrote in the 1904 *Political Science Quarterly* that "parliamentary obstruction is no longer a mere intermezzo in the history of this or that parliament. It has become an international phenomenon which, in threatening manner, calls in question the whole future of parliamentary government" (Jellinek 1904, 579).

Gloomy prophecies indeed, but stunningly wrong. Despite the concerns, parliamentary government appears to have survived, and if anything is prospering. How then was disaster avoided?

One need not invoke as weighty an intellectual presence as Michel Foucault to note that, for the most part, democratic legislatures have made the transition from punishment to discipline. Roman swords are no longer needed, save perhaps for the truly recalcitrant.[2] Instead, the secret recipe for legislative longevity has been a willingness to alter the existing rules and procedures to limit dilatory tactics. Without the dagger of archaic procedures, obstructionists have been forced to stand idly by and watch as the legislative engine continues relentlessly to churn out legislation.

The ebbing of obstruction has typically been celebrated, not mourned. We see the elimination of procedures allowing delay as a step toward legislative *efficiency*, making it easier for a set of legislators to transact *business*. The language here is not forced: references to the need for businesslike procedures can be easily found in numerous legislative sources. Dr. Josef Redlich argued in his treatment of procedure in the House of Commons that the central problem in the theory and practice of politics, "as it now presents itself, is the manner in which a parliament is to discharge the function of enabling the state to perform its regular *work*"(1908, vol. I, xxiiii; italics in original). A half century later, in a document entitled *Improving the State Legislature*, the Illinois Commission on the Organization of the General Assembly was more direct:

State legislatures throughout the nation have not developed adequate procedures to cope with the increasing problems and responsibilities they now face. There is not present in government the pressure of business competition that compels efficient operation within the private sector of the economy. As a result, modern techniques that are commonplace in industry have seldom been applied to the day-by-day operation of state legislatures. It is paradoxical that our state legislatures should lack the qualities of streamlined efficiency which are the very qualities the world associates with the concept of the American society. (1967, viii)

Efficiency, however, appears to be not as key a feature of American exceptionalism as the Illinois Commission would have us believe. In December 1993, Labour M.P. Dennis Skinner, the "Mangler of Maastricht," uttered the phrase "I spy strangers," delaying the proceedings of the House of Commons for a quarter of an hour while members voted on whether to clear the galleries. This mild act of obstruction brought down the wrath of that pseudonymous editorialist, Bagehot, who in the following week's *The Economist* derided the actions taken in the Commons as "the British legislature at its ridiculous, anachronistic, time-and-money-wasting worst" (57). The prescription for reform is clear enough: eliminate archaic rules that allow such inefficiencies.

The notion that legislative change is welfare-enhancing has held sway, not only over editorial writers and legislative professionals, but also over a number of prominent interpretations of legislative change.[3] David Mayhew (1974) suggests that "in a good many ways the interesting division in congressional politics is not between Democrats and Republicans, but between politicians in and out of office. Looked at from one angle the cult of universalism has the appearance of a cross-party conspiracy among incumbents to keep their jobs" (105). Keith Krehbiel (1991), drawing on his previous theoretical work with Thomas Gilligan (Gilligan and Krehbiel 1987, 1989a, 1989b), has argued that the institutional structure of legislatures is directed at enhancing the transmission of information. The result, he argues, is to enhance welfare: "Regardless of where the realized outcome lies, all legislators benefit from the reduction of uncertainty about the relationship between policies and outcomes" (74). Gary Cox, while recognizing that institutional changes were hardly uncontested (61–62), portrays the struggle over the rights to the floor as a tragedy of the commons. "Each MP wished to exercise the extraordinary parliamentary rights available to him in order to ventilate his, or his constituents', grievances and opinions, but when too many did exercise their rights, the cumulative effect was distressing to all MPs. . . . In order to extricate themselves from the dilemma in which they were entangled, the commons repeatedly took the most obvious way out and abolished the rights that were being abused" (60–61).

These and other scholars could be perfectly right when it comes to explaining particular procedural changes. It is certainly true that majorities and minorities are not always at each other's throats. But if procedures protecting obstruction *are* truly inefficient, then it becomes hard to understand why Roman knights needed swords, or why parliamentary government might be in jeopardy from obstruction. All one would have to do, presumably, is sit down with the obstructionists and show them how much better off they would be with a more efficient procedural structure. Faced then with the irrefutable fact of legislative gains to be had, members of all parties would more likely be expected to join together in celebration, perhaps in a moment of legislative ecstasy similar to that sweet abandon following Lamourette's suggestion in 1792 to a badly troubled Legislative Assembly teetering on the edge of revolutionary collapse that an oath of "eternal fraternity" be taken, sealed with an embrace.[4]

But eliminating archaic procedures is hardly as idyllic as this amiable picture might suggest. Rules changes in legislatures are instead often highly conflictual, bloody affairs, with charges and countercharges, entreaties and snubs, subtle insinuations and brazen rudeness, sometimes even fisticuffs and arrests, all belying the peaceful notions of welfare enhancement and Pareto optimality that we all too often subscribe to. It is more likely, in these heated moments, that legislators would approach each other not with a kiss but with a bludgeon, and with a fraternalism reminiscent, if anything, of Cain and Abel.

Majority Rule and Minority Rights

Why then is obstruction so difficult to eliminate? The puzzle becomes a little easier to solve, I will argue, if we think about the reform of archaic procedures not as the simple act of eliminating inefficiency but instead as a potential change in a system of *minority rights*. Minority rights are opposition rights, the rights of members of the opposition to challenge the actions of the majority. And this is precisely what archaic rules and inefficient procedures do: they allow the minority to gum up the works, to delay and if possible defeat legislation that they do not favor.

Of course, the set of minority rights includes much more than obstruction. The right to offer amendments can also be a minority right. So, too, the right to vote, the right to demand a quorum, the right of representation on committees—all of these might be added to a list of potential minority rights. A complete characterization of minority rights is not necessary here. Instead, all that is required is that we recognize obstruction as an important element of the mix.

If archaic procedures protect minority rights, then we shouldn't be surprised if vigorous debate ensues over attempts to eliminate these "inefficiencies." People tend to object when their rights are being taken away, especially conventional rights (see Thompson 1971). In such situations, arguments about potential gains to efficiency from those most likely to benefit are unlikely to be persuasive.[5]

But is obstruction a minority *right?* One could enter here into a long and protracted discussion of all the issues involved in a theory of rights (origins, conditions, limits, and so on). I will however be mercifully short and simply defer to the influential formulation by Ronald Dworkin (1977):

> Individual rights are political trumps held by individuals. Individuals have rights when, for some reason, a collective goal is not a sufficient justification for denying them what they wish, as individuals, to have or to do, or not a sufficient justification for imposing some loss or injury upon them. (Dworkin 1977, xi)

While this definition does have weaknesses—most notably that it fails to specify the content of rights—it does provide one important view of what a right is. And on that definition, we can see that obstruction does indeed operate as a "political trump." Collective goals such as passing a particular piece of legislation, going to sleep before 3:00 A.M., getting home for the holidays, none of these is a sufficient argument for refusing the minority party a course of action permissible under the rules. Thus the procedures of legislatures function precisely as political trumps (and thus minority rights) in Dworkin's sense.

While I will defend the notion of obstruction as a minority right, I do want to disavow two possible (mis)readings of my intentions. First, I recognize that, whatever their pretensions to populism, legislatures are often "elite" institutions, with the lack of diversity that inevitably implies. It is important to state, therefore, that I am not in this work claiming to have exposed some secret root of minority suppression. I fall quite short (for example) of a full account of how minorities of all sorts, not just partisan but also minorities with respect to race, ethnicity, religion, gender, and sexual preference, have been treated within legislatures. If the claims advanced here do turn out to be part of a broader theoretical account of minority rights outside of legislatures, it will be through the workings of chance, not insight.[6]

Second, in arguing that obstruction can be viewed as a minority right, I am not claiming that every minority should be allowed a veto in every legislature. Much ink has been spilled in attempting to set out the definitive boundary between majority rule and minority rights. I am reluctant to engage in such cartography, however, without knowing more about the terrain. Tell me more about which majorities and which minorities we might be talking about, on which issues, and I would be a bit more likely to set out markers (or better still direct you to others better able to handle such questions).

Does this imply that one need be a thorough nihilist on the question of minority rights? I do not believe so. It would be more mature and honest, I think, to view the choices involved in determining a set of minority rights along the lines suggested by Martha Nussbaum in *The Fragility of Goodness*. Nussbaum powerfully argues that part of what makes a decision moral is not (simply) the outcome but also the internal conflicts one goes through in arriving at the final decision. A Benthamite moral calculator who simply reckons that indeed, his daughter must perish for the good of the community, and with a smile and a whistle goes about accomplishing this end, would rightly be subject to scorn and ridicule.

The antiseptic portrayals of legislative changes regarding minority rights should treated with similar scorn. Even if it is agreed (by whom?) that minority obstruction must go, there is nothing to be lost in recognizing that minority rights are being eliminated, that the tools used by the loyal opposition to defend itself are being disassembled; and no glossy patina of efficiency should be allowed to take that away.

Studying Minority Rights in the House of Representatives

If we see obstruction as a minority right, then studying the changes that have taken place within the House of Representatives is quite apt. For whether we trace the conflict back to Greek concerns about force and justice or more modern reflections on the demise of the confessional state, the tension between majority rule and minority rights has certainly run, as Robert Dahl (1956) put it, like a "red thread" through much of American political thought. Indeed (although this may be damning with faint praise), Madison's proposed solution to the problem of majority tyranny is arguably the greatest gift American letters has made to the long tradition of Western political thought. And, as unlikely as it may appear, the House of Representatives is in many ways the fulcrum of that discussion.

To recall Madison's argument: with a single, popularly elected institution holding all the keys of power, there would be no checks on the potential for majorities to tyrannize over minorities. To guard against this possibility, Madison argued for expanding the set of interests:

> Extend the sphere and you take in a greater variety of parties and interests; you make it less probable that a majority of the whole will have a common motive to invade the rights of other citizens; or if such a common motive exists, it will be more difficult for all who feel it to discover their own strength and to act in unison with each other. (*Federalist* No. 10)

However masterfully this passage may seem to reconcile republicanism and empire, even extending the sphere of interests was not, it appears, adequate to guarantee minority rights. There was still the danger that legislative, judicial, and executive power would eventually collect in a single institution, something that Madison considered "the very definition of tyranny" (*Federalist* No. 47). And Madison left very little doubt as to which of these three distinct entities was the most likely winner: "The legislative department is everywhere extending the sphere [!] of its activity and drawing all power into its impetuous vortex" (*Federalist* No. 48).

To battle this legislative leviathan (to borrow a phrase), the mere division of responsibilities would not be sufficient to keep the three powers separate ("Will it be sufficient to mark, with precision, the boundaries of these departments . . . and to trust to these parchment barriers against the encroaching spirit of power?" asks *Federalist* No. 48). Instead, there is the famous formulation, "Ambition must be made to counteract ambition. The interest of the man must be connected with the constitutional rights of the place" (*Federalist* No. 51). Thus the executive, legislative, and judicial branches would be set apart, and through the alchemy of human nature each branch would jealously guard its respective terrain.

But even this did not leave Madison feeling sufficiently secure. He went still further in asserting that the legislature must be made to check itself, through the institution of bicameralism. With a Senate differing in composition from the popularly elected House, the probability of "sinister combinations" would be decreased. Furthermore,

> the necessity of a senate is not less indicated by the propensity of all single and numerous assemblies to yield to the impulse of sudden and violent passions, and to be seduced by factious leaders into intemperate and pernicious resolutions. Examples on this subject might be cited without number; and from proceedings within the United States, as well as from the history of other nations. But a position that will not be contradicted need not be proved. All that need be remarked is that a body which is to correct this infirmity ought itself to be free from it, and consequently ought to be less numerous. (*Federalist* No. 62)

This of course completes the justification for the institutional structure of American national government: a president, a Supreme Court, and a bicameral legislature composed of a Senate elected by the state legislatures and a House of Representatives directly elected by the people.

The whole Madisonian edifice is thus constructed to guarantee one outcome: containing majoritarian passions within the House of Representatives and preventing their spread outside those halls. The larger size, the relentless balancing of interests, none of this makes a great deal of sense if a popularly elected legislature were able to check any impetus toward majority tyranny. Given the Madisonian argument, then, we should expect the House to have been and continue to be a hotbed of majoritarian sentiment, occasionally boiling over, checked only by the ambitious counterdesigns of the inhabitants of the other institutions of American government.

Filibustering in the House

Surprisingly, however, the history of the House of Representatives does not bear out Madison's fears at all. Instead, throughout the first century of its existence, the House of Representatives operated under a system of rules and procedures that provided the minority with a rather formidable arsenal of tactics for delaying (if not thwarting) the power-grabbing designs of passionate majorities (Galloway 1969, 52–53).

Perhaps most infamous was the so-called disappearing quorum. The Constitution explicitly requires that a majority of members constitutes a quorum for the purpose of taking action in the House and Senate. Literary theorists will be overjoyed (well, as overjoyed as that lot ever gets) to hear that even this apparent clarity is subject to the vagaries of interpretation. While the Constitution does say that a majority constitutes a quorum, it sadly does not explicitly indicate how one should count that majority. Counting would seem to be a skill easily within the capacities of seasoned American politicians, but as qualitative researchers are fond of pointing out, there is an immense difference between knowing *how* to count and knowing *what* to count. The Constitution is silent on the question of whether members need merely be present to be counted for the purposes of a quorum or whether in addition they would also have to vote. House practice during most of the nineteenth century followed the latter interpretation. This would be a distinction without a difference if the House could compel members to vote (the House has always had the power to compel members to attend). But an 1832 precedent (established by that venerable anti-Mason and ex-president, John Quincy Adams) guaranteed that members could legitimately refuse to vote, and the House had no power to compel them to do otherwise. Thus the "disappearing quorum": a clear majority of people present on the floor, but refusing to vote and therefore not to be counted for the purpose of establishing a quorum. And without a quorum, the legislature cannot act.

The disappearing quorum is not as laughably childish as it appears on its face. Members of the opposition quite forcefully defended the practice, arguing that it merely required the majority to have enough of its members present to vote. Why, they reasoned, should the majority be able to pass legislation only with the active participation of a dissenting minority? But the force of this argument only underlines the weakness of the tactic. Since the disappearing quorum simply required the majority to get enough members together, it functioned as a relatively imprecise check on majoritarian tempers.

Much more effective was the utilization of multiple dilatory motions. Consider, for example, the debate on the Kansas–Nebraska Act. This was one of the most important pieces of legislation in the nineteenth century, and it quite likely set off a political realignment that resulted in sectional parties and eventually in the Civil War.[7] We might expect, given our constant whining about the decline of the legislative arts, that this bill would have provided ample opportunity for all the rhetorical flourishes and fireworks that the Hollywood of yesteryear and the C-Span of today have led us to anticipate from nineteenth-century politicians. There were indeed fireworks: the opposition forced more than one hundred roll calls. One addressed the weighty issue of whether the House should adjourn at 2:45 P.M. This was closely followed by another vote, on the equally ponderous question of whether the House should adjourn at 3:20. The excitement mounted, one presumes, as the House voted on whether to adjourn at 3:53, 4:08, 4:38, 5:48, 6:30, 7:30, and so on.

This example, on one of the most significant bills in American political history, shows the room offered for the practice of obstruction under the House rules of the nineteenth century. Each motion to adjourn required a roll call vote and thus the consumption of at least 15 minutes of House time. Working through the eight votes listed in the previous paragraph, therefore, would take a full two hours. But even this did not exhaust the dilatory possibilities. Members could in addition ask to be excused from voting on the motion to adjourn, a request that (of course) required its own roll call. A second is demanded on the motion to excuse: another roll call. But can't a member be excused from voting on the roll call to second the motion to excuse the member from voting on the roll call on the motion to adjourn? And so it begins again.

Even the tools designed to stop delay could, paradoxically, be used in the service of obstruction. The "previous question" is a procedure used to cut off debate and bring matters to a vote. It would thus seem to be the perfect solution to problems of obstruction. But the previous question itself of course had to be voted on and would therefore be subject to a possible disappearing quorum as well as multiple dilatory roll calls. This is simple pie, however, compared to the question of how one moves the previous question, and cuts off debate, on a debate about moving the previous question. It took minds of the caliber of Russell and Gödel to work through the problems raised by self-referentiality in mathematics and logic; as these examples show, minority members of the nineteenth-century House understood the principle much earlier, and they were a great deal more persistent in following up the practical implications.

Of course, it would be ludicrous to argue that these tactics made it impossible for legislation to pass in the nineteenth century. Majorities could pass bills, even given the ability of the minority to obstruct. But this fact alone does not indicate that minorities were powerless. Even ignoring the bills the minority prevented from being considered due to lack of time, they could still utilize the filibuster to extract policy concessions. During the 1880 Hayes–Tilden electoral contest, a political event that almost plunged the nation back into civil war, members of the Democratic party freely engaged in obstructionist tactics. One of the main features of the Scott Plan (that "Corrupt Bargain" ending the debacle and electing Rutherford B. Hayes) was the exchange of railroads and (federally) unsupervised elections in the South for an end to the filibuster (Woodward 1951). This was of course quite a price to pay to end obstruction on a single legislative action, effectively abandoning even the pretense to Reconstruction and paving the way for the disfranchisement of African American voters in the South for the remainder of that century and the bulk of the next.

While majorities in the House could always bargain with minorities, they had at their disposal an even more effective response: procedural change. Minorities were after all only able to obstruct because the rules allowed them to do so. But these rules were, then as now, adopted by a majority vote of all members of the House at the start of each Congress, and they could be changed throughout a legislative session. Consequently, by voting to change the rules, a majority in the House could, at any time, easily have eliminated provisions allowing the minority the ability to obstruct legislation. While many might fault the minority for its use of dilatory tactics, Henry Cabot Lodge knew exactly who was responsible: "No minority is ever to blame for obstruction. If the rules permit them to obstruct, they are lawfully entitled to use those rules in order to stop a motion which they deem injurious. The blame for obstruction rests with the *majority*, and if there is obstruction, it is because the majority permits it" (quoted in Haynes 1938, vol. I, 399; emphasis in original).

Majority Rule and the Timing of Procedural Change

Lodge's formulation opens up another puzzle, however. If majorities are obstructed by minorities, and if those minorities are able to obstruct only because of procedural advantages secured by the rules, and if those rules are themselves determined by the majority, then why doesn't the majority simply change the rules and eliminate the offensive minority rights? Or, to put the matter in a more empirically interesting way, why is it that majorities limit minority rights to obstruct at some times rather than others?

It may be objected here that accounting for the timing of institutional change is an unrealistic ambition. We are, after all, dealing with institutional innovation, and when we try to come up with explanations of innovation, as

Jon Elster (1983, 9) phrases it, we will inevitably veer close to treating "creativity as a dependent variable."[8] One can find numerous factors making Monet's choice of water lilies as a subject quite likely: water lilies are beautiful, they provide a dramatic contrast with reflected water, the relationship between the lilies and the water changes with the season as well as the hour of the day; one could go on. But how could we produce a theory that would tell us why water lilies instead of waterfalls? Saying "Monet was a genius" only coalesces our ignorance in a word, and attempting something more general steers us close to arguing that "Anyone could have been Monet," a position which sounds (at least to anyone who isn't a Marxist) fairly absurd. How then can we realistically hope to explain the factors leading people to come up with a particularly novel solution to a pressing problem?

This formulation of the problem, however, makes things appear more difficult than they actually are, at least when it comes to explaining many institutional changes in legislatures. We can make some headway by utilizing Schumpeter's distinction between *innovation* and *adoption*.[9] That is, we are often not really very interested in how individuals came up with a solution; instead we are interested in understanding why a particular institutional change came to be embraced. It turns out that many of the institutional changes we will explore in this book had often been formulated previously, and some were even the subject of previous collective deliberation. We are clearly not dealing with procedural changes that had to be pulled out of thin air. For others, the solution was hardly difficult to arrive at. If members are able to delay proceedings by talking as long as they want, it hardly takes a Monet or a Madison to realize that imposing a time limit on debate is a solution.

This suggests that timing is a valuable technique for gauging the reliability of our accounts of institutional change. But focusing on timing brings with it two additional advantages. The first is that timing inevitably requires that we become sensitive to historical considerations. At the most superficial level, you cannot hope to explain timing if you do not know when things took place. The second advantage is that it forces us to recognize that minority rights within a legislature *has* a history. This is hardly a novel insight: anyone who has read any of the literature on race, class, or gender can recognize that these categories are not fixed, but have changed through time. Similarly, minority rights within legislatures are not fixed; instead, what the minority is capable of (which is partially constitutive of what it means to be the minority) is significantly determined by the prevailing structure of institutional rules.

Some Alternative Accounts

Why then do majorities act at some times rather than others? We have already encountered one explanation: the press of business, which requires the "expeditious" handling of legislative demands. The nineteenth century witnessed the transformation of the United States from an underdeveloped agrarian backwater to a modern industrial state. This powerful transformation ushered in new demands for political action, such as the regulation of railroads and trusts. Members of Congress submitted bills to take care of the demands of a growing nation, but the antique system of rules in the House slowed down the consideration of these new bills. Consequently, by changing the rules, the House was able to weaken the stresses on the institution caused by the need to regulate a growing economy.

The idea that rules changes in the House are the result of increased workload demands (which themselves stem from the industrial development of the nation) can be found as early as Hinds 1899. It is presented as well in MacNeil 1963, 41; Galloway 1969, 50; Cooper 1977, 152; and Keller 1977, 299–307. Indeed, as noted above, this theory is supported by comparative evidence: procedural change within the House of Commons was effected in an effort to master the increasing workload facing this legislature (Cox 1987).

If the workload account is true, then we should be able to explain procedural changes with reference to pressing business. Another potential explanation for the timing of limits on minority rights, one putting more emphasis on the partisan elements, is provided by the notion of reciprocity.[10] Simply put, today's majorities will be dissuaded from crushing minority rights by fear of being tomorrow's minority. When that fear disappears, majorities will crush their opponents.

This position attracts a quite diverse set of supporters. Lani Guinier (1994), for example, puts it this way:

> . . . even a self-interested majority can govern fairly if it cooperates with the minority. One reason for such cooperation is that the self-interested majority values the principle of reciprocity. The self-interested majority worries that the minority may attract defectors from the majority and become the next governing majority. The Golden Rule principle of reciprocity functions to check the tendency of a self-interested majority to act tyrannically. (3–4)

Guinier calls majorities that rule but do not dominate "Madisonian" and ends her piece on the tyranny of the majority with the hope that a greater number of us will aspire to this sort of rule.

It is quite unexpected, therefore, to find the same argument being put forward by conservative Republicans such as Newt Gingrich in the days before his rise to the Speakership. Even former GOP Leader Robert Michel, hardly a bombthrower, had this to say:

> Thirty-five years of uninterrupted power can act like a corrosive acid upon the restraints of civility and comity. Those who have been kings of

the Hill for so long may forget that majority status is not a divine right—
and minority status is not a permanent condition. (Quoted in Connelly
and Pitney 1994, 86)

Indeed, it is not.

But under what conditions can we expect majorities and minorities to
cooperate? The answer has been provided in a formal treatment by Alberto
Alesina (1988). In a repeated-play framework for two-party competition, he
shows that parties can gain over the one-play game by coordinating strategies.
In essence, the parties concede getting their most preferred policy on those
occasions when they do win for getting a not-so-bad policy when they do not
win. Because the parties are risk averse, they can find some compromise
version that they would both prefer to the lottery that occurs when they
alternate between winning sometimes (and getting exactly the policy they
want) and losing sometimes (and getting the opposition's most preferred
policy). Alesina carries out some comparative statics analyses on these results
and finds that interparty cooperation is most likely when the parties are highly
competitive. This implies that when parties are large, they will have no reason
to bargain with the minority and therefore will obtain their most favored
policy.[11]

The notion that it is large majorities that limit minority rights finds
support in Thomas Jefferson's *Parliamentary Manual*. Cribbing from Clerk of
the House of Commons Thomas Hatsell (who himself only rephrased Speaker
Onslow), Jefferson wrote,

> So far the maxim is certainly true, and is founded in good sense—that, as
> it is always in the power of the majority by 'their numbers' to stop any
> improper measures proposed on the part of their opponents, the only
> weapons, by which the minority can defend themselves against similar
> attempts from those in power, are the forms and rules of proceeding;
> which have been adopted, as they were found necessary, from time to
> time, and are become the Standing Orders of the House; by a strict
> adherence to which, the weaker party alone can be protected from those
> irregularities and abuses, which these forms were intended to check, and
> which the wantonness of power is but too often apt to suggest to large
> and successful majorities.

Jefferson's *Parliamentary Manual* is officially recognized in the House rules
as a guide for parliamentary procedure.[12] It would not therefore be surprising
to find that the argument had some relevance to the history of legislative
politics.

If the reciprocity account is correct, then we should expect majorities to limit minority rights to obstruct when there is no question about their being possibly kicked out of office. Reciprocity has certainly done yeoman's service in the explanation of political events, but the mere fact that reciprocity turns out to be important in many cases does not imply that it is important in this case. In the empirical work to come, therefore, I will attempt to assess how well the reciprocity account does.

Both the workload account and the reciprocity account are closely tied to the internal dynamics of the legislature. Perhaps, however, attitudes toward fundamentals such as minority rights are not determined by the strategic position people find themselves in, but instead individuals refrain from the restriction of minority rights because they hold a certain commitment to democratic deliberation, which they understand as necessarily involving the participation of the minority.

This is the perspective taken by Robert Dahl. At least the early Dahl felt that institutional structures by themselves would be unable to restrain majoritarian tempers should they erupt. He instead placed the burden of protecting minority rights on socialization into the polyarchal norms. Teach people to value the participation of minorities, and minority rights will be preserved. Socialization holds the key.

The problem is, however, that socialization appears to be such a wonderful mechanism for inducing compliance (if it doesn't, we tautologically say they "weren't properly socialized") that its use is not restricted to the preservation of democratic values. We teach children to hold lots of values, and in the course of events some bump up against others. We say "why don't you think before you act" but we also say "don't keep people waiting all day: make up your mind." We teach them that money is good and crime is bad, and then wonder why it is that people sometimes turn to crime as a way to acquire income, or turn away from crime and suffer the loss of some valuable speculative opportunities. Minority rights in legislatures, if you will excuse the crassness, work like Van Goghs at an auction: everyone at some level wants them, they just differ on the price they are willing to pay.

For those who dislike suspense in their social science, I find that workload woefully underexplains the changes in legislative procedure that have taken place with respect to minority rights. In addition, reciprocity does not seem to be playing a very important role in explaining the timing of steps taken to limit minority rights to obstruct legislation. Furthermore, I shall argue that it is not large majorities, as Jefferson suggested, that limit minority rights to obstruct, but small majorities, those, like Cato's majority in the Roman Senate, just barely over the 50 percent threshold, that so act.

Evaluating the socialization argument is much more difficult, especially when it involves attempting to understand the often idiosyncratic political socializations taking place over a century ago and for a rather numerous and diverse set of individuals. Our model, however, might be able to shed some light on this issue. As we shall see, in many cases various individuals vote to retain minority rights, despite what the model would suggest would be their optimal strategy. We could say that they didn't mean it—that it was for public consumption—that they expected to be paid off later—that the costs outweighed the benefits—but all of these seem to turn what reads like principled debate into pantomime.

At the same time, however, there will be numerous cases to the contrary, individuals who in one legislative session will denounce the very rules that in the next section they wholeheartedly endorse, the only factor apparently responsible being that they were once on one side of 50 percent and now are on the other. We don't have to write these off as liars and charlatans. Instead we simply need to recognize that socialization overdetermines behavior here and that other considerations play a role.

Plan of Attack

Legislative workload burdens, large majorities, and socialization are hardly unknown outside the lower house of the U.S. Congress. To better understand the factors leading to majority attempts to limit minority rights to obstruct, therefore, I will in the pages that follow be looking closely at the actual deliberations that took place in a number of legislatures over the rules by which they would be governed, not only of the House but of other legislatures as well. This may seem at this point to promise an intensely soporific experience, prolonging the intolerable misery that would accompany even a simple retelling of parliamentary procedure in the nineteenth-century House. Few of us, after all, stay up late at night reading parliamentary squabbles about the appropriate form of the "previous question" or "urgency motions for adjournment."

If that is the case, then it is solely through the fault of the teller, not the tale. For parliamentary rules changes are hardly the tedious exercise we now think them to be. Indeed, the fact that we consider the issue to be technical is itself the outcome of a debate resolved in many legislatures a century ago. The winners dictate the terms, and in the parliamentary debate the winners rejected obstruction in favor of businesslike efficiency, of "getting down to work." Those sympathizing with this view have written the volumes on parliamentary procedure to which scholars and legislators still defer, and while parliamentary procedure does have its complexities, the tedium has I think been overestimated.

Of course, this is coming from someone who has already shown by the selection of subject a certain (shall we say abnormal?) interest in the archaic rules and procedures of now-forgotten legislative sessions. Consequently, I assure you that in the pages to follow we shall find not only the byzantine conundrums of procedural debate (which I will do my best to simplify) but also wars, adulteries, revolutions, personal vendettas, secret societies (and parties to oppose them), government repression, good humor, and bad taste— all the candy we have come to expect in our politics.

CHAPTER 2

A Partisan Theory of Obstruction
and Procedural Change

And how they despise the vulgar crowd whenever they bring out their triangles, quadrangles, circles and similar mathematical diagrams, piled on top of each other and intertwined like a maze, and then letters of the alphabet which they marshal in line and deploy hither and thither in order to throw dust in the eyes of the less well-informed!

—Erasmus, *Praise of Folly* (1509)

One of the enduring beliefs about politics, held by politicians as well as academicians, is that smaller parties tend to be more cohesive. The importance of party size in explaining party discipline was emphasized in political science as early as 1902, when A. Lawrence Lowell presented his pathbreaking analysis of roll call votes in "The Influence of Party upon Legislation in England and America":

The falling off in the percentage of party votes among the Liberals in 1899 was due, of course, to their being in opposition instead of being in power, and the fact that the party votes of the Conservatives did not show a corresponding increase after they took office is no doubt to be accounted for by their enormous majority, which has been a continual stumbling block in the way of party discipline. (329)

By 1942, E. E. Schattschneider in *Party Government* would, with a clear note of impatience, reiterate the point yet again:

Major parties, let it be said for the hundredth time, are complex structures held together by the fact that disunity means defeat, the fact that the opposition is strong enough to take advantage of any failure of the party in power to maintain a united front. In other words, it is easier to manage a small majority than it is to manage a large majority. (95)

It is not surprising that such an enduring observation would become the target of sustained analysis by rational choice theorists. The first formal treatment of

21

the problem was presented in the seminal work of William Riker in *The Theory of Political Coalitions* (1962). The approach I will follow here is taken from John Aldrich (1988), who places the majority party caucus as the pivotal mechanism in explaining the cohesion of small majorities.[1] Aldrich's model is particularly convincing, as it allows for the presence of multiple issues in politics and also formally incorporates an important partisan institution into formal analyses of decision making in legislatures.

Most analyses of the result on cohesion, however, have tended to concentrate on the implications for the majority party, without considering the minority party. But there are not just majorities on the one hand and minorities on the other; instead there are majorities and minorities that strategically interact. Thinking about the implications of the strategic interaction of majorities and minorities within the context of Aldrich's model (properly amended) supplies, I argue, the key to understanding majority attempts to regulate obstruction.[2]

Consider then what a minority party might do when faced with a cohesive majority. It could try to amend legislation, but if the majority party is cohesive, amendments to majority proposals will fail. Cohesion after all implies that majority members stick by their own proposals and defeat minority counterproposals. The minority could always decide to support the majority's position, but if it does, there is no problem of obstruction and thus no need for procedural change. The only strategy left to a minority who disagrees with the majority, therefore, is to obstruct. A majority either experiencing such obstruction or anticipating it will, I argue, take the necessary procedural steps to limit the potential of the minority to obstruct.

The major advantage of this argument is that it provides an account of the timing of procedural changes regarding minority rights. Once the majority party is small, it will take steps to limit obstruction. If the party grows large again (or if the other party gains the status of a more-than-minimal winning coalition), then the conditions that led to the demand for rules change, that is, majority cohesion and the resulting obstruction, will no longer be present. When the majority party does approach minimal size again, demands for rules changes dealing with obstruction will again occur, with the likely result of procedural change. Checking this account is exceptionally easy: we need only turn to a newspaper and a parliamentary record of debates to find all we need to know.

Placing the emphasis on majority/minority interactions will I hope expand on the promising research agenda established by Charles Jones in his 1970 book *The Minority Party in Congress*. Jones sets out a rich account of majority and minority tactics (richer than the one set out above). But whatever the virtues, the analysis does have one difficulty: it fails to take into account the problem of strategic interaction. The main focus of the explanatory effort is on understanding the *range* of strategies a minority pursues. Do they use multiple strategies? Do they use a moderate number of strategies? This makes intuitive sense: we would think a strong minority would utilize all of the weapons in its arsenal. But looked at from a strategic perspective, this intuitive supposition may not be correct. We aren't any better off killing flies with flyswatters, bazookas, and bowie knives than we are killing them with flyswatters alone (I assume here your average household fly). I raise this point not to criticize Jones, who has done more than anyone to bring the minority party to the fore of legislative studies, but simply to reinforce how much more there is to know about minority party strategies.

It is only recently that the project suggested by Jones has resurfaced. Paul R. Rundquist (1990) limits his analysis to a much shorter time period than Jones, but he provides a much richer data set, exploring a truly remarkable number of possible minority party strategies (I count 42 in all) from the 96th to the 100th Congress (broken down into sessions, no less). Rundquist's interest, however, is understanding when a Republican position prevails, rather than when a particular strategy is utilized in a strategic context. (For a step in that direction, however, see Rohde 1991, 120f.)

Historians have also worked on the problem of minority party strategy, mostly in times of great constraint. Peter Argersinger (1992) covers the constraints encountered by the Populists in the late nineteenth-century House, when the rules that will be discussed in this book made floor influence to a third party virtually impossible. Joel Silbey's 1977 study of Democrats from 1860 to 1868 finds a party much more vibrant than conventional accounts would suggest. But as valuable as these studies are, we need to understand the minority party outside of exceptional situations, and to draw generalizations of their behavior across time.

The desire to understand the strategic interaction of majorities and minorities by itself would be sufficient to justify the use of formal techniques.[3] I am not aware of any other theoretical tradition (certainly not functionalism, structuralism, rational choice of the constrained-maximization sort, or interpretive) that is as capable of yielding insights into strategic action as game theory. Some I think come close: the best interpretive work seems to me to be able to weigh in with a healthy respect for agency, but appears to require a degree of keen insight that I have not been able to acquire. Consequently, game theory seems the most promising avenue for exploring these issues.

Formal Theory of Obstruction and Procedural Change: Some Preliminaries

Market forces might well suggest placing a formal presentation in an appendix or dropping it out completely. Intellectual honesty, I think, requires that arguments be more than black boxes. I have attempted, however, to make the technical details in the following discussion as clear as possible.

To begin our theory of legislative politics, we need to have a legislature. Every legislature is composed of a set of people, so to keep things general we will refer to legislators by number. That is, we let $N = \{1, 2, \ldots, n\}$ be the set of members of the legislature. In some cases, we wish to talk about the generic legislator, so we will refer to that person as "i." Legislatures must make decisions over some set of issues, which we again for generality will denote by the letter X. It is typical in models of this sort to think of issues as being a set of lines (say moving from left to right). We shall assume that there are k issues at stake (which is simply to say that we are letting X be a subset of $\mathbb{R}^k$, the k-dimensional Euclidean space).

Legislators are assumed to care about issues, that is, to have preferences over the set of possible policies. One way to present those preferences is as a subset R_i (for each individual) of $X \times X$. If (x,y) is in R_i, then it can be said that "x is at least as good as y as far as i is concerned." As an example, (Eisenhower, Nixon) $\in R_{\text{Rayburn}}$ means that Rayburn thinks Ike is at least as good as Nixon. Sometimes, however, Rayburn may decide that while Eisenhower is at least as good as Nixon, Nixon isn't at least as good as Eisenhower. When that condition obtains, then Rayburn strictly prefers Eisenhower to Nixon. In notation, this simply means that if (x,y) is in R_i (x is at least as good as y for Rayburn, say) but (y,x) is not (y is not as good as x for Rayburn), then i (here Rayburn) strictly prefers x to y. We shall represent the strict preference relationship as another subset of $X \times X$, namely P_i. (This set would itself be a subset of R_i, since if i strictly prefers x to y, it follows that i thinks x is at least as good as y.)

Now that we have legislators, we will need some way to aggregate their individual preferences into some social decision. A usual method is majority rule, but in many cases other rules such as two-thirds, three-fifths, or unanimity are utilized. Given the numerous possibilities, we shall keep the argument general by saying that social choices over X are made by "q-majority rule," where $q \geq [(n + 1)/2]$ (the term in brackets is a simple majority when there is an odd number of legislators). If at least q individuals prefer x to y, then society prefers x to y. In the model to be presented, the voting rule (q) will vary with the size of the majority party.

Before proceeding, I need to say a bit more about what the set of alternatives looks like. We say that a set X is convex if for any x and y in X and any $0 < \lambda < 1$, the point $z = \lambda x + (1 - \lambda)y$ is also in X. One way to think of this is that there is always some possible intermediate position between any two possible party platforms. (Whether anyone would vote for this compromise is another matter altogether: all we need assume here is that there is one.) Sometimes we are interested in only some small part of the possible party platforms. Let A denote any arbitrary subset of X, the issue space. It is occasionally the case that the set of policy positions we have picked out is not convex. That is, we might have chosen some set of policies for initial consideration, but then found that a compromise between two policies in the set is not a member of that initial consideration set. One way to think about all the possible compromise positions that could occur with a given set A is to invoke the notion of a convex hull (denoted $H(A)$). The convex hull includes all the points in the initial set of policies (A) plus any compromise between those policies (the set of points z satisfying $z = \lambda x + (1 - \lambda)y$ for some x, y in X and some $0 < \lambda < 1$). If A is convex, then the convex hull of A is simply A. Where A is not convex (for example, a doughnut), the convex hull is any point on a line drawn between two points in the set A. (Thus the hole in the doughnut is part of the convex hull of the doughnut but is not part of the doughnut: some spiny eccentrics will of course complain that if they bought a doughnut and there wasn't a hole, they would feel awfully cheated and demand their money back, but such philosophical questions cannot divert us now.)

Convexity isn't the only property that we will be interested in. We will also be interested in having the set of policies be closed. The formal definition of a closed set is a little rough to digest (a set A is closed if for any convergent sequence x^q of points in A, the limit of the sequence, call it y, is also contained in A). An easier way to think of it is to imagine a set of issues and think about moving in some direction (since we are in multiple dimensions, we don't have to limit ourselves to east, west, north, or south; we can go off in any political direction.) A set is closed if, whenever it appears that the line is converging toward some point, it follows that the point is an element of the set. A doughnut is thus a closed set: you can get nearer and nearer to the edge of the doughnut, and even hit the edge. By contrast, a set A is open if its complement (everything that isn't in A) is closed. The hole of a doughnut is an open set, because no matter how close you get to the doughnut while you are in the hole, you can always get just a *little* closer.

It may appear that doughnuts and things like them are the only closed sets there are. But this is not the case, and mathematicians distinguish between two kinds of closed sets (and other, nonclosed, sets as well). Some are unbounded, meaning that in at least one direction the set will go off into infinity. By contrast, a set is bounded if you can find some box (metaphorically speaking) big enough to contain the entire set. The set of numbers $(1, 2, 3, \dots)$ is not bounded, because no matter how big you make a set (say you have space for $10,000,000,000$ numbers), there is always another number you cannot fit ($10,000,000,001$). But it is closed, because when you have a sequence of numbers that seem to converge to a number (such as $1, 2, 3, 3, 3, 3, 3, \dots$ out to infinity), the number that the sequence is converging to (here 3) is in the set. Some sets, on the other hand, are bounded but not closed: the inside of a circle, for example. Still other sets are both closed and bounded, a property known as being *compact*.

With this background, the following assumptions might be a little easier to understand, and they will be useful for the results I want to present here:

ASSUMPTION 1.   *(Convexity and Compactness of Issues)* X *is a compact, convex subset of* k-*dimensional Euclidean space.*

ASSUMPTION 2.   *(Continuity of Preferences) For any* x ∈ X *and any* i ∈ N, *the set* $P_i(x)$ *is open.*

ASSUMPTION 3.   *(Convexity of Preferences) For any* x *and any* i, x ∉ $H(P_i(x))$.

Assumptions 1–3 are fairly standard in the spatial literature. Assumption 1 is intended to rule out cases like voting on how much money to give ourselves: if there is no limit, then we just continue voting until infinity. Assumptions 2 and 3 are intended to provide some structure to preferences. There are preferences that do not satisfy Assumption 2, for example so-called lexicographic preferences. Suppose that I always strictly prefer more guns to fewer guns, but given the same number of guns, I always strictly prefer more butter. It turns out that this sort of preference cannot be represented by a utility function, at least of the standard (Archimedean) sort.

Assumption 3 is a bit harder to figure out. The first thing one is required to do is to pick out some policy (think of some guns–butter tradeoff). Now think of the set of policies that you strictly prefer to the policy you originally picked out. Assumption 3 says that your original policy cannot be a compromise version of any two policies that you strictly preferred to the original policy. My use of the word *compromise* here should not distract one's attention. I am abstracting here from worries about appearing weak by compromising and other strategic concerns. I am simply interested in understanding where you would stand on the issues if these were your only options and you were appointed as dictator.

The usual sorts of utility functions presented in spatial theories satisfy Assumptions 2 and 3. In addition, utility functions that allow individuals to have broad ranges of indifference (and that are not typical in spatial models) also satisfy Assumptions 2 and 3, and therefore such utility functions need not be ruled out here.[4]

Now that we have a set of individuals, a set of policies, and preferences from those individuals over policies, we need to have the individuals interact. The approach taken here will draw on cooperative game theory. A simple game is meant to capture something about coalition formation. Formally, we say that a simple game is a pair (*N,W*), where *N* (as before) is a set of people and *W* is the set of winning coalitions. For example, suppose that we have three people (Groucho, Chico, and Harpo), who must decide on the annual budget for the state of Freedonia. The set *N* is simply the names of the three Marx brothers. The set of winning coalitions, *W*, would, assuming majority rule, be equal to any coalition of Marx brothers that made a majority. There are thus four possible winning coalitions: (Groucho and Chico), (Groucho and Harpo), (Chico and Harpo), and (Groucho, Chico, and Harpo).

We now would like to know what this group is likely to do. One thing seems (deceptively, I think) straightforward: an outcome x will not stay an outcome for long if there is some coalition which (a) is a winning coalition (that is, an element of the set W), and (b) is comprised of individuals, all of whom prefer some other alternative y to x. The argument here is that if a set of people would strictly prefer something other than the status quo, and if they form a winning coalition, then they have the power to guarantee that x does not become the outcome of the legislative game. The formal expression of this thought is that x dominates y (which means that, using our notation, (x,y) is in P_i for all i in some coalition C, which itself is in W). We might be particularly interested in outcomes that cannot be defeated in this way. That is, we could be interested in cases where (a) any coalition that would prefer something else to x is not capable of unilaterally securing its choice, or (b) any coalition capable of unilaterally securing its choice is not comprised of people who all prefer y over x (that is, there is a disagreement in the coalition). If that occurs, then we say that x is an undominated outcome (undominated in the sense that we cannot kick x out given the structure of the game). There can be more than one undominated outcome, so we use the term *the core* to refer to the complete set of undominated outcomes for a particular game.

I have covered the case of majority rule, but the same basic analysis can be used for other forms of voting, such as two-thirds, three-fourths, or unanimity (more generally, for any q-majority rule game). A q-majority rule game is a simple game with n players (nothing has changed yet) in which the set W consists of all coalitions (subsets of N) with at least q players. Thus when n is odd and $q = (n + 1)/2$, it follows that the game is a simple majority rule game, whereas if $q = n$, we have a unanimity game. The letter q here stands for quota, and I shall use that term when referring to the number of individuals needed for a winning coalition in a voting game.

Intermediate Steps

A large literature has developed showing that in simple majority voting games, a core cannot be guaranteed without invoking rather stringent conditions.[5] As a result, it may come as a surprise to find that there are ways in which the voting games could have a core outcome without making hazardous assumptions either on the size of the issue space or the distribution of the preferences of political actors. The trick is recognizing that the existence or non-existence of a core is related to the voting rule as well as to the number of issues. Thus a two-thirds majority may produce a core outcome in situations where majority rule would fail. The key result was shown by Greenberg and is presented in Theorem 1.

THEOREM 1.   (Greenberg 1979, Thm 2) *Let assumptions 1–3 be satisfied. Then there is a core for the* q-*majority rule game whenever*

$$q > \frac{k}{k+1}\, n \tag{1}$$

Proof.   See Greenberg.

This may seem like alchemy, but looking at how the inequality reacts to changes in the parameters may help to bring home what the theorem is saying.

Suppose that we have only 1 issue (that is, $k = 1$). Then the fraction will be equal to $\frac{1}{2}$, and multiplied by n we have $n/2$. That simply means that to guarantee a core in a voting game with 1 issue dimension, all one needs to do is to guarantee that the number of people needed to vote is greater than half of the total set of those voting. This explains, therefore, why majority rule is able to produce a core in the voting game with 1 dimension: the quota in simple majority rule requires more than half the people voting in order for a coalition to be winning.

What then happens as the number of issues increases? Suppose that we fix n at 100. Then for a single issue, we need only have a quota be more than 50 people. But for two issues ($k = 2$), the quota now needs to be over two-thirds ($2/(2 + 1)$) of those voting, or 67 people. For $k = 3$, we need over 3/4, and so on. As k is raised higher and higher, the quota necessary to guarantee a core converges to the unanimity rule ($q = n$): in fact, for any number of issues, unanimity always yields a core outcome.

What happens as the number of voters increases here? We would expect, given the discussion of Madison in chapter 1, that by expanding the sphere we might make it more and more unlikely that a majority would form. In fact, as long as the quota is based on some proportion of the population, raising the number of eligible voters has no effect whatsoever on the likelihood of a core. Only if those new voters bring with them new issues can a current core be destabilized. This offers some rather interesting perspectives on the ambiguous nature of franchise extension.

Theorem 1 provides a sufficient condition for a core in simple voting games. But is it also necessary? The answer is no: if inequality 1 is not satisfied, we cannot guarantee that we will certainly *not* have a core. For example, if we have 2 issue dimensions ($k = 2$) and 200 million voters ($n = 200,000,000$) who vote on majority rule, then we could still have a core outcome if those 200,000,000 voters have exactly the same preferences. In such a case, there would never be a majority who could be made better off than the ideal point of all these homogeneous individuals, because no one at all would be made better off by a change.

It may be objected that we should expect this high degree of consensus to be a rather unlikely occurrence, and that is true. But we can have a core even without unanimity, if we balance everyone on the issues just right (so that attempts to move in one direction or another will be blocked by a majority on the other side). This balancing act too may seem quite unlikely, but we now have two unlikely events, and if an unlikely event occurs enough times, it stops being so unlikely. How then can we characterize the likelihood that a core will exist? There are mathematical characterizations of conditions that hold almost all the time, and it is to these that I now turn.

For the following result, we need additional assumptions. A preference relation is representable by a real-valued function u_i: $X \rightarrow \mathbb{R}$ means that $u_i(x) \geq u_i(y)$ if and only if (x,y) is in R_i. This simply means that we can attach to every policy position some number reflecting the relative valuation the individual has of that policy position in comparison to all possible alternatives.

Suppose that we had a set of utility functions for each individual who participated in our voting game. We know that we cannot guarantee that a core will not exist, but perhaps we can do the next best thing: we can guarantee that if there is a core, then for any arbitrarily small change in preferences, that core will be destroyed. To prove that, however, we have to have a notion of what a *small change* in preferences means, which in turn will require us to compare utility functions.

Mathematical functions can have a number of properties. Some functions, for example, take discontinuous "jumps" at certain values. (Example: if we code anyone making $100,000 or more as *rich* and anyone making anything less as *poor*, then we have a discontinuous function, which will jump precisely at $100,000.) Other functions are continuous, but they have "kinks" in them. (Think of a function like $y = -|x|$, where $|x|$ means the absolute value of x. This function looks somewhat like the top two sides of a triangle, with a kink in the function when x is equal to 0.) Other functions do not have kinks, and are considered differentiable. But the derivative of some functions are other functions, and these functions might well be kinked. If this does not happen, and if further the derivative itself can be differentiated any arbitrary number of times, then the function is called smooth. This will be our fourth assumption:

ASSUMPTION 4. *(Smoothness) For each* i $\in$ N, *the utility representation* u_i:X $\rightarrow \mathbb{R}$ *is smooth.*

Infinite differentiability sounds rather ominous, like the punishment meted out to an erring mathematician in Hell. But the usual Euclidean (and weighted Euclidean) utility functions in spatial models satisfy Assumption 4, as can some preferences with wide zones of indifference.

This assumption imposes a great deal of mathematical structure on the utility functions. It may be wondered why this is necessary. But one way to compare functions is to compare the value of their derivatives, with close functions having similar derivatives. This way of comparing functions is known as the Whitney C^k topology (topology is just a mathematical term for a way to talk about "neighborhoods"). We say two utility functions u and u' are close in the Whitney C^k topology if at every point in the issue space X, the derivatives of the functions up to and including the kth derivative are close. We could of course require that functions be close through all their derivatives, which means, for functions that are smooth, that they are close for all their derivatives going down to infinity. This is precisely the notion of the Whitney topology, which is like the Whitney C^k topology, but k here is set to infinity.

To put forward a hypothetical example: if two functions are quite different at the eight billionth derivative, then they are not considered "close" in the Whitney topology, even though the two functions might be identical up through the eight billionth derivative, and thus would be "close" in the Whitney $C^{7,999,999,999}$ topology. This may sound odd, but it really isn't. We often use very different notions of "closeness" in our everyday dealings. Speaking on the phone to relatives, we invite them to visit, telling them that hundreds of miles is "close." If, however, we arranged to meet someone for breakfast and they showed up at a waffle house hundreds of miles away, an excuse that they were "close by" would not be entertained. The various flavors of the Whitney topology in essence get at the various notions of closeness we might want to entertain.

We know that when inequality 1 is not satisfied, we cannot guarantee the nonexistence of the core. But the Whitney topology gives us a way to think about whether a core "almost always" exists (or when it "almost never" exists). Genericity isn't an easy property to grasp, but one way to think about it is to imagine a quilt with various squares, sewn together with an infinitesimally thin thread (in fact, we have to assume that the thread has no width at all, but if that clouds the imagination, forget it). If you placed the quilt on the wall and threw a dart at it, the chances that you would hit a thread as opposed to a square are almost nil; in fact, given a thread with no width, it *is* nil. This is because the thread is "nowhere dense": there is thread, but you cannot find any area where within a small enough circle there is nothing but thread.

To recap, we know that a core will exist regardless of how large the set of issues or how many people we have. But how fragile is this core? The following theorem provides the answer.

THEOREM 2. (McKelvey and Schofield 1986) *Let* q-*majority rule be given, with* q $<$ n *(i.e., no vetoers). Endow the space of* n-*tuples of smooth utility functions with the Whitney topology. If*

$$q < (k + n - 1) \tag{2}$$

then the core is almost always empty.

Proof. See McKelvey and Schofield.

An n-tuple is simply a list of n things, here n smooth utility functions. The restriction to the nonunanimity case is necessary in view of Theorem 1, which showed that a core would always exist if we had a unanimity rule.

One may wonder whether the failure of inequality 1 guarantees that inequality 2 is satisfied, that is, if a core cannot be guaranteed, then can it be guaranteed that the core generically does not exist? The following provides the answer.

THEOREM 3. *Suppose that inequality 1 does not hold. Assuming no vetoers, then the core will be empty generically.*

Proof. Suppose that inequality 1 does not hold, that is, $q \leq (kn)/(k + 1)$. We know that the core will be generically empty when $q < (k + n - 1)$. Therefore, failing inequality 1 will imply that the core is generically empty whenever

$$\frac{kn}{k + 1} < (k + n - 1) \tag{3}$$

But this is equal to

$$\frac{kn}{k + 1} - (k - 1) < n \tag{4}$$

or

$$\frac{kn - (k - 1)(k + 1)}{k + 1} < n \tag{5}$$

Since $k > -1$, this implies that

$$kn - (k - 1)(k + 1) < kn + n \tag{6}$$

Subtracting kn from both sides, we have

$$-(k - 1)(k + 1) < n \tag{7}$$

or

$$(k - 1)(k + 1) > -n \tag{8}$$

But as long as both n and k are greater than 0 (that is, we have at least one voter and one issue), this is always satisfied.   □

If, then, we cannot guarantee a core by Theorem 1, then we know, by Theorem 3, that it will be exceptionally unlikely that a core in the simple voting game will exist.

A Model of a Legislature with Two-Party Competition

What we need to do now is to fill out the discussion of the previous session in order to derive Aldrich's result regarding the relationship between the size of the majority party and party cohesion. We can begin by recognizing that parties do in fact exist in legislative politics.[6] To capture this, we can thus partition the set N of legislators, into two sets, M and O, with M the majority party and O the (minority) opposition. A key variable in this section will be m, the number of legislators who are members of the majority party.

I should note here that while we are assuming that a set of *individuals* are members of the majority party, there is really nothing to prevent us from visualizing these legislators organized into party *wings*. In that case, party cohesion would involve getting the agreement of the various wings of the party (assuming that the individuals within the wings acted in a unitary fashion). This is an important point to remember, especially when we come to the historical section. In various spots we will find mention of this or that faction of the majority party. This does not, however, mean that the party is not cohesive: it only means that to be cohesive, various wings must agree.

To continue, within the caucus it will be assumed that outcomes can be sustained only if a floor majority within the majority party is incapable of defeating the policy currently on the agenda. The agenda is assumed to begin with the status quo, x_o. Some individual in the party (say the Leader) makes a proposal, call it y. The proposal y is accepted if and only if it is capable of defeating the status quo by a floor majority. In other words,

$$\# \cdot i \in M \colon (y, x_o) \in P_i \mid \geq (n + 1)/2 \tag{9}$$

An outcome y^* is said to be a caucus equilibrium if there is no alternative proposal y' that could defeat y^* by a floor majority within the majority party. If y^* is a caucus equilibrium, then I assume members of the majority party will support y^* on the floor (that is, if there is a caucus equilibrium, it is binding).

There are a few aspects of the caucus worth noting. First, there is no guarantee that the caucus *will* produce a caucus equilibrium. Indeed, an important part of this work will be isolating the cases where the caucus mechanism will break down. I do not therefore assume that every time Republicans (or for that matter Democrats) go behind closed doors to hammer out a solution, a solution will be forthcoming. It is quite possible that there will be cycling in the caucus, as a policy defeats the status quo by a floor majority, only to itself be defeated by some other policy, and so on, ad infinitum.

Second, note that the caucus condition reflects the size of the majority party. It is not simply the case that any individual within a caucus can dictate an outcome and by a simple majority vote force everyone in the minority of the majority party to go along. Instead, the caucus condition is meant to take into account the fact that there might well be positions capable of gathering a majority on the floor. The caucus thus acts in a way as a coordinating mechanism, allowing a set of legislators the opportunity to build a coalition before voting actually takes place on the floor. But the ease which with such coalitions can be formed will be a function of the size of the majority.

Third, the caucus equilibrium could well be the status quo. In other words, it may be the case that no policy is capable of defeating the status quo by a floor majority. For example, suppose that half of the majority party wishes to move policy to the left of the status quo, and half wish to move it to the right. Assuming that the majority party does not hold all the seats in the legislature, it follows that there will not be a floor majority capable of defeating the status quo. Thus a party beset by crosscutting cleavages might well be unable to generate caucus equilibria: unable, that is, as long as the crosscutting cleavages result in preferences sufficiently dissimilar that a floor majority cannot agree on an appropriate course of action.[7] This result would bind the members to a strategy of legislative inaction (in chapter 6 we shall see an example of such a majority).

Fourth, the argument presumes that individuals will abide by the caucus equilibrium decision on the floor (that is, the caucus will be binding). While this is quite restrictive, too much should not be made of it. The caucus enables a floor majority within the majority party to guarantee an outcome that is strictly better for all involved than the status quo. To defect from this arrangement, therefore, one would have to find some other policy outcome that yields an outcome not only better than the status quo but better than that provided by the caucus equilibrium. Furthermore, one would have to show that this alternative policy is not itself a caucus equilibrium as defined above for the implications of the theory to be affected. Finally, one would have to assume that there is some mechanism that enables the alternative coalition to hold together the agreement in a way that is not available to the majority party. These requirements are sufficiently onerous that they leave me convinced of the essential plausibility of the model.[8]

Finally, the results do not make any assumptions about how the minority feels about the majority caucus position and the status quo. Thus, within this model, it is actually possible for a minority to be left worse off under the operation of this procedure than they would be had a caucus not been held. This of course implies that in this model, we can have inefficient legislation. Less surprisingly, this means that there could be losers (as well as winners) as a result of actions taken in the legislature.

This list characterizes a number of the features of the caucus model, but we now wish to use that model to generate the relationship between the size of the majority party and party cohesion. To do so, suppose that the number of issues to be considered in the legislature is probabilistic and is characterized by a cumulative distribution function $F:[1,k] \rightarrow [0,1]$. That is, $F(j)$ represents the probability that the legislature will consider j issues or less. With this probabilistic background, we can prove the following theorem.

THEOREM 4. (Aldrich 1988) *The probability of a caucus equilibrium is weakly decreasing in the size of the majority.*

Proof.   Let q be the quota used in the caucus. I will show that x is a q-core implies that x is a q'-core for all $q' > q$. To see this suppose not, that is, there exists a point y such that $\#|i$ in M: (y,x) is in $P_i| > q'$. But we know that x is a q-core, implying that $\#|i$ in M: (y,x) is in $P_i| < q$. The two inequalities imply that $q' < q$, a contradiction. Let $j^*(m)$ be the largest j that satisfies inequality 1. Since q is strictly monotonically decreasing in m, it follows from Theorem 1 that $j^*(m + 1) \le j^*(m)$. Since F is a cumulative probability function, it follows that $F(j^*(m + 1)) \le F(j^*(m))$, which was to be proven. $\square$

Suppose that we have two issues, x and y, with x being considered for certain and y having a .50 probability of being considered. The probability of only considering x is therefore .50, and we know that whenever there is a single issue, there will always be a caucus equilibrium, regardless of the size of the majority. The probability of considering both x and y is .50 as well. But here we would have two issues ($k = 2$), and we can guarantee a caucus equilibrium except (by Theorem 1) the number of individuals required to vote in the caucus is greater than two-thirds. If we have 100 individuals in the legislature, and 51 are members of the majority party, then the quota within caucus is the entire party, and we have a caucus equilibrium with certainty despite the fact that we have two issues. In fact, we will have a caucus equilibrium with certainty as long as the majority party controls 76 seats or less. When m grows to 77, however, the quota within caucus slips below the two-thirds necessary, and therefore the probability of a caucus equilibrium drops from 100 percent to 50 percent. The numbers here are only illustrative, but they are meant to indicate the way in which the size of the majority party determines the cohesion of the caucus.

Minority Obstruction

If there is a caucus equilibrium, then we can proceed to consider the floor stage.[9] Since this is an initial step in treating minority party strategy, I will be unmercifully narrow and assume that members of the minority have two possible strategies: they can either acquiesce, or they can obstruct. If the minority acquiesces, then the floor outcome is the caucus equilibrium. If the minority obstructs, then we will assume the outcome is the status quo.[10]

Since there are only two alternatives here, a simple majority vote within the minority will yield a determinate outcome. The minority will obstruct if the number of individuals preferring the status quo over the caucus equilibrium is greater than the number preferring the caucus equilibrium over the status quo. If not, the minority will acquiesce.

Note that instead of assuming a minority caucus, we could just as easily assume that individuals within the minority make their own decisions about whether to obstruct or not. We could let the probability of achieving the status quo increase with the number of individuals in the minority who prefer the status quo over the party caucus equilibrium. In that case, surprisingly, it would turn out that the larger the opposing minority, the more likely the status quo outcome will be if obstruction is tolerated.

This logic neatly dovetails with the majority calculations set out above. When the majority is small, it is cohesive. Correspondingly, when the minority is large, it has the greatest potential for waging obstruction. This is a point that, as we shall see, was explicitly understood by the Irish obstructionist Charles Parnell (see chapter 8) and is also highlighted in one of the rare academic papers to deal with obstruction, Oppenheimer's 1985 article on cloture. But having a large minority is not all that is required here. One also needs to have party differences. The minority must prefer the status quo over the majority position. If it does not, then we will not see obstruction.

Institutional Change

If actions taken by the minority are seen as obstructive, how then do we get to procedural change? All we need do is move one step back. Suppose therefore that in the caucus a rules change limiting obstruction is proposed. Would this proposal be adopted?

Clearly, a floor majority within the majority party would vote to limit obstruction (in the policy-based model presented here) if they preferred the outcome to be obtained on the floor without obstruction (that is, when the minority acquiesces) to the outcome that is obtained when the minority obstructs (the status quo). There would be no reason to adopt such changes if the majority party itself is conservative and resists changes in the status quo. But when the status quo is not the caucus equilibrium, then it follows that the majority *will* prefer to limit obstruction (since for a new policy to be a caucus equilibrium, a floor majority within the majority party must have preferred it to the status quo). So limitations on obstruction should occur when we have a policy change adopted in caucus, which as argued above can be expected to occur when the majority party is small.

On the contrary, when a caucus equilibrium does not exist, it is far from clear that members would vote for the procedural change. Making a more specific statement would depend upon the theory one wished to use in predicting the outcome of the multidimensional floor voting process, but it is enough to note that solutions producing uncertainty about the policy outcome to be obtained in the floor could well lead risk-averse legislators to prefer the safety of the obstructive shield. This does not mean that limitations on obstruction cannot occur when the majority is large, but I believe it does suggest that such events will be rather exceptional.

Summary and Discussion of Theoretical Results

Given the theory advanced here, a number of claims about legislative politics emerge. First, small majorities should be more cohesive than larger majorities. Second, the mechanism by which small majorities become cohesive is the caucus system. Third, minority obstruction should be linked to the size of the majority. The largest minorities will be the most likely to obstruct, in part because they are necessarily facing the smallest majorities. Fourth, procedural changes to limit obstruction will be related to the size of the majority party. Small majorities, experiencing or anticipating obstruction, will enact rules changes to limit minority rights to delay the proceedings. Finally, in order to show some agency, the debates and the votes about obstruction should break down along party lines. These results will hold for all small majorities unless a floor majority within the party is unable to agree on a direction to move from the status quo.

In evaluating this theory, it is helpful to compare other theories of procedural change and minority rights. Consider, for example, findings regarding the link between party differences and party cohesion set out in a powerful series of papers by Brady (1973); Cooper and Brady (1981); and Brady, Brody, and Epstein (1989) for the Senate. These articles link the centralization of party to the increasing divergence of the constituency bases of the Republican and Democratic parties during the end of the nineteenth century. Cleavages between the parties are, according to the theory presented here, indeed an important part of the argument. But constituency cleavages (or any other cleavages, for that matter) are not by themselves enough. First, the parties need to be engaged in somewhat of a zero-sum conflict over policy. If they disagree, but either would prefer the other's proposal to the status quo, then (absent the possibilities of bargaining postures), they will not obstruct. Second, the majority party will need to be small. If not, then the theory presented here argues that the majority itself will become divided and incapable of presenting a unified front (at least unless there is an exceptionally unlikely unity in policy views among members of the majority).

Consider also the efficiency/workload arguments highlighted in chapter 1. Even if we agree that economic and social development leads to numerous problems, it does not follow that the solution is further legislation. And even if we further agree that legislation is needed, there is no reason to think that we will both wish to move policy in the same direction. Thus there is simply no real equivalent to workload in a legislature. Bismarck's witty pairing to the contrary, there is no reason legislatures have to process laws like sausages. Instead, we need to think of workload itself as something that is *endogenous* to the political process. What makes workload seem related to procedural change, therefore, is not the concept of a body of "work" that needs to be accomplished, but the fact that cohesive majorities with ambitious policy programs will have an incentive, when faced with staunch opposition, to enact procedural changes to stifle the dissenters.

Or consider the theory of reciprocity. If fear of being in the minority truly protected minority rights, then we might wish for an intensely competitive electoral system in which parties routinely alternated majority status. But the theory advanced here suggests that the small majorities produced by competitive systems will in fact have the effect of *reducing* minority rights to obstruct. Finally, there is no need to turn to political socialization. At the very least, legislators in very different times and places should, if the theory is correct, react in similar sorts of ways, ways that are more a function of the political *present* then of the politician's *past*.

To conclude, we now have a theory of institutional change that explains the timing of majority attempts to limit minority rights to obstruct, and we have done so without appeals to efficiency, reciprocity, or socialization. But does the theory do a good job of accounting for the actual changes that have taken place in minority rights to obstruct? To answer this question, there is only one place to turn: legislative history.

PART 2

Evidence from the U.S. House, 1837–95

Mr. Covert [when his name was called]. I desire to change my vote.
The Speaker. The gentleman from New York desires to change his vote.
Mr. Covert. Let my name be called.
[Mr. Covert's name was called.]
Mr. Covert. I will vote later.

—*Congressional Record,* January 29, 1890

CHAPTER 3

Testing Assumptions and Links

For this chapter and the three following, the theory developed above will be applied to the U.S. House of Representatives from 1837 to 1895. It was during these years, conventionally identified as the "partisan era" of American politics, that the House grappled with the issue of minority obstruction and put a definitive end to many of the most important obstructive techniques available to minority members of the House (Galloway 1969).[1]

If this were a standard test of the model, I would at this point proceed directly to considering the cases of significant rules change in some legislature I had selected. If the events follow the predictions of the theory (in fact, even if they did not), then the task would be complete. I would have reached some conclusion about the empirical validity of the theory.

But the theory presented in chapter 2, like most theories in political science, is not simply the sum of its predictions. Predictions are important, to be sure, but so too are the many moving parts, hosts of assumptions as well as intermediate steps that connect the size of the majority to procedural change. What then are we to make of these moving parts, of the assumptions and links necessary to get to our "final result"?

In most analyses, these parts of the formal presentation are literally sub rosa: under the rose. The empirical relation one wants to set out is of course the rose: the rest (unwanted thorns and roots) remains hidden or perhaps consigned to some compost heap (which later generations will perhaps recycle to help produce another new rose).

This willingness to gloss over the slimy underbelly of rational choice has troubled many who have read the formal literature. For example, those who spend their lives studying institutional structures are notably unimpressed with the relatively skeletal structures of even the most well developed formal edifices. Those who think that people are heir to all sorts of cognitive errors tend to turn away from the relatively stringent conditions on choice implied by rational choice.[2] Even the most explicit mathematical presentation fails to relieve these criticisms. One always suspects a trick buried somewhere in there.

Like these critics, I too believe that the notion that assumptions can be blissfully forgotten is a tremendous methodological mistake that formal theory has been all too willing to make. Consequently, I want to first set out some views about the more appropriate role that assumptions and links should have in the evaluation of the veracity of a formal theory. I then want to subject the assumptions and links presented in that previous chapter to empirical evaluation.

Some Thoughts about the Path instead of the Destination

Every theory, we are reminded, must make some accommodation with reality. A theory which failed to make such an accommodation would have no theoretical utility: it would simply be a (particular) redescription of the world. Some element of the theory will therefore necessarily stretch reality a bit here and there.

Easily enough said, but how thin do we slice the bologna? How little of the rich reality we experience are we willing to ignore before suddenly the sandwich is not filling? One particularly influential answer to this question was provided by Milton Friedman (1953) in his classic piece "The Methodology of Positive Economics." The position in that essay was that theories were to be judged not by their assumptions, but rather by their predictions. If I have a theory which explains coups d'état in Africa perfectly (or at least better than anyone else), then I have a successful theory, and the assumptions required to make those predictions are not relevant to an evaluation of the theory.

Such a position, of course, may make Nostradamus a better economist than Kenneth Arrow or John Maynard Keynes. I think that we are correctly nervous about theories whose predictions emerge from a process that no bears no relation to anything we know about. We suspect that somehow we are being the dupes of a cunning simultaneity: that perhaps chicken entrails are good predictors of famine because when famine is on its way chickens might not get fed. Predictive success from models that we feel so ill at ease with isn't an endorsement of the theory: it is a plea to find the correct mechanism.

Further, for most social science examples, one cannot separate out assumptions from predictions in the way assumed by Friedman. Most theories in the rational choice vein, for example, are based on comparative statics results from equilibrium analysis. The argument is of course that if you change the *assumed* parameter values in the model, you change the *predicted* values of the variable you are trying to explain. The prediction of a model doesn't make sense without knowing something about what one is assuming about the parameters of the model: no tests of predictions, therefore, without assumptions.

What Friedman's argument does is to elevate one particular assumption out of the set of possible assumptions, call it (through some subjective process that is never talked about) the independent variable, and then ignore all the other assumptions. While it would be interesting to hear a defense of why that particular assumption should be so honored, I know of none. And it is not difficult to see why: deductive arguments, if they satisfy the classical mathematical virtue of making no extraneous assumptions, need *all* their assumptions for the result, not just those a particular researcher is interested in.

Furthermore, the discretion comes not only at the beginning (in elevating one of the assumptions to the state of an independent variable and ignoring the others), but at the end as well. Unidimensional models of congressional voting (and some multidimensional ones as well) predict that every vote in Congress will be won by the slimmest of majorities (the median voter being the pivotal representative). This prediction, however, is clearly false. Nonetheless, it is never talked about, banished to the attic just like Mrs. Rochester in *Jane Eyre*.

One can make an even more fundamental theoretical point: the universe of cases whose behavior one is attempting to predict is in part constituted by one's theories. I have a theory that international oil agreements are a sort of Prisoner's Dilemma, and I present a theory explaining when and where I expect those agreements to be sustained and when I expect them to fall apart (and perhaps even the nature of agreements if made). I test the theory against data on international oil agreements and find that in some small set of the cases my theory did not hold. I look at those cases, and realize they aren't Prisoner's Dilemmas: that is, the structure of the game in those cases does not resemble the way I modeled them. We might then say that I do not have a very good model of international oil agreements (since not all of the agreements look like Prisoner's Dilemmas), but this is only saying that my model is unrealistic (that is, not faithful to the facts). What I do not think we would say is that the model does not predict well: I have perfectly predicted all the cases where the theory should have been applicable. Thus what counts as confirmation or disconfirmation of a theory depends on whether the thing we are applying it to looks like the thing we are theorizing about, which is to say that our assumptions are realistic.

So it appears that we are truly in the realm of social science: some of one and some of the other. Predictive success is important, but so is realism in assumptions. Can nothing more be said? I could add an article of faith: that predictive success will ultimately be found by making models more realistic, not less, but like other articles of faith about realignment, the apocalypse, or the Kennedy assassination, this might not seem quite persuasive.

To avoid the usual tedium, therefore, let me stake out a basic position: the more assumptions that are assessed as "realistic," the stronger a theory is. To be sure, I recognize all the ambiguities and elisions in this position. For example: why should number of assumptions be privileged over quality?

how should we count assumptions? what does it mean to "assess" an assumption as "realistic"? And what do we mean by an "assumption" anyway? But the position does have the virtue of making realism of assumptions at least part of the desiderata of theoretical success, and that is what I am aiming for here.

There is one slight wrinkle here. In some theories (unfortunately, mine is one of them) there is more than one stage to the argument. A set of assumptions leads to one result, which leads to another result, which leads to a final result. At each step of the game, a result becomes an assumption for the next stage of the theory. Does testing assumptions require testing only the first part, or all the intermediate steps?

I think it has to mean testing all the intermediate steps as well. Suppose we think that A is realistic, and we find that indeed A is associated with B. If we have intermediate steps, then we are stating that there is something that A leads to that in turn leads (at least to some chain that eventually leads) to B. The theory, then, isn't simply the link between A and B: it is in addition a statement about process, about the steps that are taken to get from A to B. To avoid the cunning simultaneity discussed above (at least as much as one can, given Humean skepticism), evaluating the intermediate links as well as the initial assumptions seems to be required.

I have phrased much of this in terms of a critique of rational choice theories of politics, but there is nothing that prevents the same arguments from being leveled against many other schools of political theorizing.[3] Functionalist explanations (see, e.g., Merton 1957) are notorious for missing a realistic account of how the functions cycle back to the actions (this was the stunning critical point of Olson 1967; see also Stinchcombe 1968; Elster 1983). Interpretivist notions are often similarly silent on the assumptions necessary to get one from one regime of power–knowledge relations to another.[4] Casting methodological criticisms of course is easy; avoiding them is harder, which suggests that I proceed by evaluating the theory presented in the previous chapter along the lines suggested in this discussion.

Testing Assumptions

Happily, I feel comfortable in saying that indeed there are a finite set of legislators in the House, that there is a status quo point, that there are political issues. I also do not think it much of a stretch to assume that the set of issues in any legislature is finite. The assumption that political issues can be thought of as a set of lines, while troubling to some, seems innocuous enough.

How closely do the preferences of legislators match the assumptions standard in rational choice theories? There is some research that can guide us here. Ansolabehere and Brady (1989) were able to show that a sizable proportion of the electorate did satisfy some of the basic choice axioms of revealed preference. Empirical analyses have successfully estimated legislator ideal points both on individual legislation (Krehbiel and Rivers 1988) and on broader issue cleavages over the course of the entire history of the U.S. Congress (see Poole and Rosenthal 1991). And these results do not appear to be artifacts of statistical handling. John Kingdon (1973) found that members do eventually come to an individual voting decision. We thus do not see the perpetual instability of individual positions on issues that we might expect if members were unable to latch on to a position.[5]

The theory assumes that minorities have two strategies to pursue: acquiescence or obstruction. This they do have, but as noted previously they undoubtedly have more. Thus, while the assumptions are realistic, they are not complete. I have elsewhere made an attempt to deal with the strategy of amendment (Dion 1991), and the results are identical to those presented here. While this is surely not exhaustive, I have not been able to think of a way in which the incorporation of other minority strategies would unhinge the results here, so the gap in realism is probably tolerable.

What I believe to be the weakest part of the model (in terms of realism of assumptions) comes from the notion of a party caucus. While the House of Representatives has had a caucus system with the power to compel individuals to vote according to party positions (most notably after the demise of Joseph Cannon in the second decade of this century),[6] and while the party caucus does still operate on issues such as the election of Speakers as well as the construction of the rules (nota bene!), in general the House has not had the kind of strict party caucus that is assumed in the model. Perhaps the largest gap is that the caucus does not operate under the institutional rule assumed in the model (that one needs to have a floor majority to defeat a bill) but instead on a simple majority within the House.

I am not going to suggest that I am untroubled by this disjuncture. I clearly am. The question then is what should be done next. The first response would be to present a theory of cohesion that assumes a more realistic institutional mechanism for the creation and maintenance of party loyalty. Cox and McCubbins have attempted to move in that direction by providing a notion of party as a bond (see also Hechter 1987). This is an exciting avenue for future research, but it is not the tack I plan to use here. Instead, I want to offer a plausible account of how parties operate that is consistent with the model.

All the model is really suggesting is that the notion of what it means for there to be a majority party position within a caucus will become less clear as the party becomes larger. This is because there will be numerous policy contenders, all of which can achieve a floor majority relying solely on votes from the majority party alone. It would not be surprising that, in such situations, what exactly the "stand of the party" is will become less obvious. As long as the potential for alternative floor majorities to be created within the majority party exists, the theory would still maintain some resemblance to reality, although admittedly not enough for my taste. This resolution is not fully comforting, but those who require perfection in the social sciences will almost certainly find themselves with empty bookcases. (For those still unsatisfied, evidence of the relationship between party size and the use of the caucus will be presented below.)

I have covered the problem of inclusion, but not of exclusion: is the theory really that realistic, in that I have not considered (a) an executive branch, (b) bicameralism, (c) a committee system, (d) the role of constituents, or most importantly (e) (fill in your personal favorite here)? In some cases, those factors will influence the course of procedural change, and when they do I will point them out. There certainly is quite a story to be told about obstruction (broadly considered) and all of these factors: the reconstitution of governmental institutions in the years of Theodore Roosevelt (Skowronek 1982) overlaps with the rule of Speaker Cannon, for example. It is not hard to see that if obstruction makes life difficult for executives, they may start attempting to influence policies outside of those institutions (in bureaucracies, for example).

But the main story here will deal with the resolution of certain procedural details on the floor of various legislatures. Executives do not play a main role (at least as far as I have seen), bicameralism seems not to play a role (although perhaps something could be said about joint rules), the committee system crops up once in a while (but seems less relevant given that floor obstruction occurs after a committee has already acted), and I did not find the press of constituents to be very obvious either (but of course I could have missed it). This is not to say that these and other variables have no effect, only that I have not found much in them that would account for the timing of institutional changes regarding obstruction.

This is an important point in assessing the realism of assumptions. Saying that the president is not important for issues of procedural change does *not* mean that the president does not exist. The president does exist; so do the Federal Reserve, the stock market, the Catholic church, and so on. We think about topics like presidency, bicameralism, committees, and constituency because they are the *politically relevant* variables that come to mind. But this does not mean that they will always be relevant for everything political. And as far as I can tell they are not relevant here.[7]

Testing Links

The Friedmanite position asks us to assess no more than the ultimate predictive success of a model, regardless of the path taken to get there. But a multistep theory such as the one presented in the previous chapter offers much additional room for assessing the realism of the model. Five links seem especially crucial, if not exhaustive, for the theory presented in the previous chapter. These are, in logical order:

1. Small majority parties are more cohesive.
2. The mechanism by which parties become more cohesive as they diminish in size is the party caucus.
3. The largest minority parties will be the most likely to obstruct.
4. Procedural changes to limit obstruction will be related to the size of the majority party.
5. Final votes and debates on these changes will be along party lines.

Of these, only number 4 would be evaluated if we accepted Friedman's argument. Since I am rejecting that position, I will be forced to do a bit more work. The remainder of the chapter is therefore intended to evaluate the plausibility of these links (although the analysis of 4 and 5 will be taken up in subsequent chapters). In chapter 6, I will take up at greater length the possibility that some other mechanism (such as the growth in workload, the increase in the number of individuals in the House, and the varying level of electoral competition) may be responsible for the patterns I will attempt to set out.

A warning: the relative paucity of historical data about some types of behavior in the House during the nineteenth century limits the sort of evaluation I can perform. This will be particularly true when it comes to claim 2. If the results therefore are not as thorough as one would like, please recall that tests of assumptions are a rarity in models of this type, and that the weakness of the performance may be excused by the novelty of the action.

Testing Claim 1: Party Size and Party Voting

What causes party cohesion? Under what conditions will party cohesion be greatest? The variables of interest will depend on the questions we are asking. For the comparative questions asked by (among others) Lowell (1902) and Mayhew (1974), the variable to be explained is the great divergence between American and British levels of party cohesion in legislatures.[8] We are familiar with the relevant variables: open party lists in the United States, the institutionalization of the executive branch in the Commons in the form of the Cabinet (making parliamentary election referenda on government), and so on.

Different variables can be pursued if we ask what it is that causes party cohesion levels to rise and fall within a single country over time. This is the most relevant variable for the study here, and it is clear that many of the usual comparative signposts will not help in explaining changes in the historical levels of party cohesion in the United States (although it does, of course, enter into the constant term). But having forgone those variables, what can we use to explain changes in levels of party cohesion?

The size of the majority party is a clear candidate, especially since the work of William Riker (1962) brought the size principle to a new level of importance. Barbara Hinckley (1972) statistically tested Riker's theory, however, and found no tendency for minimal winning coalitions to form. She also found that defections from the majority party do not increase with increasing size.

Due to Hinckley's work (as well as work on coalition formation), it appeared that majority party size did not play an important role in explaining party cohesion. As a result, measures of party size began to drop out of statistical analyses. Neither Brady, Cooper, and Hurley 1979 nor Hurley and Wilson 1989 includes the size of the majority party as an explanatory variable. Even worse, their analyses begin at the latter decades of the nineteenth century, at the tail end of the era I am interested in. This implies that I needed to go back and do some party voting research on my own.

Measuring party cohesion in legislatures is one of the murkiest corners of political numerology, and there appear to be as many ways to measure party cohesion as there are stars in the sky. Rather than engage in a fratricidal and sororicidal effort to establish a best measure, I instead opted for methodological pluralism (well, of a narrow sort). Data on voting in the House for the period from 1836 to 1861 was taken from Alexander's 1967 study of roll call voting in the antebellum House. Alexander assembled a selected series of roll call votes and for most years included data only from the first session.[9] Data from 1860 on have been collected by Clubb and Traugott (1977). Since we are interested in the partisan era, only data from 1860 to 1895 have been included. It should be noted that Clubb and Traugott analyze all roll calls in their article, while Alexander analyzes only a subset of roll calls (chosen, it appears, with an eye to avoiding minor and repetitive roll calls—that is, in all likelihood, those which are obstructive).

My justification for selecting these data sets was simple: they were easily available. As a result, the variables used to measure party cohesion differ within and between these sources. It may have been more preferable, following the periodization adopted in this book, to gather data on each measure throughout the partisan era, although I do not believe that this would affect the results.[10] All of which is simply a way of saying that while I believe the results to follow are serviceable for this project, more could be done.

Between the two sources on party voting, then, we can assemble four separate time-series of party voting measures. The first, *Party90*, measures the percentage of roll call votes in which 90 percent of one party vote on the same side. This was the definition of party vote used by Lowell (1902). The larger this number, the more the votes reflect an exceptionally high degree of party cohesion. The theory would predict a negative coefficient for party size on this variable: the larger the party, the less cohesive, and thus the fewer the number of cases where we would see 90 percent of the party on the same side.

A problem with the Party90 measure is that it does not take into account the nature of minority opposition. Thus a legislature in which every single member of every party voted identically would witness a high level of party cohesion. In many theories this would be an exceptionally appropriate test, but for this theory we would want to supplement it with a measure of party cohesion that takes into account majority–minority conflict. Alexander supplied a measure that satisfies this requirement, which he called Party Agreement. This is defined as the percentage of roll call votes with at least two-thirds majority of each party on the same side minus the percentage of roll calls with at least two-thirds majority of each party on opposite sides. The larger the Party Agreement score, therefore, the larger the proportion of roll calls in which a sizable majority of both sides agree. To maintain consistency with the rest of the equations, however, I look at the negative of Party Agreement, which I call *Party Disagreement*. This measure gives the percentage of votes with two-thirds on *opposite* sides minus the percentage on the *same* side. Since our theory predicts that small majorities will tend to disagree with their opposing minorities (which occurs if the caucus reaches a decision), then we would expect a negative sign for the coefficient on party size: as the party gets larger, there will be more and more issues on which a faction of the majority party and a faction of the minority agree.

Party Disagreement may seem to require too high a level of cohesion for the majority party (two-thirds as opposed to a simple majority). The third measure, *Party50*, is therefore defined as the percentage of roll call votes in which a simple majority or more of one party opposes a simple majority of another party. This is the definition of party vote used by Westerfield (1955). Once again, the theory would predict a negative coefficient for party size given this dependent variable.

A difficulty with both Party50 and Party Agreement is that it relies on relatively arbitrary cutpoints. Our final measure of party cohesion, *Party Unlikeness*, a simple algebraic manipulation of the likeness score used by Rice (1928), tries to overcome that problem by calculating the difference between the proportion of members who vote in favor of the particular measure in the different parties on a particular measure, and then averaging the resulting numbers over the set of roll calls. One would therefore be unlikely to see members of the two parties voting on the same side in a legislature with a high degree of Party Unlikeness. Our theory would predict that the parties would be most "unlike" when the majority party is small and that this measure will decrease as the majority gets larger and larger. In other words, we would expect a negative coefficient on party size in a regression using Party Unlikeness as a dependent variable.

The measure of our major independent variable requires some explanation as well. There have been numerous attempts to determine the partisan affiliations of members of Congress. And there have been numerous difficulties involved in any such operation. What, for example, is to be done about individuals elected under the banner of one party (say, a "Fusion" candidate) but consistently voting with another? Should we ignore the "Fusion" label and lump that individual with the party they vote for, or not? And what do we do about the many individuals whose partisan affiliations we know exceptionally little about?

The definitive attempt to settle the problem of party affiliation for members of the U.S. Congress was undertaken by Kenneth Martis (1989). This work represents an incredible scholarly effort, sifting through the contorted and often confusing issues that have confounded all previous measures of party affiliation. Consequently, in all of the statistical estimations to be presented on the U.S. Congress in this book, the measure of party proportion will be based on the Martis breakdown. In calculating that proportion, I have consistently ignored third parties and vacant seats.[11]

While it would be tempting to report results from a simple regression of whatever dependent variable is of interest and the proportion of majority party seats, I have instead attempted here and throughout the book to control for the various political factors that might be in play along with the theoretically predicted majority proportion effect. For the case of party voting, there is no shortage of likely suspects. For example, changes in the proportion of new members over the nineteenth century may have altered the willingness of members to accede to party demands (although in what direction is not a priori clear). Data on turnover, controlling for increases in the number of seats during the nineteenth century, was therefore obtained from Fiorina, Rohde, and Wissel 1975. Party cohesion might also be influenced by the time that has passed since the last realigning election (Brady 1973, 182; Clubb, Flanigan, and Zingale 1986). The notion here is that the issues that first galvanized the party ebb over time, and party voting in Congress wanes with it. Divided government offers another possibility. It has been argued that party cohesion will drop if the majority in the House differs from the majority of the president (Brady, Cooper, and Hurley 1979).[12]

Standard errors here and throughout the book have wherever possible been calculated using the White 1980 correction for heteroscedasticity. To avoid misinterpretation, throughout this book I have marked coefficients passing a particular one-tailed test by pound sign ("#") and those passing a two-tailed test by an asterisk ("*"). Some people argue that the correct standard when we have theoretical expectations about the sign of statistical estimates is the one-tailed test, while others seem content only with two-tailed tests. Identifying significance levels in both ways therefore allows readers to utilize whatever standard they think is most appropriate.

Initial regressions suggested two facts. First, neither the divided party variable nor turnover in the legislature had a significant effect on party cohesion. Furthermore, dropping the variable had no effect on the value of the remaining coefficients. The divergence of these results from those of Brady, Cooper, and Hurley should not be that startling: they may simply be a reflection of the fact that the president was not as important to the internal affairs of the Congress in the nineteenth century as was to be the case in the next. In the results to follow, therefore, I have dropped the presidency variable out.

Second, a look at the studentized residuals (a test for the presence of outliers) suggested the presence of outliers. For column 1 the outlier appeared to be the 31st Congress (1849–50), while for column 2 the outlier appeared to be the 32nd Congress. Studentized residuals outside the 95 percent confidence interval were observed for the Reed Speakership in both columns 3 and 4. These are hardly average Congresses. The 31st Congress witnessed one of the greatest conflicts in Congress before the Civil War, leading to the Compromise of 1850. Party lines during this time were thus strongly undercut by sectional ties, and it should hardly be surprising to find this Congress atypical in terms of party votes. The 32nd Congress saw a sharper than normal return to partisanship, as members of the Democratic party patched up the wounds of 1849 and 1850. As for the Reed Speakership, it is comforting that the statistical test indicated what is the basic historical opinion, that Reed was one of the most, if not the most partisan Speaker in the history of the House. Consequently, a dummy variable indicating the Speakership of Reed has been included.

The results are presented in columns 1 through 4 of table 3.1. All significance levels in this book are based on *t*-statistics computed using White standard errors. Where necessary, I have corrected initial estimates for first-order autocorrelation: when this is done, it is always made clear. The results of most interest here are the coefficients on the proportion of seats held by the majority party. All four equations have the predicted signs, and three of the four are significant at the .05 level (two-tailed test). The weakest relationship appears to hold for the Party Disagreement measure, which is significant at the .10 level for a one-tailed test.[13] Using four different measures, it appears that party cohesion does drop as the proportion of seats held by the majority party declines.

TABLE 3.1. GLS Regression Results on Party Voting

	Dependent Variable and Years Covered			
Independent Variables	Party 90 1837–60	Party[a] Disagreement 1837–60	Party 50[a] 1860–95	Party[a] Unlikeness 1860–95
Constant	127.926***	103.403**	103.351***	81.258***
	(25.879)	(39.781)	(9.644)	(7.791)
Majority proportion	−1.705***	−1.198#	−0.353**	−0.310**
(Martis)	(0.465)	(0.718)	(0.128)	(0.118)
31st Congress	−29.214***			
	(4.681)			
32nd Congress		−65.400***		
		(6.428)		
Congress since 1860			−1.822**	−1.158***
realignment			(0.626)	(0.296)
Reed Speakership			28.565***	20.290***
			(2.726)	(3.642)
Number of observations	13	13	18	18
Corrected R-squared	0.418	0.562	0.740	0.591
Standard error of the regression	13.433	18.869	5.388	5.184
Durbin-Watson (Rho)	1.675	(0.188)	(0.430)	(0.143)
Mean of dependent variable	31.462	31.846	68.444	53.933

[a]Corrected for first-order autocorrelation
#significant at the 10 percent level, one-tailed test
*significant at the 10 percent level, two-tailed test
**significant at the 5 percent level, two-tailed test
***significant at the 1 percent level, two-tailed test

One may be troubled, however, by the issue of substantive significance (see Achen 1982). Compared to the other coefficients, the proportion of seats held by the majority party has a quite modest coefficient. For example, using the results of the 1860–95 time-series, party control of an additional 10 percent of the seats in the House tends to diminish either party votes or disagreement scores by only 4 percent. Why isn't this effect larger?

The results of column 1 might provide an answer. The theory of the previous section notes that as the proportion declines, the caucus will no longer be able to guarantee party unity on the floor. Therefore, one might predict that the bulk of the proportion effect would show up in a decline in the percentage of votes on which the party was almost unanimous. In other words, proportion effects might appear larger once one limited attention to fairly restrictive measures of party cohesion. That the fairly restrictive Party90 measure has the largest coefficient (a 10 percent increase in the proportion of seats held by the majority party leads to a 20 percent decline in the proportion of roll calls witnessing 90 percent or more of the party on one side) buttresses this argument.

Retesting Claim 1: The Notion of a Cohesive Core

There is nothing written in stone that states that majority party leaders have to work with all the members of their party. It is always possible to treat some individual as an outsider or irrelevant to your party—indeed, some members might prefer that status (see, for example, Huitt's 1961 essay on Proxmire). Especially in a distributive politics setting, as Riker argued, there would seem to be a great incentive to jettison peripheral members and divide the spoils among a minimal winning coalition within a much larger party.

This possibility, however, destroys the account of obstruction and procedural change I am trying to set out here. If excess members are jettisoned, then it suggests that regardless of the actual number of individuals elected under the party banner, there will always be a cohesive minimal winning coalition contained within that group, like the pit in a peach. And that cohesive majority has the same incentive regarding procedural change as any cohesive majority: to limit obstruction. Played out, this observation implies that the proportion of seats held by the majority is irrelevant in explaining rules changes.

The cohesive-core argument is a useful one in separating out work that tests predictions and work that tests links. If we were interested only in predictions, then the cohesive-core argument would be out the window: even in the twentieth century, it is clear that there are not major rules changes at every single Congress, so the cohesive-core argument fails as a prediction.

But if we are interested in the links from assumptions to that prediction, as we have been in this chapter, then things become more complicated. If there is a cohesive core, then it suggests that one of the links in our account—the link relating the size of the majority party coalition to party cohesion—is weak. And if that link is weak, then it doesn't matter whether majority party size seems to be related to procedural change: we know (a) that even if there is a real relationship between party size and procedural change, it is not the relationship suggested by the theory in chapter 2, or (b) that for all we know any relationship we might find between the proportion of the legislature controlled by the majority and procedural change is thoroughly spurious. These are hardly comforting alternatives.

Testing the cohesive-core argument is fairly slippery. We could always assert that cohesive cores form only under certain historical conditions (therefore the theory is falsified under those same conditions, assuming they aren't identical to the partisan theory) or that over time the coalition forms only on some issues (which would then require a link between the issue space and procedural change). Perhaps the biggest danger in researching a cohesive core is the ease of defining the notion so loosely that indeed it does turn up in every single Congress (an Americanist example of Sartori's 1970 notion of "conceptual stretching"). Conversely, the more of a rarity cohesive cores are, the less they are troublesome in accounting for changes in the nineteenth century. Without further intensive research we cannot know for sure how troublesome the cohesive-core objection is.

We can, however, use the results at hand to attempt at least an initial assessment of the strength of this objection. Consider, to begin, Party50, which measures the proportion of roll calls on which a simple majority of one party opposes a simple majority of another party. If there is a cohesive core within the majority party, then that cohesive core must be a majority contained solely within the majority party. If minority votes are independent of the existence of a cohesive core (which we might think they would be, if a cohesive core is always present), then the same proportion of votes should be party votes in each Congress. Since the size of the majority does vary, however, this would imply that the proportion of seats held by the majority would have no effect on the level of party voting as measured by Party50. But we have already seen that this is not the case: table 3.1 indicates that the majority proportion was statistically significant.

Further evidence that the cohesive core objection is not correct can be found by considering the measure of Party Unlikeness. As the majority party increases, the proportion of the majority party that is made up by our presumed cohesive core decreases. This implies that the Party Unlikeness measure will automatically decrease. To see this, consider the following example. There are 100 seats in a legislature. I shall assume (to keep the analysis simple) that the majority party always votes Yea on any measure, and the minority party always votes Nay. When the majority party is minimal winning, 100 percent of its members vote Yea. Since 0 percent of the minority party votes Yea, Party Unlikeness in our example would be 100. Now suppose that the majority party gains two seats. We assume all the members of the cohesive core vote Yea and the two members outside the core vote Nay. That means that 50 out of 52 of the members of the majority party vote Yea, or roughly 96 percent. Doing similar sorts of calculations for majority parties of between 50 and 70 percent of the legislature indicates that the Party Unlikeness measure should fall by 1.5 for every additional percent increase in the size of the majority party. The estimated coefficient on Party Unlikeness from table 3.1, however, is significantly less than 1.5. Therefore, using two independent tests, the cohesive core objection seems to be incorrect.

This discussion helps shed light on the rather shadowy existence that

Riker's size principle has had in studies of American politics. It is true, as Riker claimed, that ceteris paribus small majorities are cohesive, but it is not necessarily true that small majorities will always form. Riker's account of the forces of cohesion was on target, but (this would argue) his theory of coalition formation was off. Interestingly enough, this parallels the results from comparativists, who have also found that Riker's minimal winning coalition theory fails as an account of coalition formation. In the United States, however, where two-party competition can be considered to essentially fix coalitions ex ante (at least in the partisan era), this coalition formation argument is less useful.[14] Thus it should not be surprising that when looked at from the perspective of coalition formation there is not a great deal of evidence for the minimal winning coalition theory, but when looked at from the perspective of party voting, there is.

Testing Claim 2: The Party Caucus

While it is true that the theory presented in the previous chapter predicts that small majorities would be more cohesive than large majorities, it was also implied that the mechanism for inducing this cohesion is the majority party caucus. This, however, is only one possible mechanism for linking size and cohesion. If we cared only about predictive success, then debates about mechanisms might be superbly uninteresting. Given the position of this book, however, that dodge is untenable, and I will need to show that the party caucus, rather than some other mechanism, is at work in inducing cohesion.

The easiest way to accomplish this is to break the task down into two parts. The first would be a consideration of different mechanisms that would link small majorities and party cohesion. While imaginative minds could undoubtedly produce more, I will focus on three: evenly balanced parties as deep play, small majorities as core supporters, and finally the mechanism of relative deprivation. None, I argue, is compelling. I then turn to the positive project of providing evidence to support my contention that the party caucus *is* the correct mechanism.

To begin the negative project, we may first turn to Clifford Geertz to provide one alternative account of why small majorities might be more cohesive. In his analysis of Balinese cockfighting (1973, 412–53), Geertz distinguishes certain cockfights that are relatively uninteresting from others that he labels as *deep*. *Deep play* is borrowed from Bentham's description of games in which the stakes were so high that it was simply irrational to play. Deep cockfights, therefore, are high-stakes battles in which more than economic rationality is at work. For Geertz, this something else is (in this case) "a dramatization of status concerns" (Geertz 1973, 437).

While Geertz urges us to look at the Balinese cockfight as text and invokes the language of diagnosis,[15] he does suggest some conditions under which deep play is more likely to result. The more nearly equal the status of the participants, the more likely the play is to be deep, and the deeper the play,

1. The closer the identification of cock and man (or, more properly, the deeper the match the more the man will advance his best, most closely-identified-with cock).
2. The finer the cocks involved and the more exactly they will be matched.
3. The greater the emotion that will be involved and the more the general absorption in the match.
4. The higher the individual bets center and outside, the shorter the outside bet odds will tend to be, and the more betting there will be overall.[16]
5. The less an "economic" and the more a "status" view of gambling will be involved, and the "solider" the citizens who will be gaming. (Geertz 1973, 441)

Geertz also notes that the greater the status of the participants, the deeper the play (and notes that these conditions are not only sufficient but, it appears, also necessary).

Balinese cockfighting is, on any stretch of the imagination, a far cry from nineteenth-century parliamentary procedure. But we can find some similarity. Partisan conflicts in the nineteenth-century House were definitely contests between high status participants. Given Geertz's analysis, we should therefore expect that the more evenly matched the two sides in the House, the deeper the play, with all the consequences: emotional, absorbing, intense, status-oriented behavior. This sounds like a sure recipe for party cohesion, and for party conflict.

Furthermore, the stretch is not as far as some might imagine. In describing the appearance of the new Senate chamber, the *New York Times* of 1859 noted the floor "somewhat resembles a richly carpeted cock-pit" (cited in Byrd 1988, 216) And the notion of politics as a vicious battle to the death was not unknown to the nineteenth century. Walter Dean Burnham cites approvingly Richard Jensen's characterization of the political style of the pre-1896 era as "militarist," with party loyalists being "drilled" and party disloyalists being branded "traitors and turncoats" (Burnham 1970, 72–73). Jean Baker goes into far more detail, spending an entire chapter of her excellent *Affairs of Party* determining the meaning of elections for nineteenth-century Americans, and she finds the militaristic image central to the elections of that period ("The Day of Battle draws nigh / Reverence for your Patriot sires / And strike for your altars and your sires" runs one—seemingly unhummable—Maryland Democratic song; see Baker 1983, 290).

Some evidence that the cock-fighting account may not be right will be found in the following pages, when we go over the rhetoric of rules change. Generally, if we think of deep cockfights then it is difficult to understand the attempt by majorities to limit the rights of the minority through procedural changes. If it is status that the majority wants, it would seem to be easier to get it by thoroughly defeating the opposition on the "field of honor" rather than by voting to take away their arms. This is not to say that individuals did not invoke the language of fighting on the floor of the House during times of procedural change: they did, particularly in the rules changes of the latter half of the nineteenth century. But in most cases, as it turns out, it was the *minority* who wished to present legislative politics as a sort of virile contest, and they presented rules revision as an unmanly attempt to gain advantage. The majority simply said that the election was over, they won, and they had a right to rule (that is, the status contest is already over).

Another mechanism is electoral change. It could be that small majorities are more cohesive because electoral trimmings merely prune back disloyal members. When a party is reduced to a minimum winning coalition, it could be the case that only those most solidly partisan districts are represented. David Donald, for example, notes that the roughly 50 to 70 (depending on the year) Radical Republicans in the Reconstruction Congresses appeared to be remarkably similar to other Republicans, failing to differ with respect to "ethnic background, geographical origin, previous political affiliation, or age" (Donald 1965, 33). What they do have in common is that they come from solidly Republican (and therefore safe) districts.

This could be a powerful argument, except that it assumes that "disloyalty" is a personality trait and not a decision. Suppose a wave of deaths made previously disloyal members the majority. Should they still be disloyal? To what? This isn't to deny that elections may prune out the least partisan, only that the model would need to be more filled out. Furthermore, it appears that Donald's result disappears once more sophisticated methods for identifying Radicals in Congress are used (Bogue 1989, 137). Of course, this is only one Congress, hardly enough to test a general theory, but it does suggest that something is not quite right.

Or consider the mechanism of relative deprivation (Durkheim 1897; Gurr 1970; Boudon 1982). Suppose that Party A has missed being the majority party by one seat. Given how closely they came to winning the election, they may well feel more frustrated and antagonistic than if they needed 100 seats to win the majority. Given a higher level of frustration, members of the minority would be more apt to act against the majority party, using all tactics allowed under the rules, including obstruction. The majority, recognizing the new tenor of the minority's position, reacts by producing institutional changes to silence the dissenters.

I find a lot to admire in this argument, but to really nail it down, we would need to have a clearer notion of what parties *expected* and what they *received*. A party that thinks it is going to have a 30 percent minority and ends up having a 49 percent minority may not feel relatively deprived at all, but rather happily surprised. By contrast, a majority that expected to capture 70 percent of the seats and only received 60 might be upset, too. In fact, in Durkheim's formulation of the problem, a party could expect the usual 20 percent, receive a majority, and derive so much stress from the experience that they instead decide to call it quits (although not, I assume, in the sense intended by Durkheim).

Of course, even if one fails to find these arguments convincing, any or all of the proposed alternative mechanisms (and others we could think of) could be at work, and many of the results of the theory would still go through. We would have small majorities, the minority would obstruct, the majority would enact procedural changes. Nonetheless, given my stated desire to judge assumptions and links, I think I have a duty not just to supply negative arguments against alternative mechanisms, but also to present some sort of positive case for the mechanism I have identified. What evidence is there to support that the caucus is at least an important mechanism in the American Congress for instilling party cohesion?

At least one influential scholar saw a great deal of room for the party caucus in explaining the party cohesion of the nineteenth-century House. Writing in *Congressional Government*, Woodrow Wilson noted that within Congress there was "no *visible*, and therefore no controllable party organization. The only bond of cohesion is the caucus, which occasionally whips a party together for cooperative action against the time for casting its vote upon some critical question" (Wilson 1885, 80). Wilson waxed a bit more eloquent, however, about the power of the caucus in his concluding chapter:

> Moreover, there is a certain well-known piece of congressional machinery long ago invented and applied for the special purpose of keeping both majority and minority compact. The legislative caucus has almost as important a part in our system as have the Standing Committees, and deserves as close study as they. Its functions are much more easily understood in all their bearings than those of the Committees, however, because they are much simpler. The caucus is meant as an antidote to the Committees. It is designed to supply the cohesive principle which the multiplicity and mutual independence of the Committees so powerfully tend to destroy. Having no Prime Minister to confer with about the policy

of the government, as they see members of parliament doing, our congressman confer with each other in caucus. Rather than imprudently expose to the world the differences of opinion threatened or developed among its members, each party hastens to remove disrupting debate from the floor of Congress, where the speakers might too hastily commit themselves to insubordination, to quiet conferences behind closed doors, where frightened scruples may be reassured and every disagreement healed with a salve of compromise or subdued with the whip of political expediency.

"The caucus," Wilson continues, "is the drilling-ground of the party" (Wilson 1885, 211–12).

But what is the relationship between the party caucus and obstruction? We might expect that when faced with obstruction, the majority party would be especially likely to turn to the party caucus mechanism. Evidence that this is so can be found from Paul Hasbrouck, author of *Party Government in the House of Representatives* (1927), who notes that "when the opposition of the minority becomes sufficiently militant, as during the Williams filibuster in the spring of 1908, we find the Cannon régime resorting to the use of the caucus to hold the majority in line" (28). Robert Luce, too, former member of Congress and perhaps one of the sharpest analysts on the subject of parliamentary procedure, notes in his *Legislative Procedure* (1922) that the importance of the caucus tends to vary with the partisan tenor of legislative politics, and concludes his discussion with concerns that it would be imprudent to ignore

> the great probability of the next step [after caucus rule], the complete suppression of the minority. . . . Already its ominous cloud hands over Congress, where now and then we see vital problems of the most serious import handled under special rules permitting preposterous limitations of debate. Will it not presently be asked—'Why any debate at all?' The caucus has decided. We have the votes. Why waste time? (514)

Indeed, Luce reasoned, the limitation of minority rights would be eminently rational (or in his words, profitable): "If a measure is to be passed just as a caucus has agreed upon it, debate can accrue only to the partisan advantage of the minority. The public is sure to pay more attention to the attack than to the defense. . . . We love a libel" (514–15).

In terms of the House during the partisan era, Allan Bogue (1989, chap. 4) has been able to extract some information about the caucus from newspaper accounts and diaries for the Civil War era. He finds in general that the caucus did not work exceptionally well. Part of this was due, however, to the fact that Radical Republicans attempted to use the caucus as a mechanism to move individuals further than it appears they were willing to go. Not surprisingly, this occurred when the majority party was rather large. But the party appears stronger when it comes to the McKinley Houses. David Brady (1973) emphasizes in particular the use of the party caucus as a way to set priorities within the party. But it did more than that: "The party caucus not only tempered the Speaker's power before conferring that power; it also consolidated and meshed the committee and party systems" (148). One way in which this happened, at least in the very late nineteenth century (sadly, immediately after the partisan era, although there is no indication that the practice was recent), was that members would exchange blocks of votes for the caucus Speakership election in return for choice committee assignments.

These suggestions support the model by highlighting the important role of the party caucus, but one wonders whether more systematic analysis might be found. Some evidence on the importance of the caucus as an institutional form, however, has been obtained by Wayne Francis (1989) for the states. Francis surveyed state legislators across the country, asking them to indicate what institution (the committees, the party leadership, and/or the party caucus) they felt made the most significant decisions. He then regressed the proportion of individuals saying that significant decisions were made in the party caucus on chamber size and the percentage of individuals in the majority party in the respondents' legislature.

The results are remarkably consistent with the theory. Francis finds that the proportion of individuals in the majority party has a negative and statistically significant effect on the perceived importance of the party caucus as a locus for significant decisions. In his words, the caucus mechanism is "most important in small chambers with evenly matched parties" (Francis 1989, 46).

Francis is not alone in finding this result. It also turns up in Jewell and Whicker's (1994) recent study of legislative leadership. They write: "The operation of the caucuses is also conditioned by the partisan environment in the legislature. The closer the two-party balance of legislative seats and the stronger the norms of party loyalty, the greater is the likelihood that leaders can succeed in using the caucus to build a consensus on legislative issues and mobilize voters for particular bills" (99). The partisan era, with its exceptionally strong bonds of party loyalty, would surely meet this test.

A more systematic study of the caucus in the nineteenth-century House would need to be established before one felt comfortable in agreeing to the importance of the caucus as a critical mechanism for party voting. Before concluding this section, however, it is important to clarify the argument. I am not suggesting here that the party caucus is the only mechanism at work in explaining majority party cohesion. Without a doubt, there are a host of attitudinal forces at work that can add to our understanding of party cohesion, and without some reckoning of those, the theory is undeniably underspecified (at least if we care about realism of assumptions).

At the same time, however, the theory indicates what I think is a fundamental problem for large majorities seeking to impose discipline in a majoritarian institution: in the absence of extreme restrictions on preferences, there will be cycling even within the caucus. Undoubtedly, a party which cannot even caucus successfully may as well not call a caucus at all, providing some insight into the historical ups and downs of the American legislative caucus system. Whether this contention will provide a compelling account of American legislative practice can only be known with further study. Nonetheless, from the perspective of the theory advanced here, claim 2 appears to be on at least sounder footing than it was when this section started.

Testing Claim 3: Party Size and Obstruction

The third claim argues that large minorities should tend to use the strategy of obstruction. It would seem to be a simple process of determining the truth of this claim: get data on party size and obstructive tactics, and then use statistical magic to see what comes out.

But there are conceptual subtleties here, subtleties that have yet to be fully worked out in the literature. To begin, we would need to determine exactly what sort of strategies constitute obstruction. This is hardly an easy issue. One definition, the most pithy, comes from the Victorian Prime Minister William Ewart Gladstone, who defined obstruction as "resisting the will of the House otherwise than by argument."[17] But is voting "nay" therefore an act of obstruction? If not, what "argument" is being made? And what exactly constitutes the "will of the House"? Should it be considered as identical to the will of the government? If not that, what? Speaker Brand (who later in this book will play an important part) tried to pin things down a bit more: for him, the

> distinctive mark of obstruction lay in the indiscriminating and incessant resistance of an extremely small minority to proposals of the most diverse kinds. To the objection that it was nothing new for opposition to be shown to one measure for the purpose of delaying another, Mr. Brand replied that this was at best a parliamentary trick which had unfortunately been carried on in late years. (Redlich 1908, I.146)

But this will not do either. If the actions of a "small minority" are required, then what are we to do if, the theory in chapter 2 predicts, we should see *large* minorities obstructing? And small minorities under Brand's definition are free to engage in dilatory tactics without being obstructive as long as they do not aim to attack "proposals of the most diverse kind."

Determining what exactly is meant by the term *obstruction* is a difficult task, and one I do not intend to fully solve here. Doing so would require that we explore not only the full set of possible minority tactics within a legislature, but also their context. For example, is calling for the House to adjourn an obstructive device? It would be if minorities used it (as in the Kansas–Nebraska case) to impede the majority; it wouldn't necessarily be, if majority party leaders used adjournment to guarantee the presence of enough of their members to guarantee majority victory. (Or would it be?)

Even if we arrived at a suitable definition, applying it would seem to require at a minimum the equivalent of a Death March through volumes of the *Congressional Record*. Since I wanted to finish this book within the time allotted me by insurance industry mortality estimates, I opted for a more modest aim. My goal was to find some likely activities of obstruction that could be easily counted (the last refuge of the behavioralist scoundrel). The three I decided on were points of order, missing quorums, and days in session. A justification of each of these follows, but these justifications should not be seen as ironclad. A great deal more work needs to be done (as I have hopefully emphasized enough) before we have the definitive account of parliamentary obstruction in any legislature, much less the House. And one could clearly quibble with my characterization of these procedures as obstructive (for an analysis on what I consider slightly more solid ground, turn to the section on the U.S. Senate in chapter 7). But I think these are good proxies given the practical limits, and they provide a useful starting point for future work.

Points of Order

Part of the duty of the Speaker of the House of Representatives is to rule on disputes about parliamentary procedure. Once a decision is made, the decision can be appealed to the House, which votes on whether to sustain the Speaker's decision. Since voters in Wichita typically do not care how one votes on quibbles about parliamentary procedure, the vote follows party lines, and since the Speaker is the leader of the majority party, the decision of the Speaker is almost always upheld.[18] Not always, of course, although the last successful appeal from the Speaker's decision apparently took place in 1927 (Tiefer 1989, 25).[19]

Asking for a vote on a point of order would therefore fit, I think, any rough notion of obstruction that we might have. Typically, all the vote does is to consume time. Those calling for a vote know that they will lose. Admittedly, there may be nonobstructive motivations in here as well (the motivation to challenge the Speaker's authority, a tool for forcing fence-straddlers to

TABLE 3.2. Points of Order, 1869–91

Congress	Majority Proportion (Martis)	Points of Order
41	70.4	5
42	56.0	8
43	68.2	6
44	62.1	71
45	52.9	47
46	48.1	73
47	51.5	67
48	60.3	101
49[a]	56.0	17
50[a]	51.4	33
51	53.9	175

[a]Incomplete data due to missing appendix.

decide, and so on), but as long as these motivations are not correlated with obstructive intent (and I can think of no plausible story why they should be) then the results here will be informative. In addition, raising a point of order and forcing the Speaker to deal with it constitutes an excellent way to derail majority party strategies. Thus on both scores (the initial raising of the point of order and the vote), we seem to be dealing with an obstructive procedure.

The *House Journal* almost routinely includes an appendix listing the points of order decided in that particular session. A count of those points of order from *House Journals* for the period 1869–95 is presented in table 3.2. A larger sample of points of order would have been more desirable, but for purely practical reasons was not possible. The dates are not idiosyncratic, however: they represent the period from late Reconstruction to the close of the partisan era. A slight word of warning: on numerous cases the House has affirmed the precedent that the *House Journal* not include appeals to points of order that are not recognized by the Speaker (Hinds 1899, §2844). This implies that perhaps the most obstructive cases are left out, so if anything the results in table 3.2 underestimate the obstructive potential of the procedure. I have starred the data for the 49th and 50th Congresses because the *House Journal* did not contain the usual appendixes for points of order for every session: these numbers are therefore in all likelihood artificially understated. As a result, I have chosen to analyze this data dropping these cases.

This will of course raise the eyebrows of the statistical cognoscenti on at least two points. First, even without dropping the questionable data we are dealing with a very small number of observations and by dropping the data we are down to only nine cases. There are clear limits to what we can infer using conventional statistical techniques from such a small data set. Most importantly, with such small numbers, standard errors for the estimates will generally be somewhat large.

But even if we had 500 observations, the results would still be troubling because we would be dealing with analyses based on missing data. There are of course techniques to correct for missing data, the appropriate choice depending on whether one has missing data on the dependent or the independent variable (see Greene 1993, 273–77). For the former case (which is the one we are dealing with here), the key question to answer prior to any correction is whether the data are missing due to some random process or whether there is instead a systematic selection bias that has crept in.

I do not have any information on why these *House Journals* did not contain the information. Sometimes the appendixes for a particular session was included in the subsequent session's *House Journal*, but that was not the case here. The Congresses were both controlled by Democrats, but Democrats controlled half the Congresses of this era and there were after all only two Congresses in which there was a missing appendix. The size of the majority in the excluded Congresses was smaller than those in the included cases, but only mildly (53.7 percent as opposed to 58.4 percent). Perhaps there is some more subtle selection process going on, but in the absence of a specification of what that process is the data appear to fall into what Greene refers to as the "ignorable case": results run on data with missing observations will lose some efficiency (that is, will have inflated standard errors) but will be unbiased. These two considerations (small data set and missing data) should be taken into consideration when evaluating the results.

With nine observations, there are not very many controlling variables that could be included. Consequently, I began by simply regressing the count of points of order on a constant and the size of the majority party. The results are presented in table 3.3 (column 1). These results indicate that the coefficient on majority party size is in the predicted direction: the larger the majority party, the fewer points of order get raised. Furthermore, they are significant at the 10 percent level for a one-tailed test. The results stay the same when one introduces a control for the party differences (see column 2). The nonsignificance of this party difference term tells us that (at least in an additive fashion, and given the data we have) Democrats and Republicans did not differ in their use of this obstructive tactic.

Things look worse, however, when we add in a variable controlling for time. Here, the coefficient on the proportion of seats held by the majority party not only loses its statistical significance, it also has the wrong sign.

Taken strictly on its own terms, this indicates that the link between obstruction and small majority party size has not passed its first test. This could of course mean that I have picked out a relatively poor measure of minority obstruction (which is undoubtedly true). Or it could simply mean that

TABLE 3.3.   GLS and 2SLS Regression Results on Points of Order, 1869–95

Independent Variables	(1)[a]	(2)[a]	(3)	(4)[b]
Constant	190.742*	184.501#	−98.818#	748.037#
	(91.540)	(100.984)	(65.768)	(427.548)
Majority proportion (Martis)	−2.146#	−2.089#	1.060	−11.759#
	(1.361)	(1.385)	(0.983)	(7.476)
Democratic Congress		7.106		
		(24.330)		
Time			19.677***	
			(3.752)	
Number of observations	9	9	9	9
Corrected R-squared	0.23	0.11	0.770	−1.630
Standard error of the regression	48.011	51.802	26.275	88.896
Durbin-Watson (Rho)	(0.341)	(0.337)	2.296	1.568
Mean of dependent variable	61.444	61.444	61.444	61.444

[a]Corrected for first-order autocorrelation
[b]Two-stage least squares estimation
#significant at the 10 percent level, one-tailed test
*significant at the 10 percent level, two-tailed test
**significant at the 5 percent level, two-tailed test
***significant at the 1 percent level, two-tailed test

the hypothesized relationship between party size and obstruction has not been realized. If so, this cannot help but count against the theory.

On the other hand, perhaps I have been the dupe of a simultaneity problem. After all, it could well be that over time, party competition in the House drove the size of the majority downward, and that it was this downward shift in majorities that led to obstruction in the form of points of order. Indeed, Clubb, Flanigan, and Zingale (1986), in the argument cited previously, trace partisan decline to the ebbing influence of the realigning election.

I therefore reestimated the model using two-stage least squares, with a constant term and time as instrumental variables.[20] I would be more reluctant to report these results if Kennedy (1984, 115, 120) had not noted that 2SLS has been shown consistently in Monte Carlo simulations to have superior small-sample properties compared to other estimators. We certainly have a small sample here. The results are reported in column 4. Note that once the equation is purged of its simultaneity bias, majority party proportion has the correct sign and is statistically significant again.

Simultaneity, however, is only one issue. More problematic, I believe, is the problem of measurement error. There are after all numerous reasons (as noted above) why individuals might lodge points of order (even against their own party). Furthermore, the use of points of order in the Senate to get around rules raises the possibility that points of order might in some cases (although, as Tiefer shows, apparently not for the House) work as an antiobstructionist tactic. The claim that minorities resort to obstruction when faced with small minorities would be on more solid footing if we could find some independent (as well as easily available) measure of obstruction that would allow us to have a broader check on the results.

Missing Quorums

Happily, another source does exist. As noted in the introduction, minorities within the House frequently made use of the tactic of the "disappearing quorum." In 1832, the House had refrained from forcing John Quincy Adams to vote (Hinds 1899, V §5943). At the time, Drayton of South Carolina prophetically noted that this decision would set a precedent under which members of the minority in the future could impede the legislative functioning of the body. In that, he was correct.

Most legislative scholars have heard of the disappearing quorum, but there has yet been no study of the determinants of its use. This is a sign, I think, not only of how little work is done on legislative history, but also how little is known about obstruction. This study constitutes the first attempt to understand the factors associated with the use of this procedure. Were there party differences in the use of obstruction? Did the use of the tactic vary over the life of a session? Was there any trend in the use of this procedure?

Determining how often the disappearing quorum was used is difficult. House rules prior to 1890 set the quorum in the Committee of the Whole equal to the quorum in the House. The use of the disappearing quorum would therefore be as possible in the former as the latter. Since the *House Journal* records only the proceedings of the House, a thorough study of the use of the disappearing quorum would require combing through shelves of *Congressional Records*. However, without a good reason why different results would obtain in the House as opposed to the Committee of the Whole, I stuck with the House results. A note: the *Journal* does not explicitly state when a disappearing quorum has made an appearance, merely that there was an absence of a quorum, so I am assuming here that whatever systematic effects show up will reflect obstructive actions. Table 3.4 presents the data.[21]

A problem with these session-by-session measures is that they ignore the possibility that some sessions are shorter than others. So for example, the single missing-quorum in the first session of the 45th Congress is treated the same as the single missing quorum in the first session of the 49th Congress, even though the former was in session for only 50 days and the latter sat for 242 days. Consequently, I have normalized the observations by dividing the

TABLE 3.4. **Missing Quorums on Votes in the House of Representatives, 1875–95**

Congress	Party in Majority	Contested Elections	Other	Total	Majority Proportion (Martis)
43-2	R	0	2	2	68.2
44-1	D	0	3	3	62.1
44-2	D	0	0	0	62.1
45-1	D	0	0	0	52.9
45-2	D	0	2	2	52.9
45-3	D	0	2	2	52.9
46-1	D	0	2	2	48.1
46-2	D	0	5	5	48.1
46-3	D	0	5	5	48.1
47-1	R	24	8	32	51.5
47-2	R	8	2	10	51.5
48-1	D	0	15	15	60.3
48-2	D	0	1	1	60.3
49-1	D	0	1	1	56.0
49-2	D	0	2	2	56.0
50-1	D	2	5	7	51.4
50-2	D	4	6	10	51.4
51-1	R	20	75	95	53.9
51-2	R	0	11	11	53.9
52-1	D	0	32	32	71.7
52-2	D	0	8	8	71.7
53-1	D	0	14	14	61.2
53-2	D	17	55	72	61.2
53-3	D	0	0	0	61.2
54-1	R	2	1	3	71.1
54-2	R	0	1	1	71.1

number of missing quorums in each session by the number of days in that session.

Column 1 of table 3.5 evaluates the simple theory that a constant and party proportion explain the observed pattern. While the sign points in the right direction, the coefficient is not statistically significant. Columns 2 and 3 present the results controlling for party difference and for the years of the most intense fighting over the use of the disappearing quorum (the 51st through the 53rd Congresses). The negative sign indicates that as the size of the majority party increases, the number of disappearing quorums per day decreases, consistent with the theory (an effect that is significant at the .01 level for a two-tailed test). But the results do more than confirm the theory. Column 2 indicates that it is indeed true that the years of fighting over the disappearing quorum were rather unique,[22] and column 3 supports what is

**TABLE 3.5. GLS Regression Results on Total Number
of Missing Quorums Per Day, 1875–95**

Independent Variables	(1)[a]	(2)	(3)[a]	(4)[a]
Constant	0.0886	0.195**	0.307***	0.252***
	(0.1455)	(0.071)	(0.067)	(0.059)
Majority proportion	−0.0004147	−0.00282**	−0.00404***	−0.00418***
(Martis)	(0.002316)	(0.00120)	(0.00097)	(0.00092)
51st through 53rd		0.133***	0.143***	0.143***
Congresses		(0.039)	(0.026)	(0.024)
Democratic majority			−0.0588**	−0.0567***
			(0.0209)	(0.0189)
Percentage of competitive				0.00159#
seats (Brady–Grofman)				(0.00113)
Number of observations	26	26	26	26
Corrected R-squared	0.130	0.441	0.561	0.562
Standard error of the				
regression	0.0765	0.0613	0.0544	0.0543
Durbin-Watson (Rho)	(0.426)	2.177	(−0.241)	(−0.268)
Mean of dependent				
variable	0.0672	0.0672	0.0672	0.0672

[a]Corrected for first-order autocorrelation
#significant at the 10 percent level, one-tailed test
*significant at the 10 percent level, two-tailed test
**significant at the 5 percent level, two-tailed test
***significant at the 1 percent level, two-tailed test

clear from contemporary accounts: the use of missing quorums on contested elections tended to occur more when the Republicans were in control than when the Democrats held the House majority, a fact that will attain importance in chapter 5.

To determine whether these results would still hold up if controlling for other likely influences, I reran column 3 adding a control for turnover and for the percentage of competitive seats. The percentage of new members (which I do not report) turned out to have a negative but insignificant effect on the dependent variable. The percentage of competitive seats, however, was positive as well as significant (column 4), indicating that the thinner the electoral margin of individual members, the more missing quorums per day one observes.

In some ways, this makes sense. During the period in question here, the willingness of members to seek out and retain Congressional office significantly increased (Kernell 1977). Faced with the need for shoring up their support, members might well have missed a vote or two. Furthermore, missing a vote or two when the majority is small would lead to a number of missing quorums in a way that would not happen if the majority is large. Column 4 indicates, however, that even controlling for this possible effect, the size of the majority party still has a significant and negative expected effect on the missing quorums.[23]

If we treat missing quorums as an obstructive device (as is quite clear from the legislative history of the House), then these results support the theory: as the majority becomes smaller, the use of this particular dilatory tactic grows more frequent. But a critic might object that this is exceptionally obvious: we already knew that the trick of the disappearing quorum worked best when majorities are small. In many ways, then, this would seem to be a trivially easy test.

This objection, however, is not enough in itself to write off the results. Minorities could after all decide at any time not to use the disappearing quorum. The fact that they appear to have used it when the majority was small therefore suggests that something a bit more systematic is going on. But even more, even if this is the only obstructive action ever taken by the minority (which it is clearly not), it would still show that there was a relationship between size and minority obstruction, and thus would still provide small majorities with an incentive to limit minority obstruction. For a more unexpected result, however, we might turn to days in session.

Days in Session

While each Congress lasts for two years, there is no constitutional provision requiring the legislature to sit for any particular portion of that time. Theoretically, therefore, Congress could simply process all submitted legislation on the first morning, allowing members to go home to relax for the remaining 729.5 days. While to date this has not occurred, neither has the Congress stayed in session for every minute of those two years. Instead, in different Congresses, the House and Senate have sat for different lengths of time.

We might think that the number of days Congress sits is simply random. There are certainly many random components that could enter into that calculation: the weather conditions in Washington, the weather conditions back home, the number of individuals engaged to be married, and so on. Nonetheless, we might get a better handle on the forces affecting days in session if we think about things from the perspective of minority rights to obstruct.

Suppose, for example, that the minority decides to obstruct. What will happen? Well, one thing that can easily happen is that more time will be consumed. As people find more and more roll call votes that need to be pressed, or more points of orders to be raised, time gets taken up. Now technically this need not lead to longer days in session. A majority could after

TABLE 3.6. GLS Results on Days in Session, U.S. Congress, 1835–95

Independent Variables	(1)	(2)	(3)[a]	(4)
Constant	416.890***	493.020***	525.892***	490.289***
	(46.988)	(92.748)	(87.663)	(57.030)
Majority proportion (Martis)	−1.261#	−1.359*	−1.080#	−1.535*
	(0.799)	(0.676)	(0.790)	(0.686)
Impeachment (40th Congress)	385.568***	372.888***	365.51***	387.483***
	(16.951)	(22.459)	(20.628)	(15.271)
Number of Representatives and Senators		0.103		
		(0.310)		
Number of bills introduced		−0.000549		
		(0.00383)		
Turnover (Fiorina–Rohde–Wissel)		−1.934#	−2.515**	−1.250#
		(1.299)	(1.166)	(0.746)
Percentage of competitive seats (Brady–Grofman)			0.186	
			(1.152)	
28th Congress (1841–43)				127.287***
				(6.261)
53rd Congress (1893–95)				107.002***
				(12.562)
Number of observations	31	31	23	31
Corrected R-squared	0.660	0.673	0.774	0.825
Standard error of the regression	46.368	45.486	41.487	33.292
Durbin-Watson	2.193	2.0825	2.140	1.704
Mean of dependent variable	355.903	355.903	357.870	355.903

[a]Results based on observations from the 32nd through 54th Congress (1851–97).
#significant at the 10 percent level, one-tailed test
*significant at the 10 percent level, two-tailed test
**significant at the 5 percent level, two-tailed test
***significant at the 1 percent level, two-tailed test

all simply give in to the slightest amount of obstruction, drop the pending legislation, and move on. But a majority (especially a cohesive majority) has another tool at its disposal: expanding the length of the session. If we assume that the minority might eventually run out of steam at some point, then by sitting for a greater number of days, it becomes possible to wear out the opposition. If the theory presented in this book is correct, then, we should expect to see an association between the number of days Congress was in session and the proportion of seats held by the majority party. The results are presented in table 3.6.

Column 1 of table 3.6 presents a simple regression of days in session on the proportion of seats held by the majority. Since the 40th Congress (1867–69) was a clear outlier (being the Congress in which Johnson was impeached),

I have also included a dummy variable to capture the idiosyncrasies of this particular session. The proportion of seats has the expected sign and is significant, although not overwhelmingly so.

Column 2 amends the simple model by incorporating some variables related to Congressional workload. It might be argued, for example, that the number of days that Congress sits in session is driven primarily by factors such as the number of individuals in the institution, their relative level of experience, and the amount of work that they have to do, rather than anything to do with majority party calculations. Measures of these factors are easily incorporated into our data set, and the amended results are reported in column 2.[24]

The sign on the size of the majority party is still negative as well as statistically significant. This finding is supportive of the partisan theory. Of the workload variables, only one, turnover, shows a significant relationship to the number of days in session. The negative coefficient makes sense: as there are more and more members without experience in the national legislature, we should expect session lengths to diminish. Put another way, long sessions are a result of the institutionalization of the Congressional career.

The remaining workload variables do not seem to have an effect. That is, it is not true that a larger number of bills introduced (a standard measure of workload) makes for a longer session. I consider this to be an important repudiation of workload arguments. Nor does it appear to be true that the increasing size of the legislature is significantly associated with the length of the Congressional session. This latter finding is especially interesting, given that one of the conventional arguments is that the need for an end to dilatory tactics is less necessary in a small institution like the Senate than in a large institution like the House. If this argument were true, we would expect the increasing size of the House to have had some effect on days in session, but this does not appear to be the case.

Can we relate these results to reciprocity, another of our theories? Brady and Grofman (1991) present the proportion of competitive seats in the U.S. House from 1851 up through 1895 (competitive being defined as winning by less than 55 percent of the two-party vote). If a large proportion of the seats in the House are competitive, then members' expectations for long-term House service should be low.[25] Of course, in terms of the reciprocity argument, this could cut both ways. Members could be more willing to tolerate obstruction if they do not have a long legislative horizon (because they wish to protect their selfish use of obstruction) or they may be less willing to tolerate obstruction (if obstruction is thought of as a system of minority rights that is sustained through reciprocity). The results presented in column 3, however, show that *neither* of these arguments is quite right. The percentage of competitive seats has no significant effect on the number of days the House is in session. By contrast, the coefficient on proportion of seats held by the majority party continues to be high.

A look at the residuals from the various estimations (and others I have not reported) suggested the clear presence of two suspicious outliers: the 28th (1841–43) and the 53rd (1893–95) Congresses. In both cases, the statistical model underpredicts the actual number of days Congress was in session. These years turn out to be rather significant. As chapter 6 will discuss, the year 1841 witnessed the adoption in the House of Representatives of the Hour Rule, an important limitation on debate. Furthermore, the 53rd Congress saw the culmination of a Republican string of obstructive tactics and the final capitulation of the Democratic party to the so-called Reed Rules (see chapter 5). In other words, the outliers here are years in which issues of obstruction were especially salient in the House. Controlling for these outliers through the use of dummy variables yields the estimates reported in column 4. Again, the proportion of seats controlled by the majority party in the House has a statistically significant negative effect on the number of days the Congress sat.[26]

The results presented here are specific to the House, which is appropriate given the context of this chapter. However, the number of days that the Congress is in session is not determined unilaterally by the House. As a result, I have also run the equations specified above with the addition of a variable measuring the proportion of seats held by the majority party in the Senate. The results do not change significantly from the story presented above. The size of the majority in the House still has a negative and statistically significant effect. The effect of the Senate majority proportion is less clear: in the Senate-augmented version of columns 1 and 3, the sign on the Senate majority coefficient is negative, while in 2 and 4 it is positive. In no case is Senate majority proportion statistically significant even at the .10 level for a one-tailed test. While it is quite possible that further analysis will undermine these results, they do imply that the number of days the nineteenth-century House spent in session was primarily driven by partisan considerations in the House and not the Senate. This may seem to suggest that the proportion of seats held by the majority is unimportant in the Senate. This would be a hasty conclusion, however, as chapter 7 will show.

Without the theory presented in this book, I think we would be unlikely to expect any relationship between the number of days the House sat in session during the nineteenth century and the size of the majority party. The strength of the results in this section, therefore, should offer compelling evidence that the account of minority obstruction offered here is on the right track.

Testing Claim 4: Rules Changes and Party Size

Notwithstanding my skepticism about the Friedmanite position, it would hardly be comforting if, after having positively evaluated the first three claims, it turned out that majority party size had no relationship at all with procedural change.

Estimates of majority party size for the House were assembled from four sources. The first and most reliable, as argued above, is the Martis 1989 data. While it may be fine to simply conclude with the Martis data, I have, in an abundance of caution, included the CQ 1982 data, taken from the Historical Statistics of the United States. The CQ figures claim to report party affiliations as of the first day of the legislative session, while Martis looks to the party affiliations members were elected under (see Martis 1989, 16). The CQ figures thus seem more appropriate for the substantive issue here, yet Martis probably has the most reliable figures. Rather than decide between them, I include both. For comparison, I have also included data on the majority party proportion calculated from George Galloway 1969, who relies on De Alva Stanwood Alexander's 1916 work and a 1960 publication by the Office of the Secretary of the Senate.[27]

One concern with the party affiliation data is that it may be more reflective of the way policy preferences fell out during the session, and less reflective of an individual's willingness to vote with the majority on procedural issues. Thus the South American party might vote with the Republicans to organize the House, although they would be technically counted as a third party. Since it is the procedural votes which I am primarily interested in here, I needed some way to get around this problem. A clear opportunity for individuals to display their partisan loyalties on procedural questions would be on the vote for Speaker. I have surveyed the various *House Journals* for the partisan era and have calculated the percentage of votes cast for the winning Speaker for the final ballot. This would, I felt, indicate the procedural coalition in cases where the largest party does not have a majority and must turn to those outside their coalition.

My assumption here is a strong one, namely that those individuals who are willing to climb on board for a Speaker election would be willing to climb on board as well for a rule change limiting minority obstruction. Of course, one can think of many reasons why third parties would hesitate to do this. As if that weren't enough, in many cases my naive desire to find the "true majority" by focusing on a case in which a majority had to support someone was foiled: on some occasions (the 31st and 34th Congresses), the House elected the Speaker on a plurality rule.

While these series all have their differences, in general, there is a high degree of agreement among these four independent measures, as a look at the correlation coefficients indicated. In general, the CQ and Galloway data are more similar to each other than each is to the Speaker election data. This is only to be expected, since third parties are separated out in the Galloway and CQ data but can be folded into the majority coalition in the Speaker series. The weakest correlations appear to be between the Martis figures and the other three, suggesting the presence of errors in the other measures. Nonetheless, these marginal differences shouldn't negate the fact that these time-series appear to be measuring the same thing. Between the four, then, we should have a fair indication of the strength of the majority party in the House of Representatives.

Obtaining systematic data on our other variable of interest, procedural change in the House, is much more difficult. Even today, there is no complete list of the rules changes that have taken place in the history of the House.[28] A complete listing of proposed and adopted rules changes is currently being compiled by Evelyn Fink and Brian Humes of the University of Nebraska-Lincoln. In addition, Sarah Binder is independently cataloging all the rules changes regarding minority rights. Their work when ultimately completed will be an excellent addition to the historical and theoretical literature on Congressional procedure. In assessing the theory presented here, however, I have had to rely on the secondary literature, which is unanimous in noting that major rules changes during the partisan era occurred on four separate occasions: 1837, 1860, 1880, and 1890 (Galloway 1969; Damon 1971; Sullivan 1984).[29]

Table 3.7 presents the four time-series on majority party proportion. I have indicated in bold those years in which according to the existing literature major rules change took place. As is fairly clear from this table, the four major rules changes of the partisan era all occurred at times when the majority was close to minimal winning size. For those who do not trust their ability to optically determine statistical significance, table 3.8 presents the mean party size (and standard deviations) in both the rules change and non–rules change Congresses. The t-value reported is the appropriate statistic for a test of difference in means when population variances cannot be assumed identical, as is the case here. The probability that the rules change and non–rules change proportions are identical is less than one in three thousand for all four measures. This constitutes strong evidence that the pattern of institutional change in the House is associated with the strength of the majority party.

While these results do indicate that small majorities have enacted major rules changes in the nineteenth-century House, the data as presented can only go so far. Three issues in particular need resolution. First, we may have a problem of simultaneity. The proportion of seats held by the majority party was not only the thing that changed over the nineteenth century and therefore is not the only possible candidate for explaining these rules changes. I have, however, explored a number of potential alternatives—increasing membership turnover, increasing workload, realignment, divided party control—and none of them matched up with the pattern of major rules changes that occurred during these years in the House.[30]

Second, we have a potential problem of selection bias. Even granting that the rules changes involved the problem of minority obstruction and that those

TABLE 3.7. **Majority Proportion in the House and Major Rules Changes, 1835–95**

Congress	Martis	CQ	Galloway	Speaker Proportion	Major Rules Change?
24 (1835)	59.1	60	60	61	No
25 (1837)	**52.9**	**45**	**48**	**53**	**Yes**
26 (1839)	51.7	51	55	51	No
27 (1841)	58.7	55	55	55	No
28 (1843)	65.9	64	64	68	No
29 (1845)	62.3	63	63	57	No
30 (1847)	50.4	51	51	50	No
31 (1849)	48.5	49	51	46	No
32 (1851)	54.5	60	60	55	No
33 (1853)	67.1	68	68	66	No
34 (1855)	42.7	46	46	48	No
35 (1857)	55.7	50	55	57	No
36 (1859)	**48.7**	**48**	**48**	**50**	**Yes**
37 (1861)	59.0	59	60	62	No
38 (1863)	46.2	55	56	55	No
39 (1865)	70.4	78	76	79	No
40 (1867)	76.5	74	74	81	No
41 (1869)	70.4	70	70	70	No
42 (1871)	56.0	55	57	58	No
43 (1873)	68.2	65	70	70	No
44 (1875)	62.1	58	62	61	No
45 (1877)	52.9	52	53	53	No
46 (1879)	**48.1**	**51**	**51**	**51**	**Yes**
47 (1881)	51.5	50	52	52	No
48 (1883)	60.3	61	62	62	No
49 (1885)	56.0	56	56	56	No
50 (1887)	51.4	52	52	52	No
51 (1889)	**53.9**	**51**	**52**	**52**	**Yes**
52 (1891)	71.7	71	69	71	No
53 (1893)	61.2	61	62	64	No
54 (1895)	71.1	69	69	70	No

Note: Boldface indicates those years in which major rules changes took place.

changes took place at times when the majority party was small, nonetheless there are other Congresses in which the majority party was also small and yet where there do not seem to have been major rules reforms. So by interpreting the data selectively (by selecting on the dependent variable), I could have

TABLE 3.8.   Difference of Means, Majority Proportion, Rules Change and Other Years

	Mean Proportion, Rules Change Years	Mean Proportion, Other Years	t	(df)	p
Martis	50.9 (2.926)	59.3 (8.69)	−3.78	(13)	0.0022
CQ	48.8 (2.87)	59.4 (8.39)	−4.91	(13)	0.0003
Galloway	49.8 (2.06)	60.3 (7.78)	−5.81	(19)	0.0000
Speaker	51.5 (1.29)	60.4 (9.11)	−4.75	(29)	0.0001

reached an erroneous conclusion. The explicit analysis of this problem is postponed to chapter 6. In addition, part 3 of this work (extending the theory to other institutions) should go even further in suggesting that we are not faced with a fluke of the House.

Finally, and most importantly, the figures above cannot tell us anything about the content of the rules changes. In particular, they do not tell us whether those rules changes had anything to do with minority obstruction. For all we know, the rules changes might actually have *increased* the ability of the minority party to obstruct legislation. This issue is taken up in chapters 4 and 5.

Conclusion

Assumptions and links are an important part of our theories, and they should be an important part of our evaluation of our theories as well. In this chapter, I have presented evidence that allows the reader the opportunity to make an informed decision on these issues. Summing up, it appears that (1) small majority parties do seem more cohesive, at least based on roll call voting results, (2) the mechanism linking small majorities and cohesion is the party caucus, (3) the largest minority parties are the most likely to obstruct, and (4) the timing of procedural changes in the partisan era does appear to be related to the size of the majority party.

In addition, we have been able to make some initial assessments about the plausibility of other theories of procedural change and minority rights. Neither workload nor reciprocity, at least as measured here, offers much of a key to unlocking the puzzle. These theories may work well in other areas, but their power I think has been overestimated, and the results here support that conclusion. Conversely, partisan factors such as the caucus, party proportion, and the Reed years show important impacts on the variables of interest. Taken together, these results may help to calm any residual fears from chapter 1 as to the possibility of accounting for the timing of institutional change.

In addition, however, I hope this chapter has demonstrated that testing assumptions and links may well be relatively painless. There is no guarantee, of course, that having looked under the rose we will not find all sorts of insects and diseases that will make us wish we had never turned a petal. But sometimes we may, if lucky, find another rose.

CHAPTER 4

Rules Changes in the
Antebellum House

It has now become a commonplace to require that theories respect the self-understandings of the agents involved. Reifying institutional change and then imputing the motive for political action as that same reification isn't very enlightening. No one after all (pace Merton) ever died for a latent function. Instead, individuals have their own views of the world, which structure the choices they make.

Of course, the cynical will see this as a veiled plea for rational choice masquerading as social theory. But even a process of unintended consequences could be consistent with a respect for agency.[1] No one "intended" the *Hindenburg* to explode and paralyze lighter-than-air travel forever (except for football games and weddings), and yet it is transparently easy to formulate an account consistent with human agency of why people would be less willing to ride in floating gas bombs after witnessing the devastation at Lakehurst, New Jersey. This doesn't alter the importance of that tragedy for the future path of transportation.

Part of the stubbornness with which rational choice theory has stuck to the Friedmanite position is due, I think, to precisely these fears about agency. It is exceptionally ironic that rational choice, a theory which prides itself on treating individuals as autonomous actors who should be accorded the respect of at least knowing what they were doing when they did it, should be so reluctant to embrace the notion of strategic calculation when it comes to historical narrative.

I would not, however, claim that arguments about self-understandings need be central to every political explanation. The refutation of that position has already been made, to my mind stunningly well, by Jacobson and Kernell in their book *Strategy and Choice in Congressional Elections*. Jacobson and Kernell offer an account of why members retire from Congressional service. The reason that most individuals *say* they are retiring is either due to their affection for their family or a need to engage in charity work. It turns out, however, that more Democrats appear to love their families (and therefore retire) in bad political years for Democrats, and vice versa for Republicans.

Jacobson and Kernell could have been neo-Benthamites and unmasked these members of Congress as shallow frauds. But they do not follow this tack at all. Instead, they argue that these retiring members are absolutely sincere, they do love their families and want to do charity work, and that might be the largest part of their reason for retiring. So far, a clear acceptance of the self-understandings of the agents. But, Jacobson and Kernell add, most members share these concerns. What distinguishes those who run again from those who retire is therefore the marginal political calculation that they will not win, which, though a small part (perhaps even transparent) of their reasons for retiring, nonetheless plays a determining role in predicting which members are most likely to retire.

This is an excellent example and needs I think to be better appreciated. At the same time, however, what enables this result to hold is that there the love of family or charity or friends or whatever people aver as their rationale for retirement is assumed to be relatively constant. This is why those self-under-standings need not play a prominent role in the explanation of retirement decisions. If, however, some individuals did care about such things and others did not, then we would not be so quick to write off the explanations offered by the agents themselves. To put it slightly differently, the role we attach to people's explanations of their own actions depends on the questions we are asking. If we want to know why a certain set of members retired, we need to talk about self-understandings. If, on the other hand, we wish to distinguish between a set of individuals who take different paths but who all avow the same explanations of their actions, then self-understandings will be less important.

In recounting the major battles over procedural change in the House of Representatives during the partisan era, I want to show that legislators did in fact think about procedural change as a *partisan* affair engaging issues of *minority rights*. This will hopefully bring out a bit more the ways in which partisanship is so central to the issue of procedural change with respect to obstruction, and it should quiet any concerns that the theoretical claims set out in this book have only a fleeting and ephemeral relationship with real politics.

Having said that, not every single individual will be a ruthless partisan. Some will maintain their stance on minority rights, even though they might be in the majority. There are not a lot of these individuals in this account, but they are there and especially conspicuous. Rather than being an embarrassment, this strakes me instead as a striking advantage of the approach I am advocating here. In other accounts, these individuals would fade into the background; here they can take their place, their behavior highlighted by the fact that it deviates from what we might cynically expect of them.

1837: Jacksonian Politics without Jackson

The Jacksonian era witnessed the fruition of the first mass political parties in the world. However inevitable that progression may seem in retrospect, it was hardly obvious at the time. Party cohesion is something that has to be constructed: it does not rain down like manna from heaven. While in office, therefore, Andrew Jackson had worked to instill party discipline by making certain issues a matter of party policy. The problem with emphasizing the common, however, is that sometimes it isn't. Jackson's approach led to the disaffection of a variety of elements, among them Anti-Masons and Calhounites, coalescing in the mid-1830s in the formation of the Whig party. And as the opposition became more organized, the majority too found the need to turn a rather loose electoral coalition into an effective legislative party.

A key actor in that partisan transformation was Speaker of the House James K. Polk. Polk's term in that office has been described by the historian Charles Sellers (1957) in the following words:

> Never had a speaker been called to the chair under more trying circumstances than was Polk in 1835. . . . These years [1835–39, the years of Polk's Speakership] witnessed the culmination of a trend toward a rigid partisan organization of American politics and a strict enforcement of party discipline. Polk was the first speaker to be regarded frankly as a party leader, responsible for pushing a party program through the House. (304)

And Polk was not without tools for accomplishing these ends. His close ties with Andrew Jackson were of course significant, but so too was his control as Speaker over committee assignments, not just of the majority but also the minority. In addition, as chair Polk had the power to arbitrate on numerous issues of parliamentary procedure. Both of these tools, as we shall see, did not go unutilized.

This effort to instill party discipline bears none of the peaceful marks we expect from steps toward legislative modernization. Polk had in the 24th Congress suffered a continuous campaign of obstructionism and insult led by arch-rival John Bell. In this program Bell had the assistance of other individuals in his boardinghouse—Henry Wise, Balie Peyton, and Judge White, a noted Tennessee Whig.[2]

Some of the legislative fireworks can be imagined by recalling that Polk's first Speakership witnessed the enactment of a gag rule requiring the automatic tabling of abolitionist petitions. The gag rule would be one of the most contentious issues in the antebellum House. Typically, the fight over the gag rule is portrayed as political contest in which sectional affiliations crosscut parties, and it was certainly that. At the same time, however, we can see the gag rule as an attempt to limit the obstruction of important House business by the introduction of an inflammatory subject (Holmes 1988). Similar slim majorities can be found on many of the roll calls to follow in the long fight over the gag rule, as Miller's 1996 rich history of the contest shows. And we may even find a bit of partisanship lurking under the surface appearance of sectional tension. Miller writes:

> . . . the more extreme Southern spokesmen shot themselves in the foot . . . Moving to *reconsider* the referral of the Briggs petition to committee opened the floor to exactly that discussion of slavery they had been endeavoring to prevent. Or they alleged they wanted to prevent. Some Democrats and some Northerners and some Southerners from other states, too, suspected that the Highest of the High Carolinian purists [John C. Calhoun] had reasons not to object altogether to a parliamentary situation that clogged the wheels of a government they opposed . . . (42)

So let Hammond (Calhoun's lieutenant in the House) and John Quincy Adams, opponents of Jackson both, slug it out over the contentious petition issue. The end result is a thorough halt to Democratic plans. This explanation may seem even more likely when one considers the careful work of Alvin Lynn (1972), who fixed the Administration majority in the 24th Congress at a thin 53.8 percent.[3]

It was, however, in the subsequent 25th Congress that many of the rules changes to be considered here were adopted, and to which we now turn. To handle the burgeoning economic crisis, Martin van Buren called the Congress into a special session, and it was during that special session that the procedural changes we are interested in were debated and approved. The political stakes were quite high. As James Walker wrote to Polk, "the man who shall bring forward the plan to produce a uniform currency, and perfectly destroy Biddle's power, will be the next President" (*Correspondence of Polk*, vol. 4, 228). High stakes combined with rough parity in partisan strength promised a great deal of attention and maneuvering in the special session.

How cohesive then was the Democratic majority? The answer to this question depended to a large extent on the political actions of the Conservative wing of the party, which favored an end to the hard-money policies embraced by the Democrats. The policy preferences of the Conservatives were pronounced through the newly established faction newspaper, *The Madisonian*, printed by Thomas Allen.

Polk's problem as party leader was simple: he had to find some way to keep the Conservatives from bolting the party line. To do so, Polk arrived in Washington shortly before the session to coordinate parliamentary strategy with van Buren and to negotiate with the Conservative element of his party (Niven 1983, 421). The result (or nonresult) of these preparations was that Polk was elected, presumably with Conservative support, on September 4, 1837. Suspicions about the price of Conservative support for Polk were raised when Thomas Allen upset Blair, the Democratic candidate, in the race for printer.

Casual observers of politics (especially those who think of the political process from an efficiency standpoint) often find it incomprehensible that trivia like the election of a printer should assume such a high profile in the minds of legislators. But it is precisely because the stakes are so small that they are often so closely watched. If they are willing to betray you in the election of a printer, what will they do on a really important issue? Thus, looking at explanations for the outcome on the printer can tell us a lot about the way in which the majority party was negotiating its tensions.

What did the election of Allen mean? Two interpretations of these events have been given. The first, by Charles Sellers (1957, 327), takes Allen's election as evidence of the willingness of the Conservatives to abandon the Democratic party. We would therefore be seeing the majority beginning to break up, or at least seeing the Conservatives flexing their political muscle. A second interpretation, given by John Niven in both his biography of Martin van Buren (1983, 421–22) and of John Calhoun (1988, 230–31), argues that Polk sacrificed the printer in order to obtain Conservative support for his election to Speaker. If this is true, then is the election of Allen a triumph for party cohesion, not a defeat?

Which explanation works? Unfortunately, Niven does not indicate any sources for his interpretation. It appears from the *National Intelligencer* that Allen was elected by Whig votes, so if there was a bargain between Polk and the Conservatives it clearly did not involve an exchange of votes (or, if it did, Polk failed to carry through). Some support, then, for the Conservative defection argument can be found in the debate that took place over the issue. Boon, an Indiana Democrat who would shortly be named chair of the Public Lands Committee, moved that voting for the printer be made viva voce. This would allow everyone to know how everyone else voted (in contrast to the usual method of balloting) and therefore place Conservatives on the spot.

Dawson, a Whig from Georgia, recognized the move for what it was and made the following response:

> Mr. Dawson wanted to know why, after nine ballotings, it was now suddenly proposed to vote openly? Some discovery seemed to have been made; some gentlemen had not acted in conformity with the wishes of others, and it was now required that the votes of all should be known. If there was any secret fact of this sort, known only to the maker of the resolution, he wished it to be known. If it was merely intended to place in harness gentlemen who were a little chafed, and seemed unwilling to draw in the old yoke, such gentlemen were stabbed by the resolution with the imputation that they dared not act independently even in the election of a printer! (*National Intelligencer,* Sept. 8, 1837)

We might still press on, and assume that Polk was playing the printer bargain exceptionally close to his chest, perhaps by agreeing not to penalize the

Conservatives for defecting on printer issue. But if this were true, it would be difficult to explain the next stage in the game, which occurred on September 11 with Polk's announcement of the committee assignments. Sellers (1957, 327) has noted that the Conservatives were treated as harshly as the minority Whigs. There were no Conservatives on Ways and Means (the most important committee in the special session). Polk's strategy was clear: by insuring that most important committees contained loyal Democrats, he could guarantee that the Conservatives and Whigs could not utilize the committee structure to bottle up bills from the Administration, nor would they be able to draft legislation of their own. Only by excluding the Conservatives at the committee level and controlling the floor could the Administration proposals pass through the House.

On September 14, following the announcement of committee assignments (an important point that we shall come back to in a moment), the House took up the report of the Select Committee on Rules. John Quincy Adams, then a representative for Massachusetts, made reference to the change in his diary:

> All the amendments proposed by the select committee of the last Congress were now again reported, excepting one, which was, that the previous question shall be applicable to pending amendments, as well as to the primitive proposition to which they are appended. I had not originally proposed this amendment, but it was the most important to the freedom of debate of any reported by the former committee; but Hamer, of Ohio, sly as a Quaker and sour as a Presbyterian, had got upon the committee of the present session, and prevailed on a majority of them to strike it out. I had moved to restore it as an amendment, upon which a warm debate of two hours terminated in a vote of one hundred and six to one hundred and two, by yeas and nays, upon my amendment. This was a strict party vote, and may be considered as showing the Administration party majority. (*Memoirs*, vol. 9, 379)

Since this is our first dealing with historical rules changes, pointing out a few important factors may be worthwhile. First, note that the context of the rules debate is partisan. John Quincy Adams was in 1837 a venerable (and minority) Whig in a House controlled by Democrats under the Speakership of James K. Polk. The partisanship of the vote suggests that the partisan character of rules changes in particular reinforces the centrality of party considerations. Second, note that the rules changes are not original to the committee. All the changes were suggested in a previous Rules Committee report. Fears about treating "creativity as a dependent variable," brought out in chapter 1, do not seem to be very important. Third, rules changes in such environments favoring the minority tend not to be accepted. Adams's amendment requiring the previous question to apply to pending amendments would have meant that the minority had a chance to amend legislation, while under the operation of the previous question pending amendments were not included, and the bill was voted on as it stood. Finally, adoption of the rules change occurred when the majority party had an exceptionally thin lead over the minority. As I will show, these characteristics are common to many procedural changes regarding obstruction.

In all, the original report of the Select Committee proposed 17 rules changes. Two more rules changes were added on September 15. After these rules were considered, nine more changes were proposed by individual members.[4] Unfortunately, the floor debate on the rules revisions is quite skimpy in either Gales and Seaton's *Register of Debates* or Blair's rival *Congressional Globe*. Nonetheless, there is some information on the changes that were the subject of roll call votes. I plan therefore first to take up the substance of the changes and the nature of the debate, then turn to an analysis of the votes.

The first roll call concerned the attempt of John Quincy Adams to alter the previous questions, discussed above. The previous question was the principal means available in 1837 for cutting off debate and bringing the question under consideration to a vote. Since the limitation on speaking time did not occur until 1841, the previous question was an especially important tool for dealing with obstruction. The original amendment that Adams sought to modify prohibited individuals from calling more than one call of the House after a call for the previous question. Since this procedure could occupy well over half an hour of time or more (Lynn 1972, 407), multiple calls of the House represented a potent weapon for minority obstructionists.

Adams's proposed alteration required that a call for the previous question be followed by a vote on all amendments then pending. Interestingly enough, the use of amendments to obstruct a bill even after the imposition of a restrictive procedure has often occurred in legislative politics, as can be seen in the use of the so-called post-cloture filibuster in the Senate of the 1970s. This procedure involved the submission of hundreds of amendments before the close of debate, each of which would then have to be voted on before the bill itself could be considered, a wonderful example of a filibuster reaching out from the grave. While these are fascinating issues, the sources are limited: the *Register* did not report the comments of the legislators. It did, however, report the names of those participating in the discussion, and here we see a rather typical partisan pattern. Arguing for the Adams amendment were Adams, Mercer (Whig), Reed (Whig), Underwood (Whig), and Mason of Ohio (Whig). Arguing against were Hamer and Smith, both Democrats.

The second roll call involved the proposal that questions of order arising out of the use of the previous question be decided without debate. This is clearly an antiobstructionist measure, since a clever obstructionist could utilize such points of order to achieve the same effect that the previous question was meant to cut off, namely delay. In the previous Congress, Polk had made a ruling in a point of order of precisely the nature as this amendment. By casting this decision in the form of a standing rule, the Speaker's hand would be strengthened in dealing with possible obstruction. In particular, attempts at delay due to votes on points of order (an obstructive tactic considered in the previous chapter) would be ruled out with this rules change.

On this topic, we are lucky enough to have some of the discussion. Both Mercer and Patton (a Conservative) argued against the rule, although on slightly different grounds. Mercer believed the rule injurious because it would require individuals to vote without information as to the nature of the point of order. Patton rejected the rule based on its giving the chair "too despotic a power," a clear slap at Polk. In addition, Patton also argued, somewhat inconsistently, that the means existed now to cut off debate on a point of order by moving the previous question, thus seeming to be arguing that the new procedure would constitute a thorough revolution and anyhow is already in place. Clearly, Patton's concern here seems to be not with minority rights per se then, but rather with the locus of control in the hands of the Speaker.

More relevant for our discussion are the comments of two members in favor of the amendment. Hamer, while saying "he did not feel very solicitous about it one way or the other," had slightly preferred the rule because "after the demand for the previous question, it sometimes occurred that questions of order incidentally arose, and were debated at great length, which debate might go on, take up the whole day," thus defeating the intention of the House in calling the previous question. The importance of Craig's argument for this discussion requires that he be quoted at length:

> Mr. Craig pointed out the necessity of the rule, and drew the attention of his colleague [Mr. Patton] to instances where questions of order had been raised, which produced a wide and extended range of debate, having little connexion with the question itself, by which the will of the majority, in progressing the business of the House, had for a length of time been frustrated. The previous question was necessary, nay, at time indispensable, to ensure action upon the public business of the nation, by arresting unnecessary discussion, and there was but one standard in regard to its application, viz.: *the judgment of the majority*. If, then, the previous question be a rule properly applicable, and all had agreed that it was, unless abused, equally necessary was the rule now proposed by the select committee; for otherwise, a small minority might set aside the will of the House, or a very large majority of it. (*Register*, 618; emphasis added)

This quote focuses attention on the problem of minority obstruction in the rules reform. It is therefore an important piece of evidence in establishing the claim that members of the House, when discussing the prospect of procedural change, often couched their arguments in the terms of the debate between majority rule and minority rights.

The final roll call took place on the proposal to reduce the majority necessary for suspending the rules from two-thirds to one-half. The House in 1837 did not possess a standing Committee on Rules, let alone one capable of crafting special rules to move bills up the legislative queue. Consequently, the only way a majority could move a bill up for immediate consideration in the face of an obstructionist minority was through the procedure of suspension of the rules. The *Register* again failed to note the discussion that took place, noting only the participants. Here we are lucky that the outlines of the discussion were noted by the *National Intelligencer* of September 18, 1837.

> The gentlemen sustaining the proposition based their arguments mainly on the postulate that the majority of the House ought to be permitted always to control its action, in every case, while they, who opposed the adoption of the amendment, contended that its incorporation into the code by which the House was to be governed would be a virtual repeal of all rules, inasmuch as a majority could then make way for any business which was the favorite of the moment, to the suspension of other and more important concerns which might be under consideration; and inasmuch, moreover, as it has stood so long, and now stands, operates as a valuable protection of the rights of the minority, always respected in the legislative branch of every free government.

The paper notes that "the discussion occupied most of the day, and was very interesting though discursive," a frustrating description typical of early reports on the House.

Though our sources are rather skimpy, the accounts of the debates do show that issues of minority rights and obstruction were crucially important to the House and that arguments about the three rules changes selected revolved around considerations of majoritarianism. Of course, it may be that only some individuals (those willing to or recognized to speak) felt this way. Perhaps the vast majority of individuals felt that the costs to minority rights were insubstantial when weighed against gains in efficiency. It is impossible to check the beliefs of every agent in the House, but we can turn to roll call voting data in an effort to determine the configuration of representatives' revealed preferences on these rules changes.

The votes are strongly supportive of the partisan account of procedural change. To determine whether voting was partisan, I required members of the Democratic party (including Conservatives, who were Democrats after all) to take the majoritarian position on each of the three votes (which would involve a no vote on the Adams amendment and a yes vote on the other two measures), and Whigs to take the opposite stand. In all, 290 of the 291 Whigs followed the partisan prediction, while only 295 out of the 325 Democrats did. While this still leaves over 90 percent of the Democrats acting as predicted, one wonders about the defections. This is a rather strong result, and suggests the partisanship of the voting in the legislature.

But despite the high aggregate levels of partisanship, the outcome of voting was not as partisan as we might have suspected. The majoritarian position prevailed on the first and second roll call, but not the final matter regarding the suspension of the rules. What happened?

To determine how Polk's majority was unraveled, I have assembled a list of individuals whose votes were not correctly predicted (see table 4.1). As a whole, the minority acted as we would expect. The only Whig vote not in accordance with the minority position was cast by William Dawson of Georgia, a slaveholder and member of the Committee on the District of Columbia, a committee stacked by Polk with a clear proslavery majority.[5] All nine members of the Georgia delegation voted no on the Adams amendment, with Dawson the only Whig. Clearly, Adams did not have many friends in Georgia.

The Democrats, as we shall see, fared less well on party unity. On the first roll call, we see a great deal of party cohesion, with only four Democrats supporting Adams. Two of these cases, Nathaniel Borden and Taylor Webster, seem simple to explain. Borden in fact changed his party affiliation and ran on the Whig ticket for the 26th Congress, and his voting reflects the sort of mixture of majority and minority positions that should be expected from an individual engaged in changing his party identification. Webster served as the second in seniority on the Committee on Manufactures, chaired by John Quincy Adams. The remaining two voters, McKay of North Carolina and Craig of Virginia, had both voted for the censure of Adams in the previous Congress. Despite this, Craig's vote may seem difficult to explain given his earlier statement in support of the "judgment of the majority." What he objected to, it appears, was not amendment but the continual debate on amendments that prevented the majority from acting.

The second roll call (regarding debate on points of order) found four Democratic defections as well as a single abstention (Rives). Two of the defections were from Parmenter and Birdsall, both low-ranking members of the Committee on Revolutionary Claims. Being the seventh and ninth ranking members on a nine-member committee of as little importance as Revolutionary Claims probably did not leave Parmenter and Birdsall with a strong degree of obligation to the party leadership. The two other defectors from the party

TABLE 4.1. List of Individuals Not Voting According to the Minority or Majority Position, Roll Calls on Rules Changes, House, 1837

Name	Voting Record	Party	State	Committee Assignment
Defections on the First Roll Call				
Borden	Y Y N	Cons.	MA	Territories
Craig	Y Y Y	Dem.	VA	Revolutionary Claims
McKay	Y Y N	Dem.	NC	Military Affairs
Webster	Y Y Y	Dem.	OH	Manufactures
Dawson	N N N	Whig	GA	District of Columbia
Defections on the Second Roll Call				
Birdsall	N N Y	Dem.	NY	Revolutionary Claims
Garland, James	N N N	Cons.	VA	Judiciary
Parmenter	N N Y	Dem.	MA	Revolutionary Claims
Patton	N N N	Cons.	VA	Territories
Rives	N + N	Cons.	VA	Military Affairs
Defections on the Third Roll Call				
Borden	Y Y N	Cons.	MA	Territories
Bynum	+ Y N	Dem.	NC	Judiciary
Casey	N Y N	Cons.	IL	Public Lands
Cleveland	N + N	Dem.	GA	Post Office
Coles	N Y N	Dem.	VA	Military Affairs
Dromgoole	N Y N	Dem.	VA	Foreign Affairs
Garland, James	N N N	Cons.	VA	Judiciary
Glascock	N Y N	Dem.	GA	Military Affairs and Militia
Grantland	N Y N	Dem.	GA	Naval Affairs
Hunter, Wm.	N Y N	Dem.	OH	District of Columbia
Kemble	N Y N	Dem.	NY	Military Affairs
May	+ Y N	Cons.	IL	Private Land Claims
McKay	Y Y N	Dem.	NC	Military Affairs
Murray	N Y N	Dem.	KY	Indian Affairs
Patton	N N N	Cons.	VA	Territories
Rives	N + N	Cons.	VA	Military Affairs
Snyder	N Y N	Cons.	IL	Roads and Canals
Stewart	N Y N	Cons.	VA	Not Assigned
Yell	N Y N	Dem.	AR	Not Assigned

Note: Y = yes vote, N = no vote, + = not recorded as having voted

line on the second roll call were Patton and James Garland, two Virginia Conservatives. As noted, Patton was concerned with the enhancement of the Speaker's power. The two votes consequently should be understood less as votes for the minority and more as votes against Polk. Nonetheless, they exhibit a willingness to diverge from the party on procedural issues, which are typically considered acid tests of party loyalty.

The result on the third roll call (regarding suspension of the rules) found a new source for defection: the Committee on Military Affairs. To understand why members of this committee would join with the Conservatives, it is necessary to understand how the suspension of the rules process worked. Weakening the suspension of the rules, while pushing some legislation ahead, would push other legislation behind. In a Congress that was sure to be preoccupied with economic issues, military affairs might be supposed to be such an issue. Of the nine members of the Committee on Military Affairs, six voted no, one did not vote, and two voted yes (including B. A. McClellan, a Democrat from Polk's home state of Tennessee). These six were joined by individuals assigned to committees also likely to be slighted (Post Office, Territories), as well as by three individuals not assigned to any committee.

This pattern of voting on the rules changes reflects a slow unraveling of the Democratic majority, as Adams clearly recognized in his memoirs:

> . . . Hamer lost in the House another of his proposed amendments, which was, to revoke the one-hundredth and seventh rule, which requires a day's notice and a vote of two-thirds to revoke or alter any of the standing rules. Hamer and Smith, of Maine, labored very hard to carry this point, although I warned them that their majority was slipping out of their hands, and that their new screws would be turned against themselves. (*Memoirs,* Sept. 14, 1837)

While two additional proposals were introduced (one making *Jefferson's Manual* the official source of parliamentary procedure when it did not conflict with the rules; the other prohibiting the sale and display—but not the consumption!—of liquorous substances, a nod to the newly formed Congressional Temperance Society), the procedural work of the committee was finished.

This did not, however, exhaust the potential for procedural change. As we shall see in the 1880 rules change as well, proposals for rules changes opened up the possibility of floor amendment, a possibility that members quickly used to their advantage. The first three amendments (from Whigs and a Conservative) all involve questions of Speaker power and party control. Patton proposed that the Speaker be required to vote, probably an attempt to constrain the Speaker to the same sort of constituent pressures that other members felt. The amendment, however, was rejected, probably based upon the arguments of John Quincy Adams that allowing the Speaker to vote would also allow him to speak, and Thomas, who noted that the Speaker would not thereby gain any advantage (since he could already vote in ties), and "in times of high party excitement, the annunciation of his vote, especially if first given, might have too powerful an influence." Underwood proposed that the chair be required to call the committees in order as listed in the rules, a radical limitation on the agenda-setting power of the Speaker.

The final proposal of the three (from Bell) would require that no division or count of the House by tellers should be taken unless seconded by one-fifth of a quorum. I find this rules change the most interesting of all, because on its face it appears to be a limitation on the power of a minority obstructionist to demand endless teller votes. Given that in the previous Congress Bell had carried out a program of obstruction, and the Whigs were still in the minority, this appears paradoxical. I think the resolution to the problem can be obtained by considering the specific character of a *teller* vote. Typically, a division of the House would be taken by asking individuals to stand and be counted. In a teller vote, however, individuals march up the aisles to record their votes with the Clerk of the House. This slower procedure would give the Speaker more time to recognize those defecting from the party position. Furthermore, while it may be easy to stand in a group to be counted and thus evade detection, it is more difficult to stand in a line in front of the Clerk and under the disapproving eyes of James K. Polk. If this argument is correct, then teller votes might have been a means for inducing party loyalty on the part of recalcitrant representatives. By imposing a limitation on the use of that tool, Bell may have intended to make it more difficult for the majority ranks to stand together, something bound to be of benefit in a closely contested House.

Among the remaining proposed changes (including a motion on viva voce voting and the approval of a new standing committee on Mileage), a rather interesting amendment was offered by Thomas, a Democrat, requiring precedence be given to bills that did not cause debate. If the House were truly concerned with simply increasing the number of public laws enacted, then certainly this measure would have passed. But it did not, and while we do not have the details of the debate, it is not hard to understand why. If the proposed change had passed, the minority then could flood the legislature with a veritable Niagara of bills not provoking debate (assuming some notion of what that was could be worked up) and use Thomas's rule to prevent consideration of other bills. While this is conjectural, it reaffirms the ways in which the simple act of eliminating inefficiency is likely to give rise to all sorts of strategic complexities. Overall, of the various additions and changes proposed to the rules, the vast majority were proposed by Whigs, showing that debate on the floor gave the minority a valuable opportunity to ameliorate an otherwise hostile proposal.

A quick overview of the changes made here makes it clear that while steps were taken to limit obstruction, the end result was not a uniformly majoritarian alteration in procedure. The cohesion of the majority was greater during the earlier stages of consideration than the final stages. Furthermore, as I have argued, committee assignments played a pivotal role in allowing for majority party defections. Had Polk been able to hold off committee assignments and as a result bluff the Conservatives into thinking they would be granted a major part in the economic debates to come, he could have kept the coalition together.

If this strategy is so obvious, then why didn't Polk use it? Interestingly enough, this is precisely the path that he followed. Debate on the need for rules changes did in fact occur prior to the announcement of the committees. However, Elisha Whittlesey of Ohio proposed that the Speaker be required to make committee assignments, a proposal that passed the House. The *National Intelligencer* of September 8 reported that "the Chair intimated that he could not be prepared as early as tomorrow, to announce the committees; and that he should do so on Monday," an attempt to gain a little delay. With his hands tied by the House, Polk was forced to make his committee assignments in advance of the consideration of the rules, losing his ability to threaten Conservatives. Not surprisingly, Elisha Whittlesey was a Whig, and his resolution requiring Polk to announce committees was a smart minority move, depriving Polk of one of his few tools to enforce party discipline.

The 1837 rules changes then can be considered along with the committee appointments as part of a strategy designed to ensure safe consideration of administration proposals. By excluding Conservatives and Whigs from key committees, Polk would ensure the safe passage of these proposals to the floor. Furthermore, Polk could use the new tools from rules revision (especially suspension of the rules by majority vote) to confound any attempts at minority obstruction. This strategy failed, however, because a key element in keeping the Conservatives in line, the threat of committee assignments, was taken away through the swift and smart action of the minority. If nothing else, this scenario should reinforce the relevance of minority rights in any attempt to understand legislative proceedings.

The 1860 Rules Changes

> A great deal of party prejudice finds its way into this Hall. A stranger who visits the Capitol would sometimes imagine that we were divided into armed bands, each ready to give battle to the other. It is nothing uncommon to hear a member allude to another substantially as "the honorable the damned rascal on the other side."
>
> —Emerson Etheridge, M.C., Tennessee[6]

The 36th Congress convened on December 5, 1859, a mere three days after the abolitionist John Brown was hanged for criminal conspiracy, murder, and treason against Virginia. The Republicans had captured a plurality in the last Congressional elections, yet did not have the majority necessary to elect a

Speaker and organize the House. In this close political contest, our theory would predict some program of obstructionism, and this is what an anonymous writer for *Harper's New Monthly Magazine* observed:

> The most significant feature of the discussions, apart from the strong disunion sentiments avowed by some of the Southern members, was the announcement of an agreement entered into between a number of Democratic members to employ all Parliamentary tactics to prevent the House from choosing a Speaker during the whole session, rather than to permit the election of Mr. Sherman.

After Galusha Grow of Pennsylvania, the Republican nominee for Speaker in the previous Congress, withdrew, John Sherman of Ohio was the preeminent Republican in the House and the obvious choice for Speaker. But how could the Democrats prevent Sherman from being elected? Analyzing the Speaker debacle will provide insight into the workings of the House in 1860 that will be essential to understanding the rules reforms.

To organize the House, the Republicans needed the support of all the antiadministration forces, including the South Americans (Ilisevich 1988, 183). The South Americans, as their name implies, were Southern Know-Nothings who advocated a program of unity, peace, and cohesion (Sutherland 1966, 54ff.) Their party comprised approximately 24 members. With the support of the South Americans, therefore, the Republicans would easily be able to organize the House.

Since the House had not yet organized, the presiding officer of the House was James C. Allen, Clerk of the previous (and Democratically controlled) House. The retention of the Clerk created all sorts of difficulties for legislative transition in the nineteenth-century House, as partisan clerks could use their power of recognition to attempt to structure a victory for their own party (Price 1971). The 1860 session offers an exceptional example of the difficulties with this arrangement. Although the Republicans were within shouting distance of a majority, Allen as presiding officer began the session by recognizing J. B. Clark, Democrat from Missouri. Clark in turn proposed that no member should be elected Speaker who had endorsed the book *The Impending Crisis,* by Hinton Helper, an antislavery tract.

Like Elisha Whittlesey's committee assignment proposal of the previous section, the limitation on candidates for Speaker was a brilliant minority move. Many leading Republicans, including Grow and Sherman, had endorsed the book, or at least an executive summary of the book—it is not clear how many had read the actual text. Some indeed may not have even read the summary, for the titles in that summary would give even a reckless politician pause: "The North must Seize the Riches of the South," "Revolution—Peacefully if we can, Violently if we must," and "The Stupid Masses of the South" are just a sample (Crenshaw 1942, 324).

Adopting Clark's resolution would therefore have the effect of removing the leading Republicans from the competition, thus opening up the possibility for Democrats to organize the House. However, if the South Americans were willing to support Republicans for the Speakership, then by voting in a sophisticated manner they could have defeated Clark's resolution and then proceeded to elect Sherman or any other acceptable candidate. Why didn't they?

The answer forces us to recognize the limitations of sophisticated voting.[7] What made Sherman and the other Republican candidates so intolerable to members of the South was that by endorsing Helper's book they had simultaneously signaled a willingness to support slave revolts. Shelton F. Leake of Virginia phrased it this way

> We on this side, are entitled to know who it is that we are to elect Speaker, whether we are to elect a man who, while I am here in the discharge of my public duties, is stimulating my negroes at home to apply the torch to my dwelling and the knife to the throats of my wife and helpless children. He [Sherman] has not disavowed it; nor has anybody in this House disavowed the sentiment yet. (Quoted in Crenshaw 1942, 330)

This is a fairly characteristic piece of rhetoric, making more understandable the willingness of members to begin carrying knives and pistols to the floor and the prediction by James Hammond that had violence erupted, the result would have been "such slaughter as to shock the world & dissolve the Gov[ernment]!" (quoted in Crenshaw, 333).

Voting for the resolution therefore wasn't simply a tactical mistake. Given the concerns of the South Americans, it was precisely the right thing to do. There was no electoral reason to support someone who had repudiated (or at least could not be trusted to represent) the fundamental concerns of their party. At the very least, there was no payoff in *appearing* to support such an individual. As a result, the Southern Americans joined with the Democrats, and the resolution passed.

Despite Democratic hopes, the Republicans were able to organize the House, though not until February 1 when, on the 44th ballot, a relative unknown, William Pennington of New Jersey, was elected Speaker of the House. This turned out, however, not to be the victory the obstructionists might have expected. Pennington simply played a puppet's role, with the actual power in the House maintained in the hands of Galusha Grow and John Sherman. This may have been a safe thing for the Republicans: Pennington was supposedly so ignorant of parliamentary procedure that he required the assistance of House pages to make his rulings.

The battle over the election of the Speaker suggests many of the outstanding points in the congressional landscape of 1860. First, the small size of parties made bargaining necessary to legislation. Second, the crystallization of parties along sectional lines made this bargaining very difficult. These two points suggest the stalemate that eventually did characterize much of the congressional session (Sherman 1895/1968, vol. I, 180).

The problem of the Republican party therefore was very similar to the position faced by the administration forces in 1837. That is, the Republican leadership had to try on the one hand to persuade and cajole members of their supporting coalition while at the same time guaranteeing that there were few opportunities left for the remaining minority members to obstruct business. As in 1837, this required changes in the existing code of House rules. Consequently, a committee composed of the Speaker, Israel Washburn (R-Maine), Galusha Grow (R-Pennsylvania), Warren Winslow (D-North Carolina), and Thomas Bocock (D-Virginia) was set the same day as the election of the Speaker to suggest possible revisions in the rules. On March 15, 1860, the committee reported back 38 changes in the existing rules.[8]

Washburn prefaced the consideration of this report by noting that "if we carry into execution the amendments proposed, we shall save at least one day in every week—, that is, we shall do more business in five months than we can do, under the rules as at present, in six months" (*Congressional Globe*, hereafter *CG*, 36-1, part 2, March 15, 1860, 1117). These rules were claimed to be an answer to "great complaint in the House, growing out of the obstructions to business under its rules" (1178), with the result that "nearly all the business transacted by the House is done through the good nature of members, outside of the rules of the House, by unanimous consent." Needless to say, on the eve of the Civil War it could be doubted whether the "good nature" of the members could be counted on much longer. The amendments proposed received "the unanimous consent of the committee," and nearly all were included in the report of the Committee on Rules of the last session of Congress.

Although Washburn explicitly notes that problems of obstruction motivated the revision of the rules, the fact that the committee was unanimous in consenting to the report is a serious blow to my hypothesis. For if the report contained provisions that worked contrary to the interests of the minority party, then either of the two Democratic members could veto those provisions. How then could the report have stopped minority obstruction?

Two explanations are I think sufficient to explain the actions of the minority. First, members of the minority may have felt that approval of the report did not commit them on the floor. Bocock in fact explicitly stated:

If, in the course of this discussion, anybody shall show me that any of them are wrong, or improper, and will operate to the injury of the business of the House or the rights of any portion of its members, I hold myself perfectly free to vote against them, though they were reported by the committee with my approbation and consent. (*CG,* 1183)

But there was a second reason why the minority might have been reluctant to repudiate the report: the proposed changes had in fact been fashioned from the recommendations of the Rules Committee in the previous House, a committee whose Democratic majority included Warren Winslow and Thomas Bocock, now in the minority. Not surprisingly, these individuals may have found it difficult as members of the minority to urge the rejection of a resolution they had reported as members of the majority little over one year ago, at least without some "convincing."

What changes were suggested? Out of the proposed amendments to the rules, 15 are either redundant with other changes or amount to no change at all.[9] For example, the various provisions on House officers were combined into a single rule. This required eliminating the four provisions that contained the discussion now in one rule. The only change to the existing rules is that the appointees of the doorkeeper and the postmaster were to be approved by the Speaker. Consequently, out of five putative rules changes, only one substantive change was actually made. Many of the remaining categories were real changes, but unrelated to our interests here (the election of the doorkeeper and the postmaster; admission to the House; treatment of bills from the Court of Claims).

In order to organize the discussion of the remaining salient issues, I would like to begin by noting two problems encountered by the House during the 1850s, both of which are addressed by Cooper and Young (1989) in their examination of changes in House bill introduction. First, the system for bill introduction was notoriously slow. A complete call of the committees could take months, and the regular introduction of bills was often postponed for private business or other legislation. Second, there was a great difficulty under the rules in dealing with unfinished business. As they note, once in the Committee of the Whole on the State of the Union, debate was not required to be germane to the legislation at hand. Members therefore took this as an "opportunity to address the nation and their constituents on the leading issues of the day, particularly slavery" (78).

On the first score, the House adopted a variety of rules changes to make it easier for legislation to be considered. First, they created a special calendar for private legislation, so that the regular introduction of bills would not be postponed. They also limited the times one could call for a suspension of the rules. On alternate Mondays, bills would be directly referred to the Committee of the Whole. Cooper and Young (1989) characterize these changes as moves toward efficiency, which may be true, but they also work to make the problem of the minority obstructionist much more difficult. As regards Cooper and Young's second problem, the House explicitly gave preference to unfinished business, which was to be brought up as soon as the journal was read. On the committee level, bills referred to a committee during one session were assumed to be referred to it for the second session (thus the break of session would not necessitate the reintroduction of bills).

While the politics over bill introduction may seem much more neutral than we would expect, there is in fact within the rules changes one proposal that is particularly problematic for this study: a rules change proposed by the majority that in fact worked to the *detriment* of the majority party by eliminating the trick of striking out the enacting words of pending legislation.

To put this rule in context, a brief history might be helpful. In chapter 1, I noted that the consideration of the Kansas–Nebraska Act witnessed a heavy use of dilatory tactics. If these tactics were as powerful as I argued, one might wonder how the Kansas–Nebraska Act could ever have passed into law. While the Act was delayed for a quite a while in the Committee of the Whole, Alexander Stephens found a way out of the swamp of obstruction by moving to strike out the enacting words. Stephens reasoned that this left the opponents of the Kansas–Nebraska Act in a no-win position. If they agreed to the amendment, then the enacting words would be struck out, and the bill would pass from the Committee of the Whole to the House. Once in the House, any amendment could always be reconsidered and rejected, so all one would have to do would be to restore the enacting clause and thereby put the Kansas–Nebraska Act into a form suitable for passage. If, on the other hand, the amendment was not agreed to, then the bill, Stephens claimed, would be referred to the House anyway, since members would have voted to enact the legislation.

The Kansas–Nebraska Act raised great ire among Republicans, and one can understand their simmering resentment of being tricked on such an important issue. One of those who objected most strongly to the tactic was Israel Washburn, a member of the current Rules Committee. But Washburn was not unaware that by outlawing the enacting clause trick, the majority would be opening itself up to dilatory tactics. Indeed, he freely admitted as much: "if the majority desire that the bill should pass, but that there should be no discussion and no amendment of the bill, we desire that that abuse shall be done away with" (*CG*, 1180).

It is to Washburn's credit that even while in the majority he considered the practice so repugnant that he was willing to outlaw it. But we have not quite finished with the issue. Immediately after discussion of the above change, Washburn stated, "Now it may be said that, while you are depriving the majority of this power to strike out the enacting clause, you should give them some power by which they may bring the discussion in the Committee of the Whole to a termination" (*CG*, 1180). He then offered an amendment allowing the majority to vote to close debate on amendments to a section of a bill after five minutes debate had elapsed. "In this way," Israel Washburn concluded, "we thought we could remedy, as far as they could possibly be remedied by the rules, the abuses upon either side—on the one side, the abuse under which you may be called to pass these important bills without any opportunity to debate them, either in committee or in the House; and on the other side by the abuse of making Buncombe five-minute speeches—not in order, in fact—upon amendments which they may offer in Committee of the Whole" (1180).

A number of facts should be observed about this supposed "bargain." First, the provision limiting minority rights was considered before the provision on limiting majority power. If the minority was able to overturn the first part of the bargain, the second could be easily defeated. Second, the bargain favors the majority a bit more than it may appear at first glance. On the one hand, the majority is giving up a technique of great indelicacy in stopping obstruction. The tactic of striking the enacting clause would apply to all sections of the bill and thus would be a quite cumbersome procedure. What the majority gets in return is a more refined tool, one that allows the majority to amend or discuss when it chooses on any particular section of the bill as well as to close off discussion. In short, the majority gave up a tool that it would probably have only seldom utilized and received back a considerable power to stop debate.

This is only one change, however. Several other alterations were made rendering the act of obstruction a bit more difficult. For starters, limitations were placed on the motion to excuse a member from voting. This motion was sometimes used as a dilatory tactic. Examples can be found in the discussion of the admission of California as a state (Feb. 18, 1850; Hinds 1899, IV. §2900) and in the Lecompton debate (Feb. 5, 1858; Hinds 1899, IV.§2903). As Hinds notes, these motions could reach rather ludicrous limits: "On that day, Mr. John Sherman made a point of order on the following motion, submitted by Muscoe R.H. Garnett, of Virginia 'Mr Garnett moves to be excused from voting on the motion of Mr. Letcher, to be excused from voting on the motion of Mr. Cobb, to be excused from voting on the motion of Mr. Seward to lay on the table the appeal from the decision of the chair" (Hinds 1899, IV.§2903).

In addition to the limitation on the motion to excuse, the requirement for voting on a special order for an appropriations bill was reduced from two-thirds to one-half (a change leading the South American Horace Maynard of Tennessee to inquire whether under the new amendments to the rules "will it not always be in the power of the dominant majority to restrict and limit the debate to such subjects as they may see proper?"). Changes were also made in the operation of the previous question. One of these prohibited the dilatory tactic of asking for a call of the House after the previous question is seconded (except when the Speaker deems a quorum not to be present). Another guaranteed that if the majority should fail in its attempt to impose the previous question, the bill would not go over to the next day. Instead, the situation would be returned to the status quo ante, just as if the previous question had never been called. This reduced the cost to the majority from a failed attempt at the previous question. Finally, the previous question was refined so that on a motion to postpone, the previous question would apply only to the motion and not to the bill itself. The effect is clearly explained by Washburn:

> Now, when a motion to postpone is pending, if the previous question is ordered, it cuts off the motion to postpone, and brings the House to a vote upon the amendments, if any are pending, and then upon the engrossment of the bill, so that when there is a motion before the House to postpone, *there may be interminable debate upon it.* You may not want to come to a vote upon the bill, nor to hear an endless discussion on the motion to postpone. But you cannot stop that debate unless you do it at the expense of bringing the House to a direct vote upon the bill. (*CG,* 1180)

Endless discussions on the motion to postpone of course are not usually grounded in some intense interest in the particulars of a bill or of the nature of postponement, but rather are and should be seen as steps designed to obstruct the business of the House.

So far we have considered the substance of the debates. Can the roll call votes reveal anything more? Unfortunately, for this particular rules change the votes are less revealing than we might hope. Of the four roll calls on the 1860 rules changes, two were over the question of admission of ex-members of the House to the floor (see *CG,* March 19, 1860).[10] The first of the roll calls on the issue was minimally a party vote (55 percent of the Republicans favoring the admission of ex-members, 63 percent of the Democrats against), while the second indicated no party difference at all (54 percent of both the Republicans and the Democrats voted against reconsideration of the vote). A third roll call concerned whether the House should adjourn over the weekend. Since this was not a motion to adjourn immediately, however, it is unlikely to be a proxy for voting over a particular rules change (as motions to adjourn sometimes are).

This leaves a single roll call to be analyzed. Clement Vallandigham of Ohio, a Democrat who would eventually be tried by military authorities for treason and banished to the Confederate States of America, proposed that the

TABLE 4.2.   Voting by Party on Repeal of Hour Rule, 1860

Vote	Democrat	Republican	ALD	SA	Total
Yeas	53 (76%)	14 (16%)	1 (25%)	12 (67%)	80
Nays	17 (24%)	71 (84%)	3 (75%)	6 (33%)	97

rule limiting speeches on any question before the House or a committee to one hour be abolished. Repealing this rule would, of course, be a great boon for the minority party, who would be allowed the same filibustering opportunities that members of the Senate have enjoyed. The results of voting on Vallandigham's motion reveal the following patterns (see table 4.2). Note that in every party at least two-thirds of the members voted the same side. Consistent with their cohesion over the rest of the session, the Republicans suffered less than 20 percent defections, while the Democrats were a bit harder hit, almost a quarter of their forces having voted to ban the hour rule. The results of this vote are consistent with the theory: majorities will tend to vote against extensions of minority rights.

But who were these defectors? A check on previous service (see table 4.3) indicated that the Republicans generally had limited previous experience in Congress. This result, however, should be expected given that the Republicans were a new party and would generally be unlikely to have a great number of members with prior service. Of the Democrats, a comparison of electoral, regional, and prior service characteristics yielded an interesting mix. Most interesting from a modern perspective is the large number of defectors on the hour rule who were Southern representatives of long standing in the House. This is quite contrary to the modern popular caricature of the filibusterer as a ancient, drawling Southern gentleman. While they may have simply grown

TABLE 4.3.   Prior Service, Defectors on Hour Rule Vote, 1860

Party	Two or Fewer Terms	More than Three Terms
ALD/ID	5 (4)	0 (1)
South	2 (1)	5 (6)
Border	3 (2)	0 (1)
Other	4 (4)	1 (1)
Total	14 (11)	6 (9)

Note: Figures in parentheses reflect the inclusion of noncontinuous service. ALD/ID represents individuals elected either as Anti-Lecompton Democrats or as Independent Democrats.

weary of years of tiresome speeches, more likely they feared that repeal of the hour rule would allow those "fiends from hell" (the abolitionist forces, as Miller reminds us) to consume time in never-ending incendiary speeches. Whatever their reasons, the numbers were not sufficient, and the hour rule, one of the most important weapons against obstruction, was retained.

In conclusion, it seems clear that a concern with obstruction plays some part in motivating the rules changes adopted in 1860. Certainly, these changes could be argued to have made the House run more efficiently, but in the political context considered here that would mean the House running more efficiently for the Republicans in control. Once more, we find procedural change to be an intimately partisan affair.

An Interlude

The theory I have presented seems to suggest that, with the simple swing of a few seats, a small change in the composition of the House, all of the members so proudly proclaiming the need for minority rights would be instead trumpeting the virtues of majority rule. Doesn't this seem to insinuate that individuals do not have sincere commitments to either majority rule or to minority rights, and that they are, in essence, hypocrites looking for immediate partisan gain?

While this would be easy to infer from an isolated perusing of the model, this is not my position at all. I do believe that individuals hold sincere commitments to both majority rule and to minority rights. But these are not the only normative commitments that political actors can hold. They can also be concerned about the need for good public policy, or fairness, or a whole host of other things. In some cases, these commitments clash, and they get worked out in various ways. So, for example, Republican principles about Free Soil, Free Labor, and Free Men clash with concerns about minority rights, and the former wins. Let me phrase it in Grand Inquisitorial fashion: if by invoking cloture you could guarantee social equality, would you do it?

It is often difficult to determine exactly how these normative commitments would fall out, because we usually are not given an opportunity to witness individuals who are taken out of their political surroundings and put in a new situation altogether. The 1860 rules change, however, offers a slight opening for assessing these arguments. It is known that southern Democrats during the 36th Congress were quite virulent in their hatred for what they perceived as majority infringements on minority rights (Sutherland 1966). Typically, there is only one House of Representatives, and so it is impossible to tell what the Southerners would have done had they had the chance to organize the House. The Civil War, however, offered these Southern members a chance to form their own legislature, with their own rules of procedure. What happened?

The Confederate Congress did adopt rules for closing debate that were weaker than those adopted in the House. In the House, the previous question closed debate and amendment, required votes on all pending amendments, and then on the main question. Under the guidance of Alexander Stephens, the Confederate Congress weakened this to "the question," a procedure that would have the effect of cutting off debate on the pending question but would allow consideration of the topic under discussion to continue.

This reinforces the notion that the normative commitments played a role in shaping the actions of Southern members of the House. At the same time, however, we must recognize that the Confederacy was woefully short on party structure, a result that at least one historian has tied to Southern difficulties in carrying on the war effort (McKitrick 1967). In the absence of a party structure, issues of majority and minority become less clear. But as the war progressed, and especially after the passage of the first conscription act in U.S. history and suspension of the writ of habeas corpus, factional lines within the Confederacy began to form, with pro– and anti–Jefferson Davis coalitions.

Without a Confederacy-wide party system to express views, however, differences tended to be aired at the state level (Schott 1988, 401–2). The extent of obstructionism, however, was sharply limited by the precarious condition of the Southern economy. When Alexander Stephens went to the Georgia assembly at a special session to discuss the writ, members certainly had differences, but

> None of the legislators wanted a long session; daily board in Milledgeville cost more than twice what they collected in per diem. Moreover, although most of the legislators deplored the recent acts of Congress, few wanted to express their opposition as a body for fear of harming the war effort. (Schott 1988, 405)

Some effort was therefore needed to grease the wheels of the anti-writ resolution. Joseph E. Brown, the governor of Georgia and a vigorous opponent of Jefferson Davis, engaged in a bit of wheeling and dealing, selling cotton cards for 10 dollars (a discount of 75 percent or more on the going rate) and allowing members of the delegation to exchange confederate currency for Georgia state currency (a profit margin of 100 percent). Yet even these legislative blandishments were not sufficient. As Schott notes in his biography of Alexander Stephens,

> On the eighteenth the House passed the peace resolutions 88 to 49, but friends of the administration managed to have an additional resolution tacked on declaring Georgia's dedication to achieving independence. The habeas corpus resolutions also passed the House, but narrowly. On the

morning of March 19, 1864, the last day of the session, it began to look as though Brown and Stephen's effort would fail. In the House the pro-administration forces carried a vote for reconsideration of the habeas corpus resolutions. Meanwhile the senate had taken no action, except to pass a resolution that the governor impose no obstacle to operation of the conscription laws. Linton's resolutions still hung fire, and adjournment loomed. No action at all would have been as bad as defeat for the governor's plan. (410)

This would seem to be the end of the peace resolutions.

But of course it was not. To get the resolutions through, Brown threatened *another* special session, with the prospect of another stay at gloriously expensive Milledgeville. This threat brought results, with the House passing the habeas corpus resolutions again by the slim majority of 71 to 68, the Senate following suit. Whatever obstruction the Senate might have offered had been crushed. This show of defiance attracted nationwide attention, with ridicule from the Southern newspapers for what it considered a treasonous act and celebration from the North, which saw in this the crumbling of the Southern effort.

While state legislatures may have been the most prominent site for the expression of these sorts of sentiments, such parliamentary wrangling was not limited to the state legislatures. Stephens, as vice president of the Confederacy, presided over the Senate. The reelection of Abraham Lincoln and the difficulties of sustaining the war effort placed new pressures on Jefferson Davis, who reacted by proposing a new writ of habeas corpus. This passed through the House, but in the Confederate Senate the vote was tied at 10–10. Stephens as vice president could of course cast the deciding vote to kill the bill and was set to do so, but made the tactical blunder of asking if he could speak and explain his reasons. Everyone in the Senate, however, "already knew his reasons, and several declined to hear them again" (Schott 435). In a rather odd instance of cloture, one member changed his vote in order to guarantee that the resolution would not pass and Stephens could not speak. As chair, Stephens ruled this out of order, but was rejected by a vote of 16 to 3. Although the Senate did request that he address them on the issue at a secret session, Stephens was crushed by the repudiation.

One wonders what would have happened to Southern parliamentary procedure had events like this gone on. Clearly, the notion of a unified South established at the outset of the war, the promise of a more minority-friendly parliamentary procedure, was fading. And we see here numerous signs of close party (or at least factional) splits that suggest the makings of a party system and the dynamics discussed above. The Senate vote on the new writ, however, took place in December 1864, and within months the South would unconditionally surrender.

CHAPTER 5

Rules Changes in the Gilded Age

The Civil War ushered in an era of Republican control over the institutions of government. Two-party competition did not return to the United States until the 1870s. The House did attempt to reform its rules in 1872, passing a resolution to appoint a commission for this purpose, a commission that appears not to have reported (Galloway 1969, 50). However, the thorough revision envisioned in this resolution was not undertaken until 1880, the next major rules change to be considered.

1880 Revision

Of the four major rules changes in the partisan era, the 1880 change represents the most difficult test for the theory. The Committee on Rules in 1880 operated under a unanimity rule, as did the Committee in 1860. Thomas Brackett Reed, the Speaker of the House and one of its most skilled parliamentarians, has specifically charged that the 1880 rules change furthered the power of the minority (Reed 1898, chap. 19). Not surprisingly, then, the *Washington Post* predicted at the beginning of the consideration of the rules that while there might be some opposition, "party lines will not be drawn, and the squabble will be entirely of a non-partisan character" (Jan. 6, 1880, 1).

A second look at the 1880 rules change, however, might lead one to rethink these positions. While the committee report was unanimous, James Garfield, a member of the Committee on Rules, did not support the rules changes on the final vote. The rule so violently attacked by Reed stating that the motion to adjourn, to fix the day of adjournment, and to take a recess were in order at all times can be found in the rules prior to the 1880 change. The Rules Committee did in fact address the concern shared by Reed regarding the ability of dilatory tactics to kill committee bills in the morning hour. Finally, contrary to the *Post*'s predictions, the final vote was clearly along party lines.

In order to make sense of the 1880 rules change, I shall organize the argument in the following stages. First, I shall briefly summarize the political context in which the 1880 rules change occurred. Was it partisan or not? What might the Committee on Rules have been reacting to? Second, I shall look at the committee itself. Who were the members of the committee? Why did they adopt a unanimity rule in their proceedings? Third, I wish to take a look at the committee document that was reported from this unusually gifted committee. Did it take steps, as the theory predicts, to limit minority obstruction? Finally, I want to look at the floor stage. The report was considered on the floor for roughly two months, with countless amendments and speeches over topics from the most tedious grammatical points to procedural changes that would have engendered a revolution in House procedure. The floor debate thus provides a valuable keyhole for understanding the politics of procedural change in the 1880s.

Political Context

The victory of the Northern forces in the Civil War presented the political question of the terms under which the Southern states would be allowed to reenter the Union. A return to the status quo ante, with malice toward none and charity toward all, was impossible after Lincoln's assassination. The actual manner of the South's reemergence, then, was determined through the course of Reconstruction. And at the core of Reconstruction was a politically astute observation: the return of the South to national politics would give the Democratic Party a solid majority in both Houses, and therefore the power to repeal any civil rights efforts enacted by Republican majorities (Morrison, 714). Such a move would be doubly ironic: not only would the South retain political power, but it would even *gain* in strength, due to apportionment.[1]

Republicans were able to maintain control until 1875, when the Democrats regained the House. With pessimism over the Grant administration at a high level, the presidential elections of 1876 did not bode well for the Republicans. To make matters worse, the leading Republican contender, James G. Blaine, the "Plumed Knight," was under public scrutiny for participating in a questionable bond sale with the Union-Pacific Railroad. The convention settled instead on Rutherford B. Hayes, the Governor of Ohio.

Although Hayes had a public record as a Radical Republican, his feelings toward the South were beginning to mellow. Referring to his letter of acceptance of the nomination (and of the party platform), Hayes wrote, "I wanted to plainly talk of the rights of the colored man, and at the same time to say what I could for the interests and feelings of the well disposed white man" (quoted in Hoogenboom 1988, 17). Nevertheless, recognizing the political difficulties of the contest against the reform candidate Samuel Tilden of New York, Hayes urged his party to make rebellion the fundamental issue of the election.

As is well known, Tilden captured the popular vote, almost 51 percent to Hayes's 48 percent. While this would normally be enough to guarantee Tilden an address on Pennsylvania Avenue, graft, partisan manipulation, in short typical Gilded Age politics led to an electoral college outcome in which Tilden had 184 votes, Hayes 165, and 20 votes were disputed.[2] If Hayes were to receive all the disputed votes, he would win the election. If the electoral votes of even one state went to Tilden, he would win.

How Hayes was able to pull off the election has been amply documented in C. Vann Woodward's classic study, *Reunion and Reaction*. To grossly simplify a complex story, Hayes and his political agents pursued a Southern strategy in which internal improvements in the South (such as a southern railroad route to the Pacific) and the restoration of home rule to the South (with the removal of federal troops) would be exchanged for favorable resolution of the contested votes, the election of Garfield to the position of House Speaker, and assurances on the matter of civil rights. While the notion of a quid pro quo is a bit strained here, the "corrupt bargain" was sufficient to win Hayes the election.

The first breach in the bargain came during the organization of the new House, in which the southern Democrats failed to join with Republicans in organizing the House. While the organization of the House was, as Woodward states, more of a "hope and a tentative agreement" than a "positive understanding," the Democratic defection had the effect of chilling northern Republican enthusiasm for Hayes's southern policies of internal improvements and home rule. And some comments of Hayes's with respect to the Union-Pacific Railroad left southerners concerned as to whether Hayes himself meant to honor his promises.

As a result, Democrats did what any group in their situation might be expected to do: they attempted to make it impossible for Hayes to renege on their agreement. The mechanism for securing his compliance was the adoption of political riders to appropriations bills. For example, a rider to the army appropriation bill required that the funds not be used to enforce election laws. These riders placed Hayes in the difficult position of either agreeing to the rider and signing the legislation, or else having (in this case) no money for the army. Between these options, Hayes was willing to call the Democrats' bluff and would continue to veto any appropriations bills containing riders.

The problem with calling someone's bluff is that in some cases the other person is not bluffing. Hayes's vetoes of appropriations bills had led to a governmental crisis. As a result, the 46th Congress was called into a special session to break the impasse. But this did not happen: the basic pattern was repeated, as Democrats again attached political riders to appropriations bills.

Republicans countered with a two-pronged strategy. On the one hand, Hayes promptly vetoed appropriations bills with such riders. On the other hand, the minority Republicans in the House adopted a strategy of obstruction (Josephy 1979, 253–54). At the end of the session, exhausted from Republican efforts, the Democrats gave up the ghost, passing an appropriations bill without riders (although only to take up the rider cause again in the next session).

Partisanship was therefore back in the House of Representatives, and the hoped-for realignment of Southern ex-Whigs with Northern Republicans fashioned by Hayes and his political aides fell apart. Historically, the House in 1879–80 witnessed the highest levels of party voting since the Civil War, and the highest levels until the emergence of czar rule in the 1890s. The legacy of the 46th Congress has been written by Robert Byrd: "The Forty-sixth Congress was largely unproductive, marred by party wrangling and continuing impasses with the president. . . . Congress looked parochial and obstructive. It seemed intent on fulfilling Mark Twain's dictum that, had Congress been present when the Deity said 'Let there be light,' mankind would never have had any" (1988, 322).[3]

The Committee on Rules

The story so far seems consistent with the theory. We have a small majority within the House, high levels of party voting, and a strategy of obstruction on the part of the minority party. Our theory would predict that the majority would enact rules changes designed to limit the ability of minority members to obstruct legislation, which there was. This suggests that the theory was correct.

But we have not predicted just any rules change: instead, we need to guarantee that the rules changes adopted dealt with the issue of minority obstruction. We do not, however, find a partisan debacle, at least in the Committee on Rules. This set of extraordinary legislators—chair Samuel Randall, Alexander H. Stephens, Joseph Blackburn, and minority members James Garfield and William Frye—in fact worked out their committee report under the operation of a unanimity rule. This hardly sounds like partisan squabbling.

But we should not imagine an idyllic meeting of the minds either. The Committee had its differences. The most junior member, Blackburn, then serving in his third Congress, had given Randall a run for his money in the contest for the Speakership (Garfield noted in his diary that the campaign had been exceptionally bitter and was "likely to leave its dregs in the cup of their victory" [198]). In addition, Blackburn was a member of the prestigious Appropriations Committee and chair of the Committee on Expenditures in the War Department. In terms of consecutive service, Alexander Stephens had only slightly more seniority than Blackburn, sitting for his fourth consecutive Congress. But this fact masks a distinguished career that included participation in six Congresses before the outbreak of the Civil War. In somewhat failing health, Stephens held the chair of the Committee on Coinage, Weights, and Measures. Frye was serving his fifth term, holding a place on Ways and Means in addition to Rules. Both Randall and Garfield were on their ninth terms (with Garfield on Ways and Means along with Frye). All of this took place in a Congress in which almost half the membership was serving its first term.

While the Democrats had a nominal majority, it is important to recognize the limitations of the coalition. Stephens was not the archetypal loyal Democrat: he had been elected to Congress as a Whig from the 29th through the 31st Congress, as a Unionist for the 32nd Congress, as a Whig for the 33rd Congress, and as a Democrat until the eve of the Civil War. He was elected vice president of the Confederacy (as noted at the end of chapter 4) and returned as a Democrat from the 43rd Congress until his resignation in 1882. Stephens, therefore, was an old-time Whig who had converted to the Democracy. Political rivals Blackburn and Randall stood on opposing sides on the important issues of the Electoral Count and the tariff, with Randall the leader of the protectionist wing of the Democratic party and as a result finding himself at times more closely aligned with the protariff Republicans than with some of his fellow party members. Across party lines, Randall and Garfield had known each other for a number of years and had a warm personal friendship (Olcott 1916, 135). Deals between the two were not unknown: Garfield was able to work with Randall on minority committee assignments in return for his assurance that the Republicans would not join forces with the Greenbacks (*Diary*, 209).

Out of this cacophony of similarities and differences, there is one note on which all the members of the Committee were in agreement: they were all well-known proponents of fiscal restraint and centralized control over appropriations (Stewart 1989, 99). This qualification was sure to be important, since the 46th Congress started off with numerous calls for devolving the power of the Appropriations Committee. Formed in 1865 (when it split off from Ways and Means), the Appropriations Committee had utilized its power to report at any time in order to call up its legislation late in the session. Furthermore, the committee utilized restrictive procedures to limit the ability of individuals to either increase or decrease appropriations. This effort bore fruit: during this period, the federal government often ran a budget surplus. Such legislative efficiency did not, however, merit the approbation of all members of Congress, many of whom pressed for a distribution of the power to appropriate among various committees.

Given this agreement, perhaps it is not surprising that the Committee adopted a unanimity rule. But while these members may have agreed about some issues, as I have shown, they were in great disagreement about others. What can explain the adoption of this extraordinary procedure? I think two observations can be made that will help sort out the puzzle of the unanimity rule.

The first observation concerns the purpose of the Committee. The resolution authorizing the Committee on Rules to sit through the recess allowed it to do so "for the purpose of revising, codifying, and simplifying the rules of the House" (quoted in *Congressional Record*, hereafter *CR*, Jan. 6, 1880, 198). That is, the intent of the resolution was not to change the rules, but rather simply to organize what had become a quite unorganized agglomeration of mostly incremental changes. "The urgent necessity of a thorough revision of the rules of the House cannot be better illustrated and shown," the Committee report notes, "than by the simple statement of the fact that of the present one hundred and sixty-six rules sixty-three of that number, or portions thereof, were adopted prior to the year 1800, and that in the only revision and re-arrangement of the rules ever made since that time, not less than thirty rules which were practically obsolete, in whole or in part, were allowed to remain among the standing rules of the House of Representatives" (*CR*, 198). When one views the work of the committee as one of simple pruning and rearrangement, the imposition of a unanimity rule appears more understandable.

This might at least partially account for the lack of partisan spirit celebrated by Frye in his remarks on the floor:

> And first, I desire to pay a deserved tribute to the democratic majority of our committee. In these days, when party spirit runs high, when it permeates almost the whole body politic, provokes bitter hostilities, jealousies, and dissensions, incites the majority to ride rough-shod over the minority, justifies or acquiesces in the overturning of the will of the people as expressed at the polls, seizes upon the governments of the great States in the face of the Constitution and the laws, it is indeed refreshing to record one instance, at least, where this spirit has been completely exorcised, where the decree, 'Get thee behind me Satan,' has been fully executed. From the beginning of our deliberations down to the signing of the report there never has been the slightest evidence of partisanship on the part of the democratic majority of the committee; and I think they will bear the same testimony to the Republicans. There have been no heated discussions, no dissensions, no attempts to trample upon the rights of the minority. (480)

Perhaps the scenery had something to do with it: the Committee picked for the location of its deliberations the delightful seaside resort of Long Branch, located some distance away from the partisan bickering of Washington.

Second, the adoption of the unanimity rule may not have meant a great deal to this Committee. Certainly, it did not imply that they always agreed: it just meant that where they disagreed, they refrained from making a *committee* recommendation. This did not mean that they weren't free as individuals or even as a committee to suggest without recommendation procedural changes for the consideration of the full House. The Democrats, for example, had been able to block an attempt by committee Republicans to introduce a clause prohibiting riders on appropriations bills. The level of trust held by the Republicans for those in the majority can be seen from this revealing quote out of James Garfield's diary:

> The Committee met at ten o'clock and sat until one, making good progress. I offered a resolution, which was adopted, that when the session at Long Branch closed, the Committee should adjourn to meet at Washington on the tenth of November next to re-revise the whole work. *This will prevent any action by the Democrats without our presence.* (*Diary*, 278, emphasis added)

Certainly, even the good spirits described by Frye did not prevent Garfield from being a prudent politician.

So the Committee had its differences. But more than anything else, what may lead us to temper our enthusiasm regarding the unanimity rule is a recognition of how loosely the Rules Committee apparently used the term. At the adoption of the rules at the start of the 46th Congress, the Committee proposed some rules changes that would have had important implications for the role of committees in the House. Like the comprehensive 1880 revision, these rules were reported to the House as the unanimous report of the Committee on Rules (Stephens, *CR*, April 9, 1879, 326). However, immediately after the report was presented Blackburn noted that he did not approve of all the recommendations, and in his diary Garfield set out his own objections to the report (*Diary*, 213). Perhaps the Committee on Rules had a very strange definition of unanimity.

How can the unanimity rule be characterized then? The best account I can furnish was that the Committee sincerely tried to bind itself to a nonpartisan attempt at rules change. Furthermore, the committee fashioned a document that was to explicitly govern the House in all future sessions. As a result, the document the Committee produced was flawed in many respects, addressing some issues while postponing the most contentious issues to the floor.

The Committee Report

Given the presence of a unanimity rule in the Committee, one might expect it to be relatively simple for the minority (or any single member) to veto an attempt to limit minority obstruction. Yet the Committee report at several points did seek to limit the ability of one individual to obstruct the workings of the House, and the purpose of this section is to catalog these changes.

The Committee undertook a number of relatively minor changes with respect to obstruction and delay. The Committee recommended that pairs were henceforth to be announced by the Clerk rather than by members, something the committee felt would "greatly facilitate the calling of the roll, which now occupies half an hour" as well as ensure accuracy, "a matter of the first importance when the House is closely divided politically" (*CR*, Jan. 6, 1880, 199). Existing procedure allowed individuals to amend a bill with the substance of another pending bill. The Committee on Rules banned such practice, noting that it would prevent "the practical inconvenience that would result from public business being obstructed by substantive motions which had no connection with the orders of the day" (*CR*, Jan. 6, 1880, 199). A motion to reconsider made during the last six days of the session would be disposed of when made: a typical delaying tactic by minorities is to vote on the winning side in order to be eligible to move that the measure be reconsidered (thus consuming more time). The extent of delay was made more obvious by requiring that the *Journal* record the actual hour when the House adjourns rather than the time at which the motion was made. The practice of "objection days," where a single individual could block private legislation, was also abolished.

But the most important alteration was in terms of the order of business (see Cooper and Young 1989). The Committee on Rules attempted to replace the reliance on special rules for consideration of pressing legislation with a institutionalized system of bill introduction and referral. Prior to the change, bills could be introduced only by leave or through committee report. The new rules did away with that entirely. The Report of the Committee noted that there had been no restriction on the introduction of bills for many years, a fact that is brought out by Cooper and Young (1989, 87). As a result, the procedure needed to be improved.

But why should it have been improved now? What had changed? The answer, as one might expect at this point, involved obstruction. On April 14, 1879, Omar "The Great Objector" Conger of Michigan raised a point of order against the introduction of a silver bill, noting that it had been introduced neither by report of a committee nor by leave. This action was apparently unprecedented. Alexander Stephens called the point of order obstructive, and the Speaker of the House claimed that he could not remember such an objection being raised at any time during his past 16 years of service (*CR*, April 14, 1879, 246). Although Conger's point of order was overruled, he had made it clear how an enterprising individual could use the antiquated rules of the House (particularly with respect to bill introduction) to throw a monkey wrench into a fragile system. To some extent, then, Cooper and Young are right: the rules changes ratified existing House procedure. But the further question to ask was why individuals felt it necessary to ratify House procedure, and the answer has to be that there were individuals such as Conger who were increasingly willing to utilize the gap between the rules and practice for the purposes of obstruction.

The order of business was to be further improved through a streamlined procedure for the consideration of bills reported from committees. All bills except those to which there was no objection to immediate consideration would go to one of three House Calendars (the Union Calendar, the House Calendar, and the Private Calendar). The aim was to eliminate filibustering in the morning hour, a procedure by which individuals would block the consideration of a bill through dilatory tactics. Bills thus delayed could only be considered through unanimous consent or suspension of the rules. Since these procedures required extraordinary majorities, members of the minority could easily defeat bills produced by parties with slim majorities. Furthermore, such delays could impede the consideration of noncontroversial legislation. The seriousness of such delays was noted in the report, which stated that "numerous instances might be cited, during the past few years, where the 'morning hour' has been consumed by dilatory motions for days, and even weeks" (*CR,* Jan. 6, 1880, 200). The committee felt that by changing the nature of consideration such delays might be avoided.

The Calendar system itself was meant to operate in a regular fashion, with bills being taken off the Calendar in the order in which they were put on. To aid in this attempt, the Committee on Rules proposed that it no longer be in order at all times to move that the rules be suspended for the purpose of going into the Committee of the Whole on the State of the Union. Furthermore, during the consideration of the report, the Committee proposed four further and more drastic changes (see *CR,* Feb. 27, 1880, and Bach 1990). First, a motion to suspend the rules had to be seconded by a majority vote. Second, the motion to suspend the rules was debatable for 30 minutes (to be split between the two sides). Third, suspension of the rules was to be allowed only on the first and third Mondays of each month rather than each Monday (with preference going to individuals on the first Monday and committees on the third Monday). These recommendations were all accepted, albeit not without some debate.

Consideration on the Floor

While these changes are important, it is difficult to imagine that they could sustain the *two months* of amendment and debate that the report received in the Committee of the Whole. This debate was far-ranging, from points as trivial as slight grammatical alterations to the ability of committees to report appropriations bills. In the interest of space, I will concentrate here on controversies of a partisan nature. This does not exhaust the topic of rules change nor, for that matter, of obstruction (see Dion 1991), but it will help us concentrate on the issue of majority rule and minority obstruction. Two issues in particular evoked the partisan cleavage in the House: riders on appropriations legislation and elimination of the disappearing quorum.

Riders on Appropriation Legislation
Much of the partisan wrangling on the rules issue involved the use of political riders on appropriations legislation. These riders were substantive amendments which were placed on appropriations legislation as a strategy to increase the cost of a presidential veto. Technically, the 120th rule of the House forbade legislation on appropriations bills, except—and this was the clincher—in cases where they would act to retrench expenditures.[4]

Of course, there are many alterations in law that might be expected to "retrench expenditures," and it was through this provision that riders were justified. In all, seven political riders were attempted in the 46th Congress, from one provision preventing the federal government from using troops to keep the peace in congressional elections to another that would stop future payment for marshalls to merely observe elections. All were vetoed by Hayes, and in the tightly contested and partisan House the Democrats simply did not have the votes to override the veto. Dealing with the rider issue had come up in the Committee on Rules, but the committee had been unable to reach a unanimous position on this highly partisan issue, and so the rule was merely rewritten into more elegant language. However, once it was reached in the Committee of the Whole, the rule was open to all sorts of amendments. Harry White, the ranking minority member of the Committee on Military Affairs, began by proposing an amendment that would prohibit riders (*CR,* Feb. 12, 1880). After some discussion, White withdrew his amendment to allow Emory Speer of Georgia, an Independent Democrat serving his first term, to propose a related measure that would allow appropriations bills to be amended as long as the proposed change reduced appropriations. This amendment serves as a beautiful example of compromise. On the one hand, it preserves the opportunity for retrenchment that was demanded by most Democratic members. However, by limiting such changes only to alterations in the sum of money, it would prohibit alterations in the law that would work to reduce expenditures but would not necessarily change any appropriations figure. Speer, however, also withdrew his amendment so that William Lowe, a first-term Greenback member, could offer an amendment that would prohibit any amendment on appropriations that was "of a partisan nature." One might object, as did members at the time, that it would be impossible for anyone to determine what exactly a partisan amendment was. Speer's response, if ultimately not successful, indicated a clear grasp of strategy: simply look at the vote. If the vote is along party lines, it is a partisan amendment. If not, then it isn't, and it can be admitted. After allowing Lowe to offer his amendment, Speer again proposed his amendment as a substitute for Lowe's. Garfield offered an amendment to Speer's substitute that would allow sums to be struck out and lesser amounts inserted. While the amendment itself is hardly significant, Garfield offered it "to test the sense of the Committee of the Whole" (860).

And test the sense of the Committee it did. The vote on Garfield's amendment to the substitute stood at 121 ayes to 121 noes. After the vote had been taken by tellers but before the vote had been announced, Young of Tennessee voted no, defeating the amendment. While this narrow escape did save the issue for the Democrats for the moment, it showed that the sentiments of the Committee were quite close to limiting riders on appropriations legislation.

After the vote had been announced, Garfield attempted to take advantage of the momentum by pushing for a vote on the Speer substitute. The chair, however, noted that amendments were pending. One amendment (allowing for changes in law if a two-thirds vote obtained) was defeated, while another (that it be in order to reduce the amounts of money provided for by law, and only to that extent change the law) was adopted by a vote of 124 to 79. This final amendment was very carefully worded, with Garfield and others endeavoring to guarantee that loopholes and perverse effects would not follow. The success of the amendment did not augur well for the policy of riders.

The antirider forces, however, were not able to capitalize on this victory. Blackburn immediately moved that the Committee rise, and then he moved that the House adjourn. The Committee returned to the Rules five days later, on February 17, 1880.

The Speer substitute as amended went down in defeat. What had happened in the meantime to the drive against political riders? Horace Page of California, a Republican, argued that the minority would be better off with the current rules than with the Warner substitute (*CR*, 954). His argument was that with a fair construction of the rules outlandish changes in the law would not be countenanced, while the current amendment would leave the chair with no discretion but to admit even the most eviscerating amendments. The only occasion in which this fair construction was not observed, he noted, was when Committee on Rules member Joseph Blackburn held the chair.[5]

A more compelling argument might be that the Democrats had brought the discipline of party down on recalcitrant members. The *Washington Post* of February 13, 1880, noted that the Republicans were able to win on the Warner amendment to the Speer substitute with the help of the Greenbackers and a few Democrats. After the tie vote, Finley of Ohio was reported to have said "damn a Democrat who will leave his party in a pinch" (1). Furthermore, the Committee on Rules had failed to furnish an alternative measure on the riders issue, while the Democrats had. After the defeat of Speer's substitute as amended by Warner, Frye warned the members against a proposal that he thought might be coming: the Morrison substitute that would in fact win the day. Summing up the rider battle at the adoption of the rules, Garfield would note:

> On this side of the House we have made a very persistent and very earnest, and, I think, an exceedingly fair exhibition of our desire to prevent by positive enactment in the rules the presence of political riders on appropriation bills. We had re-enforcements from some of the noblest and best elements on the other side of the House, [laughter,] and for a time it appeared probably that we were going to succeed. But what happened? All the power of party discipline was brought to bear on our allies, and they were told that the point of party honor would not permit the rule in question to be changed, even if they should resolve privately that in fact and in practice there should be no political riders on appropriations bills during this session. As I understand it, though I have no authority for making the assertion, but I express it as my belief that this was the truce which brought about our formal defeat; that it was probably agreed that there should be no attempt this session to put political riders on appropriation bills if they would only let the rule remain unchanged, so that they might have the appearance of victory to cover the reality of defeat. (1256)

With Speer defeated, Price offered a substitute that would require that retrenchment specifically state the amount of money to be saved. This might be a good idea, but would hardly regulate riders, since any individual who could come up with a reasonable number of dollars saved would be allowed to attach a rider. To this substitute, Speer attempted an amendment reintroducing his substitute. He was told by the Chair, the future Speaker of the House John Carlisle, that since there were two amendments on the floor, further amendment would not be in order.

While it is not clear on the surface, this is essentially a partisan ruling. To understand why, it is important to realize that House rules prohibit amendments in the third degree (an amendment to an amendment to an amendment). It is, however, thoroughly appropriate to have an amendment, an amendment to an amendment, a substitute to the amendment, and an amendment to the substitute. Lowe had already provided an amendment. Price offered an amendment, which the chair admitted as a substitute to Lowe. It is clearly admissible to offer an amendment to the substitute, yet the chair responded to Speer's attempt to do so by saying that no amendment would be in order, "as two amendments are pending" (955), thus treating the Price amendment as a second-order amendment to Lowe and Speer as a third-order amendment to Lowe.

Clearly unable to understand the chair's ruling, Speer would (after the intervention of some other business) rise for a parliamentary inquiry. Recognizing that the chair had mistakenly interpreted Price's motion as a second-order amendment to Lowe, Speer stated that his amendment was being offered as a substitute. However, even this did not get Speer his day in court. Under the rules it is not in order to bring up propositions that have already been voted on, and so objection was made on the grounds that Speer's substitute was identical to the proposed amendment already voted on. The chair concurred and on appeal was upheld on a 129 to 100 vote.

To get around this roadblock, Speer then offered a substantially similar amendment, but one that would limit riders not only on general appropriations bills but on all bills appropriating money. After some debate, the chair finally admitted this amendment, which was defeated (120 Yeas, 121 Nays), an outcome almost identical to the previous vote on Warner. Two more amendments were attempted, but they both went down in defeat, and the innocuous Price substitute was disagreed to.

The antirider forces attempted again with the Warner substitute. During the consideration of this substitute an interesting thing occurred. Alexander H. Stephens attempted to gain the floor. However, since debate had been limited, he was not allowed to speak. The only way for Stephens to be heard would be for the Committee to rise and for the House to resolve itself into the Committee of the Whole House on the State of the Union, a trick which would allow at least an hour speaking time. Blackburn vigorously opposed the attempt, but on rather close votes the attempt to allow Stephens to speak succeeded. Since this vote took place in the House and Yeas and Nays were called, we can tell what the cleavages on the vote looked like. These are summarized in table 5.1.

This vote clearly indicates high party cohesion. We also see the Greenbacks voting with the Republicans. Of the six Democratic defectors, five were from the South (including three from Georgia, Stephens's home state). The remaining nonsoutherner was Warner, who had already aligned himself with the antirider forces.

After Stephens's speech, the House returned to the Committee of the Whole for consideration of the rules. Amazingly enough, the Warner substitute was adopted. Again, while this substitute did not eliminate riders, it did attach significant conditions to the practice. After the substitute was adopted, Mills of Texas offered three amendments that would allow certain specific

TABLE 5.1.   Vote on Motion that the House Resolve Itself Into the Committee of the Whole on the State of the Union, February 17, 1880

	Democrat	Republican	Greenback	Total
Yeas	6	105	6	117
Nays	114	0	1	115
Not voting	28	26	6	60

riders (tax cuts, retirement of national banks, and silver legislation) to be in order. None passed. The prospect for limiting the objectionable practice of riders on appropriations legislation looked good.

Were this a Greek tragedy, the subsequent actions of George Robeson of New Jersey would be more explicable. After some success had been achieved on the rider issue, Robeson exhibited the sort of overreaching ambition associated with tragic heroes and offered an amendment that would essentially chop off all the conditions that had been instituted. His desire, it appears, was to have a straight vote on the rider issue that could be taken back to the constituency for the upcoming election.

His initial attempt was ruled out of order, for the simple reason that issues already considered cannot be brought up again. Robeson therefore proposed amending some of the language in the initial report as well as removing the conditions already voted on, a slight change but one that guaranteed that his amendment was in order. His amendment passed (115 Yeas, 43 Nays), canceling out all the work that had been done to limit riders. The lack of significant objection of course signals that the Democrats had something up their sleeves.

And then came the coup de grâce. Morrison proposed a substitute that Frye had earlier warned against: it would essentially return the rider issue to the status quo ante, but would also allow individuals on the committees whose jurisdictions include the subject matter of the bill to offer riders as well. This was a brilliant stroke: it would leave the rider issue intact, at the same time alleviating concerns that the Appropriations Committee had a virtual monopoly over riders. Furthermore, Morrison proposed a substitute for the entire clause. That meant that individuals could not go back and alter what he had proposed, except to add additional language. Morrison's sweetener attracted enough votes to carry the day, 123 to 95. Garfield quickly attempted to add a clause limiting the use of riders, but was defeated, 109 Yeas to 122 Nays.

The Democrats had narrowly averted a defeat. Had Robeson offered his amendment in the form of a substitute for the whole clause, he could have cut off Morrison's challenge. By leaving some room open, Robeson allowed the

Democrats to repeal all the conditions that the Republicans had worked so hard to get. Furthermore, the Morrison substitute put the Republicans in a difficult situation. They did not want to vote for the Morrison substitute, but on the other hand they did not want to vote for the Committee on Rules version in the House either.

Faced with this difficulty, the Republicans attempted to put the best face on their loss. As noted above, Conger threatened a filibuster, but Frye and Garfield were unwilling to go along. Garfield's speech on March 2, 1880, contained some of the gems of the vanquished party. He asserted the existence of a secret deal by which the Democracy had promised its members it would not offer any riders for the remainder of the Congress in exchange for the appearance of victory. The Republicans had fought a good fight, the country knew where the parties stood now, and further bargaining would do nothing to improve things. As Garfield put it,

> Viewing these things, therefore, as I do, we are brought face to face with this problem; shall we now reopen the whole fight on the rules, only to come out of the end of another indefinitely long struggle at possibly the same place? While we are doing that, trying to adjust our blocks in the puzzle, the other party will be adjusting their blocks, the tariff blocks, the center party blocks, all revolving around in the puzzle to come out at the end in a general tangle upon the whole board. (*Diary*, 1256)

The vaunted nonpartisanship of the Committee fell apart once more. Blackburn said that he had never heard of Garfield's secret deal. Furthermore, in the glorious tradition of mudslinging, Blackburn brought up the vote of the Committee on Rules taken that morning on the Morrison substitute: Blackburn and the Speaker were for it, while Garfield, Frye, and Stephens were against it. Blackburn thus made full use of the embarrassing position the Morrison substitute put the Republicans in by reading the roll of the Committee and then saying, "Those gentleman declared their preference for the original rule as it now stands" (1256). That is, those gentleman had voted to keep the current policy on riders, hardly a moral victory for the Republicans. Frye countered that they merely felt the substitute created more problems, not that the current policy was admirable (Blackburn retorted that he was merely stating the facts). Finally, Warner, whose substitute had been trampled by Robeson's inept handling of the bill, responded to Garfield by saying that " . . . I wish to say in reply to my colleague that the 'moral victory' he boasts of is nothing more than a tactical blunder into which he himself led or helped to lead his party" (1257). Warner had offered an amendment that was agreeable, he felt, to all sides, only to have it torn down by the Republicans: "They dug their own pit and fell into it, and my colleague has not succeeded this

TABLE 5.2.   Yeas and Nays on Morrison Substitute, March 2, 1880

	Democrat	Republican	Greenback	Total
Yeas	117	0	2	119
Nays	6	100	8	114
Not voting	25	31	3	59

morning in extricating them from it" (1257). The final roll call on the Morrison amendment is presented in table 5.2. No Republicans defected, and the Democratic defections were for the most part expected (e.g., Speer, Stephens, and Warner). The Morrison substitute became the law of the House for regulating legislation on appropriations bills.

The Disappearing Quorum

The 1880 rules change also witnessed a preliminary skirmish over the problem of the disappearing quorum. Acklen took advantage of the freewheeling general debate on the rules to suggest a rules change regarding the disappearing quorum. He noted:

> I shall offer that in no partisan spirit whatever; but, after our experience in the extra session of the present Congress, I think it will strike any fairminded, candid man of the House that we should adopt some rule that will prevent, when a measure is violently advocated and strongly opposed, a minority of the House through parliamentary legerdemain in obstructing necessary legislation. It is impossible if we carry out, or if any body of men attempt to carry out, the practices which were adopted in the first session of this present Congress, for the country not to suffer. Needed legislation is certain to be obstructed by such tactics. I think it will be far better when a minority of this House shall have decided to their own satisfaction that the measure supported and advocated by a majority of this House is wrong and unconstitutional to place their opposition on record, and not to impede and obstruct legislation, but remit the whole question to the people, who in the present day of a free press have the most favorable opportunity to judge of the propriety of measures pending before Congress. (423)

Acklen's suggestion was followed up in the Committee of the Whole on January 28, 1880, during consideration of Rule 8 (Duties of the Members). Tucker, a Democrat from Virginia, then made the motion that members present but not voting be counted for the purposes of a quorum, an amendment he offered, like Acklen, in a spirit of nonpartisanship.

Whatever the intentions, this nonpartisan amendment unleashed a maelstrom of partisan conflict. Garfield noted that it would easily lead to despotism:

> This House has been the theater of all sorts of political storms and tempests. We have lived through the times of great wars, of great civil war, when there were excitements hardly parallel in the history of parliamentary annals. Yet during all these years no man before, so far as I know, no party before has ever thought it necessary to introduce a rule which gives the power of declaring the presence of members by the single voice of one person; a power that will enable him to bring from his sick-bed a dying man and put him down in this Hall, so that the Speaker shall count him, and make his presence against his will, and perhaps in his delirium, count in order to make a quorum, so that some partisan measure might be carried out over the body of that dying man. (576)

He continued, "I hope my friend from Virginia will not press his proposition to a conclusion as part of the body of our rules, for we shall be compelled to oppose it with all our might" (576).

Again, the presumed unanimity of the Committee on Rules was not in evidence on this partisan issue. Blackburn noted that Tucker's amendment did not go as far as many such proposals (it did not, for example, require that individuals not voting be counted in the negative). Furthermore, he felt that even with the rule there would be ample opportunity to obstruct legislation.

> I do not mean to commit myself to the theory that there should be no power given to a minority to impede or obstruct legislation. I know that there have been times and occasions upon which I would not abridge that power if I were able. Where the right to offer amendments has been denied, where reasonable opportunity for debate has been refused to the minority, it is not only their right but their duty to obstruct such legislation. It matters not whether I stand here with the majority or with the minority, I shall always advocate and demand that right. But I say the report submitted by this committee is not, upon any fair construction, amenable to the criticism that it is its purpose, even as supplemented by the amendment from the gentleman from Virginia, to abridge in any material respect the right that the minority should hold in this House. Take this revision, adopt it as a whole, and incorporate in it the amendment now pending, and the minority will still be amply provided with

every facility to obstruct and impede legislation where debate has been refused and the right of amendment denied. (576)

The remainder of the day continued in often passionate discussion of the amendment. One meager contribution, however, has stood out from the rest. A sophomore representative from Maine, Thomas Brackett Reed, rose to state his position on the disappearing quorum:

> It is not the visible presence of members, but their judgments and their votes, that the Constitution calls for. . . . It is a valuable privilege for the country that the minority shall have the right by this extraordinary mode of proceeding to call the attention of the country to measures which a party in a moment of madness and of party feeling is endeavoring to enforce upon the citizens of this land. And it works equally well with regard to all parties, for all parties have their times when they need to be checked, so that they may receive the opinions of the people who are their constituents and who are interested in the results of their legislation. (579)

Ten years later, Reed would be reminded of these very words as he presided over the dismantling of the disappearing quorum.

Blackburn began the day's consideration on January 29, 1880, by noting that Tucker's amendment might not pass, and that even if it did achieve a majority, the members of the Committee on Rules "are of the opinion that it may in no small measure affect the final vote on the adoption of the series or system of rules which have been submitted for the consideration of the House" (603). The argument was clear: even if the amendment wins, it loses in the end. Tucker withdrew his amendment, and the disappearing quorum would be left intact for another ten years.

Final Action by the House

The prolonged consideration of the rules of the House were brought to an end on March 2, 1880. Many of the changes made in the Committee of the Whole were ratified without objection. The Committee on Rules also proposed a number of technical amendments that also passed. Five issues, however, attracted serious enough contention so that the Yeas and Nays were called. I have already given the breakdown (in table 5.2) of the final vote on the Morrison substitute. The other four votes took place on rules changes regarding the duties of the clerk, the devolution of appropriations to Agriculture, the devolution of appropriations to Public Buildings, and the final vote on the adoption of the rules. Table 5.3 indicates the breakdown on the votes by party.

TABLE 5.3. Selected Party Divisions on Yeas and Nays, 1880 Rules Changes

	Democrat	Republican	Greenback	Total
1. Clerk				
Yeas	130	10	4	144
Nays	0	96	5	101
Not voting	18	25	4	47
2. Agriculture Appropriations Devolution				
Yeas	70	53	10	133
Nays	55	47	0	102
Not voting	23	31	3	57
3. Public Buildings Appropriations Devolution				
Yeas	44	48	9	101
Nays	84	52	1	137
Not voting	20	31	3	55
4. Final Vote on Adoption of the Rules				
Yeas	113	6	3	122
Nays	3	80	5	88
Not voting	32	45	5	82

Note: The Morrison substitute, which also received the Yeas and Nays, is recorded above in table 5.2. On Public Buildings Devolution, there is a discrepancy between the *House Journal* and the *Congressional Record*. The numbers above are from the *House Journal*. The *Congressional Record* records O'Brien, a Democrat, as not voting rather than voting no.

On the Clerk vote, which was a majority–minority issue, party lines held. The devolution issue, as might be expected, cut across party lines. A complete analysis of these last two votes is made in Stewart (1989, 109–12). His assessment is that the rural bias of the Democratic party made it difficult for electorally motivated MCs to vote the party line and defeat devolution. Party forces, despite appearances from the simple partisan breakdown, were more powerful in the area of public buildings, which for many members of the Democratic party did not have the same constituency imperative.[6]

The final vote is clearly on party lines. At least one interpretation of this is that the minority party found the document to be harmful to its interests. This interpretation, however, must recognize that prior to this final vote the irrepressible Conger made the following announcement: "I demand the yeas and nays on the adoption of these rules. I do this because it gives us the only opportunity we can have to vote against this principle of political riders" (*CR*, March 2, 1880, 1266). Although Conger's attempt to filibuster the rules report was defeated,[7] his announcement (especially in the pages of the *Record*) that this was to be taken as a vote on riders might have been difficult to resist. That the vote was taken as a symbolic stand on riders would help explain why Garfield, a member of the Committee, voted against the rules changes on the final vote. Garfield's diary entry for that day contains no explanation of his actions. As a result, it is much more difficult in this case to say that the party-line vote on adoption represents the dissent of the minority party over limitations on its procedural rights.

Summary

As noted at the outset of this section, the 1880 rules change is the most complicated such change we shall consider. The topics covered range across the board, evoking a number of cleavages in what was itself a quite complex House. The purpose of this summary is to attempt to rise above the details and to determine how well the proceedings outlined in this section accord with the theoretical expectations of chapter 2.

To introduce a bit of clarity, let me present two competing interpretations of the 1880 rules change. The first is the *obstructionist* hypothesis. This view has been held by Thomas Brackett Reed, Hubert Fuller (1909), and Ronald M. Peters (1990) in his recent book on the Speakership. The basic outline of this view goes: Randall was an obstructionist, as much when he was in the minority as when he wasn't. The combination of his presence on Rules plus the unanimity rule guaranteed that obstruction would continue unabated in the House.

The second view is the *antiobstructionist* hypothesis. According to this view, Randall was the first truly partisan speaker, the first person to attempt to alter the office to suit the needs of party leadership. The rules changes of 1880 may not have gone as far as possible, but they weeded out a convoluted and confusing system of rules, making them more coherent and practical. This weeding out process was the first step in the march toward the elimination of obstruction. This view is presented in Follett 1896 and House 1935.

Cast over both of these interpretations is the long shadow of Thomas Brackett Reed and his attack on obstruction in 1890. As a result, both seem to suffer from what Fischer (1970) has called "fallacies of narration." The obstructionist view appears to me to try to make the 1880 rules change as different as possible from the 1890 Reed changes so that the latter will appear all the more radical. I believe that the Reed changes are so patently revolutionary that there is no need to buttress their case by downplaying the steps that the 1880 rules changes took to limit obstruction. Yet the second view seems to me to go too far: it reinterprets the 1880 rules changes as a sort of 1890 in miniature, as part of a grand march toward the end of obstructionism that comes with the 51st Congress. It seems clear that the 1880 rules changes attempted to limit obstructionism. At least in the areas I have labeled partisan, these changes appear to be motivated by the concerns of majority/minority that I have been arguing all along. But the degree of unanimity and the presence of other factors (such as the appropriations issue) make the 1880 case a far cry from the sort of rules changes that are envisioned by the theory presented in chapter 2. At the conclusion of this chapter I will speculate on some of the reasons why the 1880 rules change did not go as far as the 1890 changes.

The Adoption of the Reed Rules

> What a charming life that was, that dear old life in the Navy! I knew all the regulations and the rest of them didn't. I had all my rights and most of theirs.
> —Thomas Brackett Reed, Speech before the Loyal Legion, Washington, 1884[8]

Of all the cases we shall consider in this portion of the book, the rules changes adopted in the 51st Congress (1889–90) are the most consistent with the theory. And much of the thanks for making this an easy case should go to the Speaker of the House, the Honorable Thomas Brackett Reed. Reed's single-minded determination to quash the ability of members of the minority party to obstruct legislation has left an institutional legacy that the House still operates under today. Yet Reed's success did not seem as guaranteed as it does in hindsight, and in this section I would like to discuss how "Czar" Reed was able to put the final nail in the coffin of minority rights to obstruct in the House.

There are two important aspects to the institutional changes of the 51st Congress that need to be analyzed. The first concerns the famous "quorum" ruling. The second concerns the adoption of the Reed Rules.

Reed's famous ruling on the quorum (that individuals present but not voting could be counted in determining the presence of a quorum) was made during the consideration of the contested election case of Smith vs. Jackson. It is important to note initially exactly how fragile Reed's majority was in the House. His election as Speaker over Democrat John Carlisle was determined by a vote of 166 to 154 (McCall 1914). The magic number 166 was also the minimum number of votes required for a quorum in the House of Representatives, which at that time had 332 members. Without additional members, the Republicans would be subject to continual harassment by the Democrats with the use of the disappearing quorum. To gain additional members, however, they would need to resolve some of the contested elections cases in their favor, an action that was also susceptible to the disappearing quorum.

Making this impossible appears to have been the Democratic strategy. On the question of consideration of the resolution seeking to seat Smith, the Yeas and Nays revealed 162 Yeas, 3 Nays, and 163 not voting. After announcement of the vote, Reed was treated to the quite typical abuse cited at the beginning of this part of the book. Covert's sarcastic response elicited laughter from the Democratic side. Then two individuals withdrew their votes, the Yeas and Nays standing at 161 to 2. Cowles objected that there was no quorum. Whereupon, in a revolutionary ruling, Reed directed the Clerk to record the names of the individuals present but not voting.

Reed had not told the House or the public about his plans. Nor, it appears, did he tell either Cannon or McKinley, his parliamentary lieutenants.[9] After directing the Clerk to record the names present but not voting, an extraordinary scene erupted. Reed directed the Clerk to continue counting. When the name of Breckenridge of Kentucky was called, Breckenridge shouted "I deny the power of the Speaker and denounce it as revolutionary" (*CR*, 949). Breckenridge thereupon went down the aisle and into the well, followed by "the entire Democratic side" (Busbey 1927, 177). Reed's reaction according to Cannon: "But Reed never appeared more calm, more like a big, good-natured boy in manner and appearance, as with his beatific smile he serenely gazed upon those furious, shouting Democrats and waited for the disturbance to subside" (177). When the outburst would die down, a few more names would be recorded as present but not voting, leading to another riotous scene, after which Reed would begin the cycle again. Cannon noted that it took "several hours" for Reed to complete his call (Busbey 1927, 178). After he had completed this task, he began to present his ruling.

In a well-prepared statement, Reed presented the arguments for eliminating the disappearing quorum. He began with the Tucker amendment considered in the last section, noting that the Democrats had tried to eliminate the disappearing quorum back in the 1880 rules change. He attributed their failure to do so to an unfamiliarity with the evils of the practice. He then cited two cases, one in New York state and the other in Tennessee, in which Democratic state legislatures had made the same ruling he was now making over Republican objections.[10] Even in this most intense and partisan of battles, Reed maintained his usual poise and humor. When he reached the part of his ruling where he quoted the New York legislature's characterization of the minority— "Their action is in defiance of the rules of this body, factious and revolutionary"—Reed silenced the loud round of Republican cheers with the admonishment "The House will be in order. This was not said of Democrats" (*CR*, 951). This astonishing display of grace under fire brought laughter and applause from the Democratic side.

We have the following account of the House after Reed's ruling by O. O. Stealey, a correspondent from Louisville then in the press gallery:

. . . a frantic scene ensued; the whole House was on its feet and likewise the galleries. The Republicans were cheering and the Democrats were answering in derisive yells. Many of the latter were clamoring for recognition. During all of this excitement Speaker Reed stood immovable in his place behind the table, his face pale and determined and his right hand firmly clenched around the butt end of his gavel.[11] It was fifteen minutes before the least semblance of order was restored. In the meantime, Charles F. Crisp, the well-known member from Georgia, the head of the Minority in the Elections Committee, had walked down the lobby directly in front of the Speaker's desk, and in loud tones was demanding recognition from the Speaker. (1906, 80)

At first it appeared as if the Democrats would have no chance to counter Reed's arguments. Payson of Illinois moved to table Crisp's appeal. Crisp demanded the right to be heard, noting that it was "unfair, unjust and unmanly to refuse to us an opportunity of presenting our case to our fellow members" (*CR,* 951). In a surprising move that one might not have expected from the accounts of the partisanship of the 51st Congress, it was a Republican, Butterworth of Ohio, who urged Payson to let the other side be heard. Payson withdrew his motion, and Crisp presented the minority side of the case.

The majority argument had traditionally been that the Constitution must have required that members present be sufficient for a quorum, otherwise there would be no logic to the constitutional provision allowing the House to compel the attendance of its members. To defeat this argument, the minority would have to find some ground for the practice of the disappearing quorum in the Constitution, and it had: in the provisions for the Yeas and Nays. As Crisp put it,

This is something more than a question of rules. The right to have the yeas and nays entered on the Journal is a constitutional right. It follows necessarily, when the Constitution says you must enter the yeas and nays on the Journal, the yeas and nays so entered must determine the presence or absence of a quorum. They can not be added to or taken from, but must be taken as conclusive of the question. (*CR,* 952)

Crisp followed Reed's lead in defending the disappearing quorum with a ruling from the opposing party, in this case the famous ruling of ex-Speaker and then–Secretary of State James G. Blaine during the debate over the Force Act in 1875: "The moment you clothe your Speaker with power to go behind your roll-call and assume that there is a quorum in the hall, why, gentlemen, you stand on the very brink of a volcano" (cited on 953). Crisp followed this by recounting the numerous Republicans who had supported the disappearing quorum during the 1880 rules change, beginning with Garfield and Conger, and with a wonderful rhetorical flourish ending with Reed's own arguments ten years prior. "I appeal, Mr. Speaker," Crisp argued, "from Philip drunk to Philip sober" (*CR*, 954).[12]

Crisp then veered into rather treacherous waters. He noted that the House, despite assurances from the Republicans, had gone without any formal rules for the past two months. This was in fact correct: Reed had ruled that without rules the House would be governed by "general parliamentary law," a procedure that naturally granted great latitude to Reed, who seemed to be the only person to really understand what that law implied. Crisp then began to attribute partisan intentions to Reed's ruling, an attempt that drew objections from the members and a directive from Reed that Crisp keep to the question. After numerous attempts to make his argument, Crisp finally gave up and turned to a summary, closing with the following plea:

> I leave the case with the House with the confident assurance that there are at least some Republican members of this body who can rise above partisan prejudice, who can respect and will respect the ancient usages and customs of the House, who will respect the opinions of the fathers, and who will be regardful of that Constitution whose sacredness we all acknowledge, and in which alone are secured the rights of the American people. (956)

It is not surprising that Crisp addressed his final comments to the Republican side: even a few Republican defections and Reed would be overruled.

While these arguments are compelling, there is an additional argument Crisp used that seems to me the strongest. This argument is based upon majority rule.

> If you have got a majority you can do business without violation of the Constitution; you can do business without acting in defiance of the precedents of a hundred years by simply bringing your members here and keeping a quorum in the House. It is no reply to say, 'Some of our men are absent,' 'Some are sick.' We say to you we simply insist upon our constitutional right to have the yeas and nays entered upon the Journal and to have the responses to the roll-call determine the presence or absence of a quorum. (*CR*, 953)

The disappearing quorum did not prevent a majority from acting: it merely required that the majority show enough effort and cohesion to furnish an actual majority on the Yeas and Nays. Without the construction of the Constitution favored by the Democrats, it would be possible for a bill to pass with a majority vote of a very small percentage of the House, as long as there were enough individuals "present but not voting" to make up the quorum. It was on this argument that Carlisle ended his own appeal:

> I think, Mr. Speaker, that while some inconvenience results from the rule we have always had, as inconveniences must result sometime from the operation of any rule you can have, still it is far more safe, it is far more in accordance with the character of our institutions, that we should stand by the old rule as laid down in the Constitution and allow no legislation here unless it is participated in by a majority of all the members elected to this House. It is the only safe rule, and it is the rule we ought to stand by hereafter as we have heretofore. (960)

The notion of the disappearing quorum as a safety net was even acknowledged by Cannon in Busbey's work, years after he had taken the floor to rebut Crisp:

> The filibuster was a recognized parliamentary weapon, and its use by both parties had always been regarded as legitimate. Blaine when Speaker, and he was considered one of the greatest parliamentarians of his time, had refused to use his power to destroy the filibuster. I suppose there was the feeling that however subversive the filibuster was to the rule of the majority, it was, like the knife of the revolutionary, the last desperate resort against tyranny; the majority of today might be the minority of tomorrow, and no minority could allow itself to be disarmed. (Busbey 1927, 174)

These arguments, as well as the others that have been produced from politicians on both sides of the aisle, indicate the high value placed on the disappearing quorum by practical politicians. They also indicate the great obstacles Reed was facing in his effort.

Ultimately, however, Reed won the battle of the quorum. Crisp's appeal was laid on the table, a legislative move that left Reed's ruling intact. Yet the quorum only represented one element of Reed's attack on dilatory tactics. On February 6, the Committee on Rules brought forth its proposed changes of the rules.[13] The changes proposed by the Committee struck at the heart of obstructionism in the House.

The first major change made individuals present but not voting count in determining the presence of a quorum.[14] This cemented Reed's ruling in the standing rules of the House. The second major change made dilatory motions out of order. Under this rule, any parliamentary maneuver that the Speaker deemed time-consuming and wasteful could be cut off. Since the rules change did not define what exactly a dilatory motion was, critics of the rules change were quick to comment on its rather sweeping force. The third rules change placed the quorum of the Committee of the Whole at 100 members. Prior to this time, the quorum had been identical to that of the House, that is, a majority of all members. Adoption of this rule would make it virtually impossible for members of the minority to obstruct by the use of a disappearing quorum in the Committee of the Whole. In the committee's report, the majority explained the failure of previous Houses to regulate the quorum of the Committee of the Whole by noting (somewhat disingenuously, if we remember John Quincy Adams) that the reason "the issue has never been heretofore presented is due entirely to the fact that until recent years members have not sat in their seats and refused to vote when their names were called" (*CR*, Feb. 7, 1890, 1150). Finally, a set of changes in the order of business were adopted, making it easier to take up Senate bills, finish off unfinished business or business close to being finished, select bills in the Committee of Whole from the Calendar, and introduce legislation off the floor where precious time might be taken up.

The unanimity witnessed in the 1880 rules changes was in no evidence here. The minority of the Rules Committee (Carlisle and Randall) presented a minority report that, among other things, argued that "the policy of the proposed rules is to suppress the individual member of the House as far as possible and increase the power of the committees" (*CR*, Feb. 7, 1890, 1151). The Minority Report attacked the new order of business rules, the Committee of the Whole provisions, the disappearing quorum provisions, and the dilatory motion rule.

However much one may have wished for a clash of the titans over the rules, fate intervened. Samuel Randall was in the grip of an ailment that would take his life in a little over two months. Carlisle was also ill and not able to add his voice to the Democratic side. The Democrats and Republicans engaged in general debate on the rules over the next two days, a debate that toward the end became rather stale (members making much the same arguments and reading from identical precedents). On February 13, 1890, the House began to consider the rules for amendment under the five-minute rule, with the explicit understanding that the previous question would be ordered at 5:00 P.M. on the next day.

The process began with a number of technical amendments to the rules from Cannon that were agreed to, although with some debate and attempt at amendment. Two and a half hours of the limited time of the House were thus taken up in dealing with issues that were in fact quite removed from the real sources of controversy, a rather pleasant show of obstruction on the part of the majority.

After Cannon had finished, Crisp began the Democratic response. He placed the Republicans in a difficult spot by immediately moving that a demand for the Yeas and Nays not be considered dilatory. The call for the Yeas and Nays is provided for by the Constitution, and therefore disagreeing with Crisp's amendment weakened the Republican case that their decisions on the quorum showed the proper constitutional respect. But assenting to Crisp's amendment would allow the use of the Yeas and Nays as a dilatory motion and thus defeat the whole purpose of the rules changes. Republican members attempted to get out of the box by arguing that the constitutional protections were themselves sufficient, thus rendering the proposed change unnecessary, and that in any event it was better to place the power to determine what constitutes a dilatory tactic in a Speaker who could always be overturned on appeal, a rather perverse argument.[15] The Yeas and Nays were then called on Crisp's amendment, which went down in defeat on a straight party-line vote (see table 5.4).

Taking advantage of the argument of the Republicans that the possibility of appeals from the Speaker's decision would limit potential abuses, Crisp proposed a second amendment that stipulated that the Speaker not fail to entertain a motion for an appeal from his decision. If this amendment carried, Democrats would be able to filibuster through constant appeal from Reed's decision. All they would have to do, noted Cannon, would be to make a motion to adjourn twice in a row. When the Speaker rules the motion out of order, the member could appeal the decision and then move to adjourn again, and repeat the whole cycle. Such an individual, Cannon argued, "could appeal a thousand times and compel the House to call the yeas and nays in each case, thereby exhausting five hundred hours or a thousand or five thousand" (*CR,* Feb. 13, 1890, 1294). After some more debate, the Yeas and Nays were counted, and a perfect party split was revealed.

The House then adjourned over until the next morning. Through one of the various absurdities of the legislative process, the hour before noon was still counted as the legislative day of February 13, and by agreement the hour was spent only in debate, without voting. At five minutes to noon the House adjourned, reconvening at noon on Valentine's Day, 1890, a coincidence that was the source of endless amusement at the time (the procedural changes were considered "Reed's Valentine" to the Democrats).

The consideration of the rules began again, this time with Bynum offering an amendment that would require that pension bills indicate how they would be funded. Under this amendment, therefore, every Republican attempt at pension legislation would be accompanied by a public notification of a new charge on the people. This would thoroughly transform the politics of pension bills, transforming what is essentially a distributive politics issue into a redistributive morass of the sort that members of Congress strive to avoid. An attempt by Bland to link in currency politics to Bynum's amendment failed,

TABLE 5.4. Roll Call Votes on the 1890 Rules Changes

	Democrat	Republican	Total
1. Crisp (D) amendment that a call for Yeas and Nays not be considered dilatory.			
Yeas	117	2	119
Nays	2	147	149
2. Crisp (D) amendment that Speaker shall not in any case refuse to entertain an appeal from his decision.			
Yeas	114	0	114
Nays	0	140	140
3. Bynum (D) amendment on pension bills.			
Yeas	96	0	96
Nays	18	146	164
4. Outhwaite (D) amendment to strike out provision that quorum consists of 100 members.			
Yeas	135	1	136
Nays	0	149	149
5. Crisp (D) amendment to strike out clause counting members present and not voting in a quorum.			
Yeas	136	0	136
Nays	0	156	156
6. Mills (D) amendment to strike out rule that no dilatory motion shall be entertained by the Speaker.			
Yeas	140	0	140
Nays	0	155	155
7. Vote on Adoption of the Code of Rules.			
Yeas	0	161	161
Nays	144	0	144

Source: McPherson, *Hand-book of Politics*, vol. 4, "Hand-book of Politics for 1890," 107–12.

and the Yeas and Nays were ordered. The pattern is familiar: a party-line vote, although a number of Northern Democrats crossed party lines to cast their vote with the Republicans.

An attempt was made by McMillin to return the procedure for the introduction of bills back to the status quo ante. This attempt was rejected by a vote of 100 Yeas to 110 Nays, but was not subject to a roll call vote. A roll call vote, however, was taken on Outhwaite's amendment to strike out the rules regarding the quorum in the Committee of the Whole. Here again, a partisan split was observed, as was the case with Mills's motion to strike out the language banning dilatory motions. Outside of a rather bizarre amendment to limit everyone to ten minutes speaking time and some additional technical amendments from Cannon, all that remained was final action on the report from the Committee on Rules, a vote that again was perfectly split on party lines.

Conclusion

Above I have noted the strong arguments that have been adduced in support of the procedural guarantees granted to minorities. But if this tool was so valuable as a safety net for members of Congress, how was it that Reed was able to take it away from the minority? Why 1890 and not 1880? Why was Reed able to succeed where others had failed?

The theory presented in chapter 2 suggested that obstruction is more likely to the extent that the parties differ on the appropriate departure from the status quo. When parties do not separate, then we have the possibility of crosscutting cleavages. The strong sectional conflicts operating in the Democratic party during the 1880s would be expected to make the Democratic party more accepting of obstructive practices.

This argument receives some support from Cooper and Brady's (1981) classic study of party leadership. They present evidence showing that party cohesion and centralized leadership (including the 51st Congress) were associated with a widening gap between the two parties in terms of rural/industrial constituencies. Taking their data as an indicator of the degree of party separation, their results also uphold the claim that increasing party separation is associated with decreasing tolerance for obstructive procedure.[16]

But party separation cannot be the whole story. If it were, then Democrats and Republicans would be equally likely to support the centralization of power in the House. As we have seen, however, this was not the case. Republicans were much more supportive of attempts to limit obstruction than were members of the Democratic party. Party separation therefore cannot predict why Reed was so successful.

We can, however, make some more headway by recognizing that the caucus will be successful to the extent that a floor majority within a party can find a policy preferred by all its members to the status quo. The more individuals prefer the status quo to the relevant alternatives, therefore, the more likely obstruction is to be maintained. Some suggestion that this characterizes the relative situations of the two parties is provided by no less a personage than Thomas Brackett Reed himself:

> For years rule has been piled upon rule and decision upon decision to render legislation dependent upon the sufferance of the minority. Filibustering lurked in every line. The power of obstruction was without

limit. You will naturally ask why it was that those who most of the time had the majority should so strengthen the minority. If you will consider the nature of the two parties the cause cannot escape you. The Democratic party wants no legislation. It is not charged with the progress of the world. All the Southern men who control the party want or ask for is to be let alone. When the Republican party comes into power it has work to do. If that action can be prevented what more should the Southern Democrats desire? Hence all their plans, whether in power or out of power, are centered in obstruction. (Quoted in Robinson, 1930, 222)

This quotation is from an election speech Reed gave in Maine. Yet we should not discount too much for electoral sentiment, given the number of Democrats who over the course of the debates made explicitly the same point. Holman, the Watchdog of the Treasury, noted that "many very sensible men believe that the curse of our age is too much legislation, not too little" (*CR*, Feb. 11, 1890, 1210). Lane noted that the old rules were not so dangerous as the new rules "because all that a member could do under the old rules would be to obstruct. He could not inflict upon the country dangerous, wrongful, or wicked laws, as can be done under the proposed rules" (*CR*, Feb. 12, 1890, 1252). From Wike: "The growing curse of the country is too much legislation, and the people approve wholesome restraints of it . . . " (*CR*, Feb. 12, 1890, 1263). From Hatch: "We have had too much legislation" (*CR*, Feb. 11, 1890, 1218).

The Republican view of the legislative process was quite different. Cutcheon explains the salient points:

Now what is the ground for this change [in the rules]? Why this change now and not twenty years ago? The answer is plain. First, the change of political parties; the advent into this Chamber in this Congress of a different political school from that which has been in control of the House for the past fourteen or sixteen years. The school of Jefferson, for the time being, has been retired by the people, and the school of Hamilton and Washington is placed in control. The party of strict construction has been ordered to go to the rear, and the party of broad and liberal construction and of national constitutional powers has been entrusted with the helm of the ship of state, and changes in the mode of procedure and of policy must inevitably follow this change of political control. (*CR*, Feb. 12, 1890, 1236)

Moore on February 12, 1890, noted that a growing country demanded, at least in his opinion, growing legislation. This in turns required procedural change: "with ten thousand bills on the Calendar, with thousands more already in sight, and with fifty committees of this House constantly at work sifting and revising the vast mass of legislation proposed here, the necessity is imperative that this should be a business body, governed by business principles" (*CR*, 1256). And businesses produce.

What accounts for this difference? A large part may simply be economic. The tariffs that the government relied on for revenue worked to the advantage of manufacturing interests and to the disadvantage of urban and rural consumers of manufactured goods. The task for Democratic leadership, therefore, was to guarantee that the public till would be free from assaults. Given that task, it is clear that a perfectly admirable system for checking these assaults would be a system of obstruction. An individual whose proposals are obstructed can still claim to be making every effort to protect whatever constituents might be interested in expenditures, while at the same time making sure that costly expenditures are not made. Republicans, on the other hand, had no fear of high appropriations and the ensuing tariffs and therefore could see nothing of use in the obstructive procedures. These arguments help make sense of the Republican claim that the Democratic party was afraid to trust itself (Kerr, *CR*, Feb. 12, 1880, 1240). They also make sense of the Democratic perception of Republicans as spendthrifts wedded to lobbies and syndicates (Holman, Feb. 11, 1890, 1212; Rogers , *CR*, Feb. 12, 1890, 1258). Lane quipped that the House under the Republicans was entering an "era of good stealing." With vivid imagery, Holman argued, "These new rules will leave the Public Treasury absolutely without protection so far as the House is concerned, which is made by the Constitution its especial guardian. They manacle the watchmen and arm the lobby with crow-bars!" (1212).

Unfortunately, later generations of scholars, reading these exchanges (or at least reports of them), took what was a political position for a theory. Of course procedures worked to make it easier to transact business: don't we have the quotes to prove it? Yet this interpretation does a disservice to the obstructionists and makes the whole process seem much less conflictual than is actually the case.

But interparty conflict is not the only consideration here. We also need to determine how Reed was able to keep his coalition together in a way that evaded Polk. While Reed might have had a cohesive majority, his success was never assured, especially for the revolutionary changes that he was going to make. But some tricks had been learned in the years since Polk. Rather than meeting in Washington to work out a scheme and then launching it on a stunned audience, Reed submitted his proposals to the Republican caucus, which eventually supported his position.

But this pushes the question a step back: why did members of the party abide by the action of the caucus? How was Reed able to retain loyalty? In general, the answer is that individual members of the party needed Reed more than he needed them.

Turnover in the House declined during the last half of the nineteenth century (Polsby 1968; Fiorina, Rohde, and Wissel 1975). Much of this decline, Kernell (1977) has shown, can be attributed to the desire of members to stay in the House, rather than changes in norms of rotation or party competition. Having acquired the congressional bug, however, members of Congress must go about attempting to get reelected. But to do so required the support of the Speaker of the House. In describing the Speaker's power, Chipman noted

> . . . he is omnipotent. He may turn his back upon you or upon me; and as a rule Speakers will not recognize and do not recognize the newer members of the House. As a rule, too, the Speaker, as the leader (unfortunately under our system) of the majority party in the House, has a very prompt ear and a very kind heart for the members of his own party, especially those members of his own party who are favorites with him. (*CR*, Feb. 12, 1890, 1246)

The electoral connection was made all too clear by Caruth. The new member is neither recognized for speeches on the floor nor allocated prized committee assignments. "But the people at home think he is somebody, and they are scanning the newspapers to see what he has done towards immortalizing himself" (*CR*, Feb. 12, 1890, 1248). But even before he has a chance to learn his way around town, "some ambitious individual who wants the seat he has hardly warmed by his presence pronounces him a 'stick' and 'a complete failure.'" If, however, he was lucky, he might be called upon to report a measure, "and then the people would see it telegraphed over the country that he had made this report, and 'the boys' in his district, gathering at the country stores or waiting their turn at mill or barber-shop, might talk over the distinction which had been conferred upon him and unite in the opinion that he is 'the best Representative the district ever had'" (1248).

The ability of an individual to distinguish himself in this manner, at least in the 51st Congress, was to a large extent determined by Reed. Before the days of huge caseloads and television spots, the *Record* and the newspaper accounts gave individuals one of their few mechanisms for evaluating the efforts of their members, and Reed was clearly aware of his influence in this regard. When a member asked Reed why he helped kill a bill the member supported, Reed responded "To get rid of you" (Josephy 1979, 260).

Furthermore, the 51st Congress promised to be a bonanza of legislation and spending. Opponents estimated that the Congress would spend upward of a billion dollars, an unprecedented figure and one not too far off from the actual level of appropriations passed by this Congress. This exasperated thrift-minded opponents such as Springer, who listed the bills expected to pass as a result of the rules changes and in frustration predicted that "there will be a public-building bill for each Congressional district before we get through" (*CR,* Feb. 12, 1890, 1258). Without the rules changes, there was no reason to expect the bills to escape obstruction and thus little hope for members to remain in office. Those interested in reelection or even in further political office would thus have an incentive to take the medicine offered by the Reed rules changes.

Is that all there is to these changes? A final factor, though one shudders to bring it up, is the personality of Thomas Brackett Reed. One could perhaps think of "charisma" as a human capital investment, or as a continuous parameter whose value is determined by nature. I would prefer, however, to refrain from such gross manipulation of the model and instead recognize that in some sense Reed's action represented a level of political leadership and responsibility that is difficult to theorize about. What Reed did was not totally unprecedented: other leaders with other small majorities, from Polk on, made moves to limit obstruction. Yet it is difficult to believe that any other individual would have accomplished the same results that Reed did: Cannon certainly did not believe he could have pulled it off, and he had serious doubts whether William McKinley (the third candidate in the 1890 Speakership race) would have been able to, either (Busbey 1927, 166–67).

And in many ways, Reed's dedication to eliminating obstruction went well beyond anything that would be required by practical politics. Reed himself, prior to his ruling, informed future Senator Elihu Root of his plans and noted that if he was not supported in his attempt to eliminate obstruction he would resign from the Congress and enter into the practice of law, with the understanding that he would practice in Root's firm (see McCall 1914, 167).[17] This was no idle boast: Reed would in fact resign from the Speakership in protest over U.S. imperialism. Nor were Reed's procedural opinions changeable: while a minority member on the Rules Committee in the three Democratic Congresses before 1890, Reed submitted proposals designed to eliminate obstruction. The official history of the House Committee on Rules notes that Reed could advocate such changes "knowing that the Democrats were not likely to adopt his recommendations," but also noting that Reed's "commitment to principle," especially the principle of majority rule, was unshakable (65)

Reed himself phrased it this way, when he submitted an antiobstruction resolution while in the minority:

> The rules of this House are not for the purpose of protecting the rights of the minority, but to promote the orderly conduct of the business of the House. They can have no other object. It is because in their application they have been perverted from the purpose for which such rules are intended that we have this great trouble today. (Cited in House Committee on Rules 1983, 66)

This would make for better copy had he not said this in the lame duck session of the 50th Congress, when it was clear that the Republicans would take over in two short months. But it does indicate Reed's view of procedure, and it is a view, as noted in chapter 1, that still holds sway over much of our understanding of parliamentary procedure today. The business metaphor served Reed well: who could object to a well-run business? But in doing so, Reed laid to rest an older tradition of parliamentary procedure that sought protection for minorities in the rules of parliamentary procedure. There may be no desire to go back to those old days of cumbersome procedure and ineffective majorities in the House, but there is nothing to forfeit in recognizing what has been lost.

CHAPTER 6

The Missing Rules Changes

The cases covered in the previous two chapters appeared from the existing (admittedly skimpy) historical literature to be the major rules changes taking place in the partisan-era House (see, e.g., Galloway 1969). Of course, had these Congresses seen exceptionally large majorities, the theory would hardly have seemed very compelling.

However reassuring these results might be, they may be less informative than we would otherwise think. Inferences from a set of cases such as those just considered is critically dependent on the way in which those cases are selected. The approach taken here, a critic might argue, amounts to "selecting on the dependent variable" (Achen and Snidal 1989; Geddes 1990; King, Keohane, and Verba 1994).[1] Quite simply (the charge would go), I selected a set of cases of major rules changes (my dependent variable), looked for what was in common among that small set, and then propounded a theory to explain the cases I had selected.

Why this method can lead to erroneous inferences can be understood by looking at the study of war (Most and Starr 1982, Achen and Snidal 1989). For decades political scientists have spent a great deal of effort gathering data as to conflicts. The hope was that by looking at the correlates of actual conflicts, it would be possible to understand why nations go to war—certainly a noble end, except for one difficulty: the set of cases of nations that go to war is a biased subset of all cases of international interaction. Uncovering factors that the conflict situations have in common will tell us nothing about conflict unless we compare the conflict situations to the nonconflict situations.

How closely did my own case selection follow this method? To be sure, I had some notion of when the major rules changes of the nineteenth century took place, and I did notice that those rules changes had in common the factor that they were adopted during times when the majority party is small—so far, a striking example of selecting on the dependent variable. Unfortunately, due to the lack of information in the literature, I did not (a) know whether the link between size and party cohesion would hold up in the nineteenth century; (b) whether obstruction was related to majority party size and cohesion; (c) whether in fact these rules reforms were partisan affairs; and (d) whether the rules changes in fact dealt with minority rights to obstruct (in fact, based on a line in Galloway 1969, I had erroneously concluded that obstruction was *never* dealt with procedurally until 1890—happily, reviewing the rules reforms eroded that mistaken impression). This is terribly risky social science and displays a stunning shallowness of preparation, but at least it does not display the typical pattern that critics associate with selecting on the dependent variable.

This does not exhaust the potential problems with case selection, however. While the previous two chapters have addressed periods of major rules change, it is quite possible (given the lack of a complete listing of rules changes) that other major changes affecting obstruction took place that (for whatever reason) have not been identified in the secondary literature as periods of "major rules change." If those changes occurred during sessions in which the majority party controlled a large proportion of the seats, then the theory presented here would be less compelling.

Do these problems in case selection destroy whatever insights we have obtained? Answering this question is the purpose of this chapter. I will begin, therefore, by considering what happened to those Congresses that also witnessed small majorities, then moving on to a consideration of the potential rules changes regarding minority obstruction that might have been missed.

Missing Rules Changes: Part I

Determining what might have happened to the rules regarding obstruction when the majority was small required that I have some method for assembling a set of small majorities. I therefore selected for each of the four measures of party size presented in chapter 3 (Martis, Congressional Quarterly, Galloway, and the Speakership Election) every Congress in which the majority had a proportion of the seats equal to or smaller than the largest proportion (according to that particular measure) occurring in a rules change year. Since the four measures differ, they consequently select different candidates for small majorities. In table 6.1, however, I have presented a list that indicates those Congresses in which all four of the measures agree. I have also added the other Congresses that meet the criterion for small majorities on at least one measure.

Given these results, we should be most likely to see rules changes in the 30th (1847–49), the 31st (1849–51), the 34th (1855–57), and the 47th (1881–83). The remaining Congresses may witness some rules changes, but the unevenness of the proportion data may make us more forgiving if we do not find what we expect.

In assessing these Congresses, I am interested in two questions. First, was there some push to limit minority rights to obstruct? If there were, then the theory has yielded new insights into legislative politics by leading us to cases that given the conventional literature on rule reform we would not have

TABLE 6.1. Small Majorities in the House, 1835–95

Congress	Year	Martis	CQ	Galloway	Speaker
Rules change years					
25	1837	52.9	45	48	53
36	1859	48.7	48	48	50
46	1879	48.1	51	51	51
51	1889	53.9	51	52	52
Maximum proportion		53.9	51	52	53
Non-rules change years, majority proportion less or equal to maximum on all four measures					
30	1847	50.4	51	51	50
31	1849	48.5	49	51	46
34	1855	42.7	46	46	48
47	1881	51.5	50	52	52
Non-rules change years, majority proportion less than maximum on three measures					
26	1839	51.7	51	55	51
50	1887	51.4	52	52	52
Non-rules change years, majority proportion less than maximum on one or two measures					
35	1857	55.7	50	55	57
38	1863	46.2	55	56	55
45	1877	52.9	52	53	53

studied. Second, if there wasn't an attempt to limit minority rights to obstruct, can it be explained in the context of the theory presented in chapter 2?

The Likeliest Cases

I want to start first with the four cases that are below the maximum majority party proportions for the rules change years. These cases are the likeliest candidates to either disconfirm the theory or else show that the theory is capable of leading us in directions we might not have expected.

The 30th Congress
Looking back at the 30th Congress (1847), it turns out that quite a few rules changes did take place. Rule 80 clarified the use of special orders: a special order gave preference on a particular day to the consideration of a bill, report, or resolution, but notwithstanding such an order the House could if it wished "proceed to the consideration of such appropriation bills" (*House Journal*, 30th Congress, 681). The hour rule was amended so that committees could open and close the debate. Motions to excuse a member from voting had to be taken without debate (Rule 42). The previous question was taken to include the motion to commit. A motion to reconsider a debate could not be with-

drawn the next day without consent of the House. Individuals wishing to introduce a bill on leave must give notice a day in advance. If the Committee of the Whole on the State of the Union should find itself without a quorum, the Committee was to rise and report the names of the absentees to the House. These names would be listed in the *House Journal*, therefore becoming public knowledge. Rule 135 addressed the order of business and required that the decision to consider a bill on the Calendar must be taken without debate if objection is raised. Rule 137 directed that the Speaker not entertain the motion for suspension of the rules except on Mondays. Since this motion was often obstructive, this provision can be seen as an antiobstructive measure. The list is fairly long, but we can see a continuing concern with quorums, time for debate, obstructive motions: in short, the rules changes adopted in the 30th Congress fit well into the scheme that I have been arguing all along.

A further change relating to obstruction was the passage of a rule limiting debate on amendments to five minutes for each side. Characterizing this change is actually somewhat tricky.[2] On the one hand, it could be considered a move toward minority rights, in that the right to debate on amendments was being guaranteed. But it was also a move that worked to the advantage of the majority, which had experienced difficulties in voting on bills without debate on amendments as well, as Hinds points out (1899, V.§5221). Not surprisingly, then, the five-minute rule was apparently held in high esteem, but Hinds notes in the same section that after a few years, members recognized the room available for obstruction under the five-minute rule for obstruction: by offering a series of amendments, it became possible to delay proceedings for quite a period. The use of this delaying tactic threatened to permanently delay passage of the Kansas–Nebraska Act, leading Alexander Stephens (as noted in chapter 3) to move to strike the enacting language and place opponents in a double bind.

The 31st Congress
Unfortunately, the 31st Congress does not do as well by this scheme. One change merely directed that the doorkeeper not let in anyone he did not know until a member told him that the individual was permitted on the floor and by what reason. The only other change was to the five-minute rule. After an individual spoke five minutes on his amendment.

> any member who shall first obtain the floor shall be allowed to speak five minutes in opposition to it, and there shall be no further debate on the amendment; but the same privilege of debate shall be allowed in favor of and against any amendment that may be offered to the amendment; and neither the amendment nor an amendment to the amendment shall be

withdrawn by the mover thereof, unless by unanimous consent of the committee. (*House Journal,* 31st Congress, 1607–8.)

In his magisterial *Precedents,* Asher Hinds indicates this rule had been adopted because "while the five-minute rule was generally in high favor, this practice produced much delay and irrelevancy" (Hinds 1899, V.§5221).

Hinds's comments may support the theory, but one must ask whether two rules changes, only one of which appears very important, count as support of the theory. Why didn't the 31st Congress go further? One argument is that they might have found the rules changes of the previous Congress enough. If that rules change hit the major procedural protections given to obstruction, there might be little left to do. On the other hand, in chapter 4 we have already seen that the 31st Congress was something of an outlier. The dummy variable for this Congress showed that it was well below what might have been expected in terms of party cohesion on the basis of the other variables alone. It must be remembered that the 31st Congress witnessed an eruption of sectional pressures cutting across party lines, leading to the Crisis and eventual Compromise of 1850. As noted in chapter 2, sectional pressures tend to weaken the desire for rules changes limiting obstruction. What is impressive, therefore, is not that they did not go far enough, but that they went this far at all.

The 34th Congress

The 34th Congress witnessed the smallest majority party in the set we are considering here. This Congress occurred after the breakdown of the Second Party System but before the consolidation of the Republican Party. Consequently, the Republicans, while having a plurality of seats, lacked a majority. In fact, their party was so small that this is the smallest proportion of seats held by a "majority" party throughout the entire partisan era. But this was not the end of the nascent Republican Party's problems. They also faced the problem of divided government of a particularly troublesome sort: the Democrats controlled both the presidency (under Pierce) and the Senate.

Given the double difficulties of a small party and unified opposition control of the other federal institutions, it might be inferred that the Republicans would not anticipate much potential for launching a positive legislative program. This seems to characterize their legislative strategy: as Schuyler Colfax (who would later be Speaker for much of the 1860s) noted in a letter to Charles M. Heaton Sr.,

With the Speaker & the Committees ag[ain]st us, we should be totally powerless. With them, we may effect a little & but little, but we can *resist*—& that will be something, even if we could do nothing affir-matively. (Cited in Gienapp 1987, 248; emphasis in original)

I do not think that any party having less than a majority has to adopt the position that it can get nothing done, but if such a party does see its legislative program as one of obstruction, it will, I would argue, tend not to see a great need in reforming rules favoring obstruction.

I have found only two rules changes that have occurred in the 34th Congress, both dealing with the establishment of a Court of Claims to investi-gate claims against the United States. The first dealt with bills and accom-panying reports from the Court of Claims, and required that they be referred to the Committee on Claims, which every Friday morning would be allowed to report, with the bills placed on the private calendar (*House Journal* 34 1&2, Appendix, 1647). The second established a new joint rule between the House and the Senate dealing with the procedure for the Court of Claims.

The Court of Claims shared with Elections the distinction of being the oldest standing committee of the House, both created on November 13, 1794 (Hinds 1899, IV.§4262). There had been discussion as early as 1822 on "overburdened condition of the Committee on Claims" (Hinds, 1899, IV. §3303, fn. 2). The establishment of a Court of Claims would seem to relieve the Committee of some of its burdens. I do not see anything in here that conforms to limiting obstruction: if anything, it appears to be a simple case of expediting a process that provided members with casework opportunities (see Stewart 1989, esp. 9–11, 54–58). For a new party with hardly a working majority, faced with divided government, this move seems sensible.

The 47th Congress

This leaves the final case of the 47th Congress. Since the Republicans were in charge of this Congress, the sectional tensions that plagued the Democrats were not as serious. Here, we see again the passage of a rules change limiting the opportunities for obstruction. Two important changes emerged.[3] The first was motivated by the contested election case of Mackey vs. Dibble. The Republicans had suffered losses that furthered endangered their small minor-ity, and their attempt to increase their numbers was met by constant motions to adjourn and disappearing quorums. As a member of the Committee on Rules, Reed fashioned a rules change that would essentially outlaw dilatory tactics on contested election cases.

Of course, if the minority could obstruct a contested elections case, it could obstruct a rules change to stop obstruction on contested elections cases, and Randall, now in minority, moved to adjourn. Reed made the point of order that such a motion was dilatory and that, as compared to the constitutional right of the House to decide contested elections cases, out of order. After debate, Speaker Keifer upheld Reed's point of order, and was sustained on appeal (150 Yeas, 0 Nays, and 141 not voting). Reed's change was adopted. The reaction from the minority party can be captured from this quote from *The Campaign Book of the Democratic Party*:

> May 29, 1882, should be a day long remembered in the annals of Congress, for on that day was first enunciated by a Speaker of the House of Representatives the remarkable doctrine that the majority of the House has the right to so change the rules as to deprive the minority of all rights whatsoever. (1882, 46)

Even allowing for rhetoric, the proposed rules clearly dealt a sharp blow to minority rights.

Yet this was not all. The elections of 1882 returned control of the House to the Democrats. The 47th Congress, as was then the custom, would return to Washington after the elections for the "short" session, a three-month period of lame-duck legislating. Tariff legislation was still pending, but no matter how intensely the Republicans wanted tariff revision, the possibility seemed remote. An Independent Commission had recommended significant rollbacks in duties. And the Democrats needed only to keep up the filibuster for the length of the short session. If successful, the control of tariff legislation would pass into their hands as the new majority.

Reciprocity accounts suggest that the Republicans should have been quite cordial here and receptive to Democratic attempts at delay. After all, this is an excellent case of a party that knows with absolute certainty that it will be in the minority in a short three months. What then was the Republican response?

In point of fact, rather than sitting by and cooperating, the House majority went into full partisan gear. As it turns out, the Senate had attached some legislation on the tariff to a House bill designed to decrease internal revenue. Revenue bills, however, are supposed to receive their first consideration in the House, so objection was made to the Senate bill, which languished on the Speaker's desk. Taking the bill off the Speaker's desk would require a suspension of the rules, which would mean a two-thirds vote that the Republicans certainly could not muster.

On February 24, 1883, then, a short seven days before the close of the 47th Congress, a privileged report came from the Committee on Rules that would allow the rules to be suspended by a simple majority, the bill to be taken from the Speaker's table, the House to disagree with the Senate version of the House internal revenue bill, and the bill to be referred to a conference committee. The report squeaked through the threat of a disappearing quorum and was adopted by 129 Yeas, 22 Nays, and 140 not voting.

The conference committee contained some of the most famous protectionists in congressional history. On the House side there was Kelley, McKinley, Haskell, and Randall, with Carlisle the lone House nonprotectionist. The Senate side contained Morrill, Sherman, and Aldrich. Two senators, Bayard and Beck, refused to serve, disagreeing with some of the conditions imposed on the conference by the House. While the bill reduced some duties, it raised others. Tariff revision passed the House, squeaked through the Senate, and was signed by President Arthur. This was an unthinkable turn of events, one that would have been impossible without Reed's quashing of the Democratic filibuster.

Less Likely Cases

We now turn to the less likely cases. Two of them we have already encountered. As noted in chapter 4, the 35th Congress (1857–59) produced, but did not adopt, the set of proposed rules changes that were finally adopted in 1860, and the 45th Congress (1877–79), the first after the Hayes–Tilden struggle, witnessed a debacle over the use of political riders. Since some discussion of them has already been made, and since both of these cases (as well as the 38th Congress) satisfy the selection criteria on only a single measure, I will concentrate my attention here on the other two cases, which are stronger tests for the theory.

The 26th Congress
The 26th Congress would have satisfied the critera for likeliest case, except that a single measure—Galloway's—was higher than the cutoff of 52 percent for that measure. But the 55 percent figure presented by Galloway seems exceptionally at odds with the 51 to 52 percent figures presented by the other three sources.

What transpired during that Congress? Rather surprisingly (at least for me), there was a rather extraordinary rules change adopted. On June 1, 1840, with roughly five months to go before the election, a rule was adopted that would diminish the vote necessary to suspend the rules from two-thirds to *a simple majority*. The suspension of the rules was one of the main ways in which earlier Congresses could modify the procedure of the House to reach a particular bill. Without it, obstructionists could require that the regular order be followed, which could consume a great deal of time and possibly kill the bill.

This provision stayed in the rules for the 27th Congress (discussed below), but was rescinded in the 28th Congress. In this Congress, the Democrats controlled 65.9 percent of the seats (according to Martis) and obtained over two-thirds on the vote for Speakership. Rolling the two-thirds requirement back in that session was hardly a profile in courage.

The 50th Congress

The 50th Congress was the last Congress before Reed assumed the Speakership. It has gone down in history as perhaps one of the most obstructive and least productive sessions of the American national legislature. Reed himself referred to it as the "nadir" of ineffectiveness.

Part of the responsibility for this outcome might be laid at the foot of John Carlisle. The precedents on dilatory actions assembled by Hinds suggest that while Carlisle had opportunities to limit obstruction, he did not take advantage of them. On April 4, 1888, Carlisle ruled that a motion to excuse a member from voting on a motion for recess *was* in order, even though the rules said that such a motion would be out of order on a motion to *adjourn*. The distinction between recessing and adjourning is pretty thin, but Carlisle negotiated it (Hinds 1899, V.§5712). On January 21, 1889, a bill to organize Oklahoma was considered under a special rule that ruled out dilatory motions. A motion to adjourn was made and voted down, and then another motion, this time to recess, was proposed. A member objected that these were dilatory tactics; Carlisle responded that while the special rule was designed to prevent obstruction, things had not in his opinion gotten to that point yet (Hinds 1899, IV.§3210). This view was apparently shared by those who substituted for Carlisle in the chair (Hinds 1899, V.§5745)

Before proceeding, however, we might want to take a look at that last sentence. A special rule limiting dilatory amendments in the *50th* Congress? Before Reed? Of course the precedent was on the organization of a territory that would in all likelihood be Democratic, and so the usual divisions among Democrats did not apply. But in looking over the precedents, it seemed to me that there may have been some steps by Democrats to limit obstruction, but steps that were difficult to find, occurring not on the standing rules (as did Reed's changes), but instead on some selected special rules.

This pattern makes partisan sense. Republican cohesion made antidilatory tactics written into the standing rules safe. After all, they only had to worry about obstruction from Democrats. The more divided Democrats, however, on some issues had to worry not just about Republicans, but also about members of their own party. As a result, adopting a bill-specific approach might have been preferable.[4] After all, if a particular agreement could be worked out between the wings of the Democratic party, it could be sustained by a special rule without in any way endangering each wing's rights on other issues. While this was the only example that I have been able to turn up on the Democratic use of a special rule for this purpose, and while the official history of the House Committee on Rules is clear that special rules were not exceptionally popular among Democrats, further analysis of these issues may yield surprising results (or at best, an interesting irregularity).[5]

Conclusion

This section has done more, I hope, than simply establish that the theory is capable of overcoming the objections that started this chapter. I also hope it demonstrates the utility of theories that outline simple (and easily checked) conditions for leading us in directions we might have never thought to go. Especially in a topic as convoluted as that of parliamentary procedure, we need some guides, some way to determine where one should look. The evidence here suggests that, even after taking into account the problem of selecting on the dependent variable, small majorities do appear to limit minority rights to obstruct.

The Missing Rules Changes: Part II

Even the preceding analysis, however, might not satisfy the persnickety critic. In the previous section we brought in periods that were not times of major reform. But there could be other times of minor reform, and as a result, given the data presented so far, it could well be that in *every single Congress* there were rules of the kind that I have discussed. A bit more cynically: perhaps with a little bit of "careful" looking, I could find obstruction anywhere.

There is, however, an independent source that can be of assistance here. Asher Hinds's collection of parliamentary rulings has been referred to previously in this work. It constitutes *the* guide for parliamentary procedure in the nineteenth-century House and is still (joined to the efforts of Cannon and Deschler) in use today. To make sure that I was not imagining obstruction where it did not exist, I decided to allow Hinds to do the coding, by using the voluminous index contained in his magisterial work to assemble a list of all the rulings cited under the heading "Dilatory Proceedings" that took place during the partisan era. Hinds was Thomas Brackett Reed's parliamentary assistant, and as a result (I imagined) if a precedent against dilatory motions existed, Hinds would probably be the person to find it. Furthermore, his greater experience in matters nineteenth century and parliamentary made me willingly defer to his judgment.

There is a further advantage to using Hinds. Numerous theories have been proposed to account for procedural changes in legislative institutions. These have never been subjected to systematic evaluation. With the rich dataset presented here, it will be possible to get some assessment as to how well those other theories do in explaining the pattern of antidilatory precedents. Having said that, I hasten to add that I cannot guarantee the inclusion of every single relevant precedent. There is the chance that Hinds missed some difficult cases. The results do, however, provide some sound basis for at least initial inferences, and in the absence of a thorough recoding of the parliamentary history of the nineteenth century, it seemed the best that could be done.

A note on procedure here: where a precedent is referred to in the index twice, I have counted the precedent once. Two precedents found in the "Dilatory Motions" chapter but not found in the index were also added.[6] From these, I deleted those precedents not occurring during the partisan era, as well as a case from the Senate that somehow made its way into the House precedents (III.§2123).[7] This gave me in all 37 precedents, which I aggregated into a per-Congress count. Some of the references in the index were to actual cases of obstruction. Table 6.2 presents the raw data.

The number of precedents in a congressional section is considered "count data." In dealing with such data, the statistical methods we have used so far are inappropriate. Consequently here (and elsewhere in the book where count data crops up) I have estimated the statistical model using Poisson regression.

Table 6.3 presents some initial estimates. Column 1 includes a constant as well as the proportion of seats held by the majority party, but I have found it necessary to include two dummy variables. The first controls for precedents during the Johnson presidency. When John Wilkes Booth's own act of political obstruction propelled Andrew Johnson to the highest office of the land, the nation saw a degree of tension and bitterness between the institutions of Congress and the presidency that would culminate in impeachment. These problems precipitated some rules reform in Reconstruction Congresses that had huge Republican majorities. Since the model does not entertain interinstitutional issues, and since I said in chapter 3 that when such characteristics took on prominence for our story I would point them out, the inclusion of a dummy variable seemed appropriate. The second dummy variable captures the clear break in the series at the 51st Congress.

As expected, the dummy variables for the Johnson presidency and the post-1889 sessions are positive and statistically significant. The proportion of seats held by the majority party is in the expected direction, but not statistically significant. This suggests that if the size of the majority party has any effect at all, it is in the negative direction. This is somewhat comforting, but is not quite as strong as one would like.

Column 2 begins the analysis of other theories of institutional change. One account of procedural change suggests that the rules in the House were modernized over the course of the nineteenth century as a result of the growth in House membership. The nineteenth-century House, contrary to modern practice, dealt with the problem of new states and population growth by increasing the size of the legislature. Within the partisan era, the number of

TABLE 6.2. Antidilatory Precedents, 1835–95

Congress	Antidilatory Precedents	Majority Proportion	Majority Party
24 (1835)	0	59.1	Democratic
25 (1837)	0	52.9	Democratic
26 (1839)	0	51.7	Democratic
27 (1841)	1	58.7	Whig
28 (1843)	0	65.9	Democratic
29 (1845)	0	62.3	Democratic
30 (1847)	0	50.4	Whig
31 (1849)	1	48.5	Democratic
32 (1851)	0	54.5	Democratic
33 (1853)	0	67.1	Democratic
34 (1855)	0	42.7	Republican
35 (1857)	1	55.7	Democratic
36 (1859)	0	48.7	Republican
37 (1861)	0	59.0	Republican
38 (1863)	0	46.2	Republican
39 (1865)	2	70.4	Republican
40 (1867)	1	76.5	Republican
41 (1869)	0	70.4	Republican
42 (1871)	0	56.0	Republican
43 (1873)	2	68.2	Republican
44 (1875)	1	62.1	Democratic
45 (1877)	1	52.9	Democratic
46 (1879)	1	48.1	Democratic
47 (1881)	2	51.5	Republican
48 (1883)	0	60.3	Democratic
49 (1885)	0	56.0	Democratic
50 (1887)	0	51.4	Democratic
51 (1889)	6	53.9	Republican
52 (1891)	4	71.7	Democratic
53 (1893)	10	61.2	Democratic
54 (1895)	4	71.1	Republican

TABLE 6.3. Poisson Regression Results on Antidilatory Precedents, 1835–95

Independent Variables	(1)	(2)	(3)	(4)	(5)
Constant	0.234	−3.352##	−3.422#	−3.137##	−3.558##
	(0.962)	(1.664)	(2.505)	(1.682)	(1.876)
Majority proportion (Martis)	−0.021	−0.042##	−0.042##	−0.041##	−0.044##
	(0.018)	(0.019)	(0.020)	(0.017)	(0.020)
Johnson presidency	1.694###	3.304###	3.310###	3.202###	3.329###
	(0.547)	(0.580)	(0.563)	(0.518)	(0.611)
51st Congress and after	2.883###	2.028###	2.040###	2.097###	1.977###
	(0.435)	(0.662)	(0.650)	(0.651)	(0.693)
Number of representatives		0.020###	0.020##	0.018###	0.021###
		(0.004)	(0.009)	(0.004)	(0.007)
Number of bills introduced		−0.0000619##	−0.0000615##	−0.0000475#	−0.0000735##
		(0.0000258)	(0.0000273)	(0.0000343)	(0.0000373)
Years from previous realignment			−0.00055		
			(0.106)		
Reed Speakership				−0.198	
				(0.210)	
Democratic majority					−0.169
					(0.368)
No. of observations	31	31	31	31	31
Log-likelihood	−1.543	1.235	1.236	1.311	1.322

#significant at the 10 percent level, one-tailed test
##significant at the 5 percent level, one-tailed test
###significant at the 1 percent level, one-tailed test

representatives in the House grew from 242 to 357. Such an increase, it is argued, makes it more difficult to transact business and thus necessitates the need for more "efficient" procedures. Thus James Bryce in 1890 wrote,

> The conduct of government by assemblies of men instead of by individual men is proverbially one of the most difficult things in the world. When the number of an assembly rises beyond thirty or forty, so that conversation is superseded by speech-making, the difficulty increases in proportion. When the number passes one hundred and fifty or two hundred, a new element of trouble is introduced in the excitement produced by the sympathy of a multitude, under whose influence men will say and do things which the judgment of a single man or a small group would at once condemn. (385–86)

Bertrand de Jouvenal, in a 1961 *American Political Science Review* article that is a sadly forgotten gem, provided the earliest (and also, I believe, the last) (and hence the best) formal treatment of the problem of the allocation of speaking time. His analysis revealed that

> (1) With an upper time limit for discussion m, and a lower time limit for the formulation of a speech k, the feasible maximum number of people exercising the right of speech is determined. (2) Therefore with an increasing number n, the formal right to speak is a delusion for an increasing proportion of those entitled to this formal right. (3) In any system which grants formal rights to more than can effectively be given the opportunity of exercising them, there must be some device whereby those who are allowed the actual rights are singled out from those to whom it formally belongs. (368–69)

These and similar arguments have provided a ready explanation to legislative scholars for the differences between the House and the Senate on the issue of obstruction. The Senate, with its smaller numbers, can more easily tolerate unrestrained debate than can the larger House, an argument that can be found as early as Luce (1922, 289).

Similarly, institutional changes such as those we are considering have been linked to the press of business. The number of bills introduced in Congress grew rather dramatically from 1107 in the 24th Congress to 14,585 in the 54th, over a 13-fold increase when membership had only increased by a little less than half. Faced with this onslaught of legislation, the institution had no choice but to respond. Arguments linking institutional change with economic and social change and the resulting workload have been made in numerous places, including Hinds 1899; MacNeil 1963, 41; Polsby 1968; Cooper 1977, 152; and Keller 1977, 299–307.[8]

I therefore incorporated two new variables into the model in column 1: the number of representatives in the House and the number of bills introduced in Congress. This may seem an exceptionally crass way to think about the effect of size and workload in a legislature, but I am not aware of any discussions in the literature that would suggest a way to complicate the picture.

Note that with the controls for membership size and workload, the majority party proportion variable achieves statistical significance. The findings regarding the other measures are even more interesting. The evidence supports the claim that the precedents in the House with respect to dilatory tactics increased as the size of the membership increased. But it does not appear that this is simply a workload effect. As the negative coefficient on bills introduced shows, the House reacted to a great press of business by enacting *fewer* precedents, not more.

This result bears some additional reflection. Numerous explanations of the changes in the rules of the House have claimed that the needs of a growing economy led to legislative demands, that the press of those demands necessitated changes in the rules, and that those changes were forthcoming. This society-centered view, however, receives no support here: if it were true, we would expect to see antidilatory precedents precisely at the times when the press of business was greatest. Of course, it may be possible to refine the workload explanation in some way, but the results here should reinforce the strength of partisan factors in explaining procedural change.

What then explains the impact of membership size? The answer is quite clear from an obstruction perspective. The more individuals in the legislature, as Bertrand de Jouvenal recognized, the more time that could be taken up in discussing, or more appropriately for our context, delaying the consideration of a piece of legislation. In particular, if membership increases while majorities stay razor thin, then there will be a larger body of potential obstructionists in the legislature. The response of antidilatory precedents therefore becomes more understandable.

The final three columns of table 6.3 are my attempt to determine whether a number of political variables could possibly add to the workload model. Column 3 considers the possibility that procedural change will occur as one moves further away from a realigning election. While the insights from the workload model of column 2 remain unchanged, "years from previous realignment" is insignificant. Furthermore, the sign is negative, indicating that as one moves away from the realignment, precedents become if anything rarer, not more common. This suggests that the precedents considered here were not a response to declining cohesion caused by the ebbing of realignment forces.

This result could have been anticipated, given the literature. In his study of critical American elections, Walter Dean Burnham (1970) notes the ambiguous relationship between realignment and procedural change in the House. While analysis of trends regarding seniority show sharp breaks during the critical election of 1896, "the data leave no doubt that the New Deal realignment, however massive at the grass roots and however significant in reorganizing the scope and focus of national policy, left the behavioral routines of the House almost completely untouched, at least as far as seniority was concerned" (104). That major procedural changes did not accompany the 1932 election in the House is also supported by Jones 1970. Even confining our attention to the partisan era, the relationship between procedural change and realignment is far from clear. We can see rules changes during a critical election (1860), a few years previous (1890), fifteen years previous (1880), and nine years after (1837, after the 1828 election).

Column 4 reflects my naive attempt to capture the role of charisma in a regression equation. As conjectured in chapter 5, there would seem to be ample historical reason for thinking that the role of Speaker of the House Thomas Brackett Reed was pivotal. While there is I think no denying his importance to the process, the statistical results offered here do not support the conjecture that the Reed years were unusual in terms of antidilatory precedents. In fact, the negative sign indicates fewer precedents under Reed than at other times.

Chapter 5 also offered some suggestions regarding the possibility that Democrats, the less activist party during this period, would find less need (or less support) for antidilatory precedents than Republicans. I have included a dummy variable to capture those years when Democrats held the majority. The sign on this variable is negative, consistent with the argument made in chapter 5, but it is not statistically significant. This suggests that there may be a great deal of reason for thinking that when it comes to being in the majority, Republicans and Democrats of the partisan era acted fairly similarly.

Of course, the result reported in columns 4 and 5 should raise some eyebrows. Could Reed have secretly been a pro-obstructionist? Could the Democrats have pushed for limitations in minority rights just as hard as the Republicans? These speculations seem ludicrous in terms of the legislative history. How then can we explain the results?

Two factors seem crucial to me. First, a number of the changes in the Reed years were written into standing rules rather than into precedents. It should therefore not be surprising that there were fewer precedents under Reed. This does not, however, mean that Reed was necessarily supportive of minority rights. This point I hope reinforces the argument that considerations of minority rights need to take into account all the strategic possibilities.

A second factor is more seductive, but also more speculative. We have little idea of the process Hinds used in compiling his *Precedents*. On its multivolume face, it seems exhaustive enough, but when compared to whole library aisles of *House Journals* and *Congressional Records,* it is clear that not everything that happened in Congress will fit into Hinds's work. Even if we agree that Hinds was thoroughly diligent in reading through the records of debates for clues to the precedents, that still puts him at the mercy of what was, especially in the earlier years of the Republic (as seen in the discussion on the 1837 rules change in chapter 4), a selective transcription of the events.[9]

Given our lack of knowledge, could it be possible that Asher Hinds, Thomas Brackett Reed's parliamentary assistant, might have included a few more Democratic precedents, just so that quick rejoinders to minority Democrats from their own precedents would be available? This would certainly explain the lack of significant party differences on obstruction, as well as the weak showing of the Reed variable. But a more important issue is at stake here. Raising these sorts of objections asks us to confront the possibility that the *Precedents* are themselves a political document. In conferring status on some decisions but not others, they alter our interpretation of history as much as they end up influencing the way the game is played. And I think that this tendency is quite unavoidable. If a legislature on five hundred occasions has allowed the use of the disappearing quorum, and on one occasion eliminates the use, what determines which is the true precedent? Decisions have to be made, and those decisions will reflect the political categories of their time. Rather than sinking us into a morass of relativism, however, I think this insight can give us a better comparative handle on the question. How majoritarian, for example, would we categorize a given nation's collection of precedents? How much do they respect the rights of the minority? Do the legislative incidents noted constitute a random sample of decisions, and if not, what is the selection process at work? This are fascinating, if difficult questions.

I raise these points not to question the labors of Asher Hinds, especially on such slim evidence as I have presented here. Part of what makes a set of precedents a set of precedents is a conventional understanding that they constitute the reference to which one defers, and Hinds has certainly been that for the U.S. House. But Hinds, like anyone involved in a scholarly endeavor, is liable to the missed opportunities, the unintentional gaps, the hidden biases that elude our most ruthless attempts at weeding.

But efficiency, realignment, and the other variables are only one piece of our story. Equally (if not more) significant is the possibility that the dismantling of minority rights is linked to the erosion of reciprocity. The idea that reciprocity could fence in adventurous majorities was well-known to politicians during the partisan era. One Democrat in the 37th Congress, for example, expressed it strongly (though not gender-neutrally): "Men should remember how mutable is party ascendancy, and that the bitter cup which they mix for other lips, the next may be tendered to their own" (quoted in Baker 1983, 169). Bryce (1890), no fan of majoritarianism ("A majority is the least scrupulous thing imaginable," 392), argues that the decision of the House of Commons to safeguard closure by resting authority with a nonpartisan Speaker took place because ministers were able to recognize "that they might before long become an opposition, and be silenced by the application of the very 'gag,' as its enemies called it, which they had just invented" (389).

Table 6.4 includes all of the ways that I have been able to come up with for measuring reciprocity effects. Admittedly, this is a difficult feat, and having a perfect idea of how likely members were to believe in reciprocity will be impossible. Nonetheless some inferences can be made, which I think will in total reduce the plausibility of the reciprocity account.

We can begin with an interesting technical feature of the nineteenth-century legislative calendar. As noted in the discussion of the 47th Congress above, the House in the partisan era sat in both a long and a short session, with the short session taking place after the elections. Consequently, returning members knew with moral certainty whether they would be in the majority or the minority in the next Congress. To determine whether this had any effect, I created a dummy variable that took the value "1" when the majority party knew that it would be in the minority in the next Congress (and thus was "doomed") and "0" when the majority party knew that it would retain its majority status. If the presence of a short session has a systematic influence, we should pick it up.

As can be seen from column 1, the inclusion of the Doomed Majority variable does indeed make a difference. Unfortunately, the influence of majority party proportion is now effectively eliminated (the coefficient, while positive, is not statistically significant). The other variables are a bit attenuated, but with the exception of the number of bills introduced still preserve their sign and statistical significance.

Most interesting, however, is the estimate on the Doomed Majority variable. Contrary to the expectations suggested above, it appears that majorities who perceive that they will soon be in the minority do not, as suggested in chapters 1 and 2, refrain from engaging in antidilatory precedent setting: on the contrary, they increase it. Furthermore, the result is statistically significant. What this suggests is that majorities, recognizing that they will soon be in the minority, take advantage of their fading moments to craft restrictive precedents that will have the effect of greasing the skids on majority legislation before the clock strikes them out.

TABLE 6.4. Reciprocity and Antidilatory Precedents, 1835–95

Independent Variables	(1)	(2)[a]	(3)[a]	(4)[a]	(5)
Constant	-5.715##	-6.032##	-4.611#	-3.427##	-1.151
	(2.285)	(3.222)	(2.825)	(1.885)	(1.684)
Majority proportion (Martis)	0.008	-0.024	-0.043##	-0.040##	-0.004
	(0.033)	(0.025)	(0.017)	(0.021)	(0.030)
Johnson presidency	2.703###	2.705###	3.492###	3.224###	1.864##
	(0.609)	(0.729)	(0.840)	(0.709)	(0.976)
51st Congress and after	1.637##	1.866###	2.075###	1.997###	1.733###
	(0.659)	(0.676)	(0.632)	(0.646)	(0.680)
Number of representatives	0.015###	0.019###	0.022###	0.020###	0.014###
	(0.005)	(0.005)	(0.007)	(0.005)	(0.005)
Bills introduced	-0.0000303	-0.0000542##	-0.0000858###	-0.0000747#	-0.0000632##
	(0.0000349)	(0.0000276)	(0.0000347)	(0.0000335)	(0.0000272)
Doomed Majority	0.891##				
	(0.440)				
Swing ratio (Brady–Grofman)		0.473#			
		(0.342)			
Competitive seats (Brady–Grofman)			0.0234		
			(0.030)		
Majority bias (Brady–Grofman)				1.494	
				(2.452)	
Turnover (Fiorina–Rohde–Wissel)					-0.056##
					(0.029)
No. of observations	31	23	23	23	31
Log-likelihood	-1.543	6.450	6.049	5.994	2.317

[a]Results for 32nd–54th Congresses

\# significant at the 10 percent level, one-tailed test

\#\# significant at the 5 percent level, one-tailed test

\#\#\# significant at the 1 percent level, one-tailed test

Those seeking further evidence regarding this effect would do well to concentrate on the 1875 Civil Rights Act, considered in the 43rd Congress. James G. Blaine, who presided over the consideration of this act, has gone down in history as the Speaker most sympathetic to minority rights. Peters notes that Blaine "won the esteem of Republicans and Democrats alike by his commitment to honor the rights of the minority as they were then understood. He accepted the legitimacy of the tactics of obstruction and believed that it was the obligation of the majority party to unify for action or to wait the minority out" (1990, 57). Fuller (1909, 188) also claims that Blaine refused to enact antimajoritarian rules changes that would bind the minority Democrats: "He declared that the responsibility of the majority to the nation was a sufficient safeguard to its interests" (188). As if this was not enough, he also stood fast against those who pressed for the elimination of the disappearing quorum.

So far, this is a rather inspiring example of nonpartisanship. But Hinds reports in V.§5708 that Blaine on January 27, 1875, ruled that dilatory motions on proposals to change the rules were out of order. This was not Blaine's first such ruling: in his statement he notes "the Chair has repeatedly ruled that pending a proposition to change the rules dilatory motions could not be entertained, and for this reason he has several times ruled that the right of each House to determine what shall be its rules is an organic right expressly given by the Constitution of the United States" (quoted in V.§5708). The following Monday, which "under the rules then existing was the time for introducing bills" (Hinds 1899, V.§6775), a resolution was introduced that, in addition to suspending the rules in order to allow the Committee on Rules to report, would also ban dilatory motions on the consideration of that report. Samuel J. Randall (Democrat and future Speaker) objected to the introduction, but was overruled, and later that same day (by a vote of 181 to 90) the rules were suspended and the Civil Rights Act passed. This action took place in the 43rd Congress, the second (short) session, and Republicans knew with certainty that they would in a few short months be in the minority when the next Congress was organized.[10]

While the Doomed Majority variable is helpful, it relies quite heavily on second session calculations. While assuming that parties have a good idea of the probability of maintaining their majority may be plausible, it is a rather weighty assumption to invoke without some empirical support. Additional evidence would therefore be useful in evaluating the extent to which the results in column 1 are stable. Consequently, in columns 2 through 4 I have looked at three measures of party competitiveness calculated by David Brady and Bernard Grofman (1991). The first of these measures, the swing ratio, captures how sensitive the number of seats held by a party is to changes in the national vote. If the swing ratio is high, then very small changes in the national vote can have a large impact on the party contingent in the House.

What does this mean for reciprocity? A high swing ratio means that majorities would be less robust: small changes in votes lead to large changes in seats held. Consequently, we would expect to see fewer antidilatory precedents when the swing ratio is high. This argument receives support from Alesina's model of party competition discussed in chapter 1, which suggests that high levels of party competition lead to interparty cooperation.

Column 2 presents the empirical results. Note that since Brady and Grofman present data from 1850 on, the set of cases used in the estimates had to be reduced. Nonetheless, we can still find some important effects. While majority proportion is still not significant, it at least has the correct sign. The remaining variables are all quite stable, although we now have a significant negative coefficient on the number of bills introduced—quite a puzzle for workload explanations. The swing ratio, it turns out, has a statistically significant effect, but it is the *opposite* of that predicted by the reciprocity account. The higher the swing ratio, other things equal, the greater the number of antidilatory precedents. This is consistent with the arguments made regarding the Doomed Majority variable and suggests that ephemeral majorities are, contrary to the reciprocity account, not more likely to have a respect for minority rights.

Column 3 includes a variable measuring the proportion of seats that were competitive, defined as seats won by a margin of five percent or less. This is, I think, a better measure of *personal political insecurity* than the swing ratio. Given the reciprocity argument (especially as formulated in the game-theory literature on repeated games), we would expect electorally insecure members of the House to be myopic and therefore to be less dissuaded by the threat of future retaliation. After all, there is a good chance that they will not be around to be punished. If this argument is correct, then we should see a positive relationship between turnover and the proportion of competitive seats.

With competitive seats thrown into the equation, the statistical significance of the majority proportion variable is restored. We see a bit of an increase in the effect of the post-1889 years. More surprisingly, the coefficient estimate on the number of bills has gone down, indicating that once we control for variations in the number of competitive seats, a larger number of bills introduced leads to even fewer antidilatory precedents than we had previously estimated. The effect of the proportion of competitive seats is positive, providing some evidence consistent with the reciprocity account, although the coefficient is not significant.

The final measure from Brady and Grofman concerns bias. This term measures the difference between the proportion of the seats going to the two parties given that they each obtain exactly half of the national vote. If bias is positive, this indicates that the Democrats would gain a greater share of the seats with 50 percent of the vote, while if the bias is negative, it indicates that the Republicans would gain the greater share of the seats. A majority should, I conjecture, feel relatively more safe if they came to power due to an election in which the prevailing bias tilted in their favor. And if the majority feels safer, according to the reciprocity account, it will enact more antidilatory precedents.

To determine, therefore, whether bias had this effect, I kept the magnitude of the bias effect calculated by Brady and Grofman, but set the sign as positive if the prevailing bias in the electoral system worked in the majority's favor, and negative if the prevailing bias worked against the majority. The results are presented in column 4. They are exceptionally similar to the estimates of column 3. The new majority bias variable is positive, again consistent with the reciprocity argument, but again not statistically significant.

The final measure that seemed to capture reciprocity considerations involves turnover: the proportion of new members. The argument here would be that a high degree of turnover reflects a rapidly changing membership and therefore a more difficult time for reciprocity. If this account is correct, we should see a positive relationship between turnover and antidilatory precedents (since this would represent a breakdown of interparty reciprocity). Column 5 reestimates the model but including the Fiorina, Rohde, and Wissel measure of turnover, a measure that corrects for the admission of new states. Unfortunately, the addition of this variable eliminates the statistical significance of the majority proportion variable (although the sign remains negative). Turnover, however, has a negative coefficient, indicating that high times of membership change led to fewer, not more, antidilatory precedents.

Summing up, the results presented in table 6.4 show that the support for the reciprocity hypothesis is exceptionally thin. Considerations of reciprocity simply do not seem to lie behind the calculations made by majority members as to whether it is a prudent time to limit obstruction. And outside of the number of representatives effect (which is consistent with obstruction), workload–efficiency arguments do not seem to be working either. And while the results regarding the proportion of seats held by the majority party is not as supportive as the estimates presented in table 6.3, nonetheless, in all the estimations where majority proportion is found to have a significant effect, the coefficients show a surprising uniformity, supporting the notion that party size is an important element in accounting for the pattern of procedural change (at least with respect to obstruction) in the House of Representatives during the partisan era.

The One That Got Away

One significant rules change has not surfaced in either our discussion of small majorities or our discussion of precedents. This is the adoption of the hour rule in 1841, which limited individuals in the Committee of the Whole from consuming more than an hour, either in general debate or in amendment. The adoption of the hour rule marks one of the most significant ways in which the procedures of the House differ from those of the Senate.

Unfortunately for the theory, however, the majority party was hardly tiny. Three of our sources–the Congressional Quarterly, Galloway, and the Speakership votes–show a surprising unanimity in placing the majority position of the Whigs at 55 percent, and our most reliable source, Martis, places the number even higher. How can this be explained?

The 27th Congress was the first Congress in which the Whigs came to power, controlling not only the House, but also the Senate and the presidency (although the Tyler presidency certainly caused some detours in what should have been a smooth Whig parade). But while 54 percent may have been more than 51 percent, it was still less than the two-thirds vote that the majority would need to take a bill from the Committee of the Whole under suspension of the rules. And if a bill could not be taken out of the Committee of the Whole, it would stay there, because at the time members of the House were allowed to speak as long as they wanted.

Being talked to death seemed the fate of the bill to appropriate the proceeds of sales from public lands. Consideration of the bill in Committee of the Whole began on June 22, 1841, and continued until July 6, and apparently would have gone on for much longer thanks to the Democratic party's delaying tactics. In order to guarantee that Whig legislation would go through the House, therefore, two important changes had to be (and were) adopted.

First, the Committee on Rules was for the first time given the right to report at all times. This would bypass any delays stemming from the cumbersome procedures for bill introduction and referral then in place (Cooper and Young 1989). The ability to report at any time has given the Rules Committee a clear edge over obstructionism. The final vote on this resolution was 119–103, hardly a wide margin.

Second, using the new power to report, the Committee on Rules introduced a resolution that would allow suspension of the rules and closing of debate by a majority vote. To add injury to insult, the chair, John White of Kentucky, ruled that to adopt the report would itself only require a majority vote. The reaction of one observer to the session at the time, quoted by Hinds, was that he believed "chaos were come again" (Hinds 1899, V.§5221). There was an objection made, but White's decision was sustained—by majority vote. The whole operatic scene must have been beautifully enhanced by the thunderstorm raging outside as the majority approved the rules resolution. After this fine example of steamrolling, the public land bill was a done deal. The hour rule was adopted that very night.

Hinds's postscript on this rule is remarkable given the events just related.

After recounting the gory details and noting that it was a time of "high party excitement," he then states

> The method of closing debate in Committee of the Whole by resolution adopted by a majority in the House was continued at the next session of Congress, since business could not be transacted without it. (Hinds 1899, V.§5221)

As if this was all there was to it!

Conclusion

In this chapter, I have carried out two operations. First, I determined whether, during times when the majority party was small, steps were taken to limit minority obstruction. The answer appears to be yes, except in those cases in which it is reasonable to conclude that the party caucus condition is not met. The second operation was determining whether a full survey of parliamentary rulings would contradict the theory. In general, the majority party proportion has a strong and expected effect: large majorities tend to enact fewer limitations on minority rights than smaller majorities.

But most importantly for this work, it appears that neither the workload notion of procedural change (that rights to obstruct were eliminated due to the crush of business) nor the reciprocity claim (that majorities fearful of being the minority in the future would protect minority rights) works well in accounting for the pattern of antidilatory precedents. A larger press of business (measured by number of bills introduced, the usual measure of workload) in fact *decreases* the likelihood of an antiobstructive precedent, a finding that is strong and holds consistently through numerous specifications. This turns the conventional wisdom on its head. Similarly, "doomed" majorities, contrary to the reciprocity account of minority rights, seem *more* likely, not less likely, to restrict minority rights to obstruct than continuing majorities.

These are surprising findings, and they reinforce the centrality of partisan calculations to the process of procedural change on minority rights to obstruct. Unless the partisan element of procedural change is confronted, we are liable to get a very incomplete picture of the process of legislative change. Even more bothersome, however, without more attempts at empirical assessment, we can easily convince ourselves that the act of procedural change is a rather placid one, in which individuals calculate the likelihood of being in a future minority or sensibly sit down to work through the common program of legislation. Neither, it appears, is correct.

PART 3

Evidence from Other Institutions

But in the case of M. de Norpois there was above all the fact that, in the course of a long career in diplomacy, he had become imbued with that negative, methodical, conservative spirit, a "governmental mind," which is common to all governments and, under every government, particularly inspires its foreign service. He had imbibed, during that career, an aversion, a dread, a contempt for the methods of procedure, more or less revolutionary and at the very least improper, which are those of an Opposition.

—Marcel Proust, *Remembrance of Things Past*

CHAPTER 7

The U.S. Senate

Case studies lead a rather uncomfortable existence in political science. For the most part, they are often treated as poorer cousins, country bumpkins who "haven't seen the world." When they tell us their little stories about life back home, we nod appropriately and look for exits. Some, of course, through the sheer force of erudition, gain notice, no doubt with the same attending gaze of uncertain awe the Parisian aristocracy must have given to Benjamin Franklin in his beaver hat. "Yes, yes, a genius, but . . . "

I do not own a beaver hat, and I have certainly failed to live up to the standards set by the giants of the case study. But having returned from the dreary underworld of the unimpressive case study, I can safely report that it is not quite as bad as it is sometimes made out to be. While no one in their right mind would doubt the value of comparative analysis, the results of such analyses must be taken with the appropriate note of inferential prudence. The mere fact that a theory fails to extend to all four corners of the earth doesn't mean that it is not the correct explanation for *one* of the four corners of the earth. This seems to me the scholarly equivalent of believing that because not everyone likes grits, it must therefore follow that no one could like them.

The fear that case study arouses stems primarily from a concern that one has somehow misanalyzed even the small world one is interested in. The bumpkin assures us that the addition of eggshells produced his fine grapes; we wince knowing the quality of the grapes had nothing to do with eggshells and everything with weather. We turn to comparative analysis, then, as a way to check to see whether variables that seem important locally really are as important as we might believe. If we find that local conditions do not seem to be particularly helpful in explaining other cases, then we drop the theory.

But the mere fact that a theory doesn't travel well does not mean that it fails to have admirable domestic properties. And those can be of exceptional interest. To see this, consider the following thought experiment. Suppose that by some fluke every legislature in the world was blown up except for those in which my theory proved correct. I would then have (by default) a theory that "traveled" exceptionally well, but nothing has really changed. My point here is that we should view comparative exercises not as disposing of theories, but only disposing of (or at least refining) a particular theory's claim to universal validity. Of course, since no one but economists with too little sleep or physicists with too much ego (or is it the other way around?) have ever claimed universal validity, this isn't much to give up.

But certainly, the response goes, we would want to insist that a theory be capable of explaining as many of the cases as there are out there. The problem here is that the cases aren't "out there": the set of cases to which a theory applies is determined by the theory itself (you can't use arms race theory to determine if you really did see an up quark). It isn't unreasonable, therefore, when area studies experts tell us that "political culture" is important in explaining why a theory doesn't work in their country. This could simply be a shorthand way of saying that the assumptions of the theory simply don't seem realistic.

In fact, we might gain more knowledge about politics and an appreciation for the idiosyncratic if we looked more carefully at places where the theories come apart. An argument that the personality of Margaret Thatcher was particularly important in explaining political proceedings in the House of Commons attains greater weight when projected against a backdrop that suggests that those changes would not have taken place. Thus theories that do not travel well can still be useful in formulating counterfactuals against which we can test various local accounts. If done well, this could increase our respect for the idiosyncratic in politics, not diminish it.

Unfortunately, many social science theories will be of limited help in enhancing our appreciation for local irregularities. If each of us insists our narrow corner of the world is totally unique, then idiosyncrasy becomes a constant, hardly of interest. The situation is not much improved for theories that aspire to great generality. One of the perverse results of the adoption of falsificationism is that it has inspired a universal dread of being falsified. As a result, theories are propounded containing various rubrics such as "pivotal entrepreneurs" or "social prerequisites" enabling all possible local behavior can be quickly filed away while still maintaining the illusion of refutability. Filing systems haven't as yet filled me with the awe of the particular. What is therefore required are disposable theories, theories that work well enough to have some claims to generality but that do not submerge all behavior in their titanic wake.

The theory presented in this book functions quite admirably for this purpose. Whatever the dangers of the "monocausal" view, we get more appreciation for the richly varied nature of procedural change if we project a theory easily disposed of against a large variety of other institutional settings. At the very least, this is the quickest method for generating anomalies and thus for focusing greater attention on explaining the puzzling features of minority rights within legislatures.

In this chapter and the next, therefore, I will see how well the theory does in accounting for procedural changes with respect to minority obstruction in institutions beside the House. This of course raises the question: where else?

The House of Commons Survey of Foreign Legislatures

On the eve of World War I, when one might have thought they would have had better things to do, the House of Commons ordered the publication of a report from the Select Committee on Procedure. This Committee had been charged with improving the legislative procedure of the Commons. To aid in that effort, a survey was sent out to various foreign legislatures, with (harsh task this) follow-up visits to Paris, Berlin, Vienna, Brussels, Budapest, and the Hague. A memorandum of the results was submitted along with the report, as well as the responses from the various legislatures (12 nations, 13 legislatures in all). This is an invaluable document for understanding what writers at the century's turn meant when they feared for the future of parliamentary democracy.

I have gone through those responses to compile a list of references to appeared (at least to me) to involve changes in procedure relating to obstruction. The results are presented in table 7.1. A bit more systematically, table 7.2 presents a list of cloture rules by nation. To be sure, this source is not without its difficulties. The House of Commons is not on the list: unconcerned with the needs of future scholars, the Commons found it unnecessary to survey itself. Yet this same institution struggled famously with the question of minority rights to obstruct, struggles that in part inspired the survey. The response from France might also be troubling. Jeremy Bentham castigated the French in his *Political Tactics* for their urgency decrees, which he claimed "may well be remembered with dread: they were formed for the subjugation of the minority—for the purpose of stifling arguments which were dreaded" (quoted in May 1893, 323). Like Bentham's cadaverous remains at University Hospital, this francophobic argument too appears to have been trotted out over the years for public display: Josef Redlich in his history of British parliamentary procedure refers to an 1882 Commons debate in which Conservative Ashmead Bartlett labeled closure "a French invention and only suitable to Frenchmen, who had never known the meaning of real liberty as between man and man, and class and class" (Redlich 1908, I.171). On the other hand, Guizôt, a master observer of the French legislature, in testimony given to the House of Commons in (of all years) 1848, claimed that the majority in France had never abused its powers of clôture in the 34 years of the procedure's existence (Luce 1922, 282).

These observations will I hope show the amount of additional work that needs to go into the comparative and historical study of legislative politics. Recognizing these limitations, however, we can use the list to provide some

TABLE 7.1. Rules Changes Regarding Obstruction, by Nation, 1915

Nation	Year	Description
Austria	1897	During period of obstruction in November, the *Lex Falkenhayn* was used. Members were removed from the Assembly room by the police.
Austria	1902	Attempt made to prevent delay in passing the Budget by allotting speeches to various parties, with speaking order determined by lot. Since the speeches were not time-limited, this method proved ineffective.[a]
Austria	1908	Debate on second deliberation limited to 200 hours, divided among parties in proportion to seats with allocation left to party leaders. *Vote en bloc* used on various parts of the Budget to save time.[a]
Austria	1912	President empowered to reserve discussion of Urgency Motion to end of sitting. This due to the fact that such motions were used for the purposes of obstruction.
Germany	1902	Resolution passed in Reichstag that there would be a *vote en bloc* during the second and third discussions of the Tariff Law.[a]
Hungary	No date	The president can take a number of steps given against an individual who obstructs debates, up to and including expulsion.

Source: Select Committee on House of Commons (Procedure). 1915 (Appendix, various pages).

[a]The Memorandum notes these as "isolated efforts" made "to deal with measures which were exceptionally complicated or encountered exceptional resistance" (246).

TABLE 7.2. Cloture Rules, by Nation, as of 1915

Nation	Who can Initiate	Amount of Debate Allowed	Frequency of Application
Austria	Any member	Two speeches	On all important debates
Belgium	20 members	No limit	Practically disused
Denmark	President or 15 members		Rare
France	Any member[a]	One speech in opposition	Practically disused
Germany	30 members	None	Frequent
Holland	5 members	None	Rare
Italy	10 members	One speech on each side	Rare
United States	Any member[b]	None (unless if topic has not been previously discussed, in which case 40 minutes)	Frequent

Source: Select Committee on House of Commons (Procedure). 1915, 247.

[a]President must be sure that a substantial part of Chamber wishes cloture.

[b]As long as member in charge of bill does not claim to speak.

insights into valuable cases to study. Judging from the tables, it appears that of the 13 legislatures surveyed by the House of Commons, Austria, Germany, the United States, and (I would add) the House of Commons had by far the greatest experience with obstruction and the greatest degree of procedural change to limit obstruction.

Having already studied the U.S. House, a study of the Senate was in order. This is especially appropriate given that the Senate did not adopt a cloture rule until 1917. Explaining the pattern of procedural changes prior to that period therefore presents a quite tough case for the model. Analysis of the Senate case (both in the nineteenth as well as the twentieth centuries) will consume the remainder of this chapter. Regarding non-U.S. legislatures, I must admit to being constrained by language difficulties. The House of Commons was of course an easy selection, but my ignorance of German made a full study of Germany and Austria impossible.

Quite miraculously, however, I have been able to find a truly exceptional account of the Austrian parliament's struggles with obstruction from a rather singular English-speaking eyewitness—the American novelist Mark Twain. Twain was present in the gallery during the intense struggle culminating in the adoption of the *Lex Falkenhayn*. Thanks to this source, I will be able to provide some comments regarding the Austrian case, although the bulk of the analysis will have to be confined to the Commons. To make the presentation more manageable, I defer consideration of these cases to chapter 8.

The Senate and Obstruction

Patricia Hurley and Rick Wilson introduce their statistical analysis of party voting with the remark that they will engage in "an endeavor that is all too rare in our discipline: a replication for the Senate of research conducted in the House" (1989, 234). But if legislative politics means more than a study of House politics, then our theoretical accounts should be able to travel, at the very least, down the hall.

One might infer from the prominence of filibustering in the Senate that there would be a wealth of academic work on the topic. Surprisingly, however, obstruction in the Senate has remained a woefully understudied topic. The last full-length book treatment of the topic published, a work by Franklin Burdette, is now over half a century old. While one can find some discussion of the procedure in scattered papers and a single unpublished dissertation, for the most part the filibuster has eluded the intensive scrutiny of legislative scholars.[1]

But lack of prior work is only one reason why we might be leery of studying this case. The Senate is, after all, famous for its tradition of unrestrained debate. Individual senators are often asserted to be free to block up or delay proceedings. Thus in many ways we see in the Senate a continuation of the pattern of respect for minority obstruction that reigned in the House in the previous century.

Nonetheless, this respect for tradition has not prevented the Senate from attempting, at various times, to limit the room for unfettered debate and delay. Rather than be dazzled by the history the Senate likes to tell about itself, we need to more fully engage the historical record to determine exactly how majorities even in the Senate might have made attempts to diminish the rights of the minority to obstruct legislation.

The Senate in the Partisan Era

We begin by considering the partisan era. Even a tantalizing cursory look suggests that there might be more here than we imagine. In the only history of the filibuster published thus far, Franklin Burdette (1940) notes that "in the last two decades of the nineteenth century storms of obstruction had swept the chamber: and, while filibustering early in the twentieth century was hardly so spectacular as that in the years immediately preceding, the practice continued without parliamentary restraint" (79–80). Burdette's argument is confirmed by DeNardis (1989, 70f). And Rothman (1966) has argued that the Senate began this period with a great deal of room for individual action and ended with strict party control.

These claims acquire a bit more significance for this book when viewed against the pattern of majority party proportions in that era (table 7.3). This was an era of exceptionally tight Senate majorities, beginning on an ominous

TABLE 7.3. Party Composition
in the U.S. Senate, 1881–99

Congress	Year	Proportion of Seats (Martis)
47	1881	48.7
48	1883	50.0
49	1885	55.3
50	1887	51.3
51	1889	58.0
52	1891	53.4
53	1893	50.0
54	1895	48.9
55	1897	48.9
56	1899	58.9

note with the 47th Congress. Electoral returns showed that the Democrats would control 37 seats, while Republicans controlled 37 seats. Two independents remained, one of whom (David Davis of Illinois) had announced his intention to side with the Democrats. The lone holdout was George Mahone, a Virginia Readjustor. If the Republicans could convince Mahone to support their party, then the vote would stand at a tie and Chester Arthur (the Republican vice president) would cast the deciding vote. Mahone's price was high: the chairmanship of Agriculture, the right to appoint the Sergeant-at-Arms and the secretary of the Senate, exclusive control over federal patronage in Virginia, and Garfield's assistance in suppressing Republican competition for Readjustor votes in the next election. Nonetheless, the Republicans did receive their slim majority (Byrd 1988, 324).

This observation may be fascinating, but how much can we trust this anecdotal evidence? More systematic data, however, seemed unlikely to exist, and I believed, especially after my work on the House, that it would be an exceptionally difficult undertaking to compile a list of major Senate rules changes regarding minority obstruction. Even if I carried this Herculean task out, I could do nothing about the appearance of impropriety: having the individual responsible for the theory coding all the data tends to arouse suspicions.

Luckily, however, the Congressional Research Service, that invaluable institution, has already compiled a list of attempts to limit debate in the history of the Senate.[2] While this does not reflect the entire universe of obstructive tactics, it does provide an important first look at that most unique feature of the Senate—its toleration of debate. The raw data are presented in table 7.4.

Since the limitation of debate is a dichotomous variable, I estimated the statistical relationships using probit. Outside of that change, my main aim was to replicate the analysis undertaken for the House. The statistical estimates are set out in table 7.5.

In this case, the partisan theory is soundly supported. In all five equations, majority proportion has the correct sign and is statistically significant. Furthermore, a dummy variable for the Johnson years (as in the House analysis) and for the late Reconstruction (which was a clear outlier, as can be seen from table 7.4) are both significant. Outside of those systematic relationships, however, little else appears to be related to the timing of the Senate's attempts to limit debate. Neither workload (measured by the number of Senators and the number of bills introduced), years from realignment, nor the presence of a Democratic majority in the Senate performed very well. Most disappointing is the performance of the Doomed Majority variable.[3] Majorities about to be replaced do not to any significant degree perform any differently than other majorities in the Senate. This of course makes sense—since only a third of the Senate is up for reelection at any one time, two-thirds of the members can expect to stick around regardless of how the election turns out.[4]

**TABLE 7.4. Majority Proportion and Attempts
to Limit Debate in the U.S. Senate, 1835–95**

Congress	Year	Majority Proportion (Martis)	Attempt to limit debate according to CRS?
24	1835	50.0	No
25	1837	67.3	No
26	1839	57.7	No
27	**1841**	**55.8**	**Yes**
28	1843	55.8	No
29	**1845**	**58.6**	**Yes**
30	1847	63.3	No
31	**1849**	**56.6**	**Yes**
32	1851	58.1	No
33	1853	61.3	No
34	1855	62.9	No
35	1857	62.1	No
36	1859	55.9	No
37	1861	62.0	No
38	1863	63.5	No
39	1865	72.2	No
40	1867	83.8	No
41	**1869**	**83.8**	**Yes**
42	**1871**	**75.7**	**Yes**
43	**1873**	**63.5**	**Yes**
44	1875	60.5	No
45	1877	52.6	No
46	**1879**	**55.2**	**Yes**
47	**1881**	**48.7**	**Yes**
48	**1883**	**50.0**	**Yes**
49	**1885**	**55.3**	**Yes**
50	1887	51.3	No
51	**1889**	**58.0**	**Yes**
52	1891	53.4	No
53	**1893**	**50.0**	**Yes**
54	1895	48.9	No

Note: Boldface indicates sessions in which attempts were made to limit debate.

TABLE 7.5.   Probit Analysis of Attempts to Limit Debate, U.S. Senate, 1835–95

Independent Variables	(1)	(2)	(3)	(4)	(5)
Constant	5.537##	4.430	4.792#	5.407##	6.302##
	(2.735)	(4.447)	(3.335)	(2.822)	(3.153)
Majority proportion (Martis)	−0.106##	−0.078#	−0.096##	−0.090##	−0.117##
	(0.048)	(0.056)	(0.053)	(0.050)	(0.054)
Johnson presidency	−1.638##	−1.922##	−1.648##	−1.658##	−1.589##
	(0.818)	(0.846)	(0.824)	(0.844)	(0.832)
Late Reconstruction (41–43rd Cong.)	6.921###	6.298###	6.759###	6.840###	7.041###
	(1.319)	(1.554)	(1.372)	(1.360)	(1.397)
Number of Senators		−0.013			
		(0.044)			
Bills introduced		0.0000667			
		(0.0000968)			
Years from previous realignment			0.022		
			(0.061)		
Democratic majority				−0.278	
				(0.647)	
Doomed Majority					−0.552
					(0.622)
No. of observations	31	31	31	31	31
Log-likelihood	−14.936	−14.5055	−14.871	−14.834	−14.534
Percent correctly predicted	70.968	77.419	67.742	70.968	67.742

#significant at the 10 percent level, one-tailed test
##significant at the 5 percent level, one-tailed test
###significant at the 1 percent level, one-tailed test

The replication of the House results for the partisan-era Senate has, therefore, shown an even stronger level of support for the partisan theory. Small majorities in the Senate as well as the House attempt to limit the rights of members of the minority to obstruct legislation. Furthermore, neither workload, reciprocity considerations, nor other political variables seem to be capable of explaining the data. This presents the first evidence that the theory outlined in this book works outside the U.S. House.

Furthermore, the results presented here help highlight what is truly unique in the Senate case. Think how easy it would be to conjecture that the attempts to limit debate during the late Reconstruction Congresses were a sign of how changed the institution had become by the pressures of an unusual time, even to the point of attempting to limit the Senate's proud tradition of unlimited debate. But attempts to limit debate weren't all that unusual: they took place at other times too. However, Reconstruction is unusual in that the attempts to limit debate took place at a time when we would, ceteris paribus, not have expected such changes to have occurred. This enhances rather than diminishes our respect for the uniqueness of these Congresses.

Cloture in the Modern Senate

Although the Senate did have the use of the previous question in the early republic, Joseph Cooper (1962) has carefully and to my mind definitively shown that this procedure could not in any way be considered a mechanism for cloture. And while the partisan era may have seen attempts at limiting debate, these were only attempts. The most important limitations on obstructionism in the Senate took place after the partisan period, with the introduction of the cloture rule. In table 7.6, I have gathered together a brief list of the major changes made to the cloture rule in the Senate.

The most important change took place in 1917, in the middle of World War I.[5] After a German U-boat sank the now-forgotten U.S.S. *Housatonic*, Woodrow Wilson asked Congress for the authority to arm merchant ships. Congress's willingness to accede to the president's request was significantly accelerated by the release of the famous "Zimmerman Note," a communiqué from the German foreign minister suggesting that Mexico would receive large parts of American territory if it would agree to align with the Germans against

TABLE 7.6.   Major Changes in the Cloture Rule, U.S. Senate, 1917–85

Congress	Year	Action Taken	Majority Proportion[a]
65	1917	Two-thirds of Senators present and voting for cloture on pending measure	56.25
81	1949	Increased requirement to two-thirds of all Senators, but extended cloture to cover "motions and other matters pending"	56.25
86	1959	Reduced requirement to two-thirds of Senators present and voting and extended cloture to apply to debate on any matter, including rule changes	65.0
94	1975	60 percent vote necessary to secure cloture on any measure but a rules change	60.0
	1976	Altered cloture to allow for consideration of amendments after cloture if submitted to Clerk	
96	1979	Limit postcloture filibuster	58.0

[a]excludes vacancies

the United States. The vote on the Armed Ship bill took place in the House on the very day that the memorandum was released and passed in a vote of 403–13. This was, however, March 2, and the 64th Congress would come to a close on March 3. Given the short amount of time, those advocating neutrality in the Senate—in particular Robert M. La Follette Sr. and George Norris—adopted the most efficacious course a minority faced with a cohesive majority in the twilight moments of the legislative session could select, which was to filibuster.

The filibuster was successful, at least in guaranteeing that the 63rd Congress ended without the passage of the Armed Ship Act. This was, however, hardly the close of the play. Woodrow Wilson, in his inimitably quotable way, referred to those who had filibustered as "a little group of willful men" who had rendered the United States "helpless and contemptible." Public sentiment was thoroughly inflamed against the obstructionists—Robert Byrd in his history of this period notes that one town in Arkansas sent their filibustering senator, William Kirby, thirty pieces of silver, noting that "if Judas Iscariot earned his so have you" (Byrd 1988, 417).

What options did Wilson have in this situation? As we have seen in discussing the 1837 rules changes in the House, one of the institutional prerogatives attached to being president is the ability to call the Congress into special session, and while March 3 was the final day of the 64th Congress, Wilson convened the Senate into special session a mere two days later in order to amend the rules. This session resulted in the "two-thirds" rule, meaning that upon the assent of two-thirds of the Senators present and voting, each Senator would be limited to only one hour of debate, and amendments would not be allowed except by unanimous consent. The rule also included a ban on the offering of any "dilatory motion, or dilatory amendment, or amendment not germane" after the invocation of cloture. The new cloture rule thus dealt not only with speaking limits but also with the sort of dilatory motions addressed by Thomas Brackett Reed in the House. This important rule was rather quickly adopted on a vote of 76 to 3.

Those with calculators will quickly realize that 76 divided by 79 is a much higher number than the 50 percent majorities that we have been observing so far. Even the overall majority proportion—a bit over 56 percent—is still somewhat high given the other cases we have considered. How then can we account for the passage of cloture?

A usual explanation is to invoke the exigencies of war. In ordinary times, the Senate would never contemplate changes in the tradition of free debate. But war by itself won't work: none of the many wars from 1789 on—the War of 1812, the Mexican–American War, the Civil War, the Spanish–American war, not to mention the armed efforts to displace Native Americans—resulted in a cloture rule. We could up the ante and assert that it takes a world war to force the Senate to change the rules regarding debate. Even that ploy falls short, however: there was no further limitation adopted on speaking during World War II.

What then changed that made cloture possible? A bit of history will help us out here. Rather than concentrating on 1917, we can follow Robert Luce in tracing the roots of the change a bit earlier, to what he calls "the crowning filibuster" over the Ship Purchase Bill in 1915. The obstructive pyrotechnics displayed over the bill required superhuman effort and resulted in the longest continuous session that the Senate had ever experienced. The filibuster succeeded in killing the bill, and Luce remarks,

> Senator Lodge was quoted afterward as attributing success partly to the fact that the Senate was *almost equally divided* at the start, and partly to the fact that there was no general support for the bill throughout the country, but on the other hand a strong opposition developed. This filibuster brought near an end the long, slow crystallizing of sentiment against unlimited debate in the Senate. Public opinion, as far as it was voiced in the press, seemed to be almost solidly against filibusters. (Luce 1922, 294; emphasis added)

The attempt to filibuster on a relatively similar bill two years later does suggest a possible antecedent for the 1917 effort. It would, however, be a little too convenient for my story to argue that 1917 was simply a delayed reaction to 1915. Clearly, public opinion had an impact, but why would public opinion seem to crystallize in 1915 and reach fruition in 1917?

The answer is clear: direct election of Senators. Prior to May 1913, when William Jennings Bryan as Secretary of State signed the 17th Amendment, Senators were elected by state legislatures. This provided an intermediate step between public opinion and the electoral consequences resulting from the actions of individual Senators. The first election of Senators under the new electoral procedure occurred in November 1914. The Ship Purchase Bill filibuster occurred in February 1915. Not surprisingly, this is the period when it appears that "public opinion suddenly crystallized."

In retrospect, this observation may seem easy, but I have been unable to find the link in any of the literature I have read on the filibuster. Luce (1922, 294–95), cited above, discusses the adoption of cloture, but makes no mention of direct election. Burdette (1940, 127) finds the story of the adoption of cloture uneventful, as does Byrd (1988, 417). Neither links cloture to direct election. DeNardis (1989, 86) does note that the initial use of cloture occurred in 1919, a year that he also notes "coincidentally was the first year that all Senators were products of direct election in their states." Perhaps the "coincidentally" is ironic here—he does not link direct election back to the 1915 filibuster, however.[6]

Direct election need not be the only factor at play. The passage of this rule becomes a bit easier to understand when it is realized that the rule wasn't expected to be all that successful. Luce again writes that the 1917 cloture rule "could hardly be called a drastic rule. Very rarely does either party control two thirds of the votes of the Senate, and on any bitterly contested matter of partisan nature it was believed there would be no stifling of speech under such a rule" (Luce 1922, 295). Cloture therefore represented the minimum necessary to get constituents off the Senators' backs without having catastrophic changes in the way the Senate did business. This approach seemed to work, as cloture remained an unused tool in the Senate (despite ample opportunities) until the imbroglio over the Treaty of Versailles.

The cloture rule would not be altered again until 1949, when the majority once more held 56 percent of the seats. The impact of this change as far as minority rights, however, was not clear. On the one hand, the revision did close loopholes in the old cloture rule. For example, the rules of the Senate made a motion to amend or correct the *Journal* what is known as a "privileged question," meaning that it took precedent over all other business. Thus while cloture might stop debate on a bill, it could not apply to debates over amendments of the *Journal*. This provided an opening for obstruction, an opening fully utilized by opponents of the Anti-Lynching Bill in 1922. But opposition to the strengthening of the rule led to the adoption of a compromise package in which two-thirds of all Senators would now be required to vote for cloture, as opposed to the old rule of two-thirds of those present and voting. Given low attendance, cloture becomes incredibly difficult to adopt.

The cloture rule stayed unchanged for another 10 years, when in 1959 the compromise version was undone and cloture was returned to the 1919 requirement of two-thirds present and voting. This occurred, as one would expect given the theory presented in this work, when the majority was 65.0 percent: exceptionally close to a minimal winning coalition under cloture of 66 percent. The adoption of this rule came at the end of four Congresses in which the size of the majority party never got above 51 percent, a stunning series of incredibly small majorities. Yet having achieved a larger majority, it was clear that even if all the members of the majority showed up, cloture would be impossible to obtain: they would fall short by one vote. Consequently, a rules change from two-thirds of senators to two-thirds present and voting gives the majority a chance to limit debate. Given the theory, the adoption of the cloture vote in this Congress makes sense.

The next major change, and the most significant since the 1917 adoption of cloture, was the reduction of the voting requirement from two-thirds to three-fifths in 1975. And as the theory would predict, this occurred at precisely the time when the majority had 60 percent of the seats: a bare majority under a three-fifths rule.

While further changes were forthcoming, they were essentially mopping-up exercises. A change in 1976 was adopted after a vote on cloture unintentionally cut off the ability of the majority to offer further amendments. By fixing this problem, however, the majority only created a new one: the post-cloture filibuster. Senators could propose literally hundreds of amendments knowing that, even if cloture was invoked, it would take weeks for the Senate to work through them all. This opportunity did not stick around for long, for in 1979 a rules change was adopted that eliminated the practice.

As a result, both of the truly significant changes in the cloture rule—the drop to two-thirds present and voting, and the reduction to sixty percent—occurred when the majority party was respectively roughly two-thirds and sixty percent. This is in keeping with the prediction of this model.

But anyone who isn't my relative will undoubtedly be inclined to question the lack of detail. Aren't we missing some fairly important procedural issues here? For example, the 1975 change did reduce cloture to three-fifths, but only on matters *not* dealing with a change in Senate rules. In those matters, the requirement stayed at two-thirds. And certainly the complex politics of the filibuster in the 1950s did not resemble the closely divided party lines assumed in the model: this was a period in which the Democratic majority in the Senate was split between conservatives and liberals.

Note, however, that in raising these questions, all we are doing is confirming the claims made in chapter 3: that it is not enough simply to pick out one independent and one dependent variable (here the proportion of seats held by the majority in the Senate and the alteration of cloture) and say that predictive success is all we care about, assumptions be damned.

There has to be more to the story, therefore, than I have been able to spin out here. Even if the size of the majority party turns out to be a significant variable in the explanation of changes in the cloture rule, unraveling the full story of cloture over the course of the twentieth century would require a great deal more research and space than I can muster. But we can assess a bit more easily the theory's validity when it comes to the use of the cloture motion itself, the topic of the next section.

Cloture Votes

In evaluating the theory, we are not simply limited to understanding the changes that have taken place in the cloture rule itself. If, as I have conjectured, steps to limit minority obstruction should occur when the majority is small, then the number of times cloture is voted on in a session should be related to the size of the majority. The effort here is worthwhile at least for novelty: these results constitute the first statistical analysis of cloture in the Senate.

Once again, data on cloture were obtained from the volume prepared by the Congressional Research Service. I have reproduced this information in table 7.7, along with the Martis measures of the majority proportion in the Senate. Since cloture votes, like precedents, fall under the heading of "count data," I estimated the statistical relationship using Poisson regression.

In terms of independent variables, there is, of course, the proportion of seats held by the majority party. But certainly majority party size is not the only variable related to cloture votes. One would expect that the various reforms of the cloture procedure might also have an effect on the number of cloture votes taken. To investigate the effect of each reform, I created three dummy variables. The first variable (1949 Rule) took a value of 1 for the 81st through the 85th Congresses, inclusive. This represents all the Congresses that operated under the 1949 version of the cloture rule. The second dummy variable (1959 Rule) took a value of 1 for all Congresses from the 86th to the 93rd (the reign of the 1959 version of the cloture rule). The final dummy variable (1975 Rule) took a value of 1 for all Congresses after and including the 94th. Unfortunately, the estimation process experienced convergence failure whenever I included the 1975 Rule dummy. Rather than force the impact of the 1975 reforms into the constant term, I opted to confine the data to the period running from 1919 through 1974. To determine whether there were any party effects, a dummy variable was included for those Congresses in which the Democrats controlled the Senate.

Before proceeding, I would like to address a possible difficulty that needs to be kept in mind. An anti-obstruction device, if thoroughly credible, would hardly be needed. Minorities would immediately recognize that any attempt at filibustering will result in the use of the procedure. Anticipating this reaction, the minority may decide to refrain from filibustering. This would of course mean that there would be no cloture vote to enter into the count, but this hardly constitutes evidence that the cloture rule was not effective.

Before we make too much of this, it may be useful to think about whether the logic outlined here would really work. Given that the minority has decided that a strategy of delay is optimal (that is, in a situation in which the minority *would* want to delay proceedings), I can see little reason why the minority would not wish to obtain at least a minimal stretch of delay by forcing the majority to go through the time-consuming paces of invoking cloture. Working out the complete logic here will require a much fuller model of strategic interaction than I have worked out, but my intuition is that the objection raised here is not pivotal.

Table 7.8 presents the statistical estimates. Column 1, the simple model,

TABLE 7.7. Majority Party Proportion and Cloture Votes in the U.S. Senate, 1919–85

Congress	Year	Majority Proportion (Martis)	Cloture Votes
66	1919	51.0	2
67	1921	61.5	1
68	1923	55.2	0
69	1925	56.25	7
70	1927	50.0	0
71	1929	58.3	0
72	1931	50.0	1
73	1933	61.5	0
74	1935	71.9	0
75	1937	79.1	2
76	1939	71.9	0
77	1941	68.75	1
78	1943	59.4	1
79	1945	59.4	4
80	1947	53.1	0
81	1949	56.25	2
82	1951	51.0	0
83	1953	50.0	1
84	1955	49.0	0
85	1957	51.0	0
86	1959	65.0	1
87	1961	64.0	4
88	1963	66.0	3
89	1965	68.0	7
90	1967	64.0	6
91	1969	57.0	6
92	1971	54.0	20
93	1973	56.0	31
94	1975	60.0	27
95	1977	61.0	13
96	1979	58.0	21
97	1981	53.0	27
98	1983	54.0	19

TABLE 7.8.   Poisson Regression Results on Cloture Votes, U.S. Senate, 1919–74

Independent Variables	(1)	(2)	(3)	(4)	(5)
Constant	2.237	4.299*	5.035###	5.911***	6.444***
	(1.770)	(2.171)	(1.911)	(1.886)	(1.803)
Majority proportion	−0.0164	−0.0479#	−0.0885###	−0.0984***	−0.113***
(Martis)	(0.0263)	(0.0329)	(0.0364)	(0.0343)	(0.0343)
1949 Rule		−2.352***		−1.383##	−1.966**
		(0.842)		(0.802)	(0.906)
1959 Rule			2.610***	2.323***	1.711***
			(0.573)	(0.538)	(0.484)
Democratic majority					0.935
					(0.796)
Number of					
observations	28	28	28	28	28
Log-likelihood	28.059	43.510	90.975	94.234	95.905

#significant at the 10 percent level, one-tailed test
*significant at the 10 percent level, two-tailed test
**significant at the 5 percent level, two-tailed test
***significant at the 1 percent level, two-tailed test

shows the expected negative sign on majority proportion, although the coefficient is not significant. As can be seen from columns 2 through 4, however, controlling for the various procedural regimes in the Senate allows a significant party proportion effect to come through, and most importantly in the correct (negative) direction.

The results also shed some light on the impact of the various procedural changes. Looking across the table, it appears that the 1949 reform had a negative effect on cloture votes. That is, all other things being equal, there were fewer cloture votes in the 1949–58 era than one might otherwise have expected. One may wish to attribute this to the fact that cloture was much harder to obtain during a period in which the majority party never rose above 51 percent.[7] The equation, however, controls for the size of the majority party, suggesting that the effect is attributable to changes in the procedure.

The period from 1949 to 1958 has come to be known less for its small majorities than for the towering presence of Lyndon Johnson, leader of the Democratic Party in the Senate for much of this period. Much has been made of Johnson's legislative abilities and in particular his expertise as a practitioner of that occult art known as the Johnson Treatment:

> The Treatment could last ten minutes or four hours. . . . Its tone could be supplication, accusation, cajolery, exuberance, scorn, tears, complaint, the hint of threat. It was all of these together. It ran the gamut of human

emotions. Its velocity was breathtaking, and it was all in one direction. Interjections from the target were rare. Johnson anticipated them before they could be spoken. He moved in close, his face a scant millimeter from his target, his eyes widening and narrowing, his eyebrows rising and falling. From his pockets poured clippings, memos, statistics. Mimicry, humor, and the genius of analogy made The Treatment an almost hypnotic experience and rendered the target stunned and helpless. (Rowland Evans and Robert Novak, quoted in Byrd 1988, 617)

Johnson pressed these abilities into service when faced with the problem of avoiding a filibuster, in particular during Strom Thurmond's 24 hour, 18 minute record filibuster of the 1957 Civil Rights Act.

Robert Byrd has referred, too kindly, to Johnson as "the pivotal man in the civil rights struggle" (Byrd 1988, 615). He argues that

If he [Johnson] had joined with other southerners or had even chosen to remain neutral to protect his popularity in his home state, the coalition of Eisenhower Republicans and liberal Democrats who supported the civil rights legislation would have lacked both the numbers and the expertise to break the filibusters on the floor. (615)

Johnson's efforts here were not solely selfless. Richard Nixon (the clear Republican candidate for the 1960 presidential race) believed with others (among them, it appears, Martin Luther King Jr. and Ralph Abernathy—see Branch, 220) that the 1956 electoral results signaled that new African-American voters would be solidly Republican. Nixon consequently made overtures in that direction (among others, agreeing to a summit with King).[8]

Nixon's tactics here were not the result of an overheated imagination. The political calculation was set out by Roy Wilkins:

Senator Eastland's name is not on the ballot. We did not make him chairman of the Senate Judiciary Committee, where he has life-and-death power over civil rights bills. But up here we can have something to say about the party that made Eastland chairman of a Committee which can choke up. Up here we can strike a blow in defense of our brothers in the South, if necessary by swapping the known devil for the suspected witch. (Quoted in Lawson 1976, 161)

But Nixon was not the only potential presidential candidate. Lyndon Johnson was playing that game as well. But Johnson (rightly) feared that if a Senate filibuster destroyed the civil rights bill (a bill proposed by a Republican president) then not only would the Senate and the Democratic party suffer a massive loss of legitimacy, but his own political chances for advancement would be destroyed as he became too clearly a sectional candidate (Kearns 1976, 149). The stakes were high. But how could Johnson stop the filibuster and pass the Civil Rights Act?

A sticking point in the negotiations was the demand by the opponents that individuals held in violation of the law be given a jury trial. It was widely perceived at the time—correctly, it turns out—that this would essentially eviscerate the legislation, since few thought that southern juries would willingly prosecute southern political officials for violations of African-American civil rights (Branch 1988, 220–21; Caro 1990, xviii; see also Garrow 1978, 12–13). Nonetheless Johnson agreed to this provision. But to make sure that his concession did not undercut the bill, Johnson also engineered a logroll: Western votes on civil rights in exchange for Southern support on the Hell's Canyon power project (Lawson 1976, 189–90). Even this seems to have fallen somewhat short. Nonetheless, with sufficient cajolery—and the apparently midnight conversions of Henry Jackson and John F. Kennedy—the amendment was approved by a roughly minimal winning coalition of 51 to 42, and the first Civil Rights Act since 1875 passed the Senate.[9]

This use of personal influence and skill may seem a bit odd. Why, after all, rely on such personal tactics? Why not reform the filibuster? Part of the key here is given by the problems of party cohesion. As noted above, the civil rights coalition was composed of Northern Democrats and Republicans. Therefore, the split in the party made the caucus mechanism unworkable. Had the civil rights issue not cut across party lines, things might well have been quite different. But this is simply to repeat what is well known.

Cloture was reformed in 1959. Column 3 again presents the Poisson regression of cloture votes on party proportion, this time controlled for the influence of the 1959 rules changes. The 1958 elections saw an incredible increase in the Democratic fortunes, with the party majority rising to 64 (as opposed to the Republicans 34). This was a fairly large majority, which would suggest that it would be difficult to maintain cohesion, but as noted above it was also one seat short of a minimal winning coalition under the old cloture rule. Indeed, there were splits in the party, as Robert Byrd has noted

> Mr. President, there were two distinct periods of Lyndon Johnson's majority leadership. From 1955 to 1958, the Democrats controlled the Senate by a slim one- or two-vote margin. There are many observers of the legislative process who contend that the closer the margin, the easier it is for a Majority Leader to keep his ranks in line. Lyndon Johnson certainly subscribed to that theory; but the election of 1958 caused a dramatic change in party fortunes. . . . This [the Democratic Majority] was the largest majority for any party since World War II, and the greatest trans-

fer of seats from one party to another in the entire history of the Senate. The first sign of discontent came immediately after the election . . . (620)

Byrd's view is shared by Ornstein, Peabody, and Rohde (1989), who also find that "with the election of 1958, the ability of a leader to 'strong-arm' the Senate declined dramatically," a result they link to "the larger number of independent freshman Democrats" (22–23). Much of that criticism dealt with the continued inability of the Senate to deal with the problem of obstruction.

In response, an effort was made to reduce the vote required for cloture to a simple majority. Indeed, Richard Nixon as president of the Senate actually ruled that the Senate could, at the start of the session, adopt whatever rules it saw fit by majority vote. This would of course open the path to radically altering the cloture rule, since Nixon had in essence ruled that the Senate was not a continuing body to be bound by the rules of the previous Congress. Johnson, however, was able to head off the drive for majority cloture by again suggesting a compromise version. On the one hand, the votes necessary for cloture would be based on two-thirds of those voting rather than two-thirds of those present, but on the other hand the Johnson resolution wrote into the rules an explicit recognition that the Senate was a continuing body and that a new Congress carried over the rules of the previous Congress.

Column 3 includes both the 1949 rules change as well as the 1959 changes just described along with majority party proportion. In this full model, the proportion of seats held by the majority party has the expected negative effect: the larger the party, the fewer the number of cloture votes one sees. The result is statistically significant at the .01 level (for a two-tailed test). Furthermore, both of the changes in the cloture rule had a significant effect, as one would expect, on the pattern of cloture votes. This suggests that the reforms were not merely shams, or even ratifications of current practice, but instead real substantive changes.

The results so far ignore the possibility of party differences in the willingness to engage in cloture votes. Column 5 therefore adds to column 4 a dummy variable for Democratic control. As one can see, the signs of the various coefficients remain the same, as do the statistical results. There is a positive sign on the coefficient, indicating that if anything the control of the Senate by Democrats has a positive effect on cloture votes, but the results are not statistically significant. Controlling for party basically leaves the other effects unchanged.

A difficulty with using Poisson regression is that the coefficients cannot be interpreted as straightforwardly as can those of an ordinary least squares regression. One way around this is to present the predicted number of cloture votes for various scenarios. This, of course, requires that we pick one of the

TABLE 7.9. Predicted Number of Cloture Votes Under Various Procedural Regimes

Majority Proportion	Procedural Regime		
	1917 Rule	1949 Rule	1959 Rule
50	2	1	25
55	2	0	17
60	1	0	10
65	1	0	6
70	0	0	4
75	0	0	2
80	0	0	1

above models on which to base our estimates. Since Democratic majorities in the Senate do not have a statistically significant effect, I based my estimates on the numbers presented in column 4.

The predicted number of cloture votes for the various procedural regimes are presented in table 7.9. The first column sets out the number of cloture votes expected for various majority proportions under the procedural regime adopted in 1917. Confirming the historical analysis above, we can see that there are relatively few cloture votes under this regime. The second column presents the expected number of cloture votes for the same majorities given the 1949 rules. Here we see that if anything the procedural changes of 1949 diminished the number of cloture votes that could be expected. Given the history presented above, it seems safe to suggest that the 1949 rules change, despite its ambiguous nature, essentially enhanced the opportunity of minorities to obstruct.

The most provocative finding emerges from the final column, representing the 1959 regime engineered by Johnson. Lyndon Johnson has been presented in the literature of the era as an opponent of increasing restrictiveness on cloture.[10] In his history of the King era, Taylor Branch notes that once the remodeling of his office was completed

> Johnson moved quickly to place his personal stamp on the new Senate by controlling its most volatile institutional issue—the cloture rule, which governed the changes of civil rights bills. One by one, he summoned the incoming senators to flatter, cajole, or intimidate them. No matter how many liberals had been elected in 1958, Johnson told each one, he would never permit the radical relaxation of the cloture rule that reformers now

thought possible. It would ruin the party in the South, he said, and worse, it would play into the hands of Vice President Nixon, who was using liberal Northern Democrats in a scheme to win Negro votes for the Republicans. In an impressive display of personal influence, Johnson induced many supporters of civil rights to help him crush the cloture reform movement in the new Senate. (248)

While these results cannot speak to the question of what would have happened to civil rights in this country had the Senate voted to allow cloture through a simple majority vote, they do suggest that the notion that Johnson's resolution was a subterfuge that left legislative politics in a pre-1959 state seems incorrect. The estimates presented here suggest that, especially for small majorities, the 1959 reforms (other things being equal) enhanced the tendency of the majority to attempt cloture. Of course, such quantitative evidence cannot uncover intentionality: who is to know whether Johnson's scheme just backfired?

The analysis so far has been based on the notion that the number of votes is a sign of cloture efficacy. This need not be the case. It is quite possible, for example, that the 1959 reforms did in fact make cloture more difficult to obtain, thus necessitating numerous additional votes in order to get the clunky procedure to yield results. I then mindlessly point to these additional votes (actually a sign of the weakness of the procedure) and suggest how significant the reforms were in making cloture easier!

Dealing with this objection is straightforward. The Congressional Research Service volume also provides information indicating whether cloture was successful or not. I have therefore replicated the analysis presented in the previous section, this time however taking as my dependent variable the number of cases in which cloture was successfully invoked. The estimates are presented in table 7.10.

As can be seen, in every estimation majority party proportion had the expected negative sign and was statistically significant. This suggests that a declining proportion of seats held by the majority does not simply increase the number of cloture votes without accomplishing anything of substance: it also makes it easier for the majority to successfully invoke cloture. The results on the effect of procedural reforms hold up as well. The 1949 reforms, once again, appear if anything to have made successful cloture harder to achieve, but the impact is not significant. The coefficient on the 1959 reforms is positive and significant: not only did those changes significantly increase the number of cloture votes that were taken, they also made the securing of cloture easier. This confirms that Johnson's reforms may not have been as inconsequential as some have suggested.

TABLE 7.10. Poisson Regression Results on Successful Cloture Votes, U.S. Senate, 1919–74

Independent Variables	(1)	(2)	(3)	(4)	(5)
Constant	2.911#	4.488*	7.425***	7.885***	7.866**
	(1.765)	(2.444)	(2.554)	(2.807)	(2.850)
Majority proportion	−0.0554*	−0.0863**	−0.158***	−0.163***	−0.163***
(Martis)	(0.0278)	(0.0382)	(0.0531)	(0.0539)	(0.0568)
1949 Rule		−1.385		−0.473	−0.428
		(1.219)		(1.312)	(1.058)
1959 Rule			2.650**	2.493**	2.554***
			(0.961)	(0.979)	(0.907)
Democratic majority					−0.0714
					(0.981)
Number of observations	28	28	28	28	28
Log-likelihood	−25.470	−23.383	−12.390	−12.238	−12.236

#significant at the 10 percent level, one-tailed test
*significant at the 10 percent level, two-tailed test
**significant at the 5 percent level, two-tailed test
***significant at the 1 percent level, two-tailed test

Conclusion

The analysis presented here can hardly do justice to the rich history of the filibuster. Nonetheless, the results do suggest that the pattern of behavior witnessed in the House—in particular, the tendency for minimal winning coalitions to limit minority rights to obstruct—does have at least surface plausibility in the Senate. I have no doubts that with further analysis, many of the arguments presented here (especially on the explanation of changes in the cloture rule) may have to be radically overthrown or tossed out. But the regressions on attempts to limit debate during the nineteenth century and the actual use of the cloture procedure in the twentieth century seem stronger to me and suggest that there is a relationship between small majorities and steps to eliminate obstruction, even in the U.S. Senate.

The evidence presented here also shows the possibilities inherent in statistical analysis for clarifying historical problems. Certainly anyone simply looking at the text of Johnson's changes might expect that they would have a minimal effect. In legislative politics, however, even minimal changes in procedures can have a lasting effect. Statistical analysis makes it possible, if not to judge why individuals adopted a change (that still requires, it seems to me, the usual historical methods), at least to indicate the effects (intended or not) of that change.

My main worry is that I have failed to take into consideration the problem of anticipated use of the cloture rule. This is not a paralyzing difficulty, since, as I have argued, a dilatory minority might still wish to force the majority to go through the steps of cloture, but it does present a challenge for further work to overcome. Do the results shown here change once we take into account the fact that a filibuster liable to fail may not even be started?

We need not rely as heavily as we have on claims about an enduring tradition of free debate in the Senate. Even granting that this tradition has an impact, it is (like most traditions) hardly static. What constitutes "intolerable constraint" changes with the changing institutional practices of the Senate. Thus, even acknowledging that the political culture of the Senate might differ considerably from that of the House, there is still room, as these results show, for more systematic analysis into the Senatorial filibuster.

CHAPTER 8

Going Abroad: The House of Commons
and the Austrian Parliament

No reviling or nipping words must be used, for then all the house will cry 'it is against the order'; and if any speak unreverently or seditiously against the prince or the privy council, I have seen them not only interrupted, but it hath been moved after to the house, and they have sent them to the Tower. So that in such multitude, and in such diversity of minds and opinions, there is a great modesty and temperance of speech that can be used.
—Sir Thomas Smith, *De Republica Anglorum* (1581)

How well does the theory presented in this book work outside of the American Congress? We have already encountered one case: the trial of the Catiline conspirators that began this book. There we saw the Roman Senate split between Optimates and Populares. Cato was just able to keep the wavering troops in line. Caesar's response was to obstruct, producing just the reaction we would expect: an attempt to limit obstruction, in that case using force.

I hope references to Caesar and Roman methods will not inspire any suspicions about my claims to world-historical conquest. I do not believe that the theory presented here will work in every legislature since the dawn of recorded history. But the test of the theory presented in chapter 2 could not be complete without some reference to the activities of non-American legislatures. Do they behave as we would expect from the theory? What is different? Most importantly, what was it about the activities in these legislatures that made contemporaries, as noted at the start of this book, fear for the future of parliamentary democracy?

The bulk of this chapter will be taken up with the case of the House of Commons during the nineteenth century. From there I will move on to Mark Twain and the stirring times he witnessed in Austria.

The House of Commons in the Nineteenth Century

While obstruction has not disappeared from the House of Commons (as the story of Labour M.P. Dennis Skinner in chapter 1 showed), the Commons has

189

over the past two centuries acquired a number of tools with which to limit the rights of minority members to obstruct. Many of these were formulated in the nineteenth century, a time when, as Gary Cox has shown in *The Efficient Secret*, party discipline was being forged. While I will look at some of the same period that Cox addressed, much of my concern will be directed to the latter half of the nineteenth century, in particular the struggles in Parliament over Irish obstruction.[1]

A Conventional Story

> The rules of Parliament are designed to afford every legitimate opportunity of discussion, to ensure reasonable delays in the passing of important measures, and to guard the rights of minorities; and freedom of debate has been maintained and observed by the rules and usages of both houses, with rare patience and self-denial. But, of late, these salutary rules have been strained and perverted, in the House of Commons for the purposes of obstruction.
> —Sir Thomas Erskine May (1893)

There is a conventional story about British parliamentary history that goes something like this: in the old days of Peel and Wellington, when members of the Commons were drawn from the same elite social circles, there was a gentleman's understanding of the balance to be struck between majority rule and minority rights, an understanding that was buttressed by the recognition that today's majority would be tomorrow's minority. This was made easier due to the existence of what Walpole called "fashionable young gentlemen" (Redlich 1908, I.81), representing "rotten boroughs" with few constituents to worry about.[2] The Reform Acts unhinged all that, but British determination stuck by minority rights and adjusted to the needed changes in the Commons. It was only when that Irish upstart, Charles Parnell, along with a bare handful of followers in the 1870s and 1880s, began systematically carrying out the prolonged attempt to destroy the House of Commons by the means of obstruction, that the House, regrettably, was forced to turn to restrictive procedures.[3]

This conventional story deals a rather harsh blow to the claims advanced in this book. If it is true that Parnell and his small minority were the causes of attempts to limit minority obstruction, then the theory advanced in chapter 2 can hardly be correct for the British case. We can think of all sorts of reasons why the Commons might differ from the House or other American legislatures: the Cabinet as executive-in-legislature, the incremental nature of suffrage extension, perhaps even (if we are truly desperate) the presence of a feudal past. But before we go to the stock of ready explanations, we need to determine whether in fact this conventional account is true.

Obstruction and Procedural Change in the House of Commons

> Once he had seemed callous and indifferent to the House of Commons, Foster had accused him of abetting assassination, but when he came among his followers his hands were full of blood, because he had torn them with his nails.
>
> —William Butler Yeats (1916)

> —This is Parnell's anniversary, said Mr. O'Connor, and don't let us stir up any bad blood. We all respect him now that he's dead and gone—even the Conservatives, he added, turning to Mr. Crofton.
>
> —James Joyce, "Ivy Day in the Committee Room," *Dubliners* (1916)

Telling the story of obstruction would be impossible without reference to the "Uncrowned King of Ireland," Charles Stewart Parnell, the leader of the Home Rule party. In a letter to Isaac Butt, the leader of the Home Rule party, Parnell explained his position:

> If Englishmen insist on the artificial maintenance of an antiquated institution, which can only perform a portion of its functions by the 'connivance' of those intrusted with its working in the imperfect and defective performance of much of even that portion—if the continued working of this institution is constantly attended with much wrong and hardship to my country, as frequently it has been the source of gross cruelty and tyranny—I cannot consider it is my duty to connive in the imperfect performance of these functions, while I should certainly not think of obstructing any useful, solid, or well-performed work. (Redlich 1908, I.142–43)[4]

Bringing this point home to British legislators would take up most of Parnell's political career.

The above quote may help explain why Parnell obstructed, but it cannot explain what it was about that obstruction that led Speaker Brand in 1878 to claim before the Select Committee on the reform of rules that obstruction "was an offence new in the annals of Parliament" (Redlich 1908, I.146). Everyone agrees that, even concentrating exclusively on the case of the Commons, Parnell did not invent delay. There was apparently some obstruction that took place during the Grand Remonstrance at the time of Charles I (Nov. 22, 1641). Over a century later, in 1771, Edmund Burke, whose noble views on politics we are sometimes urged to emulate, called in one sitting for a total of 23 divisions in order to postpone the consideration of a proposal to publish parliamentary debates. Despite maligning the French as a "nation of game-sters" in his *Reflections*, Burke felt no pangs of remorse over his own efforts in that regard: "Posterity will bless the pertinacity of that day" (Redlich 1908, I.138). Other cases can be easily added: Castlereagh and friends filibustering in 1806, Sir Charles Wetherell in 1831 delaying the First Reform act by calling for eight divisions and keeping the house in session until 7:30 in the morning, delays on private bills—the list could go on, all of which could be narrated without mentioning the name of Charles Parnell.

What then was so novel about Parnell's behavior? What made him stand out? For the British, it was his willingness to obstruct *all* legislation, not just those dealing with the affairs of Ireland, that made him a legislative revo-lutionary. The rhetoric here is not overblown: in a speech on obstruction, Gladstone told the House of Commons that they were engaged in an epochal struggle:

> "the House of Commons has never since the first day of its desperate struggle for existence stood in a more serious crisis—a crisis of character and honour, not of external security." (Quoted in Redlich 1908, I.158)

Considering the number of crises the Commons has suffered through, the charge is really quite substantial. Could filibustering be as bad as all that? It would appear so. Members worried that Parnell's dilatory tactics were making a mockery of British parliamentary democracy at the very time when that nation was asserting its hegemonic position throughout the world. The timing is seductive: Parnell's decision to follow a course of obstruction was made in the same year that Victoria was crowned Empress of India. Being humbled by the provincials in one's own Parliament, it appears, does not play well in the colonies.

Charles Parnell's view of his actions were, as one might expect, quite different. For him, the shrill nature of the reaction to his use of obstructive tactics was British prejudice, plain and simple. He set out his position in 1877 in a letter published by the *Times:*

> There seems a disposition to indict me for something. Is it for not being as other members are? I have not been as other members are. I have worked in the House instead of stopping in Ireland or amusing myself in London . . . I have studied the measures submitted to the House and

endeavoured to improve them, instead of blindly voting without knowledge or caring anything about the question. But I have done worse than this. There is an unwritten law, hitherto acquiesced in by the Irish members, that no Irish may interfere in English and imperial concerns—at any rate, if they do, their interference must be in homeopathic doses, well covered up with sugar. I have transgressed this law. I have taken a part in those English matters when I have thought it right to do so, and have not troubled myself about the sugar. (Quoted in Lyons 1977, 66)

Speaking before the House of Commons, Parnell was a bit more succinct: whenever an Irish member takes interest in English laws, there are cries of "Obstruction" (Redlich 1908, I.144).

Both the letter to the *Times* and the quip before the Commons indicate the trait that probably vexed the British the most: Parnell's irritating ability to straddle the line between constructive criticism and systematic obstruction. His colleagues in the Home Rule party recognized this skill: one member wrote that Parnell "excelled all of us" when it came to "obstructing as if he were really acting in the interests of the British legislators" (Redlich 1908, I.141). For the British it was a different matter. "We feared him because we never knew what he was up to," said one English viceroy (quoted in Kee 1972b, 69).

Both views, however—Parnell as Savior and Parnell as Antichrist—do him a disservice, because they rob his actions of their context. Parnell may have been the most visible obstructionist, but even among the Irish he was neither the first nor the last. Similarly, we need to see the actions by the majority within their historical context as well. Neither tends to happen: actions taken on both sides of the dispute attract words like "unprecedented" and "unheard of." Were they really?

To answer this question, I compiled a chronology of references to obstruction (especially references to procedural changes dealing with obstruction) taking place from 1832 to 1904. These references were taken from a variety of sources: Cox 1987, Kee 1972b, Lyons 1977, May 1893, Parnell 1914, and Redlich 1908. I have tried to be comprehensive, but given the technical complexities of the procedural arguments, I have no doubt missed some cases and given short shrift to others. At the very least this will provide some account of the major steps taken in the Commons to limit minority rights to obstruct legislation.

Such a list is worthless, however, without information on the proportions of seats held by the various parties. I rely here on the percentages calculated by Craig (1989, 52). Party proportions are tricky: in the early years there is the question about who really aligned with whom (Bulmer-Thomas 1965, I.85f.), and even for later years there are the inevitable changes in proportion due to sickness, deaths, by-elections, and the like, but the Craig data offered at least a foothold. I will however occasionally introduce some figures from Bulmer-Thomas where relevant (especially for the fourth Gladstone administration).

To impose structure, I will be breaking the discussion along the conventional periodization: 1832 to 1846 (from the first Commons elected under the Reform Act to the repeal of the Corn Laws), 1847 to 1867 (which brings the story up to the Second Reform Act), 1867 to 1886 (the defeat of Gladstone's Home Rule bill), and 1886 to 1905 (the rise of the Labour party).

It will be impossible in the context of a single chapter to present a comprehensive overview of Commons history. In particular, and again for purely practical reasons, I have obtained few final vote tallies for the rules changes, especially for the earlier cases. This suggests that without further analysis much caution should be taken in inferring a particular partisan dynamic into the findings I will present here. As if this weren't enough, many of the tallies I did assemble exhibit exceptionally large majorities at apparent odds with the theory. Lest this appear too startling, I should note (and will discuss at greater length below) a technical feature of voting in the House of Commons that would make lopsided majorities (especially in the cases I am considering here) an act of obstruction and thus an imperfect signal of individual preferences *over* obstruction.

1832 to 1846

The election of 1832, the first under the Reform Act, found the Liberal party in control of the majority. The size of that majority, however, is not absolutely clear. According to Craig, the Liberals held 67 percent of the seats. But Bulmer-Thomas (1965, I.69), who warns about stuffing members into partisan categories at this date, calculates that out of 658 members, 360 were Whigs with 70 Radicals and 70 Irish normally supporting. This would work out to a majority proportion of 75.99 with Radicals and Irish, and 54.7 without.

Certainly the Irish and the Radicals could not be trusted to sit by after the introduction of Earl Grey's Irish Coercion Bill. Daniel O'Connell, the original "Uncrowned King of England," began obstruction on the Coercion Bill the very first day of its consideration, and with the assistance of other Irish members as well as the Radicals and other Irish members was able to use up the entire month of March before the bill made it through a third reading (Redlich 1908, I.139). The results here are a mixed bag for the theory, however. Redlich states that the Irish and the Radicals faced Whigs and Tories, hardly the party-line squabble predicted by the theory. We do, however, fail to see any steps for procedural reform (although, to be honest, a procedural reform in the Commons during this period would be rather exceptional).

The election of 1837 brought the Liberals a slim 52 percent majority, the smallest majority of the period we are considering in this section. Consistent with the theory, the government (under Melbourne) formed a select committee with Mr. Poulett Thompson as chair "to consider the best means of conducting the public business with improved regularity and dispatch," this a mere five years after the passage of the Reform Act (Redlich 1908, I.78).

The "best means of conducting business" was apparently taken by the committee to mean the best way to guarantee that the government set the agenda. Correspondingly, one of the major reforms proposed was intended to establish the right of the government to have precedence on Monday and Friday. In general the government was able to consider legislation on these days, but the Committee recognized that this convention,

> "resting not on the rules but on the desire of the House to assist the Government, had been subjected to serious interference by the practice of the House; that, in fact, the orders had, in the then current session, been perverted in one way or another in the proportion of one third of the whole number of days of sitting, and that to the disadvantage of the Government." (Quoted in Redlich 1908, I.79)

One "perversion" the Committee went after was the ability of members to introduce amendments on any subject at any time. This procedure, according to the Committee to be reserved for use only on the most urgent issues, was abused by members in order to introduce whatever individual initiatives they were interested in (Redlich 1908, I.79; Cox 1987). Note here how "urgent business," even at this early stage, becomes equated with "the Government's agenda."

But the right to offer amendments in this fashion was hardly the product of a few individuals pursuing pie-eyed reforms. It was, instead, a traditional device used in Parliament for raising grievances against the government or for asking questions (Redlich 1908, I.79). By ruling such motions out of order, the Committee was doing more than simply guaranteeing a conventional right of the government: it was instead writing what had been a courtesy into a law, and in the process stifling an opportunity for dissent.[5]

The Committee also suggested changes making it more difficult for ordinary citizens to alter the legislative agenda. From 1800 on, there had been an increase in the number of petitions presented to the Commons, and for each of these petitions there were four regular motions, all of which could be debated. This was a perfect opportunity not only to bring up new issues, but also to delay, a tactic used by Lord Brougham to delay the maintenance of the tax on income (Redlich 1908, I.76). In 1839, therefore, the House voted to ban debates on petitions, although only as a sessional order (Redlich 1908, I.77).

The next election, occurring in 1841, brought the Conservatives to 55.7 percent of the seats. This was the second smallest majority during this period, and as expected by the theory, we do see procedural changes. The ban on debate on petitions was made permanent by inclusion into the standing rules in 1842 (Redlich 1908, I.77). This did not eliminate the specter of obstruction, however. In 1843, there were 44 divisions in committee on the Irish Arms Bill, promulgated by an exceptionally small minority of 5 to 20 individuals. Lord Palmerston, reflecting on this in 1844, derived the following lesson: "Experience has shown that a compact body of opponents, though few in number, may, by debating every sentence and word of a bill, and by dividing upon every debate, to obstruct the progress of a bill through Parliament that a whole session may be scarcely long enough for carrying through one measure" (Lord Palmerston, quoted in Redlich 1908, I.139). No doubt in recognition of the problem, an order was made in 1846 setting Monday and Thursday as government days.

Palmerston's lesson here is important because it shows, decades before Parnell arrived on the scene, that members believed it possible to conceive of obstruction lasting through a whole session and totally frustrating business. It also shows, quite early on, the easy identification of Irish opposition with dangerous obstruction. But there were good reasons to be fearful: the possibility of imminent civil war in Ireland was escalating daily.[6] Daniel O'Connell had organized a number of "monster meetings," the one at Tara having as many as 750,000 people (O'Connell himself claimed one and a half million). Such mass meetings do not make states very confident, and the government asked O'Connell to bring the meetings to a halt. O'Connell complied, and in return was arrested, tried, and convicted of conspiracy. In retrospect, therefore, the obstruction acquires a certain sinister disposition, even if we are willing to accept the possibility that obstruction was salient to Palmerston simply because it was Irish.

The final majority to consider, resulting from the election of 1835, brought the majority 58.5 percent of the seats. This is (with the exception of the larger estimate for 1832) the biggest majority in the period. While silence does not constitute evidence, I have been unable to locate any reference to procedural reform in any of the sources that I have consulted. Given the tedious attention to detail in Redlich, I would have rather high confidence that a rules change did not occur.

In the period between the First Reform Act, then, and the repeal of the Corn Laws, the two smallest majorities witnessed procedural changes designed to limit obstruction, while the two largest majorities witnessed no attempts at procedural change. This pattern is consistent with our theory.

1847 to 1867: The Age of Uncertainty

Peel's proposal to repeal the Corn Laws was successful, but the result of his antiprotectionist stance was to split the Tories, thus beginning a hiatus in party politics that lasted until the passage of the Second Reform Act in 1867. Gary Cox has argued that "the agenda in the 20 years after the repeal of the Corn Laws was largely negative, aimed at preventing the schemes of the Radicals in the House from coming to fruition" (125). As discussed in chapter 2 and throughout this work, a party that sees its position as one of protecting the status quo is unlikely to take steps to limit minority rights. Even so, did the Commons take steps to limit minority rights to obstruct?

The election of 1847, following hard upon the split, produced the smallest majority during this second period, 49.5 percent for the Conservatives. The very next year, as both Cox and Redlich observe, Mr. John Evelyn Denison's Committee proposed and House adopted an abolition of parliamentary maneuvers that enabled private members to get their bills before the House. This would make it difficult (but as we shall see, not impossible) to obstruct the government's agenda. The discussion of procedure was also notable for a proposal from the Speaker that votes on motions to adjourn be decided without debate. Since a motion to adjourn was always in order, the ability to debate such a motion made it possible for individuals to take up time and introduce issues of their own. Redlich also notes that this Committee provided the first occasion in which closure had been suggested by "any responsible party," although the proposal made by the Speaker was not considered by the committee (Redlich 1908, I.78, I.88; Cox 1987). A final change occurred on June 25, when on the eve of the July general election an order was adopted adding Wednesday as a third government day, expanding the ability of the government to prosecute its agenda.

From there we move to 1852, which saw the Conservatives edge just barely above a simple majority: 50.5 percent.[7] And the very next year saw the adoption of many of the limits on obstruction proposed during the 1848 session, including a provision that took away the ability to debate the merits of a bill on each occasion that the House went into committee for discussion. This too was another form of delay: by arguing the merits of a bill again and again, opponents could, if not sway opinion, at least delay proceedings long enough potentially to kill the bill.

The reforms of 1853 did not seem to go far enough, however, so in 1854 Sir John Pakington's Committee was set up. Present to give evidence was Sir Erskine May, the foremost authority on parliamentary procedure. He had numerous suggestions for reform that, as characterized by Redlich

> were mainly directed to saving the limited and previous time of the House by the discontinuance of unnecessary forms, and the abolition of all such methods of conducting business as lent themselves without difficulty to underhand use of an obstructive tendency. (Redlich 1908, I.90)

As was noted numerous times over the course of procedural debates, the consideration of a bill took numerous formal motions. Each of these motions was itself subject to debate and therefore represented numerous opportunities for opponents to postpone (perhaps indefinitely) the consideration of the legislation. To combat this problem, the Committee proposed a number of changes. Nongermane amendments could no longer be offered in the Committee of the Whole without a change of title. The extraneous questions for a second and third reading of a bill in the Committee of the Whole were eliminated. Reports from the Committee of the Whole would be brought up without the raising of any question (another opportunity for obstruction gone). Finally, bills were to be considered without the interposition of the archaic motion that the chairman leave the chair. These changes all simplified the process to be sure, but they did something else: they limited the expression of dissent. All were adopted into the standing rules.

A majority of 54.4 percent was obtained by the Liberals after the general election of 1859, followed two years later by the appointment of Sir James Graham's Committee. The conclusion of their report speaks directly to the question of minority rights:

> "Your Committee, like preceding committees on the same subject, have passed in review many suggested alterations, but like them have come to the conclusion that the old rules and orders, when carefully considered and narrowly investigated, are found to be the safeguard of freedom of debate, and a sure defense against the oppression of overpowering majorities." (Quoted in Redlich 1908, I.103)

There is no need to invoke cynicism here. Members of the Committee did, it appears, wish to retain the traditional functions of the rules. But by this they meant order: "Order is their [the rules'] sole object; and without order, freedom of debate and prompt despatch of business cannot long exist" (quoted in Redlich 1908, I.104). Order was contrasted with its parliamentary antonym, "uncertainty." Speaker Denison in the 1861 report phrased it this way:

> "Besides the delay which is occasioned by these proceedings, there is great uncertainty in every step in public business. The great complaint of members is that they never know what business is coming on, and this uncertainty is, I think, the great evil at present to be corrected." (Quoted in Redlich 1908, I.98–99)

The language here is eerily similar to that presented in the book by Stanley Bach and Steven Smith (1988) on the adoption of restrictive rules in the 1980s House of Representatives. Bach and Smith argue that restrictive rules provided a mechanism for inducing stability in a frequently chaotic postreform House. But (as Bach and Smith note) these rules were also subject to condemnation by the minority side of the aisle. Despite differences of over a hundred years and thousands of miles, the arguments are the same: it is not particularly clear to the minority what it is that "order" is buying.

This does not mean that the Speaker is trying to pull a fast one over on the minority. Members come before the individual responsible for the conduct of business in the House and talk about the fact that they never know what legislation is coming. A reform is therefore proposed to make consideration of legislation more orderly. But how is that to be accomplished? Putting it in the hands of every member to set the agenda would only invite chaos. But putting that power in the hands of a responsible majority would guarantee the certainty that members desire. Q.E.D.

But the steps taken to induce order look very much like antiobstructive moves. It was proposed that on all days (except Thursday and Friday) when estimates from the Committee of Supply were the first order of the day, the Speaker would leave his chair without putting any question. A proposal was also made that when the House adjourned on Friday to meet again on Monday, this would also take place "without question put." These were all adopted by the House.

Once the 1861 measures passed, a Select Committee on rules for the House of Commons did not meet again for another ten years, as Redlich observes.[8] What he does not observe, however, is that in between these two committees was the general election of 1865, which produced a majority of 56.2 percent. That majority was exceeded in size during this second period only by the 57.6 percent of the seats attained by the Liberals in the general election of 1857. These were the two largest majorities in the period between the repeal of the Corn Laws and the passage of the Second Reform Act. Neither witnessed any procedural changes.

1867 to 1886

With the Second Reform Act, we begin to enter the pivotal period in the history of the Commons' dealings with obstruction. That era begins with the largest majority in this set of elections, a Liberal majority of 58.8 percent from the general election of 1868, which is also the largest majority given in a general election since the election following the passage of the First Reform Act.

Despite this, members witnessed both obstruction and rules changes, though not of the sort to occur soon enough. The Ballot Bill of 1871 mandating the secret ballot was "delayed by that practice of talking against time which has more recently become famous under the name of obstruction" (McCarthy *Own Times* IV. 1880, lix. 313; cited in OED-2 on CD-ROM; see also Buxton 1892). The year 1871 also witnessed the first appointment of a

Select Committee on parliamentary procedure since 1861, under the chair of Mr. Robert Lowe.

The procedural reforms coming out of this committee, however, were notably weak. A major limitation on obstruction—prohibiting the obstructive device used by Dennis Skinner of clearing the House of strangers discussed in chapter 1—failed to pass the House. A limitation was finally put on motions to move into the Committee of Supply, discussed but not adopted in 1854. While that measure passed, it applied only to the case where the Committee was to consider estimates, and it left open for obstruction situations where the Committee would consider supplementary estimates, a report of supply, or the motion to go into the Committee of Ways and Means. Other proposals (such as the Speaker's suggestion for limiting dilatory sittings) were not adopted.

One change was adopted, however, which would soon end up having an impact. The 12:30 rule prohibited the Commons from taking up new business that was opposed after 12:30 A.M. The rule was ostensibly designed to guarantee a "shorter duration of sittings, the length of which was becoming a menace to the health of members" (Redlich 1908, I.109).[9] Adopted as a sessional order, the 12:30 rule would, as we shall soon see, not have the salutary effect the majority had envisioned. Summing up, this rather large Liberal majority produced few procedural changes of substance, and those that were produced were (with the exceptions noted above) turned back.

The next general election, taking place in 1874, brought the Conservatives back into power, though with a majority of only 53.7 percent. Present in the House were 59 nominal Home Rulers elected from Ireland. Like many minorities, the Home Rule party disagreed on the precise tactics it should follow for success. The leader of the party, Isaac Butt, while not a lackey for British colonial interests, was nonetheless committed to opposition by the usual constitutional means. This required amendment, debate, and most of all patience.

A much different theory of opposition was proposed and carried out by Joseph Ronayne and Joseph Biggar. The idea for pursuing obstruction appears to have originated with Ronayne, who suggested in 1874 that the Home Rulers "show them [the British] that if we are not strong enough to get our own work done, we are strong enough to prevent them from getting theirs" (quoted in Lyons 1977, 50). But it fell to Biggar, a Belfast pork butcher (one is, it appears, required to mention this fact) and a member of a secret society known as the Irish Republican Brotherhood, to carry out the legislative strategy. In this he was admirably suited: John Howard Parnell (1914) in his biography of his brother writes of Biggar: "He hated the English parties, despised the rules of the House, and feared nobody" (143).

Butt disagreed with these tactics, and argued that Irish members could only lose by engaging in such provocation. Had major Irish legislation been passed during this period, his hand might have been strengthened. But this was not to be: from 1874 to 1875, Irish issues did not advance. Indeed, in 1875 the 12:30 rule was brought back in specifically for the purpose of killing Irish bills. This worked exceedingly well: since the government now retained a great deal of control over the agenda, it could use up time in consideration of its own measures, postponing Irish legislation to the nighttime where they could be easily disposed of by the 12:30 rule. Without concrete results, Butt's constitutional opposition began to lose its glow, and more members began looking toward a program of obstruction.

Biggar was on April 22, 1875, engaged in obstruction—four hours worth on the Irish Coercion Bill—when Charles Parnell took his seat as a first-term member of the House of Commons. Parnell did not exactly take the commons by storm. In fact, he was so ill-schooled in parliamentary procedure that he was unable, after making his maiden speech, to formulate a question (the response was awkward silence, as members waited for him to provide a question he did not know he had to provide).

There is evidence that Parnell was opposed to Butt's "gentlemanly" approach even before his election (see Lyons 1977, 48), but his resolve to adopt obstructionist tactics did not come until after Parnell paid a visit to the United States on its centennial (Parnell 144–45). While it would be wonderful to trace Parnell's decision to the filibustering going on in the Congress around that period, the transformative experience seems to have occurred not in Washington but in New York: "I have lately seen in the city of New York a review of the militia in which five or six thousand armed and trained men took part . . . If in Ireland we could ever have under Home Rule such a national militia . . . " (quoted in Lyons 1977, 57).

Whatever the causes, 1877 did see Parnell turning to obstructive techniques. His timing was impeccable: Great Britain was busy fighting in the Russo-Turkish War. Obstruction would therefore seem especially ominous given that one of the plans of Clan na Gael, the secret organization of Fenians in America, was to foment an Irish insurrection during a time when British forces were occupied elsewhere (Lyons 1977, 72).

The fight began on February 13, 1877, when the 12:30 limitation on opposed business was again renewed as a sessional rule (Kee 1972b, 59; Lyons 1977, 59). Biggar and Parnell immediately turned the new restrictive rules against the majority, submitting notices that they objected to *every* major bill desired by the Ministery (Lyons 1977, 59). Since consideration of opposed legislation ceased at 12:30, any Irish member could, by prolonging debate on the bills submitted by the government, guarantee that the 12:30 time was reached, and therefore end action on the bill. The range of legislation thus obstructed was exceptionally broad: army estimates, the Prisons bill, and even (Lyons notes) a measure dealing with threshing machines.

But stating objections was not the limit of Parnell's obstructive efforts. During consideration of the Mutiny Bill, Parnell, Biggar, and other Irish members kept the Commons occupied with numerous motions and divisions. An example shows why obstructionism is not necessarily compatible with "efficient" legislation. When moved to report progress, a member of the government responded that the provisions in the bill to which no objection had yet been made by the obstructionists would be considered as having already been acted upon. This of course is a red flag, and Biggar and Parnell thereupon began debating each and every one of the "unobjectionable" provisions, consuming even more time.

The decision to obstruct would have momentous consequences for the Irish Nationalists. While the filibustering was taking place, Butt walked in and stated before the Commons his regret "that the time of the House had been wasted in this miserable and wretched discussion." While he could not control Parnell, he had "a duty to discharge to the great nation of Ireland and I think I should discharge it best when I say I disapprove entirely of the conduct of the honourable member for Meath" (Kee 1972b, 70).

Butt had made a tactical blunder by criticizing a fellow countryman on the floor of the Commons. Parnell quickly exploited the opening:

> The instinct of snobbery, which seems to compel some Irishmen to worship at the shrine of English prejudice, and to bow down before the voice and censure of the English press, will never gain anything for Ireland, and will only secure for such panderers the secret contempt of Englishmen. (Lyons 1977, 60–61)

If anything, Butt's criticism stimulated Parnell to continue his obstructive ways. On July 2, he kept the house in session on the Army Reserve bill from 4:00 in the afternoon to 7:15 the next morning (Parnell 1914, 150). His tactic for sustaining this effort was precisely the strategy that Thomas Brackett Reed attacked in his comments on the 1880 rules change: Parnell would cycle over privileged resolutions, in this case the motions that "that the Chairman do now leave the chair" and the motion "to report progress." The session came to an end only when the government backed down (Redlich 1908, I.143).

Later that month, on July 25, Parnell began obstruction on the South Africa Bill. This time, however, he appears to have crossed the line. His statement during that debate—"I feel a special satisfaction in preventing and thwarting the intentions of the Government"—incensed members of the House (although Parnell did point out that he had said "Government" and not "House," an example again of his ability to edge between opposition and obstruction). Sir Stafford Northcote moved that Parnell should be suspended for the remainder of the session, but that resolution did not carry.

This did not mean that Parnell was out of the soup just yet. Speaker Brand warned "that any member willfully and persistently obstructing public business, without just and reasonable cause, is guilty of a contempt of the house, and would be liable to such punishment, whether by censure, by suspension from the service of the house, or by commitment; as the house may adjudge" (May 1893, 323; Redlich 1908, I.143). Despite this warning, Parnell continued to obstruct, leading Northcote on July 27 to propose that a member declared out of order twice should be suspended, and that the obstructive motions "to report progress" and "that the Chair do leave the chair" could only be moved once by each member during debate (Parnell 1914, 151; Redlich 1908, I.144). These were supported by overwhelming majorities, not surprising considering that the minority numbered only seven.

The resolutions, however, had no effect. The second part of the resolution only limited one kind of obstruction: there were others, as the Commons would soon find out. But even this lacked teeth without the first part of the resolution, which was equally impractical: to suspend a member, as Redlich 1908 (I.147) observed, would require a *motion* to suspend. Under House rules, that motion would be open to debate and amendment. Attempting to sanction the obstructor, in the kind of parliamentary irony one comes to expect when dealing with the politics of delay, therefore made obstruction easier, not harder.

The South Africa Bill was still being delayed on August 31, 1877, when Parnell forced the House into a continuous session of over 20 hours.[10] While the resolution only allowed one motion per member to report progress, it did allow one, and at 5:00 P.M. O'Donnell proposed it, followed by thirteen formal motions for adjournment (a dilatory tactic not addressed by the new rules) and lengthy speeches on each motion from the Irish side, whose numbers never rose above five (Redlich 1908, I.144). The Irish finally relented, and the bill passed, but the session concluded a few days later, eliminating the need for further obstruction (Redlich 1908, I.145).

The government was not about to sit on its hands. In 1878, a Select Committee headed by Sir Northcote, the very member who had moved to suspend Parnell, was formed to revise the rules (May 1893; Redlich 1908, I.111). With this background, it becomes a little easier to read the answers given by Speaker Brand to questions put by the Committee—indeed, without knowing the background they seem patently inoffensive:

> "[Mr. Knatchbull-Hugesson] Which do you think is the more important, that every individual should have an opportunity of airing a crotchet, or of bringing before the House that which he may imagine to be a grievance, but which the great majority would not consider to be such, or that greater facility should be given for the important business of the country being carried on with due expedition and certainty?

[The Speaker] The first object, of course, is to carry on the important business of the country, which is at present very much hindered." (Quoted in Redlich 1908, I.113)

Finding limits to obstruction proved difficult. Dealing with the technical means employed by Parnell and the Irish members was tricky. The motion to adjourn utilized by Parnell was also used by other members to bring up issues before the government. This would occur especially when members wished to engage the government in debate. But debate could occur only on a motion, so a member would "put himself right" (that is, be in nominal conformity with rules) by moving an adjournment and then engaging in debate on the issue of interest. Would it be possible to find some modification that would silence Parnell without at the same time making it appear that the government was unwilling to engage in debate? And if dealing with the technical means proved elusive, dealing with the punitive angle also had difficulties. Motions to make suspension easier raised the concerns of Radical members, who saw in such steps a dangerous precedent that could be applied to their own party if the majority so decided (Redlich 1908, I.147).

The Committee was able to come up with a report on July 8 providing three proposals for limiting obstruction. The first of these would force obstructors to choose between two obstructive strategies (reporting progress or moving that the Chair leave the chair), rather than allowing members to employ a single instance of both, reducing the potential number of obstructive strategies from two to one. A second change solved the problem of obstruction on punitive measures by banning all debate and amendment on a motion to suspend a member. While the rule seems to make motions to suspend a member immune to obstruction, it prevented only debate and amendment: a motion to adjourn (as used by Parnell) would still be in order. Thus the third rule: on a motion to adjourn, the Speaker could require members to stand and be counted. This would take up less time than a full division, which would require members to leave their seats. I shall have more to say about divisions in a bit; for now it is enough to point out that none of these were adopted when the bill was considered on February 24, 1879, although a rule reducing obstructive possibilities on the motion to go into the Committee of Supply or Ways and Means did pass (although weakened by an amendment).

One may feel that more actions against obstruction are required by the theory at this point. If we truly have 300 cohesive individuals or more facing 7 intransigent obstructionists (or 5, depending on how many Parnell could muster), why then did the majority refrain from voting in support of these resolutions?

The explanation is to be found not with the majority but with Parnell, who decided at this very moment to limit his parliamentary activities. A post–

South Africa meeting of the Home Rule party showed a bitter division between Parnell's forces and the old guard, a division without any apparent hope of decisive resolution. Rather than slug it out, Parnell decided that his best chance for success was to help elect other Irish members who would share his sympathies.

Adopting an electoral strategy, however, placed Parnell in a difficult strategic bind. If he moved too far to the right, strengthening his profile in the Commons, he would lose the support of the Fenians, who, being good revolutionaries, tended to distrust the sham of parliamentary democracy. But if Parnell swung too far to the left in search of Fenian backing, he might well lose the broader electoral support he was seeking.

Such a conundrum might paralyze a lesser politician. Parnell, however, cut through the difficulty in a decidedly bold way: he decided to abandon obstruction. This would convince those worried about obstruction that he was a serious legislator. Indeed, part of the reason for the letter to the *Times* quoted at the start of this section was to buttress that perception. At the same time, by abandoning obstruction and disengaging from parliamentary politics for a spell, he could portray to the Fenians that he was distancing himself from parliamentary politics.

To buttress his position, Parnell went before the February 1879 Home Rule conference to state that in his opinion it would be imprudent to attempt obstruction with less than twenty members (Lyons 1977, 86). Despite this apparent olive branch, other members of the conference set out to oust Butt from his leadership position. Butt was able to hold on, but the fight split the Home Rule party. This experience left Butt much worse for the wear, appearing broken, contracting bronchitis, and dying three months later. Butt's demise, however, failed to elevate Parnell to the leadership of the party. Instead, William Shaw, a moderate, was elected, if only for the session, a result that reinforced Parnell's calculation that to be effective he would need to expand his base of support.

The crisis in the Home Rule party just described occurred in early February (Lyons 1977, 632). The Northcote Committee reports were considered in late February. The rules changes were thus considered with the knowledge that the Home Rule party was in difficult straits and that Parnell had essentially indicated that he would refrain from obstructing. The threat evaporated, all that was really left was an attempt by the government to impose a further limitation on members, which attracts (as we shall see) precisely the sort of opposition expected given the theory.

Meanwhile, Parnell turned his attention toward home. The threat of famine was resurfacing in Ireland for the first time in 30 years due to a combination of poor weather and bountiful American corn exports. With the threat of evictions and mass starvation appearing on the horizon, the National

Land League was formed on October 21, 1879, with Parnell as its president (Kee 1972b, 77). Engaged in speech making for the League for much of the autumn, Parnell left Ireland in December, traveling to North America to raise additional funds.

Two events are especially relevant for the account presented here. First, while Parnell was in the United States, he had a chance to address the House of Representatives. His speech took place on February 2, 1880. I will discuss this more in chapter 9, but here let me simply recall that this was precisely in the middle of the protracted disputes in the House over the proposed parliamentary changes that culminated in the revision of 1880. Second, while Parnell was away, the House discussed procedures for sanctioning members for obstruction. This discussion took place from February 26 to 28, 1879. Redlich notes that the debate was "lengthy," but finally approved by "an overwhelming majority" (I.155).

The change adopted was important because it placed the onus of determining what exactly constituted obstruction on the Speaker of the House, who would initiate sanctions by moving to suspend the member, a motion that would be determined without debate, amendment, or motions for adjournment. This rule made the Speaker focal for resolving obstruction, a fact that will acquire greater significance as the story unfolds.

Parnell's trip to North America was cut short by the dissolution of Parliament and the need to campaign for the elections to be held in April 1880. The Liberal majority captured 54 percent of the seats.[11] The election brought 63 Home Rulers to Parliament. Of the remainder, a majority of members who had taken a stand were Parnellites (24 to 21), with the undecideds over time leaning in the Parnell direction as well. Parnell's movement to the electoral realm in order to solidify his parliamentary position had paid off. Even if the remainder of the party refused to support him, Parnell had the 20 members he had previously felt necessary for sustained opposition.

This opposition turned out not to be necessary, at least not just yet. Gladstone assumed office on April 29, 1880. With Irish agrarian troubles brewing, Home Rulers introduced a compensation bill to halt evictions. This bill proceeded up to a third reading when the Liberal government, anxious to avoid the appearance of being caught behind the Irish on this issue, introduced their own Land Bill on June 18. The ability to alter the course of the government's agenda was considered a major coup for the Irish forces (Lyons 1977, 132).

With the Land Bill in consideration, any motivation for Parnell to obstruct was taken away. Conservative forces do not appear to have obstructed the consideration of this bill, but perhaps they refrained from this behavior because they knew that they held the trump card: the House of Lords. Their predictions were borne out as the Lords, the stronghold of Conservatism, rejected the Land Bill on August 3, 1880.

John Dillon, an Irish member of Commons, had predicted on August 10 that with the rejection there would be "bloodshed and massacre to come" (Lyons 1977, 133). Violence did increase, as individuals came armed at eviction attempts. Dillon's speech (and a follow-up that urged the Irish to arm themselves) set off a debate in Commons that preempted Parnell's plan to obstruct on the Irish estimates (Lyons 1977, 134). While some obstruction did take place, for the most part Parnell sat back and waited to see whether Gladstone would produce another Land Bill. The session ended, however, on September 7, without the expected bill.

Parnell may seem to be fading from center stage here. His withdrawal at the time may be a little clearer once some facts are known about his personal life. While love assumes a rather low profile in social science (to be referred to, I suppose, as an "opportunity cost" or, worse, part of the "error term"), it has been known to happen. In July 1880, Parnell met Katherine O'Shea, wife of Captain O'Shea. By October, he was addressing her in letters as "my own love." The steps of their journey from acquaintanceship to intimacy to eventual marriage, as well as the question of what Captain O'Shea knew and when he knew it, is taken up in thorough detail in Lyons's biography of Parnell. The public revelation of their affair would ruin Parnell's career. In 1880, however, this was all years away.

Violence continued to escalate in Ireland, and Gladstone reacted with the introduction of the Irish Coercion Bill. On January 24, 1881, Gladstone requested a suspension of the standing orders to give the Irish Coercion Bill priority over all other business. The result was the inevitable return of Irish obstruction. Tensions only increased when, on January 27, an indiscretion on the part of the government disclosed the contents of the bill, and obstructive efforts were intensified. While "not subtle," Lyons writes, obstruction in this session "was more effective than ever because it now had the stamina of over twenty members to sustain it" (Lyons 1977, 145). Evidence of this stamina came when Parnell and his associates defeated their old record by forcing the house on January 31 into continuous session for 41 and a half hours (Redlich 1908, I.153).

Liberals and Conservatives both wished to silence Parnell—that was clear enough. But they disagreed on the means for accomplishing this end. Gladstone wanted to locate the responsibility in the hands of the majority. The Conservatives, however, wanted the power located in the hands of the Speaker of the House of Commons, who (unlike the Speaker of the House of Representatives) was considered a nonpartisan figure. Neither appeared willing to budge.

Faced with this debacle, the Speaker on his own initiative ordered the question put, an action without precedent in the history of the Commons. While it is true that Speaker Brand was a Liberal, there is no need simply to assume that he was acting as a partisan in this matter. He had for years complained of the problem of obstruction, which must have been excruciatingly dull to the individual who had to preside over these protracted affairs. More important, however, Brand considered it his duty as Speaker to resolve the situation and right a great indignity to the House.

Partisanship, however, appears to have influenced Brand sufficiently enough to lead him, before making his ruling, to consult with Gladstone. At that meeting, Brand extracted two promises. The first was that debate would continue until the following morning, "my object in this delay being to mark distinctly to the outside world the extreme gravity of the situation and the necessity of the step which I was about to take" (Brand's diary, quoted in Redlich 1908, I.157–58). The second was that Gladstone consider a change in the regulation of business. Gladstone agreed to both and called the Cabinet together.

Brand then communicated news of his plan to Sir Stafford Northcote, the Conservative leader, although according to his diary only after first obtaining Gladstone's permission (Redlich 1908, I.158). The leader of the minority expressed, according to Brand, surprise but not disapproval. With all the preparations made (including consultation with Sir Erskine May), Brand made his ruling.[12]

This was bad enough for the Irish Nationalists, but the very next day (February 3) there were rumors that the Home Secretary had ordered the re-arrest of Michael Davitt, one of the Irish members. Asked on point, he confirmed the rumors, this immediately before Gladstone was to put forward the rules for parliamentary procedure worked out by the Cabinet. Obstruction was still a possibility, however, although in a somewhat desperate key: when Gladstone rose, the Irish member John Dillon also rose and moved that Gladstone not be heard, an act resulting in his being "named" by the Speaker.[13] Dillon refused to leave until at last five messengers came in, a number apparently sufficient to induce him to depart on his own volition. Gladstone attempted to start again, but this time O'Donoghue interrupted. He was not heard, however, so Parnell stood up and moved that Gladstone be no longer heard. Parnell was named and suspended by a vote of 405 to 7. In this vote the Irish violated Commons' rules by refusing to leave their seats for the division. Gladstone therefore moved that the members were in contempt, a motion that was interrupted by another call that Gladstone not be heard, followed by another division in which the Irish did not leave their seats. At this point, Gladstone began to weary of the game and called for the removal of the members en bloc. But even this did not eliminate delay: as the Speaker called each member, they refused to leave until superior force made refusal impossible. In all, 36 members were suspended (Lyons 1977, 146).

With the obstructive Irish members suspended, Gladstone was able to continue with the proposals for procedural reform. Redlich goes too far in saying that the new rules made the Speaker a dictator (Redlich 1908, I.164), but they did go quite far, allowing a minister of the Crown to move that a particular bill, motion, or question was urgent (hence the name "urgency motions"). Urgency motions were not subject to debate, amendment, or a motion for adjournment, thus removing much of the potential for obstruction. If sustained in the motion by the Commons, debate would proceed under rules to be determined by the Speaker. Redlich notes that while the Conservative opposition did introduce some alterations, the vote (with the exception of the Irish Nationalists and the Radical member J. Cowen) was essentially unanimous.

I cannot say that reading about these events filled my heart with glee. It seems to stand in complete contradiction of the theory presented in chapter 2. Exceptionally small minorities, exceptionally large majorities (at least on the issue of obstruction), no party division—and yet we still see obstruction and procedural steps to limit that obstruction. And this on the well-known high point in the history of British parliamentary procedure!

But a closer look at the resolution passed by the Commons reveals that there is much less here than meets the eye. True, urgency did enable the Government to set the agenda, but the resolution as passed required (in the convoluted language necessary in a legislature where a quorum is 40 members) that if it appeared to the Speaker that the Nays "had it," he could not be challenged, but if he perceived otherwise, then

> "a division may be forthwith taken, and if the question be resolved in the affirmative by a majority of not less than *three to one*, in a House of not less than 300 members, the powers of the House for the regulation of its business upon the several stages of bills, and upon motions and all other matters shall be and remain with the Speaker, for the purpose of proceedings with such bill, motion, or other question, until the Speaker shall declare that the state of public business is no longer urgent, or until the House shall determine, upon a motion which, after notice given, may be made by any member, put without amendment, adjournment or debate, and decided by a majority." (Quoted in Redlich 1908, I.164; emphasis added)

In the entire history from the First Reform Act (1832) on, the House has seen a majority capable of utilizing this procedure only once: in 1931, when a coalition of parties was able to hold 84.9 percent of the seats. The requirement that

300 individuals (almost half the House) be present prevented any chance of a sneak attack by the majority. As a result, the only case where the resolution might be of use would be those involving, not surprisingly, Irish obstruction-ists, who never captured a quarter of the Commons. Yet even this level of security was apparently not enough for members of the Opposition, who added an "escape clause" allowing a simple majority to negate urgency (Redlich 1908, I.164–65). Speaker Brand's ruling was thus clearly not the end of obstruction, as some have argued.[14]

The new rules required that the Speaker set the rules under which ur-gency motions would be considered, and the Speaker announced those rules on February 4. These were apparently not enough to stop obstruction, because six additional rules were added on February 9. "In spite of these provisions, as experienced parliamentarians had prophesied, the Coercion bill was ob-structed with as much success as ever . . . " (Redlich 1908, I.166).

Undoubtedly frustrated, the Speaker produced three new rules that in essence constituted the procedure that came to be known as the "guillotine." These rules would have the effect of setting a definite limit to consideration of a bill, obstruction or no. This apparently cut too close to the bone, for Redlich notes that the new rules were not "well received" in either the press or the Commons (Redlich 1908, I.167). Indeed, Cowen, the Radical member who had refused to go along with Gladstone's original proposal, did not see why the proposed rules stopped where they did, and he informed the House of his intention to move that whenever government bills were declared urgent, they should be voted on without any discussion whatsoever (Redlich 1908, I.167). All of these criticisms occurred despite the fact that the three-quarters rule would still apply to the guillotine. With these rules in place, closure was authorized for the first time by an urgency rule on February 23, and on February 25 the Coercion Bill passed, followed by the Arms Bill on March 21, 1881.

Further changes in procedure would not be seen until early 1882. For on April 7 Gladstone introduced a new Land Bill. The Home Rulers were divided on the bill, some wishing to amend and hopefully improve the measure, while others simply wanted to exert every effort to kill it. A policy was formulated that would give something to both sides: the party would first attempt amend-ment, and thereafter pursue defeat. The Irish forces did work toward amend-ment, but as Lyons (1977, 161) notes, refraining from combat "obscured" Parnell's reputation as a parliamentary firebrand. To help that reputation along a bit (and to have political capital for solidifying forces at home), Parnell picked a fight with the Speaker, and on August 1, 1881, was duly suspended (about which more later).

Back in Ireland on August 2, Parnell made a number of speeches throughout the country urging tenants not to avail themselves of the possibilities for rent reduction in the Land Act until the Land League could select some test cases to see how the system would work. This heightened the concerns of Gladstone's advisers, who were considering action against Parnell. Parnell only made things more difficult by continuing to denounce the government in exceptionally harsh terms, including referring to Gladstone as a "masquerading knight-errant, this pretending champion of the rights of every other nation except those of the Irish nation" who ruled Ireland "with no moral force behind him" (Lyons 1977, 167, 168). The government responded in October 1881 by taking the extraordinary step of arresting Parnell and other Irish leaders under the terms of the Coercion Act and placing them in Kilmainham Gaol.

The House of Commons did not suspend its sitting, however. Perhaps buttressing his position, Gladstone in early February made two significant speeches broadly suggesting the possibility of Home Rule for Ireland, this at a time when tensions were rather high between the Liberals and the Home Rulers. Four days after the second of these speeches, on February 20, 1882, Gladstone once more took up the issue of procedural change in the Commons.

After recognizing that the three-fourths resolution passed by the Commons did not deal as serious a blow to my theory as I had anticipated, I thought to myself, "how long until the reduction to a simple majority?" Not, as it turns out, very long. Gladstone proposed to introduce closure as a permanent institution, and to allow votes on closure to be determined by precisely the simple majority vote one would expect from the theory. This was a radical departure from the three-fourths rule adopted previously, and thoroughly consistent with the view that small majorities enact such changes. The response was just as predictable: the measure attracted the sort of fighting along party lines that we would expect, as well as some dissent from the Radical wing of the Liberal party.

It is important to dwell on these changes in comparison to the much more publicized act of Speaker Brand and the subsequent pyrotechnics surrounding Parnell. Having established a precedent for closure, Gladstone now intended to turn it into a weapon of the majority. This was consistent with his previous position—he had after all wished to retain control of obstruction in the hands of the majority all along—but it also suggests exactly the sort of majoritarian calculations suggested by our theory.

Gladstone, however, still had an opposition to fight, and in doing so he made two arguments. The first was that, while he would also be opposed to the limitation of debate without qualifications, merely having the rule on the books would be sufficient to significantly shorten debate. The second, less persuasive (if such a thing is possible), was that in the House of Commons, a misuse of power was inconceivable. The two are of course a bit at odds: the first says the procedure would never be used, while the second says it will be used wisely. Despite this, Gladstone was able to achieve a victory of sorts by defeating Marriot's amendment that the House would not tolerate closure on the basis of a simple majority. His margin of victory, however, was a scant 39 votes, showing precisely how thin his procedural majority had become. While this vote did reveal a commitment on the part of Liberal forces to a majority vote, final action on the rules was not reached, and the session closed without reform.

In the meantime, delicate negotiations were going on between the Parnell forces and the Gladstone Cabinet (involving numerous individuals including both the O'Sheas) for the release of the jailed members. These negotiations produced what has come to be known as the Kilmainham Treaty. In return for release from prison, moderation on future Coercion Acts, and an extension of the Land Act to cover those individuals who were behind in their rents, Parnell agreed that the agitation he had engaged in before being arrested would stop and that he would work with the Liberals on Irish issues (which, according to Kee 1972b, 86, meant home rule).

The hopes raised by this agreement, however, were dashed just four days later when Lord Frederick Cavendish and T. H. Burke, the Undersecretary, were killed by members of an Irish secret society known as the Invincibles. The murders called forth demands for a new Coercion Bill, placing Parnell in a difficult spot. He would necessarily be required to oppose the bill, but by delaying too much he might endanger the Arrears Act that was part of his payoff in the Kilmainham Treaty. Parnell therefore communicated through third parties to Gladstone that he was in a difficult position, caught between the government and the secret societies, but that the Irish would oppose the bill on "honest parliamentary lines" (that is, no obstruction) if a set of Irish amendments were adopted (Hammond 1938, 295).

This offer was rejected. Gladstone's advisers, able to compete with their boss in tossing out contradictory rationales, felt that the Irish were looking for an excuse to fold and that concessions would only embolden them. As a result, obstruction started up again and on July 1, after 28 hours in continuous session, 25 Irish members were suspended. They apparently withdrew "in disgust" after this event and were not present to vote on the Coercion Bill, which passed within two weeks (Hammond 1938, 294, fn.1; Lyons 1977, 225). The Arrears Bill followed soon thereafter.

Since the House did not act on Gladstone's proposals for procedural reform in the preceding session, Parliament was called together again on October 24, 1882, to meet exclusively on this topic. The proposed changes in procedure were similar in their antiobstructive tone to those considered earlier. The government would acquire the right to go into Committee of Supply on any day. Urgency would be included as part of the standing rules, and the Speaker would be allowed to rule dilatory motions out of order if he considered them to be an abuse of the procedures of the House. The changes also limited the ability to use the motion to adjourn for purposes of delay and gave the Chair the ability to dispense with divisions if requested by fewer than 20 members (Redlich 1908, I.171–73).

Consideration of these proposals was highly contentious. "The session lasted six weeks, and the work of procedure reform was only accomplished after a long and bitter struggle" (Redlich 1908, I.170). In that struggle, Gladstone fought off an attempt to raise the requirement on closure from a simple majority to two-thirds. His effort to defeat this guarantee of minority rights succeeded by a vote of 322 to 238 (57.8 percent of the vote, reflecting 49.4 percent of the House).

What of the Irish? As it turns out, they supported the reforms (Redlich 1908, I.171–72). A few weeks before the session began, Parnell sent a proposal through Katherine O'Shea to Gladstone suggesting a link between procedural reform and Irish issues: "if he were assured that this programme were likely to meet the views of the Government, he would feel justified in urging his party to support the Closure and other proposals of the Government" (Hammond 1938, 309). Gladstone's response did not give Parnell what he wanted, but it did make an overture toward Home Rule.

No doubt the Irish members were more impressed by the argument Gladstone made in the middle of the struggle over the voting requirement for closure:

> "On the 8th of November, Mr. Gladstone replied to his assailants in a very effective speech. He ridiculed the idea that the closure would be the death-knell of parliamentary freedom, and pointed out that the country had for a long time been demanding more work from the House: he warned the Irish that the great reforms they desired could only be achieved by means of a radical improvement in the method of work adopted by the House." (Quoted in Redlich 1908, I.171)[15]

In the context in which this remark was made, it could hardly be misinterpreted: continue to bloc cloture, and you can wave your policies goodbye.

The debates on procedure coincided with a particularly difficult time for Gladstone, so difficult in fact that he seriously considered stepping down: "It would be of no good to anyone that I should remain on the stage like a half-exhausted singer, whose notes are flat, and everyone perceives it except himself" (Hammond 1938, 328). In terms of procedural changes in the legislature, nothing more was accomplished. Parnell's interest during this period was primarily in seeing which of the two parties would grant him the largest concessions. Nonetheless, the final years of Gladstone's term were not without incident: the Third Reform Act, reducing restrictions on voting, was passed.

With a defeat on the government's plan to tax beer and spirits but not wine, Gladstone was toppled, and the Conservatives under Lord Salisbury formed a caretaker government.[16]

The first election under the new Reform Act resulted in a Commons balanced between Liberals on the one hand and Irish and Conservatives on the other, thus giving the Liberals a plurality of only 47.6 percent. In part this was a result of an accord reached between Parnell and the Conservatives about Irish legislation. Parnell's part of the bargain was to urge his followers to vote Conservative in the election. This he did, including references to the Liberal Party as "perfidious, treacherous and incompetent" (Lyons 1977, 302).

Since no party had emerged with a majority, the Salisbury government remained in power. A new scheme of procedural reform was apparently put forward only a few days before its short life ended on January 27, 1886 (Redlich 1908, I.175). After publicly committing to Home Rule in the "Hawarden Kite," Gladstone was able with the votes of Irish Nationalists (and despite 18 defections among the Liberals), to form a new government. Following soon after, on February 22, Gladstone made a proposal to reform the rules.

> The motion met with complete approval from the other side of the House. It is well worthy of note that both Mr. Gladstone and the leader of the Opposition laid it down that reform of procedure had passed beyond the stage of being concerned with punishment or discipline, that it had long ceased to be a party question and had become a technical problem to be solved by the united efforts of all parties in the House. (Redlich 1908, I.176)

The Committee reported on June 10, a bit too late since two days earlier the Gladstone government had been defeated on the second reading of the Home Rule bill by a coalition of Liberal Unionists and Conservatives. By July 17, the election was over, and the Conservatives would be back in power.

1887 to 1905: The Balfour Reforms[17]

While Conservatives were able to form a new Government, they were able to do so only with the assistance of a full 77 Liberal Unionists (Bulmer-Thomas 1965, I.142). The return of the Liberal Unionists after the defeat of Home Rule was made significantly easier by a Conservative pledge that Liberal Unionists who had voted against Home Rule would not be contested by Conservative candidates. The degree to which that restraint bound Liberal Unionists is hard to say; there appears to have been no agreement that this state of electoral cooperation was to remain permanent.

The Conservatives planned to introduce a new Coercion Bill during this session, which of course raised the threat of Irish obstructionism. Consequently in late February 1887 the House took up a number of antiobstructive devices. Despite Gladstone's claim of a year ago that procedure had become a merely technical issue rising above party politics, the debate was predictably partisan given the content.

Much of the concern of these new rules was the limitation of the power of the Speaker. A short time before the dissolution of the House of Commons, Peel had resigned as Speaker. An election was held in which the Liberals nominated Gully, who won over the Conservative candidate by an 11 vote margin. This result provoked the outrage of Conservative members such as Salisbury, who observed that "ever since John Russell carried the chair by storm in 1835, every Speaker has resigned at a moment when his party was in a majority: and consequently each successive Speaker has been a Liberal" (cited in Bulmer-Thomas 1965, I.156). This accounts for the extraordinary step taken by the Conservatives, apparently in violation of tradition, to run a candidate in opposition to Gully in his constituency of Carlisle (Redlich 1908, II.133). If the Speaker is partisan, why should he be treated with electoral kindness?

Even more importantly for our discussion, with Speaker Gully in the chair, Conservatives could not be completely certain of the outcome of deliberations on the Irish Coercion Bill. The appropriate response was to alter the rules in such a way as to prevent the Speaker from following in Brand's footsteps by taking a decisive role in shaping procedure. In fairness, the Conservatives did allow the Speaker to decide whether to put forward a motion for closure by an individual member. But this provision was without real effect: if the Speaker refused the majority's request, maintaining the appearance of nonpartisanship would be difficult (and probably only lead to calls for the Speaker to step down), while agreeing to put forward the majority's request meant that this stage of the process would be innocuous. Neither path seemed particularly appealing, and Gladstone criticized the new rule and the burdens it would create, burdens Gladstone considered "alien to his [the Speaker's] office" (Redlich 1908, I.179). Others recognized the difficulties as well: "Mr. Whitbread pointed out that, as the enforcement of the closure would always take place on the request of the majority, the consent of the Speaker would inevitably make him appear a tool of the Government of the day" (Redlich 1908, I.178). The older procedure had avoided this since initiation was solely by the Speaker, and even though the context may have appeared, to those of a suspicious cast, partisan (as in Brand's ruling in 1881), propriety was still observed in form. The new procedure would eliminate that entirely.

Other changes were more significant. Under the proposed rules, a motion of closure could be made by any member, rather than the Speaker as the rules had required. Also proposed was the use of the guillotine to limit time on consideration. It may be recalled that the guillotine had already been authorized, but only as one of a set of procedures to be used by the Speaker for guiding business under closure. The norms of the House of Commons require that the Speaker remain above party politics, a position that is given a little more substance than a similar announcement would receive in the House of Representatives by the fact that on numerous occasions the Speaker *was* a member of the minority party.

This debate over procedure seems to have reenergized Parnell. Fellow Irish M.P. Healy wrote that not "since his earlier struggles has Mr Parnell developed more energy or watchfulness than he is showing now, throwing himself into the discussion of every technicality as if he were as friendless and unsupported as in the days when everything depended on his single arm" (quoted in Lyons 1977, 374). Some of the amendments the Irish proposed for limiting the operation of closure were truly remarkable (and quite obstructive). One suggested that closure not be allowed on legislation for "increasing the severity of criminal law in Ireland" (Redlich 1908, I.179), which was after all the whole purpose of the exercise. Another would prohibit supply bills from gaining closure, or proposals to change procedure (which would of course make it possible to infinitely postpone the proceedings that the Irish members were attempting to infinitely postpone).

My own favorite Irish innovation, though perhaps the interpretation is too cynical, called for closure to be invoked only after four members in opposition had been heard. This sounds eminently reasonable, but it would theoretically enable the Irish members to obstruct in perpetuity simply by never going above four members in opposition. Even if this proved too much a strain on the members so chosen, nothing prevented the Irish from presenting themselves as "supporters" of the bill, offering friendly amendment after friendly amendment, and pointing out that as four opponents had not yet been heard, closure could not be invoked. Of course, if I could see through this ploy, so could the majority, and the amendment was rejected. (One amendment, calling on the Speaker to refuse to allow the proposal for closure if he felt it to be an infringement on minority rights, did pass. This too was an artful amendment: if it failed due to Conservative votes, it would be tantamount to a Conservative admission that they were in fact perpetrating a gag rule.)

These rules passed, as Redlich notes, by a rather large majority of 221, although he does not note the party breakdown or the abstentions (Redlich 1908, I.179). Buxton, managing in 1892 to write an entire piece about obstruction without once using the word "Irish," assures us that the rules adopted in 1887 have struck at the root of obstruction, and by limiting the hours of sitting, have put an end to the system under which it was physically impossible for members satisfactorily to carry on the business of the nation. (149)

With the passage of these reforms, work could begin on the new Coercion Bill. But once more, "the prophecies of many of the experts on parliamentary procedure were verified; it was found that closure was no satisfactory protection against relevant obstruction of the kind developed by the Irish under Mr. Parnell's leadership" (Redlich 1908, I.180). After 35 sittings on the Coercion bill, the government proposed a guillotine measure. This passed (after discussion on the new procedure received closure) by a vote of 245 to 93. Here we do know something of the vote, or at least of the parliamentary strategy of the opposition: Bulmer-Thomas reports that "when the guillotine was employed on the report stage of the Criminal Law Amendment bill, the Liberals withdrew from the chamber and the Irish Nationalists disdainfully looked down from the gallery" (I.148). This helps us understand the lopsided character of the vote. "Slowly and inexorably the Criminal Law Amendment Bill ground its way through parliament in the teeth of Parnellite obstruction, becoming law by mid-July" (Lyons 1977, 378).

The remainder of the Unionist time was uneventful as far as procedural reforms went. A Select Committee under the Marquis of Hartington was appointed in 1888 to consider procedure on estimates, but Redlich reports that only "trifling suggestions for reform" were forthcoming (Redlich 1908, I.187). May (1893, 301) does cite a precedent from July 31, 1888, positing that the chair can put the question if it appears that dilatory motions are being utilized.

This brings us, however, to December 24, 1889, the day that Captain O'Shea filed divorce papers and Katherine O'Shea's relationship with Parnell became public knowledge. There is considerable evidence that Captain O'Shea was quite aware of their relationship and in all likelihood had suggested their initial liaison as a way to advance his political career (Lyons 1977, 151). Financial troubles, the death of Katherine's rich aunt and a likely contestation of her will, prompted O'Shea's actions after roughly ten years of silence.[18] The case did not reach trial until fall of 1890, however, and in the meantime Parnell and other Irish obstructionists scuttled Balfour's land bill, introduced in April 1890 (Lyons 1977, 436).

These comments provide the context in which Mr. Goschen's Committee on procedure met, the final Select Committee to be assembled in the century. The committee was charged in Redlich's terms "to inquire whether by means of an abridged form of procedure, or otherwise, the consideration of bills partly considered in the House could be facilitated in the next ensuing session of the same Parliament" (Redlich 1908, I.186). By this point of course we can more readily understand what such language entails. The Committee considered various ways of carrying over legislation. The solution finally settled on was to allow a resolution carrying over legislation. This was "only adopted in the committee after a close division, and was strongly opposed by a minority headed by Mr. Gladstone" (Redlich 1908, I.187). In the House, the measure was to be rejected, not because of any great respect for minority rights, but rather because of concerns that the adoption of such a procedure would inspire the House of Lords to follow suit. If the Lords could carry over legislation from session to session, it was felt, then they would be able to permanently delay measures passed by the Commons.

Parnell, however, had enough troubles. The scandal raised by O'Shea's revelations (especially given that Parnell was the Protestant representative of a Roman Catholic country) set the wheel of decline in motion, and on December 1 1890, the Irish Nationalists gathered in Committee Room Fifteen of the House of Commons. Obstructionist to the end, Parnell asked for delays (which no doubt would give him time to shore up his support back in Ireland). But Parnell wasn't the only Irish member schooled in the strategy of obstruction, and the majority withdrew in an act that split the party. Parnell would die less than a year after, on October 11, ostensibly of rheumatic fever, and was placed in a lead casket contained within a wooden casing, a burial arrangement that fueled speculations that the coffin had been filled with rocks and that Parnell was still alive (Lyons 1977, 601–3). (One individual even claimed to have seen and heard Parnell—appropriately enough at a performance of Wagner's *Götterdämmerung*.)

Politics, as always, went on, and the scandal surrounding Parnell reduced the expected Liberal majority in 1892. This is not quite surprising if the sermon of one priest is typical: he warned parishioners that Parnellism

> "is a simple love of adultery and all those who profess Parnellism profess to love and admire adultery . . . beware of these Parnellites when they enter your house, you that have wives and daughters, for they will do all they can to commit these adulteries, for their cause is not patriotism—it is adultery—and they back Parnellism because it gratifies their adultery." (Quoted in Kee 1972b, 117)

So much for negative campaigning being a by-product of television.

Although Conservatives maintained a plurality, the coalition of Irish Nationalists and the Liberal Party produced a small majority of 52.9 percent (Bulmer-Thomas 1965, I.150).[19] On the agenda was Home Rule, the issue that had split Liberal Unionists from the party in 1886. The possibility of enactment was sufficiently remote while Great Britain still had a House of Lords, but this did not prevent vigorous debate on the bill. In a speech in Belfast reported in the *Times*, Balfour, then in the minority, stated,

"I do not come here to preach any doctrines of passive obedience or non-resistance. You have had to fight for your liberties before. I pray God you may never have to fight for them again. I do not believe you will ever have to fight for them, but I admit that the tyranny of majorities may be as bad as the tyranny of Kings and that the stupidity of majorities may be even greater than the stupidity of Kings . . . and I do not think any rational or sober man will say that what is justifiable against a tyrannical King may not under certain circumstances be justifiable against a tyrannical majority." (Quoted in Kee 1972b, 124)

A speech much less extreme than this one landed Parnell in Kilmainham Gaol. But, even more startling, speeches on majority tyranny sound fairly hollow from an individual who would soon engage in a systematic attempt to rout out the last vestiges of minority obstruction in the Commons.

Consideration of the 1893 Home Rule Bill would be quite prolonged. As Kee noted in his history of the era,

the 1893 Home Rule Bill eventually occupied more parliamentary time than any other bill in the history of the century—eighty-two days altogether compared with forty-seven for the Reform Bill. Four hundred and thirty-nine speeches were made for it in the Commons and nine hundred and thirty-eight against. (Kee 1972b, 124)

Given the length of consideration, it is interesting that none of the relevant sources I consulted—not Redlich 1908, I.189; not Bulmer-Thomas 1965, I.150; not Kee 1972b, 124; not even Hammond 1938, 692—stated that there was any obstruction on the bill. Hammond comes closest: "Such knowledge of the fate of a Bill [that is, that Home Rule was destined to be voted down in the House of Lords] has two effects. It takes the heart out of its supporters and it removes any vestige of scruple from its opponents." (692) All the sources I consulted were I believe aware of the number of speeches, and (at least judging from what I read) none (with the possible exception of Redlich) displayed any noticeable antipathy toward Irish obstructionism. On the contrary, a great deal of warmth and sympathy is shown. Somehow, a testament, however ill-placed, to Parnell's influence, the link between "Irish" and "obstruction" is easily made while obstruction by other parties is not. Perhaps Parnell was correct after all: when the Irish meddle in British affairs, it is considered obstruction.

The Second Home Rule Bill passed through the House by a small majority of 31 votes. Seven days later, on September 9, 1893, the House of Lords did what everyone knew it would do and defeated the bill by a vote of 419 to 41. Kee (1972b, 125) finds Gladstone worried about the small size of the majority in the Commons and as a result postponing the election. With Gladstone's resignation, however, a new general election was not long in coming, resulting in a new Conservative majority occupying 61.4 percent of the seats.

One of the first battles involved, strangely enough, the election of a Speaker. Conservatives, tired of a long string of Liberal Speakers, selected 1895 to make their case. Liberals, however, did not see things this way. No agreement between Liberals and Conservatives was worked out, and Bulmer-Thomas notes that "after a sharp contest the Liberal nominee, Gully, beat the Conservative by eleven votes" (I.156), a rather ominous and partisan way to start a session.

In subsequent sittings and even after the general election of 1900, Balfour continued to introduce a number of procedural changes designed to limit minority obstruction. Redlich's discussion of these changes takes up pages 189 to 203. It would be impossible to reproduce that discussion here, but a few highlights must be included. In 1896, Balfour proposed a revision to the procedure dealing with the Committee of Supply estimates that would in essence impose a guillotine by standing rule rather than require a motion (see the text of the rule in Redlich 1908, III.253). In debate, Balfour defended the measure in the following way:

> The modern generation's desire to speak, and the belief, which might perhaps be called an illusion, that the Opposition ought to hamper the Government programme to the full extent of its power, has led of late years to an enormous lengthening of debates in supply. . . . He anticipated the objection that the scheme would render certain the voting of large sections of supply without discussion, and answered that such was already the case; the new procedure [allowing consideration of most important votes first, regardless of the class into which they fell] would have the advantage of allowing many, if not all, of the important votes to come up before the "guillotine" came into action. Statistics showed [!] that twenty days was a fair assignment. (Redlich 1908, I.190)

Opposition to this plan came from the Irish, who called it a "muzzling order." But more important is Redlich's observation that "the most eminent financial experts of the Opposition . . . agreed in the main with Mr. Balfour's suggestions, save that the latter [Sir William Harcourt] spoke strongly against the application of the guillotine to supply" (Redlich 1908, I.191).

This procedure was adopted (by a vote of 202 to 65). Others followed over the years, including a reduction of the opportunities for debate (and thus obstruction) on the motion to go into the Committee, and the removal of the formal motion that the question be put (also the occasion of dilatory tactics).

In 1902 Balfour, striving "to give to the majority of the House of Commons a greater control over its own business and a greater control over the men who insult and outrage it" (Redlich 1908, I.193), proposed a series of procedural reforms. It being "long impossible, in the time allotted to the government by the rules, to accomplish even the most necessary legislative and administrative tasks" it was therefore "indispensable" that more time be allocated to government sittings (Redlich 1908, I.194). Note here how political decisions of the state now become "necessary legislative and administrative tasks" that must be carried out efficiently. The Clerk was to dispense with writing down the names of the minority asking for "frivolous" divisions, the Chair was to leave at the end of the session without question being put, penalties for disorderly members were to be increased, and the right to submit questions orally was to be limited. In the search for control, the new rules specified that sittings would commence at 2:00 P.M. and end at 7:15 but no later than 8:00, after which at 9:00 business would resume and continue to 12:00 or 1:00, this to occur on all days but Friday, which would be for the use of private members and extend from 12:00 P.M. to 6:00 P.M. Leading members of the Opposition, presented with this plan, referred to it as a "parliamentary railway time-table" (Redlich 1908, I.195). Indeed, that was precisely what it was.

One additional alteration provides perhaps the oddest entry in the entire list of proposed changes:

> The old traditional rule that money bills must be submitted to preliminary discussion in committee of the whole House was not actually to be abolished; but debate on the report of a resolution allowing the introduction of such a bill was to be forbidden, and the question that the House do agree with the committee in such resolution was to be put forthwith. (Redlich 1908, I.196)

I have read that paragraph a number of times and still cannot understand exactly how it does not abolish preliminary discussion of the resolution.

Half of the reforms proposed were adopted. Not adopted were the harsher sanctions against members (enthusiasm apparently vanishing when McKenna showed—by statistics!—that there was no need for it, few members having been sanctioned). Some of the proposals apparently went through without much delay, such as the changes in the schedule and a new method for introducing bills (the details of which Redlich is a bit sketchy on). The new restrictive supply rule passed by a vote of 222 to 138. Debate continued until nearly morning on the issue of printed questions to the government, but once the logjam broke, other procedural changes followed (although Redlich does not cite those numbers).

Another, more impressive procedural feat was being accomplished at this time, albeit without any change in the standing rules. Based on a little-known and seemingly insignificant precedent preventing members from bringing forward a motion "which anticipates a matter already set down or appointed for consideration by the house" (May 1893, 264), the practice of "blocking" emerged.[20] Private members were prohibited from even *introducing* issues to be taken up, giving the government the ability, as long as the topic remained to be addressed, of closing down all discussion on the matter. Redlich cites a case on June 22, 1904, in which a Liberal member wished to present an urgency motion for investigation of an epidemic of beriberi resulting (it was argued) from Chinese workers in South Africa. This was ruled out of order by the Deputy Speaker (another of Balfour's innovations) because the (highly contentious) topic of Chinese labor in the Transvaal had already been blocked out (Redlich 1908, I.205 fn1).

There is no need to assume either that the minority member who introduced the beriberi resolution did not understand what he was up to (artfully circumventing the limits placed on the minority) or that the Deputy Speaker was simply being ruthless (blocking after all was the accepted practice based on May). We need not miss the irony of a minority member proposing an urgency motion, or fail to sympathize with a poor Deputy Speaker who is probably wondering "what should I be doing here?" But none of this need distract our attention from the fact that the subject of these intricate parliamentary gambits is a rather mild minority right: the right simply to present a motion, a motion that could always be voted down.

Conclusions and Reconsiderations

The discussion of the period between the First Reform Act and the final Conservative government of 1905 has taken us through a number of twists and turns. But in looking over the evidence, a few points bear attention.

First, while the ability to initiate legislation may have diminished among members by the 1860s, the ability to alter the course of legislation through the act of obstruction had not. Members could use the power raised by obstruction to force policy concessions. And majorities could react to that obstruction. It is no mere fluke that Gladstone placed the Arrears Bill *after* the Coercion Bill: by doing so, he imposed a clear cost on those who would obstruct.

Second, contrary to the rough impressions of the period, the steps taken to limit minority rights were not driven exclusively by the desire to silence Irish members.[21] While Parnell's actions were clearly at the root of much of what is going on, it is difficult to understand the preoccupation with obstruction during those periods in which Parnell "behaved," or why Gladstone's proposals for reform would have met party-line resistance from Conservatives, or more importantly any of the antiobstructive efforts that took place before Parnell's arrival. This suggests that there may be a larger story to obstruction here than simply a Gaelic one and that a study of minority party strategies in the House of Commons from the perspective of this theory might enhance our understanding of the factors leading to the construction and dismantling of a system of minority rights.

Third, at least from 1832 to 1886, the steps taken to limit minority rights did seem to occur when the proportion of seats held by the majority party was small. When the majority was large, committees were not proposed, and the rules were left in place. These are, however, general statements regarding the link between majority party proportion and procedural change. On many occasions when we looked at the actual vote breakdowns, we failed to see the close votes typical in the House. Even more damaging, however, the relationship between majority party size and procedural change seems especially uneven during the Balfour years. In what follows, therefore, I wish to present some additional evidence regarding these two criticisms.

Small Minorities
How can the rather large number of lopsided divisions observed in the House be consistent with the theory of small majorities advanced in this book? Further analysis will be necessary to back up the claim I want to make, but I hope it is at least compelling enough to warrant a moment's reflection.

Making the argument requires that we know something about the method the Commons utilized in voting (Redlich 1908, II.235–36; May 1893, 341–43). Upon the call for a division, members would leave their seats and proceed to one of the two lobbies, the right if voting yes and the left if voting no. Two clerks in each lobby (one for letters A through M and the other for N through Z) would record the names of those individuals in the lobby as they passed. After having their votes recorded, members would then reenter the House, and two tellers (one from each party) at the door would count the number of those exiting from their particular lobby. Despite what appears to be a rather cumbersome process, Redlich assures that a division could be completed in about ten minutes or perhaps fifteen.

This would be true, Redlich notes, with the exception of situations in which there was an exceptionally small minority. In that case, the two tellers and the two clerks in one of the lobbies have little work to do (it not taking long to count seven people). But the tellers and clerks on the other side must (given a good turnout) record the names of almost the entire House, a process that could consume as much as thirty minutes. Sir Erskine May criticized these obstructive divisions in his testimony before Mr. Robert Lowe's Select Committee of 1871, and proposed that 21 individuals be the minimum required to demand a formal division, a result that would exclude small Irish minorities (Redlich 1908, I.107–8).

Consequently, even if one supports the obstructionists or simply wishes to frustrate the government, the best way to do so is not to vote with the obstructionists (and save the time of the clerks and tellers), but instead to vote against them and so increase the work and time required to take up a division. Such a vote would have been easy for Conservative members, who could simultaneously go on record against Irish obstruction while at the same time frustrating the wishes of the Liberal government (and the same logic works the other way as well). This is of course speculative, but it does suggest a reasonable explanation for why small minorities might be observed on divisions dealing with issues of obstruction.

Statistical Evidence on the Balfour Years

Was there a relationship between the size of the party and obstruction during the years after the Liberal split? The analysis presented suggests not: even with relatively large majorities, Balfour and the Conservative governments under Salisbury continued to make changes. But we cannot forget that Balfour did not exactly start de novo with the problem of obstruction. He had other devices, crafted by previous majorities, for dealing with the problems of delay. How were they used?

Some insights along these lines can be obtained thanks to a serendipitous change of political style. Members during this time (at least judging from Redlich's account) would frequently refer to statistics to support their claims. While some of these arguments were on target (the need for additional punishments), others were painfully naive. But we can be happy at this lack of sophistication, for it meant that members would simply produce the data and speculate. Nothing prevents us from doing the same.

Of the statistics presented, three are relevant to assessing the link between small majorities and obstruction in the Balfour era. The first is a count of the number of closure motions from 1887 to 1904 (Redlich 1908, III.54). If the theory is correct, then even in what I have been calling the Balfour years we should see the use of closure associated with small majorities. A second source of data involves urgency motions for adjournment over the same time period (Redlich 1908, II.252). The rules of the time set exceptionally tight limits on the use of this motion, but some obstruction was still possible, and there is variation in its use. If the theory is correct, then these motions should be associated with small majorities. The final source of data is the count of suspensions of members. The data here will cover only up to 1902; Redlich's source (McKenna; see Redlich 1908, I.201) did not include data for the 1902–4 period. Since suspensions were, as we have seen, generally the last straw in attempts to deal with obstruction, we should expect, if the theory is correct, that members would be suspended when the majority party was small.[22]

In terms of the independent variables, for the purposes of these tests, the proportion of seats controlled by the majority was taken from Craig except for the general election of 1892 (see note 19). I have also utilized a time trend to determine whether there was any secular increase or decrease in the use of any of these motions, as well as a dummy variable taking the value "1" if the coalition (or majority in power) contains the Conservatives, allowing me to determine whether there were any partisan differences in the use of these procedures.

A final independent variable needs a bit more explanation. In his analysis of the use of the guillotine procedure in the French National Assembly, Huber (1992) found that as the time to the end of the session diminished, there was a greater tendency to use the guillotine. Since the British electoral calendar runs on a five year clock, the closer to five years there has been since the last General Election, the greater the electoral pressure on the party, and consequently (one could argue) the greater willingness to push through legislation over any attempts at obstruction. An exhaustive analysis of the British case would of course attempt to separate out when the next regularly scheduled election would be from when the next anticipated election could be. In the absence of a reliable measure of that variable, I have simply used the time until the next regularly scheduled election as a proxy. (Those still bothered by the uncertainty about the timing of elections can simply substitute in "years since the last election," which would count 1,2,3,4,5 instead of 5,4,3,2,1. The substantive implications will be identical.)

Closure Motions

Josef Redlich refers to the motion to invoke closure in the Commons as one of the "weapons in the arsenal of an impatient majority" (Redlich 1908, III.196). How then were these weapons used?

While the data is technically in the form of a count, the large number of two-digit observations suggests that a Poisson regression (as I have used elsewhere) is not appropriate. I estimated the equations using generalized least squares (again, for robust standard errors) with corrections for first-order autocorrelation where appropriate.

Column 1 of table 8.1 presents the results from a simple regression of closure motions on a constant and the proportion of seats held by the majority party, corrected for first-order autocorrelation. Those results show that party proportion has the expected negative sign and is statistically significant at the .10 level. This result is stable even if one controls for the possibility of secular increase as well as for the number of years until the next regularly scheduled election, as columns 2 and 3 show. It is only when one controls for party (column 4) that the proportion variable loses its significance—but then, in that equation, nothing is significant.[23]

I could of course say that three out of four is hardly poor. But the results

**TABLE 8.1. Initial GLS Regression of Closure Motions,
House of Commons, 1887–1904**

Independent Variables	(1)	(2)	(3)	(4)
Constant	315.171**	321.614**	275.817*	263.752#
	(132.594)	(142.953)	(132.043)	(183.691)
Majority proportion	−4.320*	−4.457*	−3.863*	−3.332
(Craig)	(2.228)	(2.456)	(2.173)	(3.454)
Time		0.170		
		(0.682)		
Years until next regularly			3.931	
scheduled election			(3.967)	
Conservative				−8.111
				(29.171)
Number of observations	18	18	18	18
Corrected R-squared	0.27	0.22	0.24	0.22
Standard error of				
regression	32.551	33.592	33.154	33.582
Rho	−0.380	−0.379	−0.399	−0.379
Mean of dependent				
variable	60.667	60.667	60.667	60.667

#significant at the 10 percent level, one-tailed test
*significant at the 10 percent level, two-tailed test
**significant at the 5 percent level, two-tailed test

seem to suggest that there is a specification problem involved. A look at the
scatterplot of proximity of elections and closure motions made the elusive
relationship clear. Table 8.2 sets out the data, which reveals a nonlinear
relationship between time before the next election and closure motions. In

**TABLE 8.2. Closure Motions by Majority Size and Proximity of Election,
House of Commons, 1887–1904**

Years Before Election	1887–91 (Salisbury) (58.7)	1892–94 (Gladstone-Roseberry) (52.9)	1895–99 (Salisbury) (61.4)	1899–1904 (Salisbury-Balfour) (60)
5	37	49	29	23
4	84	168	99	82
3	43	36	75	96
2	87	—	23	20
1	39	—	33	69

TABLE 8.3. GLS Regression of Closure Motions, House of Commons, 1887–1904

Independent Variables	(1)	(2)
Constant	201.240#	215.991**
	(116.097)	(95.877)
Majority proportion (Craig)	−3.750#	−4.036**
	(2.179)	(1.700)
Years until next regularly scheduled election	61.460***	61.507***
	(15.022)	(15.073)
Years until next regularly scheduled election, squared	−9.463***	−9.464***
	(2.569)	(2.566)
Conservative	−2.3925	
	(20.143)	
Number of observations	18	18
Corrected R-squared	0.40	0.44
Standard error of regression	29.490	28.421
Rho	−0.517	−0.518
Mean of dependent variable	60.667	60.667

#significant at the 10 percent level, one-tailed test
*significant at the 10 percent level, two-tailed test
**significant at the 5 percent level, two-tailed test
***significant at the 1 percent level, two-tailed test

general, early years see few closure motions. In the middle years, however, their use increases quite rapidly. In the final years, they drop again.

To determine the possible effects of this nonlinear relationship, I included a squared term for the number of years before the next regularly scheduled election.[24] Table 8.3 presents the results for this new specification, with results again corrected for first-order autocorrelation. Column 1 indicates that with the correction for the nonlinear impact of elections, proportion has the expected sign and is statistically significant, even when one introduces a control for party differences (the Conservative term). The results suggest that if anything Conservatives used the closure procedure less than Liberals in the Balfour era, but the exceptionally high standard error hardly makes this claim worthwhile.

In general, it is not a good idea to drop variables if they are correlated with the undropped variables, even in the case where they are not found to be significant, due to the problem of omitted variable bias. In this case, therefore, dropping the insignificant term on the dummy variable for the Conservative party may induce bias given that party is correlated in this era with party size (Gladstone's administration had the smallest majority in the entire era and was also the only Liberal government.) While I am content with these results, I risked possible bias by reestimated the model in column 1 dropping the dummy variable for Conservative administrations. The coefficients (as one can see from column 2) change very slightly. But this second, simpler equation has a smaller standard error of the regression than the model estimated in column 1. Furthermore (important for this discussion) the sign on the proportion of seats held by the majority party is still negative (conforming to the theory) and is now statistically significant at the .05 level (two-tailed test). Knowing just two facts, then—the size of the majority and the number of years until the next regularly scheduled election—we can do a reasonable job in predicting (or better, postdicting) the number of closure motions that we will observe in that year.

This story is much too simple of course—all the interesting things are in the error term, I am sure—but if the analysis holds up in the face of a richer understanding, two facts emerge regarding the use of closure rules in the late–nineteenth century House of Commons. First, the use of these procedures was affected by electoral calculations, but in a slightly complicated way. We do not see a linear increase or decrease in the use of this device. Instead, the use of closure peaks toward the middle of the electoral cycle, a bit over three years before the next regularly scheduled election.[25]

Second, the results make it clear that the size of the majority is an important variable in explaining the use of restrictive procedures to eliminate obstruction during the Balfour years. When the size of the majority party diminishes, then, consistent with the theory, we tend to see the greatest number of motions for closure. .

Urgency Motions for Adjournment

The motion to adjourn was one tactic through which members of the Commons could derail the government's agenda. Redlich devotes pages 248 to 252 of his second volume to tracing out the history of the limitation in this right. Numerous conditions had to be satisfied before such a motion could take place: motions must be submitted in writing at the start of the afternoon session; 40 members must support the motion unless leave of the house is given; the motion cannot be used to make in order subjects that wouldn't normally be in order, such as "blocked" legislation; the urgency motion for adjournment cannot be moved again on a matter that has already been the subject of such a motion; only one motion would be allowed per sitting.

This imposing list of qualifications does not even exhaust the procedure. Of the many remaining conditions, the most important was the right given the Speaker to determine whether the urgency motion for adjournment was in order. This, however, appears to open a bit of room for minority rights:

On the whole the Speaker's practice in exercising his discretion has leant towards favouring the minority; he has never forgotten that the opportunity of moving the adjournment is an indispensable expedient of party tactics now only available in a much weaker form than in earlier days. (Redlich 1908, II.251)

The image one gets, therefore, is of an obstructive practice that is exceptionally hemmed in, although still able to be invoked in a nostalgically dilatory way once in a while. All of this is watched over by an indulgent and impartial chair. Of course the minority must be careful: "Any attempt to turn them [urgency motions for adjournment] into engines of obstruction would be met at once by the Speaker's absolute refusal to allow them to be moved" (Redlich 1908, II.152).

Despite the impression this laundry list of constraints conveys, there were in fact a number of urgency motions for adjournment that were made in each session. As a result, Poisson regression again did not seem appropriate, and so I utilized ordinary least squares with robust standard errors, corrected for the presence of first-order autocorrelation. Column 1 of table 8.4 shows that the proportion of seats held by the majority party has the expected sign and is mildly significant. Column 2 includes the nonlinear electoral effect,

TABLE 8.4.   GLS Regression, Urgency Motions for Adjournment, House of Commons, 1887–1904

Independent Variables	(1)	(2)	(3)	(4)
Constant	35.315*	23.790#	54.8935***	83.687***
	(19.700)	(14.243)	(16.871)	(18.366)
Majority proportion (Craig)	−0.477#	−0.427*	−1.031***	−1.621***
	(0.329)	(0.238)	(0.322)	(0.374)
Years until next regularly scheduled election		6.139**	6.251**	6.659***
		(2.305)	(2.231)	(1.934)
Years until next regularly scheduled election, squared		−0.918**	−0.924**	−0.952**
		(0.411)	(0.387)	(0.3325)
Conservative			5.035#	8.707**
			(2.946)	(2.979)
Time				0.200**
				(0.071)
Number of observations	18	18	18	18
Corrected R-squared	0.13	0.16	0.19	0.26
Standard error of regression	4.048	3.978	3.919	3.738
Rho	−0.292	−0.434	−0.446	−0.517
Mean of dependent variable	7.278	7.278	7.278	7.278

#significant at the 10 percent level, one-tailed test
*significant at the 10 percent level, two-tailed test
**significant at the 5 percent level, two-tailed test
***significant at the 1 percent level, two-tailed test

used above. These motions are most likely to occur when the majority party is small, an effect that is statistically significant. The nonlinear effect of the coming election is again clear and significant. Using calculus, the peak of motions for adjournment occurs a bit more than three years before the next regularly scheduled election.[26] Column 3, however, shows that we are not to have a perfect replication of the results on closure motions. Conservative administrations tend to see a greater use of these obstructive procedures than Liberal governments. Since the only Liberal administration in the Balfour era had the assistance of the Irish Nationalists in passing the Second Home Rule Bill, it could well be that these results are specific to the historical period (which, we must remember, does *not* make them unimportant).

Column 4 adds a control for a secular increase in the use of the procedure. We might expect this time variable to be positive, for example, if as a result of Balfour's reforms, members of the minority were forced to rely more and more on the one tactic available to them. The time trend is significant and positive: from 1887 to 1904, we would witness an increase of three to four urgency motions. By contrast, an increase in the size of the majority from Gladstone's proportion of 52.9 to the 61.4 percent of the subsequent Salisbury administration decreases the number of urgency motions by a total of roughly 14 motions. If a suitably small minority could be assembled to guarantee a half hour consumption of time in division, this would work out to over seven hours of legislative time, or roughly a day's work, that would be used up, not counting any other incidental uses of time (and this is only on a single procedure).

Suspension of Members

Suspension of members constitutes the most severe of the antiobstructive devices that could be used. For suspension is an admission that things have proceeded to the point where words must give way to force. The majority must, like Cicero in the Catiline conspiracy, "call in the troops." By doing so, of course, we are not simply depriving an obstructionist of the opportunity to practice his trade. We are also punishing the obstructionist's constituency, who are being denied representation in the legislature through no fault of their own.

Suspension is, however, also a recognition that procedures do, at least at some level, require the willingness of members to play within the rules. This should not be taken in a normative sense: I am not saying that the mere existence of a procedure means that people are morally obligated to "play within the rules." Even holding that position becomes a bit complex when the rules are changing, when the meaning of "playing within the rules" is a function of "how you have played the game so far." Instead, I merely make the observation that a member who stood before the legislature and set fire to every parliamentary document used, while being a clear obstructionist, would leave legislatures little room for procedural refinement. What could one do, after all—write a procedure saying do not burn up any more bills and resolutions—especially this one?

Suspensions are rare events, even in the British House of Commons in the Balfour years. The high point occurs in 1901, when 12 members were suspended:

> A vote on account of more than £17,000,000 was under discussion, and about midnight the Prime Minister moved the closure: the Irish members, who had not as yet been able to join in the discussion resented the proposal so strongly that they refused to leave their places for the division, thus committing an act of disorder; the Speaker was summoned, and, on the continued refusal of the refractory members to comply with the rules, he named twelve of them: Mr. Balfour moved that they be suspended. On this motion being carried they refused to obey the order to leave the House, and one after the other they were removed by the Serjeant-at-arms and his assistants. (Redlich 1908, I.192)

Suspensions, therefore, are not necessarily the result of a few anarchic crazies who set fire to resolutions. Sometimes the actions meriting suspension are themselves provoked by the actions of the majority, once again suggesting the need to take into account the ways majorities and minorities strategically interact. Since suspension, unlike the other two procedures considered above, is a fairly rare event, the appropriate method for estimation here is Poisson regression.

The 1901 suspensions discussed above are a clear outlier in the data (the next largest number of suspensions in a year is five). Interestingly enough, 1901 was also the year that Queen Victoria died. We might be inclined to write that off as a simple coincidence. But is that all it is? A quick check of dates revealed that the Queen died in January of that year and the Irish members were suspended on March 5. Victoria, despite the constitutional ban on the involvement of the sovereign in party politics, had openly aligned during the latter portion of her reign with Disraeli, the Conservative Prime Minister. Family differences in this case were also party differences, with the Prince of Wales (the future Edward VII) showing a clear preference for Gladstone and the Liberals (Bulmer-Thomas 1965, I.160). Could the suspensions be a signal to the new king that Liberals and their Irish sympathizers could expect no great kindness in the Commons? Without more evidence, it is hard to say, but since as much information is contained in the tag "Death of Queen Victoria" as in "1901," I have named the dummy variable in her honor.

Column 1 of table 8.5 presents the simplest model consistent with the

TABLE 8.5. Poisson Regression of Member Suspensions, House of Commons, 1887–1901

Independent Variables	(1)	(2)	(3)	(4)
Constant	−9.446	−16.208*	−14.054**	−11.910
	(7.6760)	(8.565)	(6.209)	(12.668)
Majority proportion	0.158	0.197#	0.198*	0.156
(Craig)	(0.131)	(0.113)	(0.103)	(0.2405)
The death of Queen Victoria	2.433***	1.967***	1.549***	1.522***
	(0.400)	(0.4965)	(0.342)	(0.381)
Years until next regularly		2.201	0.502*	0.502*
scheduled election		(1.761)	(0.272)	(0.267)
Years until next regularly		−0.245		
scheduled election, squared		(0.252)		
Four years from next			1.095*	1.102*
regularly scheduled election			(0.530)	(0.534)
Conservative				0.416
				(2.079)
Number of observations	15	15	15	15
Log-likelihood	4.963	7.960	9.173	9.193

#significant at the 10 percent level, one-tailed test
*significant at the 10 percent level, two-tailed test
**significant at the 5 percent level, two-tailed test
***significant at the 1 percent level, two-tailed test

theory while still accounting for the Victoria outlier. There is an unexpected (but not significant) positive sign on majority proportion, suggesting that as majorities get larger they suspend more individuals, but it is not significant.[27] The death of Queen Victoria in this equation, as in all the other equations to come, has a statistically significant and positive effect: when Victoria died, suspensions in the Commons increased (although our data does not extend much beyond the time of her death, and thus we cannot trace out the lasting impact of her demise on parliamentary politics).

Column 2 includes a nonlinear term for the influence of coming elections used in the previous section. The coefficient on majority party proportion now attains statistical significance, but it is the electoral calculations that drop out. This could suggest that suspensions are such an awesome step that the influence of elections does not enter into the decisions. On the other hand, it could simply mean that the specification I have chosen doesn't quite match the relationship in the data.

After looking at the observations a bit more closely, it seemed that the evidence for an *n*-shaped relationship between proximity of elections and suspensions did not hold up. In part this is due to the fact that the data as presented stop at 1901, so that the final Salisbury-Balfour government has only two data points, which suggests (of necessity) a linear relationship. There did, however, appear to be an effect occurring when the next regularly scheduled election is four years away. This gets at some of the nonlinearity of electoral influences (although the use of a squared term in the previous formulation allows the peak to be endogenous). Column 3 reports the estimation with the dummy variable for four years from the next election substituted for the squared term in column 2.

Two comments are worth bringing up about the estimates in column 3. The first is that while the coefficient on the size of the majority still has the unexpected positive sign, it is no longer statistically significant. Second, with the introduction of the four-year dummy, the electoral variables are now statistically significant. As elections become more remote, the number of suspensions increases, with an extra bump in the second year of a new government.

The electoral effects here are surprising. My expectation would have been that members of both the Majority and the Opposition might gain from suspensions close to an election. Minority members could convince constituents of how "dangerous" they were, while members of the majority could reassert their resolve. There is, however, good reason (although in need of further documentation) why the suspensions would diminish as elections became closer. The data here are taken from the Balfour years and thus under the operation of the Third Reform Act. This act extended the vote to county householders, and as a result numerous Roman Catholics living in England (many of whom had emigrated from Ireland) were now able to vote. If we assume that the suspended members were typically Irish, then the results make more sense. While a majority may be able to get away with a few procedural changes regarding obstruction (how many constituents, after all, were going to be concerned about the latest restrictions on the urgency motion for adjournments?), suspending members would be a much more conspicuous and inflammatory act that could easily be communicated to the voting public. This might account for the hesitancy to suspend in the later years of a government's term.

One difficulty with the model as estimated in column 3 is that it ignores any possible party differences. I have included a dummy variable for Conservative governments in column 4. There are no significant party differences (given the high standard error on the Conservative dummy variable), and the proportion of seats held by the majority party remains insignificant. The introduction of this control has no real effect on the importance of electoral factors in member suspension.

Statistical results such as these are often criticized for flattening our view of politics. We no longer appreciate the twists and turns. But results such as these help alert us to things we would not otherwise look for. To see this, we can revisit the discussion above regarding the legislative events of 1881, a period outside of the data analyzed in this section. Between the May 26 and July 27, 1881, Gladstone's Land Bill was taken up in committee. An agreement among Home Rulers to try to amend the bill (and thereafter defeat it) enabled the Irish members to actively participate in the writing of the bill. During this period Parnell even made a suggestion to Gladstone for an end to "land agitation" in exchange for the acceptance of particular amendments to the Land Bill (Lyons 1977, 161). Gladstone after consulting with the Cabinet turned the offer down, but it does suggest how nondisruptive Parnell was being during the consideration of this legislation.

Indeed, it appears that he might have been a little too nondisruptive. After the fate of the bill seemed secure, Parnell set out to "refurbish his reputation, latterly somewhat obscured, as a parliamentary extremist" (Lyons 1977, 161). He therefore began using the obstructive possibilities under the rules to force a day for discussion of arrests that had taken place in Ireland as a result of the adoption of the Coercion Act. He was called to order and responded with a rage that Lyons says was "almost certainly synthetic":

> "The minister of the day of course always gains the sympathies of the powers that be, in this House, and if we may not bring the cause of our imprisoned countrymen before the House, I may say that all liberty and regard of private right is lost in this assembly, and that the minister of the day has transformed himself from a constitutional minister into a tyrant." (Quoted in Lyons 1977, I.161)

For which outburst he was promptly named. He did not stay for the vote—"I will not await the farce of a division." But he did exit with a parting shot. "I will leave you and your House, and the public will see that there is no longer freedom of discussion left to the Irish members" (Lyons 1977, I.161– 62). This speech resulted in suspension for the remainder of the session.

Parnell's suspension occurred on August 1, 1881. Gladstone had assumed office on the April 19, 1880. While Queen Victoria was still quite alive, it was the second year of Gladstone's administration, and there were only four more years to go before the next scheduled election.

Austria

> Here in Vienna in the closing days of 1897 one's blood gets no chance to stagnate. The atmosphere is brimfull of political electricity. All conversation is political, every man is a battery . . .
> —Mark Twain

It is appropriate that we end with Mark Twain.[28] For Twain was not only a brilliant novelist and humorist, he was also the close friend and sometimes sailing companion to Thomas Brackett Reed.[29] Twain of course had little patience for politicians, and particularly members of Congress (he once wrote that one could prove, he was sure, by figures and statistics, that the only native criminal class in the United States were the members of Congress). Indeed, when Reed retired from politics, Twain congratulated him for abandoning his dissolute lifestyle. Reed's portrait was taken by two great American artists— John Singer Sargent and Mark Twain—and it is difficult to say which is the better (sadly the portrait by Sargent seems universally agreed to be "not one of his best" and isn't even reproduced in books devoted to the artist; Twain's portrait didn't include anything below Reed's mustache since Twain had, as he put it, difficulty with mouths). [30]

In an occurrence too surreal to have been fabricated, Twain happened to be in Austria in 1897. His incisive perceptions of the turbulent politics in that country are recorded in a short essay entitled "Stirring Times in Austria," which includes, miraculously, an exceptionally dramatic recounting of the institution of the *Lex Falkenhayn*. Twain was an eyewitness to events in the Austrian Parliament, and said of that experience that while he knew he had not seen abiding history made twice before his eyes, "I know that I have seen it once" (235).[31]

The Adoption of the *Lex Falkenhayn*

To understand the circumstances that made such a great impression on Twain, the following history may be helpful. After the defeat of Napoleon, the Congress of Vienna redrew the map of Europe and created what would be the Austro-Hungarian empire. In part this was the brainchild of Metternich (as in "age of"), who thought that by consolidating central Europe under a Habsburg monarchy he could create the hegemonic power necessary to keep Europe at peace. Of course, the empire so assembled was a vast cacophony: Austria, Hungary, Polish Galicia, and Venetia (and thus the city of Venice). The centrifugal pressures reached a breaking point in the annus mirabilis of 1848, at which time Hungary, under the leadership of Ludwig Kossuth, formally declared itself a republic, ejecting Franz Joseph, the Habsburg emperor. While Franz Joseph was able (with the assistance of Czar Nicholas I) to put down the insurrection and reintegrate Hungary into the empire, keeping the former republic there proved increasingly difficult, especially after Austria's defeat at the hands of Prussia in 1866.

On May 29, 1867, therefore, the *Ausgleich*, the Hungarian Compromise, was signed, creating the Dual Monarchy of the Austro-Hungarian empire. In this arrangement Hungary retained relative domestic autonomy under its king, who was Franz Joseph, the emperor of Austria. In foreign affairs, however, its freedom was somewhat circumscribed. Hungary had no army or customs houses of its own—these were controlled by Austria with Hungary sharing some portion of the costs of imperial government. These sorts of intricate arrangements, of course, involve numerous details, and the *Ausgleich* had to be bargained over and renewed every ten years: if not, Hungary would become an independent country (although ruled by the same person who was king of Austria), an outcome Austria sorely wanted to avoid.

Eighteen ninety-seven was therefore a critical political year, a year for the renewal of the Hungarian Compromise. To accomplish this feat, the new settlement would have to pass through the Austrian Parliament, a task easier said than done. The patchwork nature of the Austrian empire resulted in a rather huge conglomeration of peoples and parties. This was exacerbated by suffrage reform, passed in June 1896. The first election under the new law (held in March 1897) saw a Parliament composed of Constitutional Landowners, Bohemian Federals, a Czech Club made up predominantly of Young Czechs, a Polish Club, a German People's Party, a Progressive Party, Christian Socialists, Social Democrats, and so on: 25 parties in all. The job of passing the *Ausgleich* despite these political complexities fell to the Polish governor of Galicia, Count Casimir Badeni, appointed Minister President by Franz Joseph.

In announcing his government, Badeni noted that he "was preserving a completely free hand *vis-à-vis* the parties" (quoted in Macartney 1969, 663). The imperative of passing the *Ausgleich* and the attending necessity for a stable majority, however, made him tie these free hands a bit more tightly than he might have liked. To gain support for renewal, Badeni arranged a logroll with the Young Czechs, who controlled 60 of the 425 seats in the Austrian Parliament. In return for Czech votes on renewal, Badeni would issue Ministerial Enactments making Czech an official language (along with German) for the bureaucracy of Bohemia and Moravia.[32] The result was described by Twain: " . . . Badeni secured his majority. The German element in parliament was apparently become helpless. The Czech deputies were exultant" (212).

The result of these decrees was a political upheaval not seen since 1848. Germans throughout Austria went to the streets, some waving German flags and carrying portraits of Otto von Bismarck. The rioting continued, going to such lengths inside and outside the government that Franz Joseph, for the first time in 28 years, issued an extraordinary decree closing Parliament (Marek 1974, 346). Parliament remained closed throughout the summer of 1897, returning only in autumn, with Badeni's majority "ready to carry it through" (Twain 1898, 212).

We can attempt to see how much of the theory appears to be at work here. First, do we have a cohesive majority? It would appear within the Austrian context that this was about as cohesive a majority as one could hope for. It certainly seemed to be solid enough for Badeni to contemplate passage without engaging in further deals with other parties.[33] Second, is the majority of minimal winning size? Given Badini's stated independence from parties, it is not possible in the Austrian case (as in the British case) to simply check to see whether the prime minister's supporting coalition is large or small. Nor have I been able to obtain, from the English-language sources I consulted, what the size of Badeni's majority was.[34]

Still, some evidence that the majority could not be reduced comes from Mark Twain, who notes that "Badeni's government could not withdraw the Language Ordinance and keep its majority" (231). This suggests that there was no other option open to Badeni (for example, cutting off the Czechs and forming an alternative, smaller coalition) that would preserve the majority. If Twain is correct, then it appears that Badeni indeed had a minimal winning coalition. Of course, citing Mark Twain for factual accuracy may indicate a certain gullibility about sources: I leave this embarrassing admission as an invitation for correction to those more knowledgeable about Austrian political history.[35]

Our theory would thus predict that we would (a) see obstruction, and (b) see attempts to limit minority rights. And this is precisely what did occur. Twain notes that "the minority was determined to obstruct it and delay it until the obnoxious Czech-language measure should be shelved" (212). They seemed to have a good shot at success: if they could delay the agreement sufficiently long, Twain argued, "the government would doubtless have to withdraw the hated language bill or lose Hungary" (213).[36] And they had a number of tactics at their disposal, including the motion to adjourn, votes on the motion to adjourn, the old favorite of verifying the minutes of the preceding day, and, most important of all, the ability to talk for as long as they wanted, which was quite possible given the absence of limits on debate in the Austrian Parliament.[37]

News of the impending filibuster began circulating the very morning of October 28. Word spread around Vienna that the government would make the *Ausgleich* the special order of the day and that fireworks could be expected. All Vienna appeared to congregate at the Parliament, and the mood of the evening was, to use a word, Straussian. A man not easily impressed, Twain wrote that "no other Senate House is so shapely as this one, or so richly and showily decorated. Its plan is that of an opera-house" (213).[38] The galleries filled up with well-dressed Viennese out for an evening of politics (as well as at least one American, whose dress went unreported). This sophisticated dress is compared to those of the members of the Parliament—"down on the floor there is no costumery"—a simplicity that reminds Twain of the House.

Twain then introduces the major players, especially the demonic Presi-

dent David Ritter von Abrahamowicz, the chair and the "object of the Opposition's limitless hatred. . . . [his manner of sitting] makes you think of
Richelieu. . . . a colorless long face, which in repose suggests a death mask,"
and which, when not in repose, displayed a toothy grin that presented "a
mixed worldly and political and satanic cast" (214). Abrahamowicz is sitting
above the other members, in a seat on the president's terrace, with the chairs
of the other members stretching out fanlike in front of and below him. The
stage set, the villainous Abrahamowicz, after a full day of parliamentary
affairs, recognizes Dr. Lecher at 8:45 P.M.

Dr. Lecher then began to speak, and spoke some more, and continued
speaking for twelve hours, an act that as Twain put it constituted "the longest
flow of unbroken talk that ever came out of one mouth since the world began"
(213). This performance was even more exceptional than it might appear.
First, the rules of the Austrian parliament, while not limiting the time for
debate, did require that the speaker stay on topic. Filibusterers the world over
have, like Joseph Biggar in the Commons, relied on government reports,
constitutions, phone books, and holy documents to supplement their efforts:
Lecher had nothing but a few notes and his own intellect. If he ever strayed
from the topic, he would lose the floor, and the filibuster would be over.
Second, the rules also required that speakers continue standing. "To merely
stand up in one spot twelve hours on a stretch is a feat which very few men
could achieve," wrote an approving Twain. To be honest, Twain is callously
exaggerating here. Lecher did have one rest—a five minute break at 1:45,
after five *hours* on his feet. And he did receive some sustenance, in the form
of "three glasses of wine, four cups of coffee, and one glass of beer—a most
stingy reinforcement of his wasting tissues, but the hostile Chair would permit
no addition to it" (222).

Finally, this superhuman effort was delivered in the midst of extraordinary pandemonium. Whatever the virtues of the Austrian Parliament, they did
not include a sergeant-at-arms. As a result, normal parliamentary order was
almost impossible to obtain. Members shouted out their demands for adjournment, approval, disapproval, all in a veritable hurricane of noise thoroughly
drowning out Lecher's speech. (Unable to hear Lecher, the Chair would check
with the stenographers to guarantee that Lecher was staying on point.) Indeed,
one member found a new medium for self-expression. "Each desk has an
extension consisting of a removable board eighteen inches long, six wide, and
a half-inch top. A member pulled one of these out, and began to belabor the
top of his desk with it. Instantly other members followed suit, and perhaps you
can imagine the result. Of all conceivable rackets it is the most ear-splitting,
intolerable, and altogether fiendish" (216–17).

It is difficult to appreciate what this maelstrom was like unless we listen
to the voices of those who shouted, both at this and at other times in the
Austrian Parliament.

From Twain's account, it is pretty clear that the language of the Austrian members was a bit loose, if not in bad taste. "Political Mountebank," "East-German offal-tub," "Brothel-daddy," "word-of-honor breaker," "infamous louse-brat," "pimp," and the clever "Your grandmother was conceived on a dungpile" were just some of the epithets exchanged on the floor. Twain had a discretion that I lack, for he left that final insult in the original German:

> It would not be judicious to translate that. Its flavor is pretty high, in any case, but it becomes particularly gamey when you remember that the first gallery was well stocked with ladies. Apparently it was a great hit. It fetched thunders of joyous enthusiasm out of the Christian Socialists . . . (227)

It would be incorrect, however, to characterize these individuals simply as harmless funsters. More ominous (especially when projected a few decades forward) were the racial and national slurs typical of their era (and, all too often, ours): "Jew-flunky," "Polish Dog," "I would rather take my hat off to a Jew than to Wolff."

Religion played a significant part in the most bizarre example of unparliamentary language that I have come across. One member had argued in a report that religion should be kept out of the public schools, being a matter best confined to the private sphere. This inspired Deputy Gregorig to ring out "What about free love?" bringing the reply from Deputy Iro that rocked the Parliament: "Soda-water at the Wimberger!"

Did we miss something? It is fairly difficult to understand how a sentence as diluted (if you will excuse me) as "Soda-water at the Wimberger" could have resulted in a parliamentary brouhaha. Twain lets us in on the joke: the soda-water incident dealt with "a matter of town gossip which made Mr. Gregorig a chief actor in a tavern scene where siphon-squirting played a prominent and humorous part, and wherein women had a share." After Iro had learned of this incident, he mailed a number of postcards to Gregorig's business address (where everyone could read them) as well as to Gregorig's wife. One of the postcards read, "Much respected Madam Gregorig,—The undersigned desires an invitation to the next soda-squirt" (225). It is easy to laugh now because almost a century has passed, and these people are (unless possessed of a truly awesome constitution) deceased, but at the time it was highly insulting. Furthermore, as Twain notes, this level of discourse was not an aberration: comments like these regularly took place, and in the presence of a mixed-sex audience, a factor that to Twain makes the insults utterly audacious.[39]

But who are these individuals? These were not guttersnipes or badly socialized demagogues. They were, instead, drawn "from all walks of life and from all grades of society" (223). Twain notes that "the title of Doctor is so common in the House that one may almost say that the deputy who does not bear it is by that reason conspicuous. I am assured that it is not a self-granted title, and not an honorary one, but an *earned* one . . . when an Austrian is called Doctor it means that he is either a lawyer or a physician, and that he is not a self-educated man, but is college-bred, and has been diplomaed for merit" (223).[40]

Was the legislature then simply waiting for the emergence of professional norms (Polsby 1968)? As a matter of fact, it seems that they have stepped backward: "A gentlemen who was at the head of the government twenty years ago confirms this [that the current low condition is new], and says that in his time the parliament was orderly and well behaved. An English gentlemen of long residence here indorses this, and says that a low order of politicians originated the present forms of questionable speech on the stump some years ago, and imported them into parliament" (231). One might be inclined to write these comments off as clearly self-serving, ideological, and eccentric, but Twain also cites an editorial in the *Neue Freie Presse* of December 1, 1897, that makes the same point.

This argument is important, because it suggests two things about the process of institutional change. The first is that the teleological notion of institutionalization is quite clearly wrong. Institutions can go forward and backward, keeping and abandoning norms of courtesy as conditions warrant (see Uslaner 1993).[41] Second, it makes the path between socialization and legislative behavior extremely contingent. The mere fact that legislators live in a period in which, say, professions are booming does not automatically translate into institutionalization. Working out the subtleties here, particularly from a comparative perspective, could inform the perspectives of the "organizational synthesis" view of American history (Galambos 1983).

Despite these sorts of interjections, Lecher's speech did finally (like all things, good and bad) come to an end. He closed by directing his words to his opponents: "in any case, gentlemen of the Majority, make sure of this: henceforth, as before, you will find us at our post. The Germans of Austria will neither surrender nor die!" Wave after wave of applause from the Left greeted this finale. In triumph, Lecher left the Parliament and proceeded home, where he took some nourishment (Twain says his meal consisted of "five loaves and twelve baskets of fishes," 222), slept for three (!) hours, and then returned to see the close of what eventually became a 33 hour session. The filibuster was thoroughly successful, and the government was handed a stunning defeat. To recoup energies (as well as to calm aroused tempers), Parliament was adjourned for a week.

The delay does not appear to have improved matters. Indeed, if anything, parliamentary affairs were even worse. A stalemate took up much of November, with tensions so high at one point that a fight ensued. "It was a surging, struggling, shoulder-to-shoulder scramble. A great many blows were struck"

(231). But Twain doubts the sincerity of the fighters, noting that the only blood spilled that day appeared quite unintentional: "a professor was flung down and belabored with fists and choked; he held up an open penknife as a defense against the blows; it was snatched from him and flung to a distance; it hit a peaceful Christian Socialist who wasn't doing anything, and brought blood from his hand" (231). Had this been a real fight, "better results would have been apparent."

Still the delay in approving the *Ausgleich* continued. How could Badeni and his majority accomplish their ends? The theory presented in this book suggests that it would be impossible without a change of the rules, and that is what happened, in a particularly narrow and ruthless way, with the adoption of the so-called *Lex Falkenhayn*. When I first encountered this phrase in the report from the House of Commons, I was sure that it had to relate to some sort of ancient Teutonic rite from that primeval forest where bad historians find the birthplace of democracy. A false tradition has never been so easily created, as the Falkenhayn referred to was the quite nonancient Count Julius Falkenhayn, minister for defense under the previous government and later to play an important role in the Austrian military effort during World War I.

It was Falkenhayn who on Thanksgiving Day of 1897 strode in to Parliament and "in a voice heard only by the President of the House and the official stenographers" (Macartney 1969, 664) proposed that the president be given the ability to punish deputies who continued to engage in disorder with ejection for a period of three days, an exclusion of up to thirty days possible if so voted by the House. Falkenhayn also proposed that the Chair be given the command of whatever means necessary to accomplish this end, thus making him in effect the Sergeant-at-Arms, "and a more formidable one, as to power, than any other legislature in Christendom had ever possessed" (Twain 1898, 232).[42] After proposing this outrageous procedural change, Falkenhayn sat down, and other members, typically out of their seats anyway ("to have," Twain noted, "a better chance to exchange epithets and make other noises," 232), rushed to his side to applaud or condemn. The president thereupon moved that all those desiring to vote in the affirmative should stand up. "The House was already standing up; had been standing for an hour, and before a third of it had found out what the President had been saying, he had proclaimed the adoption of the motion. And only a few heard *that*" (232). And in this rather brusque manner, the *Lex Falkenhayn* was born.

The passage of the new procedure did not exactly endear Badeni to his opponents. The next day, the Socialists stood in front of the ministerial seats, and in a show of force crashed through the gates and made their way to the president's chair, throwing papers and the president's bell in an episode that reads much like the raising of the flag on Iwo Jima. Things certainly sounded quite feral: one professor (of law, no less) obtained a bugle and blew it into another delegate's ear, while still others threw desks and inkstands. Georg Schönerer, a "doughty eccentric" (Macartney 1969, 653) who in addition to being a German nationalist and virulent anti-Semite also holds the dubious honor of inaugurating the use of the word "Heil" as a greeting, fiercely attacked the upholstery with a pair of scissors. The president and vice president, after failing to fight off the Socialists, made an escape through a door. "And now we see what history will be talking of five centuries hence," wrote Twain (234). Sixty gendarmes entered the Parliament and arrested eleven members. The members were dragged out forcibly, Schönerer apparently kicking the police and screaming "Hail Germania" (Marek 1974, 349).

In the wake of the arrests, Viennese workers and students took to the streets. They assembled before the Parliament, where they found their progress impeded by an array of soldiers mounted on horseback. Unable to press forward, the workers and students (joined by others) simply stayed put, at times singing, at other times simply milling around. This peace was to be short-lived, however. At the stroke of noon, the soldiers took their sabers out of their scabbards and thundered through the crowd, slashing as they went. Even this level of brutality, it appears, was insufficient to stop the unrest. A panicky Badeni pleaded for stronger measures, but Franz Joseph, finding it impossible to sanction the use of firearms against the citizens of Vienna, declined. Badeni's resignation was forthcoming.

This of course should be the moment in which Franz Joseph (or some other illustrious personage) is supposed to miraculously reanimate the Parliament, stepping in and saying that indeed lessons have been learned and minority rights will no longer be imperiled in the legislature. But we are dealing with the real world here, where such graceful endings are not to be expected. When Parliament reconvened, obstruction did continue to take place. But, as Marek notes, it had no effect. Franz Joseph

> could make himself believe that he had honestly attempted a constitutional monarchy but that it had not worked. What he attempted henceforth was the exercise of absolute authority within a legal structure of constitutionalism. . . . henceforth, to the end of his reign, whenever parliamentary agreement could not be reached, Franz Joseph fell back on Article 14 of the Constitution, which enabled the Emperor to rule by emergency. Article 14 was employed too often in the coming years. (1974, 350)

It was precisely this sort of outcome that made contemporaries fear for the future of parliamentary government.

PART 4

Conclusion

The filibuster is a physical test. . . . and in essence no whit different from trial by battle, the ordeal, the duel, war itself. Do you say the determining of right and wrong by physical sacrifice is folly, with no shred of reason, a disgrace to humanity not deserving one word of defense? Do you say its record should be read with nothing but grief and scorn? Or would you think it better still to blot out that record, lest it might incite misguided youth to emulate countless generations of ancestors in making physical sacrifice the noblest of ideals? Then blot out nine tenths of recorded history. Drop the greater part of the names of the Saints from the calendar. Ask yourself what was the nature and purpose of the supreme sacrifice made by the founder of the Christian religion.
                          —Robert Luce, *Legislative Procedure* (1922)

CHAPTER 9

Final Thoughts

It occurred to him to focus his hobby on the European balance of power, because of whose long pathology he had labored, deeply, all hope of waking lost, in the nightmare of Flanders. He started in on a mammoth work entitled *Things That Can Happen in European Politics*. Begin of course, with England. "First," he wrote, "Bereshith, as it were: Ramsay MacDonald can die." By the time he went through resulting party alignments and possible permutations of cabinet posts, Ramsay MacDonald had died. "Never make it," he found himself muttering at the beginning of each day's work—"it's changing out from under me. Oh, dodgy—very dodgy."
—Thomas Pynchon, *Gravity's Rainbow*

The main story here is compellingly simple: small majorities are more cohesive, cohesive majorities lead to minority obstruction, minority obstruction leads to procedural changes on the part of the majority to limit obstruction. The evidence from a number of time periods and a number of legislatures has supported these claims.

This is not to say that the model contains everything. The model did not predict that Polk's attempt to change the rules would run afoul of a resolution for committee assignments. The model did not take into account the fact that the Zimmerman note might be released. The model didn't suppose anything at all about Queen Victoria, either her existence or her demise.

But the fact that those things are important becomes evident only after having some clue about the way in which the restriction of minority rights to obstruct legislation works. Without the theory, they sit dumbly in the background with a million other bizarre facts (Emerson Etheridge would attempt a conservative coup during the Civil War; Parnell had a beard; Mark Twain sailed with Thomas Brackett Reed). This seems to me the best justification for engaging in the use of formal theory: you see the contingent so much more quickly.

In doing so, I may seem to be violating the dictum that tells us that the whole reason for formal theory is to find systematic relationships. But we can never know what is systematic until we know what is idiosyncratic, and conversely what is idiosyncratic cannot be known until we have some clues about what is systematic. Taking sides—which is more important—seems to be missing the point. You cannot have one without the other.

Having said that, in this conclusion I want to present observations on what I have found, some of which will be horribly idiosyncratic and speculative and others of which will I think be more systematic. I will begin with a consideration of theories of majority tyranny, move on to some observations about obstruction, and then finally hit on the topic of the interdependence of legislatures.

Theories of Majority Tyranny

This book began with a set of claims about the conditions that led majorities to limit minority rights. Majorities might find procedural changes regarding obstruction to be necessary in a move to meet workload demands (the efficiency argument), when they believed they were unlikely to be in the minority themselves (the reciprocity argument), and due to the political socialization of majority members with respect to minority rights. How well did these accounts work in the cases we have looked at here?

Again, before starting, I wish to repeat my warning that the relationships I have found here characterize any and all attempts by the majority to limit any sort of minority rights. This is a question that needs to be addressed in numerous settings, of which this book is only one. My comments should thus be considered solely as a contribution to a discussion, highlighting some things that I have found on my journeys that others might be interested in.

For the lion's share of the analysis, there is convincing evidence from a number of institutions that it is small majorities that tend to adopt limitations on minority rights. The argument behind this claim is not simply based on the majority party on the one hand, or the minority party on the other. In seeking to explain the mechanism behind this result, we cannot think about the majority in isolation from the minority, or the minority in isolation from the majority. Instead, we have to consider both the majority and the minority, strategically interacting. Because small majorities are more cohesive, minority obstruction follows as a reasonable response. And because obstruction occurs on the part of minorities, limitations in the rights of minorities to obstruct follow, again as a reasonable response.

This finding has two implications, and in my attempt to be scrupulously fair I will present both. For majorities, it suggests that the time to limit minority rights to obstruct is when the majority is small. Leaders of parties should not, if these arguments are true, wait around for a larger majority to come along to provide that "cushion of security" for a convincing vote, since that cushion of security brings with it the threat of disunity. And with the disunity of the majority party, in which no individual knows whether they will be in the majority or out, limitations to minority rights become much more difficult to adopt.

For legislative minorities, the results suggest a certain caution with respect to stunning victories. When the minority comes within striking distance of the majority, this should not breed complacency. Nor should apparently welfare-enhancing changes be supported. Even the most minimal changes in procedure, those that on their face simply make it easier to get things done, make the job of the obstructionist that more difficult. Every hour saved by the adoption of "efficient procedures" is another hour that an obstructionist will have to kill.

Indeed, if nothing else, the account of the politics behind these procedural changes should make anyone reluctant to invoke the language of legislative efficiency. These procedural changes could not, by any stretch of the imagination, be considered as enhancing the welfare of all members. They were, instead, deliberate attempts by the majority to limit the rights of the minority, attempts that the minority powerfully resisted.

Nor should we think that procedural changes are necessary given a "press of business." There simply is not such a thing as a "demand for legislation" or a "need for laws to meet a new situation." This is not to say that people do not have real demands or real needs. But it is instead to recognize that whether those needs are best addressed within the context of legislative politics is itself a political question. Those who have eliminated obstruction have worked quite carefully to erase any hint of their agency. "Oh no, we don't want to limit minority rights, it is just that we need to fix the nation's problems." This may be true, but we do not want to treat legislators as mere conduits. They have goals, beliefs, discretion: we should not pretend otherwise.

Socialization does not appear to play a large role in explaining the changes in minority rights either. We are (or at least I am) only interested in socialization to the extent that it helps us understand the attitudes that individuals come to hold about minority rights. But the ease with which politicians could argue (and vote) on both sides of the issue suggests that socialization is a rather weak reed on which to hang the protection of minority rights. This is not because politicians lack respect for minority rights (or any value other than their career interests): it is instead because they possess respect for minority rights as well as numerous other things.

If a socialization effect is to be found, I think it will most likely emerge in a cross-sectional analysis. Nothing in this book can explain why similarly sized majorities in different legislatures might come to adopt different procedures with respect to minority rights. This does not mean that the theory addressed here is useless for cross-sectional analysis. But it does mean that before we begin tracing cross-national (and intranational) differences back to socialization or even political culture, we need to make sure that those differences are not attributable to different levels of party competitiveness. If a country historically characterized by large majorities has a healthier respect for minority rights than a country historically characterized by small majorities, we should not assume that socialization lies behind the difference. Again, this is not to denigrate cultural explanations, it is to make them appear even richer. A country with small majorities *and* a healthy respect for minority rights—that would be something.

Of all the results in this book, those on reciprocity seem the most surprising to me. Judging by the evidence presented here, majorities do not seem to worry too much about the possibility of being in the minority in the future.

I have thought of numerous ways to try to square this with the generally favorable evidence on reciprocity in political science. Perhaps majorities feel that they will almost certainly be in the majority forever, and in an act of hubris limit minority rights. Alas, that won't work: we have evidence that even when the majority *knows* it will be in the minority, it still limits minority rights. Perhaps this level of coordination becomes more difficult as the number of representatives gets larger. This hardly does much justice to the British case, however. There the size of the membership was relatively constant (a fact, by the way, that Americanists would do well to remember before they too eagerly rush to decipher House–Senate differences by appealing to the ubiquitous "the Senate, with its smaller size" argument). In any event the notion that increasing the number of players always makes cooperation more difficult seems to be false (Pahre 1994).

What then could be at work here? Why *doesn't* reciprocity play a bigger role? While I have not included any dynamic component to the model, perhaps part of the difficulty here is that cohesive majorities face the following options: they can either allow the minority the power to obstruct (and risk being labeled a "do-nothing" party and winding up in the minority), or they can trim minority rights to obstruct, pass some programs, and have a chance at being in the majority again. The likelihood of future interactions in this setting is therefore not exogenous (as it is in most formal models of reciprocity): instead, it is endogenously determined by the actions the players take.

In addition, perhaps we should begin to take a bit more seriously, as Richard Fenno (1973) and Keith Krehbiel (1991) have both powerfully argued, the role of public policy concerns. It is not out of the realm of possibility, for example, that members of the House during the debates over the 1875 Civil Rights Act decided that the goal of freer elections in the South justified precedent-setting decisions limiting minority rights. Charles Sumner, on his deathbed, begged his colleagues "You must take care of my civil-rights bill—my bill, the civil-rights bill, don't let it fail" (Byrd 1988, 303). We could imagine that he was forced at gunpoint to say this by friends seeking electoral advantage, or that he anticipated a stunning recovery allowing him to reap the benefits of his public position-taking. But it seems much easier to simply recognize that Sumner, dying, wanted to do some good. And in some cases, doing good requires sacrificing some principles in order to achieve others.

The final possibility would be that reciprocity works, but not at the margins. That is, there is a baseline level of respect for minorities that cannot be explained but by the mechanism of reciprocity. Certainly, no one was killed over parliamentary obstruction. Ridiculed, deafened, suspended, thrown in jail, threatened with swords, hacked with sabers, maybe even a little ptomaine in the eggnog, but not, as far as I can tell, actually killed.

The results on reciprocity may seem depressing. But they need not be: to put another face on it, the problems with reciprocity invite us to think about other strategic possibilities. To take just one example, consider the following analysis. In 1992, the American Enterprise Institute and the Brookings Institution produced a program for legislative reform in a volume entitled *Renewing Congress*. The report identified and condemned

> an intense and destructive partisanship, especially in the House, born of the near permanent majority status of the House Democrats, the frustration of Republicans, the legacy of battles between the executive and Congress, and the use of procedure and symbolism to embarrass the opposition in a quest for partisan advantage. (1992, 5)

But why has this intense and destructive partisanship invaded the House at this particular time (and why the House more than the Senate)? The report argues that the absence of party competition is the cause of both the desire by the majority to crush minority rights and the willingness of the minority to obstruct legislative proceedings. The (then) almost forty-year control of the House by the Democrats has meant that "the majority has no memory or experience as a minority, and the minority has no memory of any role other than to oppose" (1992, 55). Through campaign finance reform, elections can become more competitive, there can be a greater alternation of parties in control of the legislature, and in result the minority will learn to appreciate the majority position, and the majority the minority.

If the results presented in this book are correct, however, this is precisely the wrong suggestion to make. More competitive elections will not produce less partisanship. Instead, as in the nineteenth-century House and elsewhere, they will produce more and more majorities of smaller and smaller size, all of whom will be intensely partisan. Fear of being in the minority in the next session would, judging from the results, only enhance the willingness of the majority parties to limit minority rights. All told, then, adopting the suggestions of *Renewing Congress* would, therefore, exacerbate partisanship and ironically *reduce* respect for minority rights.[1]

We need, therefore, to think about alternatives to reciprocity. Reciprocity may be an intellectually powerful tool, but it is precisely its intellectual power that seduces us into thinking it applies where it does not. A healthy dose of resistance may free us to explore other ways that majorities and minorities interact, an outcome that would be good not just for the study of legislative politics, but also for the understanding of majority rule and minority rights in numerous other situations. Thinking about alternatives to "just you wait" may be challenging, but also important: can we live in a post-reciprocity world?

A Handbook of Political Fallacies
(with apologies to Bentham)

While we are thinking up alternatives, we may wish to come up with some alternatives to some of the arguments that have been used to defend as well as to attack obstruction. Having studied the topic of obstruction for some time, I think I have developed a fairly healthy view of the kinds of claims made in such cases, and especially those claims that merit retirement. The following list presents what seem to me to be the most decrepit specimens.

The Unhealthy Strain Fallacy. One of the sublimely ridiculous arguments, used quite a bit in Britain but capable of being applied anywhere, is to refer to the toll that filibustering is taking on the health of members. It can be found in many places, Sidney Buxton giving a typical example:

> Though these rules [1882 rules] were unquestionably of much use, the forms of the House still adapted themselves so readily to the delay of business, that though each government session by session, encroached more and more on the time allotted to private members, the length of the sittings appreciably increased, and the strain on the strength and health of members gradually became intolerable. (147)

I have no doubt that staying up late, sleeping on couches, drinking bad coffee, and listening to loud noises emanating from the next room wears on the health—a moment spent in the average college classroom will convince anyone of that. And if some have died through having to listen to filibustering, I offer my condolences to their loved ones. But all this argument does is to force the act of obstruction (which after all is just protracted speech) into the realm of *assault*. I have no wish to enter here into the tricky debate regarding the relationship between speech and harm, but I do want to point out that it becomes infinitely easier to use force against obstructionists when they are perceived as murderers. Before such claims are advanced in parliamentary debate again, I would ask that an impartial tribunal of medical experts thoroughly examine the victim(s) in question.

The Internationalist Fallacy. This argument seeks to convince the listener that the eyes of the world are fixed on the legislature, and that the inability to deal with obstruction will produce a devastating blow to national security and prestige. Redlich waxes eloquent along these lines:

> . . . the assembly whose efficiency was the object of attack was not the parliament of one of the mock constitutional countries of the Continent, created as an ornament to the supremacy of the crown, the bureaucracy and the army, with power of advice and a convenient share in responsibility; what was now endangered was the dignity, the very existence of a body from which proceeded all the political authority of the government of a world-empire, in the orderly discussions of which the administration of a great state found its supreme control and direction. (I.155)

Before this argument could be used again, I would demand a question be placed on the World Values Survey assessing whether the eyes of the world really are on the legislature in question. If not, the user of this specious argument should be thrown in jail. (I will, however, gladly repudiate this argument if someone can show me statistical evidence that links obstruction in the legislature to imperial ruin.)

The "Edge of the Volcano" Fallacy. It seems only right to turn to an obstructionist fallacy. This fallacy argues that any steps taken, however trivial, to limit the rights of the minority will inevitably end in the total collapse of democracy as we know it. Representative Blount provides us with an example during the debate in the House of Representatives on the disappearing quorum:

> Mr. Speaker, I say that the genius of our institutions, the genius of the Anglo-Saxon civilization, which has never permitted it in England for centuries, and has made it absolutely a nullity here, will revolt at this monstrosity. The scene of members brought in and fastened. How? In the discretion of that body, by whatever means it sees fit, kept here under the dictation of that majority and required to remain in that sort of condition as legislators to make a quorum to transact business. Sir, you will have facilities for legislation; you will have your committee of 100 as a quorum. That committee may close debate on any proposition in five-minute debate. It may go to any stretch it pleases; it may combine for the purpose of making many and excessive drafts upon the Treasury. The moneyed lords will be gladdened when the sanctity of the Constitution is gone, when the long-barred bolts of the Treasury are broken, and when they may imprison the Representatives of the people if needed to consummate their wicked schemes. (*Congressional Record*, Feb. 10, 1890, 1186)

Excessive imagery like this should be invoked only when necessary for the production of compelling scholarly anecdotes, and when used should be highlighted in order to expedite location of same.

The Dodginess of Procedural Change

In this work, I have treated legislative units as independent. We have the story of one legislature followed by the story of another. And as far as the theory is concerned, this is absolutely the correct way to proceed.

Politicians, however, have a nasty habit of ignoring the neat boundaries that political scientists attempt to lay out for them. They sometimes decide that what they are doing in Congress will determine their party's chances in the electoral college (James 1992); how they are doing militarily affects their domestic political stability (Skocpol 1979); how they are doing domestically affects their international situation (Iida 1993)—the list could easily continue.

If politicians are capable of rudely making these great leaps over our subfields, then certainly members of legislatures would presumably be able to take some notice of what was going on in other legislatures. Reginald F. D. Palgrave, C.B., the Clerk of the House of Commons (and presumably a prime contender for a future Merchant–Ivory film) had this to say about the disappearing quorum:

> I therefore, though an insular outsider, assert that the mischief which caused that congressional crisis sprang from the flabby treatment of their voting power which seems habitual to their representatives of the United States. (1890, 370)

A crisis such as occurred in the House of Representatives could not occur in the Commons, Palgrave asserted, because "indignant constituencies would call to quick and sharp account any weak kneed politician who refused to back his opinion by his vote" (375).

This air of Anglo-Saxon condescension is a bit surprising considering the low attendance on many divisions in the House of Commons, the principle obviously being that it was fine not to show up, but flabby to show up and not vote. But leaving that point aside, it is clear that Palgrave knew of (and had thoughts on) the affairs going on in the United States. And information flows both ways: Thomas Jefferson's treatment of parliamentary procedure drew what we might now consider excessive inspiration from British parliamentary authority John Hatsell.

The possibility that legislatures might talk to one another, or at the very least be cognizant of each other's proceedings, complicates the story I have been attempting to tell here. How might legislatures react to other legislatures? What did they know and when did they know it? Does the pattern of institutional change bear some relationship to a diffusion model, in which procedural fixes circulate throughout the democratic community? I do not believe, to be sure, that legislatures unthinkingly adopt whatever the procedural fashion might be, but neither should we believe that when a good thing comes along, they ignore it.

There is evidence that such interlegislative piracy (or more kindly, inspiration) takes place. In the middle of the 1880 rules change, as pointed out in chapter 8, Charles Parnell gave an address before the House of Representatives (Lyons 1977, 109). While members debated about the problem of obstruction before Parnell's arrival, it was on February 3, the day after Parnell's speech, that a weary Joseph Blackburn first called for a limitation on the already protracted debate. It also appeared to be the first clear example of obstruction on the rules report itself. Is it too much to suggest that the arrival of the most famous obstructionist in the world the day before had played some role in this contest, and perhaps in moving the 1880 rules reform to its ultimate partisan complexion?

Take another example. Some of the most intense parliamentary debate in the U.S. House of Representatives occurred over the issue of the so-called gag rule banning the House from accepting abolition petitions (Miller 1996). This ban was adopted as a temporary rule for some time until finally, in 1840, it was enacted as a permanent rule (only to be eliminated four years later). By contrast, the House of Commons was engaged in its own debate about petitions, and it too would enact sessional rules until finally, in 1842, it too would adopt a permanent rule banning debate on petitions.

Do I simply have a good nose for coincidence? Two final pieces of evidence may help persuade even jaded readers that there may be something here. Table 9.1 presents an analysis of the pattern of antiobstructive procedures in state legislatures as of 1954.[2] If the partisan theory is true, we would expect to see these procedures positively associated with legislatures having three central features highlighted by the theory: two-party competition, a strong party system, and a vibrant party caucus.[3] If the claims I have advanced regarding the interdependence of legislatures is true, then we may well see what I will term the "Stinchcombe effect": the structure of an organization is not driven primarily by the particulars of what the organization does, but rather by the prevailing organization structure at the time of its creation (Stinchcombe 1965). In terms of legislative politics, the Stinchcombe effect would suggest that we would see a link between the restrictiveness of the procedures adopted in a state's legislature and its date of admission to the union.[4] Table 9.1 supports both of these views. The first column shows that the partisan theory helps explain the adoption of cloture.[5] At the same time, the significant results on the date of admission as a state shows that we cannot

254   Turning the Legislative Thumbscrews

TABLE 9.1. Adoption of Cloture and Previous Question, U.S. State Legislatures, 1954[a]

Independent Variables	Dependent Variables	
	Cloture Rule in All Houses	Previous Question in All Houses
Constant	−12.478	−25.866##
	(11.071)	(11.992)
Two-party/strong cohesion/caucus system	1.411##	−0.026
	(0.610)	(0.515)
Date admitted as a state	0.00634	0.0144##
	0.00597	(0.007)
South	1.022##	0.687
	(0.558)	(0.638)
Log-likelihood	−28.014	−24.138
Percent correctly predicted	68.75	81.25

[a]Includes Nebraska.
#significant at the 10 percent level, one-tailed test
##significant at the 5 percent level, one-tailed test
###significant at the 1 percent level, one-tailed test

assume the procedural histories of legislatures to be independent. What happens in one legislature depends on what has happened in others before.

The second piece of evidence looks beyond the states to the American national legislature. I have put together the data on Senate attempts to limit obstruction and antidilatory precedents in the House during the partisan era.[6] The results are startling (see table 9.2). In every case, House–Senate differences disappear. Column 1 presents the usual method for determining whether there are intergroup differences within a pooled time-series (which we have here): the estimate of the House constant and the Senate constant are identical. Column 2 sees whether there are House and Senate differences in terms of sensitivity to the proportion of seats held by the majority, the pivotal variable in this study. Other things being equal, does a 51 percent majority in the House attempt to limit minority rights less or more than a 51 percent majority in the Senate? The estimates are consistent with the partisan account, significant, and indistinguishable.[7] Column 3 adds a control for the number of bills introduced, the key variable in workload accounts. The estimates on majority party size in the House and Senate are again consistent with the partisan account, significant, and indistinguishable.[8] Column 4 includes the "Doomed Majority" variable for majorities that were subsequently replaced, the best variable I have been able to come up with for reciprocity in the pooled data

TABLE 9.2. Probit Estimates of Anti-Minority Attempts, U.S. House and Senate, 1835–95

Independent Variables	(1)	(2)	(3)	(4)	(5)
House	1.959# (1.472)				
Senate	2.035# (1.570)				
Constant		1.967# (1.505)	0.971 (1.541)	1.784 (1.580)	1.978# (1.496)
Martis proportion	−0.044# (0.027)				
Majority proportion in the House		−0.043# (0.028)	−0.030 (0.027)	−0.042# (0.028)	−0.051## (0.029)
Majority proportion in the Senate		−0.043## (−0.026)	−0.032 (0.025)	−0.041# (0.026)	−0.051## (0.026)
Johnson presidency	5.166## (0.639)	5.125### (0.672)	5.079### (0.621)	5.187### (0.650)	5.065### (0.691)
Late Reconstruction	5.263### (0.693)	5.280### (0.685)	5.159### (0.641)	5.279### (0.677)	5.261### (0.687)
51st Congress and after	4.874### (0.525)	4.835### (0.552)	3.903### (0.652)	4.879### (0.551)	5.162### (0.738)
Bills introduced			0.0000557# (0.0000355)		
Doomed Majority				0.190 (0.397)	
Unified Congress					0.640# (0.418)
Number of observations	62	62	62	62	62
Log-likelihood	−31.929	−31.950	−30.618	−31.833	−30.652
Percent correctly predicted	70.968	70.968	75.806	70.968	74.194

#significant at the 10 percent level, one-tailed test
##significant at the 5 percent level, one-tailed test
###significant at the 1 percent level, one-tailed test

set.[9] The estimates on majority party size in the House and Senate continue to be consistent with the partisan account, significant, and indistinguishable. The final column in table 9.2 is an attempt to capture the "dodginess" of procedural change. If we are right in treating legislatures as independent entities on their own procedural trajectory, then it should not matter whether the House and the

Senate are controlled by the same party or not.[10] The results in column 5, however, show that attempts to limit minority rights are more likely when the same party controls the House and the Senate than they are when different parties control these institutions. And as might be expected at this point, the influence of majority party proportion for the two bodies is once more consistent with the partisan account, significant, and indistinguishable.

This result is worth some attention. Broadcast and print media constantly bombard us with armchair observations about the distinction between "being a Senator and being a Representative." We are told time and again that we should not mistake the politics of the House for the politics of the Senate. The Senate—small, collegial, give-and take; the House—large, streamlined, no room for debate: every legislative scholar can recite this litany. If such (in truth, cultural) differences were to show up anywhere, we would certainly expect them to show up in House–Senate differences on the willingness to limit debate. That they do not—that the House and the Senate operate in a quite similar way—suggests that we might employ a bit more caution in employing the ready-made explanations of House–Senate differences.

In raising these issues I do not aim to banish forever the study of isolated legislatures. You do not need to speak French to make french fries. Nor do I presume that there is some Unified Legislative Theory that will incorporate all behavior, past, present, and future, into one overarching account. My only desire in presenting the arguments contained in this section is to suggest directions that the study of legislative politics has tended to avoid and that may be worth a closer look.

Some Final Words

I have no closing inspired thoughts on the proper balance of majority rule and minority rights, no magic solution that would allow minorities full room for dissent while still preserving the right of the majority to act. Nor would any words I have be appropriate: this is a struggle that continues every day in legislatures, as majorities and minorities make the tactical decisions that keep parliamentary democracy moving, let's not be Whiggish and say *forward*, but at least along.

We have not, I think, treated the individuals involved in this struggle with the degree of compassion and insight that we always seem able to find for comprehending our own actions. Instead, when members throw fistfights, or impugn each other's good name, or use up time calling for roll call after roll call, we never look beyond the strategy to see the intention. We instead write them off as premodern, as childish, as lacking in the norms of professionalism that politicians should possess. We want them to get with the program, to settle down to "business." We call them "primitive." When they refuse to set aside their political views for the "economic and social demands of a changing time," we scratch our heads and shrug our shoulders and move on. This is not to say that whatever an obstructionist does is heroic. They are often crass, racist, tedious, pompous, rude, mindless, and to say the least long-winded. But they have a story, and they bring a certain passion to politics that needs to be recognized.

In making the obstructionists out to be discourteous adolescents, we have not only done them a disservice, but we have done those who fought them daily on the floor of the world's legislatures a disservice as well. It was not, contrary to whatever grand mechanism of economics we care to imagine, a given that obstructionism would perish. Some like Thomas Brackett Reed carried it off with a grace and elegance that is rare in politics; others like President David Ritter von Abrahamowicz were less adept. But none were simply flunkies for the needs of a growing economy, the mindless hirelings of parliamentary history. They took risks in meeting a crisis that they believed would threaten democratic government. In these days of democratic optimism, it is all too easy to forget that parliamentary struggle.

Notes

Chapter 1

1. To conclude the story, Cato won the day, and the conspirators were strangled by executioners in the Tullianum, a dark, stinking hole twelve feet below ground, "hideous to behold" (Sallust, *Cat.* 55). While I have relied on Suetonius (who is not known for his critical evaluation of sources), views of the Catiline conspiracy and the occurrences in the Senate differ. Butler and Cary (1927, 57) feel that Suetonius was wrong in placing the movement of the *equitum* (Cicero's "special constables") inside the Senate and that Plutarch and Sallust are right in having it take place outside the Senate, although Kahn (1986, 175) in his biography of Caesar has the equestrians at the door, as does the Clough edition of *Plutarch's Lives* (1875, 263). But following Sallust has difficulties of its own: his clear (and conservative) political motives make him a questionable source for accurate information about Catiline (see Macdonald's 1977 introductory remarks to his translation of Cicero's *In Catilinam*). Perhaps we are best left off with Bailey's 1971 position that "accounts of the debate are inconsistent in detail and unreliable in general" (33), although I have found no contradictions of Suetonius's characterization of Caesar's filibustering, nor is there any disagreement that Caesar was at least in peril from Cicero's guards. For further work on the Catiline conspiracy, see Hardy 1924 and Odahl 1971 for conventional treatments. Hutchinson 1966 presents a far more balanced view of Catiline and provides some additional critical perspective on the political goals of the classical authors (in particular Sallust).

2. This is not to assert that physical responses to delay have not had their place in more modern legislative proceedings. During one long filibuster, La Follette of Wisconsin maintained his strength by drinking a concoction of milk and raw egg. He refused to drink one glass dispatched by the Senate restaurant: later analysis revealed it to be laced with a fatal dose of ptomaine (Burdette 1965, 88).

3. See also Jack Knight's excellent book *Institutions and Social Conflict* for a critique of the efficiency view of institutional change. The first four chapters of this book should be required reading for anyone interested in these issues. I differ from Knight, however, in seeking to explain how groups become cohesive, whereas (if I read him correctly) Knight sees group cohesion as exogenous. For an early paper emphasizing the fact that institutional changes regarding delay in legislatures create winners and losers, see Hedlund and Hamm 1976.

4. See Darnton 1990; also Schama 1989, 610ff., for the unfraternal aftermath.

5. The arguments over the elimination of obstruction mirror the arguments over the

elimination of the artisanal workshop. There, too, arguments of efficiency were unpersuasive to those who understood what change would bring, and those opposing these forces were similarly branded as opponents of progress. See Sewell 1980 and Wilentz 1984 (not to mention Engels 1845).

6. If we take a nonessentialist view, however, perhaps studying an elite institution may be more informative than we might think. Social theorists have taught us to look at the categories of gender, race, and class as socially constructed (to telegraph a voluminous literature: on race, see Crenshaw 1988; on gender, Scott 1988; on class, Thompson 1963). But this is something they share with partisanship: as Jean Baker (1983) has written, no one is born a Democrat. If partisanship is not reducible to gender, race, or class (as McCormick 1986 and others argue it isn't) then there is something to be found in studying majority rule and minority rights within the context of socially constructed identities of partisanship.

7. See Holt 1978 for a masterful discussion of the 1850s realignment and the central place of the Kansas–Nebraska Act. The tactical exchanges over the Kansas–Nebraska Act are recounted in all their gory detail in Nichols 1963. Of course much more goes into a realignment (not to mention a civil war) than a single bill, however pivotal; see Foner 1970, Bridges 1984, and Gienapp 1987 for the 1850s case.

8. In point of fact, people seem to do a decent job of treating creativity as a dependent variable every day, as the racks of self-help paperbacks and productivity manuals in any bookstore will attest.

9. See Freeman 1986, chapter 10.

10. See Axelrod 1984, Fudenberg and Maskin 1986.

11. Large majorities could coordinate in Alesina's model, but such an outcome would require that the majority alternate back and forth between two parties each of which captures a lion's share at every election, a rather unlikely situation.

12. Jefferson's *Manual* was intended for use in the Senate. While never used in that body, Rule 42 of the House (and its historical predecessors) specify that this book will comprise the rules of the House "in all cases to which they are applicable, and in which they are not inconsistent" with the Rules of the House or the joint rules of the House and Senate.

Chapter 2

1. See also Aldrich 1994.

2. A great deal of work has been done recently in legislative politics on the role of party (Baron 1993; Cox and McCubbins 1993; Dion and Huber 1996; Dodd and Oppenheimer 1989; Huber 1992; Kiewiet and McCubbins 1991; Rohde 1991; Sinclair 1989, 1993; Weingast 1989). These works have been primarily concerned with the issue of how party leaders rule their own parties and not how majorities and minorities interact (although Rohde is an exception). Nonetheless, this work indicates a growing interest in giving political parties the same high profile in legislative studies they have taken in legislative practice. Of course, no argument is without opponents: for the strongest criticism, see Krehbiel 1993.

3. Despite the possibilities, there has been little formal work done on the interaction of party majorities and minorities. Cox and McCubbins (1993) provide one of the fuller models incorporating a party element. Since their interest is in issues of leadership and scheduling, however, they treat (in their chapter setting out their theory of legislative parties) being in the minority as a fixed payoff. But certainly (and I am sure they would agree) the payoff to being in the minority depends on what the majority does, and vice versa. A nonformal treatment, but very much in the spirit I am proposing here, is given by Brady (1973, 186). After noting that party leaders assembled before session to set priorities, he continues, " . . . the majority of congressmen were asked to examine and vote upon legislation which was unfamiliar to them. The most obvious voting cue was, did the speakership favor such legislation? Since the Rules Committee could facilitate swift passage, the minority was left with only opposition on the vote as an alternative" (186).

4. For an argument about the political importance of such preferences, see Dion 1992.

5. This is a large literature: the basic citations include Plott 1967; McKelvey 1976, 1979; Cohen 1979; Schofield 1983; and McKelvey and Schofield 1986. Le Breton 1987 has a superb piece dealing with some topological problems in these results; see also Fiorina and Shepsle 1982.

6. For an answer as to why they exist, see Aldrich 1995.

7. The fact that the cleavages need to cut across the status quo is important. It is not sufficient, in this view, simply to categorize the various cleavages that persons belong to, and then determine how many of them crosscut. Cleavages crosscut all the time, but only some of them are sufficient to prevent majorities from forming.

8. For those still not convinced, I suggest thinking about a caucus equilibrium as a necessary condition for majority party cohesion. That is, if there isn't a caucus equilibrium, then there is no policy outcome that can be considered the "majority party's position."

9. I do not address here what occurs when the caucus is not binding, that is, when there is a large majority. For conditions under which risk-averse individuals would prefer obstruction when the majority is large, see Dion 1991. I am currently working on a more complete model of floor consideration that I hope will fill this lacuna.

10. Of course, the minority could adopt a strategy of amendment and offer its own policy proposals. If the caucus is binding, however, such proposals will be defeated. See Dion 1991 for a model along these lines.

Chapter 3

1. The "partisan era" refers to a periodization of American political history that recognizes the continuities in the antebellum and postbellum eras, particularly in the organization of politics around parties. For a discussion of partisanship in this era, both in American political culture as well as in the legislature, see Silbey 1967; Burnham 1970; Price 1971, 1975; Keller 1977; Skowronek 1982; Baker 1983; Thompson and Silbey 1984; and McCormick 1986.

2. This is true even though rational choice has shown a much greater willingness to deal with the fundamental criticism of social psychology from Simon on: that rational choice had no place for incomplete information. See Calvert 1986 and Banks 1991 for monograph-length reviews of the huge and growing literature on incomplete information models of political behavior.

3. After having been sufficiently tough on the my own tribe, let me also critique the infuriating tendency to lob criticisms at rational choice that apply with equal weight to the research tradition that the critic is coming from. I wish I had a dime for every critic of the unrealistic assumptions of rational choice who had no qualms about assuming that errors are homoscedastic, or who wrote off rational choice as a tautology and then turned to discussing the "pivotal position of entrepreneurs."

4. Foucault has some comments on transition in *Discipline and Punish,* but these are left relatively underdeveloped, a token I think of how unimportant this part of the argument appears to be in the grander scheme. This whole discussion may seem to suggest that in my narrow positivist way I have missed the whole point of interpretive work: that there may be no master process at work explaining these cognitive shifts, and believing in one is a modernist fantasy. Exploration of these issues should be left to someone more knowledgeable than I, but if this is the case, then why should rational choice be criticized for failing to do something that it seems is not necessary?

5. Note that the question of the cycling of individual preferences is analytically distinct from the cycling of social preferences. The fact that members have well-defined preferences is all that is at issue in this section of the argument.

6. On this period, see Hasbrouck 1927.

7. We think of an actor's (a real actor, one who plays parts on stage—not the generic social science character) portrayal as realistic if it conveys the essence of what is going on. When critics say that Harvey Keitel's performance in *Bad Lieutenant* is "darkly realistic," they do not mean that there are actual police officers out there who look exactly like Keitel and have said and done the same things that he said in the film. Nonetheless, we know immediately what they mean.

8. It is a testament either to Lowell's intellectual weight or to the anglophilic nature of much party research that comparisons with other legislatures are infrequent. See Huber 1992 for an exception.

9. The exceptions are the 25th and the 27th Congress, where he presents both. For the first case, I used the data from the first session. The second case presents more of a problem. The election of 1840 resulted in Whig party winning, not just control of one institution (which they had never accomplished), but control of the House, the Senate, and the presidency under William Henry Harrison. Given this unique opportunity, Henry Clay proposed that a special session be called to pass Whig legislation. Harrison (apparently reluctantly) agreed (Byrd 1988, 164). The Congress did not turn out to be the Whig-fest one might have predicted: "Tippecanoe" Harrison caught pneumonia and died on April 4, roughly two months before the start of the special session. John Tyler turned out to be far less of a Whig than one might have thought, and the special session was doomed to interinstitutional fighting. Given the special history of this session, to include it might have been to include an apple with an orange. In the regression results presented here, I have therefore used the Party90 and the Party Disagreement scores for

the first *regular* session, which is the second session of the 27th Congress. I have also run all of the regressions using the special session of 1841 and also an average (weighted by number of roll calls) of the two sessions for both variables. The results stay the same.

10. If we follow the partisan periodization (that is, that the period before and after the Civil War contains important historical continuities that exceed their differences), then it follows statistically that all we are losing in breaking up the time series is efficiency.

11. My aim in doing this was to determine as far as was possible what Charles Jones (1968) has referred to as the procedural majority.

12. For a contrasting opinion, see Mayhew 1991, 126.

13. Since we have theoretical expectations about the relationship between majority size and Party Disagreement, it can be argued that the appropriate standard to employ is the one-tailed test. As noted in the table, the coefficient does pass this arguably more reasonable standard. For nonstatistical types, the fact that the coefficient passes the two-tailed test means automatically that it would pass a similar (indeed, even a more restrictive) one-tailed test.

14. I am not here asserting the absurdity that coalitions within the U.S. Congress can never cross party lines. But especially on procedural votes, the coalitions are a bit more fixed along party lines than might otherwise be the case. For an in-depth analysis of how the transition from partisan politics to issue politics took place, see Hansen's (1991) study of the emergence of the Farm Lobby.

15. Geertz suggests that we think of social science as a diagnostic, rather than predictive science. See Geertz 1973, 3–30.

16. "Center" bets are the bets between the principals (the person owning the cock and his coalition). Outside bets are between third parties. Geertz ruminates over the finding that betting between principals is always even money, while betting between third parties is not. At the risk of sounding like every other rational choice theorist, might this not simply reflect the fact that taking odds on one's own bird would signal some private information (for example, my bird is sick today) to every other party?

17. *Daily News*, January 12, 1893. Quoted in *Oxford English Dictionary 2* on CD-ROM.

18. Asher Hinds records a particularly bizarre case occurring in the 1852 consideration of the Homestead Bill. Henry Hibbard of New Hampshire, the chair of the Committee of the Whole, refused to vote yes on a 63 to 64 vote to uphold the chair (a result which could tie the vote and therefore sustain his own decision; although Hibbard himself felt that a tie would mean losing the question, that is, overruling his ruling in any event).

19. Tiefer also notes that this differs from the practice of the Senate, where overruling decisions on points of order is used as a technique to get around "inconvenient" rules: it would be fascinating to determine the historical evolution of this procedure in the two branches of Congress.

20. Not being a member of the Political Methodology group, I cannot be kicked out for statistical heresy.

21. I would like to thank David Crampton for compiling this information.

22. The positive coefficient indicates that this period in fact had significantly more missing quorums than would otherwise be expected. This may sound strange to those who think that the Reed Rules finished the disappearing quorum. But the variable here reflects both the uses of this obstructive tactic in the Congress in which Reed made his ruling, and the heavy use by the Republicans under the following Democratically controlled Houses.

23. Clearly, the effect of the proportion of competitive seats, or for that matter the percentage of new members, could well have an interaction effect with the size of the majority party. To determine whether this was the case, I multiplied each of those two measures by the proportion of seats held by the majority. As this number gets higher, therefore, it shows that there is a smaller majority composed of less safe members (or newer members). I also tried squaring the interaction in case there were nonlinearities. Since these interaction terms did not alter the basic story (in all cases, the sign and statistical significance of the proportion of seats held by the majority party being identical to that reported in column 4), I opted to present the simpler model.

24. Information on the number of measures introduced was obtained from *Historical Statistics*. The number of Representatives and Senators is taken from Martis. The percentage replacement figures are reported in Fiorina, Rohde, and Wissel.

25. This would be true either if the size of the electoral margins was related to low desire to return to office (the static ambition argument of Kernell) or increased party competition.

26. Before moving on, it should be noted how the results of this subsection alter the findings regarding the use of missing quorums. In that section, the number of missing quorums was normalized by the number of days. But we have found here that the number of days is itself a function of majority party size: the more obstruction, the more days the Congress sits in session. Therefore, to get significant effects from majority party proportion, it is necessary to overcome the attenuating effect of an increase in the number of days in session. To put it another way, even if the use of the missing quorum was related to the size of the majority, the effect might well disappear if our dependent variable controls for the number of days and if the majority response to a large number of missing quorums is to increase the number of days. The fact that significant effects are picked up despite this possible attenuation is additional evidence for the strength of the theory.

27. In the course of checking Galloway's figures, I found a discrepancy between the total number of representatives reported for the 53rd Congress and the sum of the various categories (Republican, Democrat, Other, Vacancies) making up that Congress. Since the calculations I make do not rely on the total number of representatives, I have assumed that Galloway's party breakdown is correct.

28. A complete list of the entire spectrum of rules changes has apparently been compiled by Richard Damon in his doctoral dissertation (Damon 1971). This work, however, is organized into substantive categories making it impossible to assess the completeness of the presentation. Stanley Bach of the Congressional Research Service has informed me that his search for either Damon or the list of rules changes came up empty. It was only after I finished obtaining the data I needed on obstruction that I

realized the obvious solution to determining Dr. Damon's whereabouts: contacting the Columbia Alumni Affairs office.

29. In addition there have been, according to the literature, major changes in the rules outside of the era I am studying, including the years 1811, 1822, 1909–1911, 1946, and 1970–1975 (Damon 1971, Jones 1970). The later period seems to me not to have much to do with the issues of floor obstruction that I am concerned with here (a reminder that we should not assume that rules reform is of a piece). The earlier period is part of ongoing research by Sarah Binder and promises to introduce some new wrinkles into the account of why cohesive majorities (even, from all appearances, *large* cohesive majorities) restrict minority rights.

30. The results (as well as comparisons with other theories) are presented in Dion 1991, 14–38.

Chapter 4

1. The term *agency* is used here to refer to the capacity of individuals to act in the world, as opposed to simply inferring that they are ciphers for some larger historical process.

2. For a discussion of the relevance of boarding arrangements for congressional politics, see Young 1966. A thorough critique of this work is presented by Bogue and Marlaire 1975. It is probably safe to state that while mess arrangements did not cause agreement, the close proximity obtained in the boarding house reduced the difficulties involved in designing a parliamentary strategy such as that undertaken by Bell, Wise, and Peyton.

3. This differs from proportions reported in chapter 3, which were much higher for the 24th Congress. Much of the difference is probably attributable to Lynn's interest in forces that supported the administration, as opposed to those who defined themselves for electoral purposes as Democrats.

4. A discussion of the specific rules changes is included in the appendix to Dion 1991. Included there is an important change in the rules regulating the introduction of bills (discussed in Cooper and Young 1989) and appropriations. The cost of not investigating this and the other rules changes is that one might miss cases where abilities of agents to obstruct were either enhanced or diminished. On the other hand, the fact that these rules changes did not lead to roll calls and were not considered important enough for comment in the records of the debates indicates that they were probably changes that all parties found either pointless or beneficial.

5. The District of Columbia has historically had a rather unique place in national politics, since it is an area where claims regarding "state sovereignty" have no weight. Members of Congress before the adoption of home rule could not avoid contentious issues like slavery by saying that they were local problems and unrelated to the concerns of the national legislature.

6. Despite the fraternal tone of this message, Etheridge would three years later (in 1863) as acting clerk of the House take advantage of a loophole in a bill regulating the

admission of members to attempt a Conservative coup in the House of Representatives. He was foiled, however, when S. S. "Sunset" Cox was unable to deliver the conservative vote. Afterwards, Whitelaw Reid was at the White House, and it was proposed that he write something disparaging about Etheridge. Abraham Lincoln commented, "No, Reid, I would not do it. Emerson ain't worth more than a squirrel load of powder anyway" (Belz 1970, 564: see that source for a further discussion of the Etheridge conspiracy).

7. See Denzau, Riker, and Shepsle 1985 for further considerations of the relationship between homestyle and sophisticated voting.

8. These are listed in the appendix of Dion 1991.

9. For an argument that these rules changes are inconsequential, see the appendix to Dion 1991.

10. In 1857, the House had moved into a new hall, and the rules then adopted restricted a variety of individuals, including ex-members of Congress, from access to the floor. They were, however, free to take a spot in the gallery. The rules changes debated in 1860 were meant to allow these former members back to the floor.

Chapter 5

1. Prior to emancipation, slaves were counted in the census as three-fifths of a person. With emancipation, each freedman would count as a whole person. Disfranchisement of African-Americans therefore would leave Southern whites with a larger proportion of House seats (due to the additional two-fifths of a person) while at the same time maintaining political control.

2. The disputed votes were from South Carolina, Florida, Louisiana, and Oregon.

3. The Republicans, however, were not unwilling to pursue nonobstructionist strategies. Garfield's *Diary* notes that the Republican caucus in fact had voted not to obstruct the Army Appropriations bill "except to procure sufficient time for debate" (IV, 207). All references to Garfield's diary in this chapter are to the fourth volume.

4. For the text of the 120th Rule and a complete recounting of activities on the floor, see Dion 1991.

5. Blackburn retorted, "I simply desire to say that if at any time in the past I have made a ruling, or shall at any time in the future be fortunate enough to make one, which incurs the criticism of the parliamentarian from California, it will only strengthen my conviction of having been right in that ruling" (955).

6. While I have no quarrel with this analysis, it does bring up the question why the devolution of appropriations power to Public Buildings, though ultimately failing, was able to pass in the Committee of the Whole. I think the answer can be found in the comments of Calkins: " . . . if beaten I think it is best not to waste time by further resisting the continued action of the committee. Let us get along with these rules. Let us make a stand on the proposition made by the gentleman from Pennsylvania [Mr. Clymer], and let us from that extract a few crumbs of comfort" (730). This suggests that Public Buildings devolution was able to pass because of its symbolic value as a last stand for devolution. After the vote on Military Affairs and Post Office, it was clear that

the piecemeal approach was probably doomed to fail, despite the promising beginning with Agriculture. Rather than diminish Stewart's constituency-oriented arguments, I believe this interpretation makes sense of the shifting fortunes of Public Building devolution. Robbed of its symbolic importance, Public Buildings devolution could not on its own merits provide the votes to carry the day.

7. The *Washington Post* of March 3, 1880, noted that "The most notable event in connection with the adoption of the revised code yesterday was the flattening out of the flatulent Conger" (2).

8. Cited in McCall 1914, 31–32. The unusual contraction is in the original.

9. L. White Busbey, Joseph Cannon's amanuensis, registered Cannon's recollections: "He sent no word either to McKinley or to me. He had previously told us to be constantly in readiness for he did not know when the time for action would come, but on that eventful morning we went into the House and sat at our desks with no premonition that before the day was over history would be written" (1927, 175–76).

10. One of the minority members of the New York legislature, Frederick Lansing, just happened to have been elected to the 51st Congress. When Springer noted that Lansing and others had attacked the ruling as unconstitutional and revolutionary, Lansing replied, "I desire to say that I was entirely convinced by Governor Hill's argument." To which Springer responded, "It seems not to have converted you until this time" (*CR*, Jan. 29, 1890, 955).

11. The careful reader may be jarred: Cannon says Reed was "calm" and "beatific," while Stealey has him "pale" with fists "clenched." Adjudicating the dispute is difficult, but since Cannon was able to get closer than Stealey, and in any event had a closer acquaintance, I would be more willing to trust Cannon. Of course, there is nothing preventing Reed from being beatific at one moment and then a bit pale at the next.

12. This remark drew a great reaction from the Democrats. "The House will have the kindness to be in order," Reed remarked.

13. When the House was considering how many copies of these proposed rules to have printed, one member offered an amendment "that 1,950 copies of the general parliamentary law under which it is alleged that the House of Representatives is governed, be printed for the use of the members of the House" (*CR*, Feb. 6, 1880, 1109).

14. The appendix to Dion 1991 contains a description of the minor rules changes.

15. In a humorous note, one member, frustrated with Crisp's attempts, proposed an amendment that "This rule shall not be construed as abrogating the Constitution of the United States or the right of George Washington to be called the Father of his Country" (*CR*, Feb. 13, 1890, 1293).

16. This is not to say that the Republicans did not also have sectional tensions. The East/West split in the party broke open during the consideration of the Sherman Silver Purchase Act, and led to a rare procedural defeat when Reed's attempt to refer the bill to the Committee on Coinage (without letting the House know) was revealed and reversed. In this case, Reed did what any good politician would do: delay the proceedings until enough supporting his side of the issue could come back to town. With their support, the Sherman Silver Purchase Act was passed as a compromise measure (Peters 1990, 70).

17. What Reed actually said was that if his *party* did not support him, he would resign.

Chapter 6

1. For further comments about selecting on the dependent variable, see Dion (forthcoming).

2. My thinking about the 1850 case has been influenced by the work of Sarah Binder (1992).

3. The account here follows Robinson 1930, 85–96.

4. For the advantages of a bill-specific approach, see Krehbiel 1991, 98–9, 250–51.

5. Some additional evidence: On February 4 1892, during the 52nd Congress (which is universally presented as a return to obstruction), a rule was allowed that would limit to one motion to adjourn any obstructive attempt on the vote for consideration of a report from the Committee on Rules (Hinds 1899, IV.§4621).

6. These two were V.§5723, a rather weird precedent in which the chair on August 31, 1842, apparently refused to entertain an appeal he considered trivial, and V.§5752, which describes a case where the Speaker overruled a point of order that it was time to recess (since it was 5:00 Friday) and allowed a vote on suspension of the rules. Hinds's index covers more cases of dilatory proceedings than are simply contained in that chapter, however.

7. This precedent dealt with the impeachment of Secretary of War William W. Belknap, who was apparently bribed through a third party in $1500 increments to allow John S. Evans to run a trading establishment at Fort Sill, Oklahoma. The incident is referred to as having produced "unprecedented" obstruction, but on closer reading it appears that the "unprecedented" obstruction came from Belknap's attorney. It therefore did not seem of a piece with the other precedents, and so was excluded.

8. Both Brady 1973, 7, and Cox 1987 present versions that are more explicit about the political mechanisms accounting for the transformation of these pressures into procedural reform.

9. What accounts for Blaine's enduring reputation? At least part of the answer is that Democrats looked to rulings made by members of the opposite party to buttress their own procedural arguments. And of the Republicans? Thomas Brackett Reed, a fellow citizen of Maine, seems to have been friendly enough (McCall 1914, 90), but it was in reference to Blaine's nomination for president in 1884 that Reed quipped those immortal lines to Henry Cabot Lodge: "Well, it is a great comfort to think that the wicked politicians were not allowed to pick the candidate, and that the nomination was made by the people. The politicians would have been guided only by a base desire to win" (McCall 1914, 91).

10. In which direction might the selection bias go? Selection rules that favor recent (in 1899) Democratic precedents would have the effect of oversampling on large majorities and of attenuating whatever relationship there might be between majority party proportion and the precedent count, a good point to remember in judging the results on that measure presented above.

Chapter 7

1. See Shuman 1969; Wolfinger 1971; Oppenheimer 1985; Herzberg 1986; Sinclair 1989; Rohde 1991, 177–79; and especially Smith 1989, chapter 4. The dissertation is DeNardis 1989. Subsequent to writing these words, the new and much welcome treatment of Binder and Smith (1996) was released. I have unfortunately been unable to incorporate their work into the discussion here.

2. This information is contained in the volume *Senate Cloture Rule* printed for the Committee on Rules and Administration of the Senate, 99th Congress, 1st Session (Y4.R86/2:S.prt.99-95).

3. I lacked corresponding Senate measures for the other reciprocity variables considered in chapter 6. Nor did I feel the need to gather the data—the remaining terms seem to me to be quite specific to the House and therefore of little interest in a study of the Senate.

4. To replicate the House analysis, I have also rerun columns 3 through 5 with the addition of the measures for number of Senators and number of bills introduced. The results were unchanged. I then reran columns 2 through 5 with a new variable representing the number of bills introduced per Senator (replacing the two workload measures presented in the table). While this seems quite reasonable, this measure too had no effect, and the substantive pattern displayed in table 7.5 remained unchanged.

5. My account here follows Byrd 1988, 414–18.

6. The interaction of legislative politics and electoral rules is a rich field that has already yielded substantial insights. Gary Cox's work on Victorian England emphasizes the critical role played by the Reform Acts in ushering in procedural changes in the House of Commons. And Theda Skocpol's *Protecting Soldiers and Mothers* finds important shifts in social policy (such as the Shepherd–Townshend Act) occurring when women were first extended the vote. She argues that the uncertainty about the power of women given suffrage led to a window of opportunity for the passage of social policy.

7. A sign of how close these majorities were: the 83rd Congress saw the Republicans at 48 seats and the Democrats at 47, with Wayne Morse a lone Independent. Morse agreed to vote with the Republicans to organize the Senate, which allowed the Republicans to control committees. However, the death of Robert Taft and his replacement by a Democrat placed the Republicans at 47 seats and the Democrats at 48, leaving the Republicans nominally in charge but without a majority. My account here follows Byrd 1988, 608f.

8. In a letter to Earl Mazo written a year later, King expressed his opinion of the future president: "I would say that Nixon has a genius for convincing one that he is sincere. When you are close to Nixon he almost disarms you with his apparent sincerity. . . . And so I would conclude by saying that if Richard Nixon is not sincere, he is the most dangerous man in America" (quoted in Branch 1988, 219).

9. The narrative here simplifies tremendously; for an exhaustively thorough account, see Shuman 1969.

10. See as well DeNardis 1989, 91, who refers to the 1959 rule as a "modest revision."

Chapter 8

1. Cox does mention filibustering (46), but it is safe to say that the story of obstruction, particularly Irish obstruction, is not Cox's main concern (see especially page 4). While some discussion of the earlier rules changes will overlap with Cox's treatment, we come at the issue from different angles.

2. The worst example of a rotten borough I have encountered is in Bulmer-Thomas: "The elder Pitt sat for Old Sarum, where there was not a single inhabited house and sheep grazed peacefully on the mound that marked the site of the ancient city" (1965, I.75). It is not every legislator who can deal with quarrelsome constituents by eating them.

3. This story can be inferred from May, but is available at an excessively amplified length in Redlich. It is also presented in Bryce 1890, although he does note a prior case of obstruction in 1872 on purchases for the army ("resisted by a group of members in the interest of the officers" [386]) and posits a few other reasons besides social ties as well. Compare Kee 1972b: "In the summer of 1877, taking advantage of the generous rules of debate and the latitude then given by gentlemanly custom to individual members to assert their rights against the government machine, Parnell and his small group of half a dozen or so supporters began holding up government business to a point where ministers desperately sought the help of Butt [the Irish leader] himself in restraining them" (69–70). Even earlier, J. L. Hammond wrote, in a passage approvingly cited by Bulmer-Thomas (1965, I.137): "Wellington and Peel established a tradition that survived for half a century, the tradition that governed and limited the range and methods of party conflict. It was agreed that it was the duty of an opposition, when a controversy reached a certain point or a problem assumed a certain character, to seek to limit the mischief that might be caused by a reform that was distasteful, rather than to prolong resistance by methods that might provoke revolution" (1938, 455–56). This tradition lasted, he argued, until 1886 and the Home Rule debate. Thanks to Cox, political scientists now know that at least part of this formulation was incorrect. Limitations on individual member initiative began much earlier than the appearance of Parnell, indeed quite soon after the adoption (and obstruction) of the First Reform Act in 1832.

4. I have here (and elsewhere) excised what is clearly Redlich's own interpolation—"he wrote, in characteristic words"—between "insist" and "on" in the first line.

5. Dissent would not be totally stifled, however. Tuesdays through Thursdays were still possible, although Saturdays had been unavailable ever since the House obliged Horace Walpole's desire to hunt over the entire weekend (Redlich 1908, II.69).

6. My account here follows Kee 1972a, 202–21.

7. John Blysma (1977) has argued that voting patterns during this period displayed a surprising degree of party cohesion. This runs counter to the opinion of most historians about this period, a fact that Blysma attributes to their attention to the machinations of party leaders rather than patterns of voting. Thus, even within a period not known for party, we see party cohesion at the moment we should expect: when there is a bare majority.

8. Redlich notes in footnote 4 a list of seemingly insignificant changes that were adopted, but no major reforms took place during this time. There was a Joint Committee set up in 1871: Redlich is not clear on the details, and it need not concern us here.

9. This is not as ludicrous as it sounds. As late as 1892, only 30 members out of 670 apparently received a salary (Buxton 1892, 149). As a result, the traditional practice of the Commons was to begin its sittings in late afternoon to accommodate those with businesses to run.

10. Estimates on the length of the filibuster vary. Kee (1972b, 70) has it as 26 hours, Redlich (I.145) places it at 20 hours and 50 minutes, while Lyons (1977, 64) puts the continuous sitting of the Commons at 41 hours and the obstruction on the South Africa Bill at 21 hours.

11. Bulmer-Thomas (I.126) places the number at 347 Liberals out of 652 members, for a proportion of 53.2 percent. The Home Rule party (as was customary) sat with the opposition (Kee 1972b, 80), although two nominal Home Rulers did sit with the Liberals (Lyons 1977, 123).

12. Parnell (1914, 189) has his brother and the Speaker trade words, after which the Speaker agrees that he needs to go and consult the precedents.

13. This form of discipline reaches back to the days of Speaker Onslow, who repeatedly threatened a disorderly member with being named. When asked what would have happened had the member in question been named, Onslow responded "the Lord in Heaven only knows" (Redlich 1908, III.72).

14. Kee (1972b), for example, argues that by putting the question on his own initiative, the Speaker suspended the "time-honoured rules of the House and forced the closure of the debate. This called the bluff of obstruction, and a formal reorganization of the House's rules later in the year confirmed the eclipse of obstruction as an effective technique" (82).

15. On pages 170–74, as well as 168–69, the text in Redlich alters typeface in the way reserved for quotations, but no references are presented. I have been unable to find any indication of whether these additions were those of Sir Courtenay Ilbert, who wrote an introduction and supplementary chapter; later additions made by Redlich; or a printer's error. I have therefore cited the author of these sections as Redlich.

16. Redlich (I.175) disparages the procedural reforms made under Gladstone, noting that they were "tacitly abandoned" and never "really put into force." This seems, however, to assume (a) that there was an occasion in which the procedures were needed, and (b) that members did not anticipate the use of these procedures and act accordingly.

17. While Salisbury was Prime Minister for much of this era, his nephew, Arthur James Balfour was, at least as presented by Redlich, the real force behind the reforms of the era, hence my handle for this era.

18. Ten years is a long time, but as Lyons points out (458) "Aunt Ben" was 88 in 1881, and there was ample reason to suspect that her demise would be imminent. It appears that all parties involved must have continued throughout this time to make the rational calculation that she could not hold out for much longer. Ex post, of course, the situation looks like a farce. For a recent discussion of these sorts of problems see Akerlof 1991.

19. Craig presents the party majorities for Conservative, Liberal, and Other. Since this did not give the specificity needed, I have relied here on Bulmer-Thomas.

20. The edition of May that I relied on (the tenth) has the precedent taking place on May 25, 1875, on a ruling by the Speaker on a motion of Mr. Dillwyn (May 1893, 265). Dillwyn was a Radical Member who had raised the ire of Palmerston when he proposed to speak to the issue of the Irish Church as a private member, a position that Palmerston apparently found inconceivable for someone speaking from the Treasury Bench (Hammond 1938, 78–79). While the practice may indeed have accelerated around the turn of the century, the rather imposing list of cites in May seem to suggest that the ruling is not as insignificant as it appears. In the supplementary chapter to the third volume of Redlich, Sir Courtenay Ilbert finds the earliest edition of May referring to the problem cites a precedent from 1871 (221).

21. After reaching this conclusion, I came across this quote in Redlich: "The reforms of the eighties were directed only against the Irish enemy in the House: but the closure, the parliamentary 'guillotine,' in short all the weapons in the arsenal of an impatient majority, were soon applied to the varying of purely English measures against keen party resistance" (III.196). After making this argument, however, he lapses back into the workload view: "Such action amounts to an admission of the sheer technical necessity of the modern form of procedure: the House of Commons, like the parliaments of all other modern great states, needs it in order to cope with the overloading which it has to bear, in order to counteract the dissipation of strength caused by the splitting up of modern party life, which, in its turn, has arisen from the infinite divergence of social and economic interests at the present day" (196).

22. For those interested in pursuing the story back a bit, both the data on suspensions and adjournment go back to 1882.

23. I also tried various permutations, but in general either nothing was significant or else party was. In no case did party ever switch sign.

24. Thus the value of the variable when the election is 5 years away would be 25, the value for 4 years 16, and so on. While the post-Gladstone years indicate the possibility of a cubic term (note the slight increase at the end), I decided to attempt a simpler form used here.

25. Calculus allows us to determine the precise moment at which the use of closure should peak. Taking the first derivative of the estimated equation with respect to the election variable and setting the result equal to zero, and assuming a 30 day month, it turns out that the use of the closure motion reaches a peak 3 years, 3 months, 1 day, 3 hours, 7 minutes, and 20 seconds from the time of the next regularly scheduled election, a finding doubtless ripe with numerological significance.

26. In fact, if we want to get precise, the peak seems to occur roughly one month further from the election than the peak for closure motions. In other words, based on these estimates (and ignoring all the problems of statistical confidence here), it would appear that obstructive motions reach a peak, and then closure motions begin to come. This is thoroughly naive, of course, but I raise it in hopes that those who have greater time-series skills than I (and who doesn't?) will be inspired to clarify the relationship.

27. If one omits the dummy variable, proportion is significant, but the log-likelihood takes a precipitous drop.

28. I may be transgressing some solemn MLA protocol, but I will stick throughout this section to referring to "Mark Twain" rather than "Samuel Clemens."

29. One yachting occasion took place after a dinner held in Twain's honor. Reed (who had lost 40 pounds from his Speakership days but was far from thin) remarked that he was the only person on the yacht "who had real gravity that was calculated to keep the ship in order and keep her down" (McCall 1914, 274).

30. When Reed died, Twain wrote an exceptionally beautiful memorial. A selection: " . . . now he is gone from us, and the nation is speaking of him as one who *was*. It seems incredible, impossible. Such a man, such a friend, seems to us a permanent possession, his vanishing from our midst is unthinkable; as unthinkable as was the vanishing of the Campanile, that had stood for a thousand years, and was turned to dust in a moment. I have no wish, at this time, to enter upon light and humorous reminiscences connected with yachting voyages with Mr. Reed in northern and southern seas, nor with other recreations in his company in other places—they do not belong in this paper, they do not invite me, they would jar upon me. I have only wished to say how fine and beautiful was his life and character, and to take him by the hand and say goodby, as to a fortunate friend who has done well his work and goes a pleasant journey" ("Thomas Brackett Reed," 1902, in Twain 1963, 312).

31. As it turns out, Twain *was* to see history made twice. In September 1898, while Twain was in Austria, Empress Elisabeth was assassinated by the anarchist Luigi Lucheni (who, by way of explanation, stated that he would have preferred to assassinate King Umberto of Italy, but lacked the requisite 50 francs to make the trip to Rome—Marek 1974, 374). Twain wrote in a letter to Reverend Joseph Twichell that the Empress was "killed by a madman, and I am living in the midst of world-history again" (Twain 1963, 535–36). Incidentally, the original has "any eyes" (rather than "my eyes"), which is undoubtedly a misprint.

32. This simplifies tremendously: technically, responses had to be phrased in the language used by the person making the first contact, and with the administrative, judicial, and bureaucratic branches, all written correspondence had to be in the language used when that particular branch of correspondence first started. This would require all civil servants in those two regions, therefore, to be conversant in both Czech and German. For a penetrating discussion of the relationship between state formation and language, see Laitin 1992.

33. I assume that had Badeni attempted other gambits, my sources would have reported it.

34. Macartney gives an incomplete breakdown on page 663, noting that while he was basing these figures on Kolmer, "no two lists ever agree exactly"; frustratingly, he reports the full figures for the February–March 1891 election five pages earlier.

35. Some sources: Dr. Gustav Kolmer's *Parlament und Verfassung in Osterreich*, an eight volume work from 1902, and E. Czedlik, *Zur Geschichte der Kaiserliche und königliche OesterreichischMinisterien, 1861–1916*, a much shorter (four volume) treatment. These sources (and the even shorter *Oestereich von Vilàgos bis zur Gegenwart* by E. Rogge, three volumes from 1872) give, according to Macartney, "every detail man could want of party and Parliamentary manoeuverings in Cis-Leithania" (854).

36. Twain is probably being too optimistic. If the government could have passed the *Ausgleich* without the language provision, it would have done so. The only appreciable cost to doing this that I can see is that it would clearly alienate the Czechs, who might subsequently revolt and perhaps as a result break apart the Austro-Hungarian empire, the very outcome that renewing the *Ausgleich* was supposed to avoid. He clearly recognizes this a few pages later (231).

37. To be sure, the Germans did not invent obstruction in the Austrian parliament. The Young Czechs and the Social Democrats had practiced obstruction against the previous government under Prince Alfred Windischgraetz, effectively ending all non-essential legislation.

38. How tastes change! The *Ringstrasse* architecture admired by Twain would later earn the wrath of Loos and others.

39. I have not attempted to find out whether the tolerance of Viennese men and women for these sorts of comments was higher than that of Twain. I suppose knowing the reaction of the Viennese to Freud makes me hesitant to think that Twain is wrong.

40. Twain may have been a dupe here: Marek (1974, 8) assures us that the plethora of titles was an innocent deceit.

41. Marek 1974 finds that "bits of excessive and meaningless politeness sat like stones in the rivulets of Viennese conversation" (9). I tend to distrust statements like this, and to be sure this is Vienna and not the whole of the Austro-Hungarian Empire, but if it is true, then it presents a puzzle for linking the comity within legislatures with the comity within society.

42. Macartney, curiously, finds the rule change unobjectionable, calling the measure "mild enough" (664). This seems to me quite an understatement.

Chapter 9

1. These words were written in the summer of 1994, just prior to the astounding election that catapulted the Republicans to their first House majority in decades. That subsequent events have not borne out the predictions of the *Renewing Congress* report is, I hope, clear. Nor, it seems, has socialization worked. Mere weeks after a bipartisan civility retreat in the amiable resort of Hershey, Pennsylvania, the House witnessed a physical altercation between Republican Tom Delay of Texas and Democrat David Obey of Wisconsin, during the course of which reference to "chicken shit tactics" was apparently made. The topic in question was campaign finance reform, an issue that, with its continual reference to "politicians getting down to working together like the people who sent us here want us to do," is tailor-made for the workload account. More relevant than workload, reciprocity, or socialization, it seems, is the razor-thin majority that supported Newt Gingrich in his election as speaker.

2. In 1954, the Committee on Legislatures of the American Political Science Association, a collection of scholars and legislative professionals under chair Belle Zeller of Brooklyn College, published the results of their four-year research into assessing the level of modernization of state legislatures. Chapter 7 of that useful report presents the results of a survey of the rules of procedure utilized in all 48 states. From

that chapter I have compiled a data set on the adoption of the previous question and cloture rules in various state legislatures. The dependent variables were coded "1" if every house of the state legislature had the restrictive procedure in question, and "0" otherwise.

3. All of these variables are coded based on the information presented in the Committee on Legislatures report.

4. If new legislatures borrow their rules from other legislatures (as Loewenberg and Patterson 1979, 117, point out), then there should be similarities regarding the restrictiveness of procedures of different state legislatures created at the same time. To make sure that statehood was not idiosyncratic, I also ran the model using date of organization as a territory or colony. No substantive differences emerged.

5. The dummy variable for the South was intended to capture the possibility that Southern legislative procedure (especially given one-party dominance, not to mention the history of civil rights filibustering) may diverge from Northern and Western procedure.

6. Data on majority attempts to limit debate in the Senate is already in a dichotomous form. Regarding the House, data on the count of antiobstructive precedents was transformed into a dichotomous variable ("1" if this House witnessed a precedent limiting minority rights to obstruct and "0" if no precedent was set). A note here: I am lumping together actual *decisions* in the House with mere *attempts* in the Senate. Nothing in what follows can indicate why the actions in the Senate had no impact (if in fact that is true). At the same time, however, if our primary interest is in explaining what it is that leads majorities to attempt to limit minority rights, then throwing both of these in the same data set is not as perverse as it might seem.

7. I also ran the equation with the party proportion and Senate party proportion variable. The latter was not significant, which strengthens the statistical case.

8. Surprisingly, workload actually seems to have a positive effect. There may be some kick in the theory after all.

9. Other measures seemed to me idiosyncratic to the House. Note that contrary to the reciprocity theory, it appears that doomed majorities are if anything *more* likely to enact limitations on minority rights, not less (although the coefficient is not significant).

10. I am not saying here that unified party control of both houses of Congress is irrelevant. Clearly it is not: all sorts of implications arise when the same party controls both the House and the Senate. What I am after here is the question of whether shared party majority influences the path of institutional changes with respect to minority rights to obstruct.

Bibliography

References for the epigraphs that introduce sections and chapters occur after the relevant bibliographic entry. (Arthur Onslow is quoted in Hatsell; Reed is quoted in McCall; Sir Thomas Smith is quoted in Redlich; Etheridge is taken from the *Congressional Record.*)

Achen, Christopher H. 1982. *Interpreting and Using Regression.* Sage University Paper Series on Quantitative Applications in the Social Sciences, Series No. 07-029. Beverly Hills: Sage Press.

Achen, Christopher H., and Duncan Snidal. 1989. Rational Deterrence Theory and Comparative Case Studies. *World Politics* 41:143–69.

Adams, John Quincy. 1969 (first published 1874–77). *Memoirs of John Quincy Adams.* Edited by C. F. Adams. Freeport, NY: Books for Libraries Press.

Akerlof, George. 1991. Procrastination and Obedience. *American Economic Review* 81(2): 1–19.

Aldrich, John. 1988. Modeling the Party-in-the-Legislature. Duke University Program in Political Economy Papers in American Politics, Working Paper Number 46.

Aldrich, John. 1994. A Model of a Legislature with Two Parties and a Committee System. *Legislative Studies Quarterly* 19(3): 313–39.

Aldrich, John. 1995. *Why Parties?* Chicago: University of Chicago Press.

Alesina, Alberto. 1988. Credibility and Policy Convergence in Two-Party Systems with Rational Voters. *American Economic Review* 78(4): 796–805.

Alexander, DeAlva Stanwood. 1909. *History and Procedure of the House of Representatives.* Boston, MA: Houghton Mifflin Co.

Alexander, Thomas B. 1967. *Sectional Stress and Party Strength.* Nashville, TN: Vanderbilt University Press.

American Enterprise Institute and the Brookings Institution. 1992. *Renewing Congress: A First Report.* Washington, DC: AEI/Brookings.

Ansolabehere, Stephen, and Henry E. Brady. 1989. The Nature of Utility Functions in Mass Publics. *American Political Science Review* 83:143–63.

Argersinger, Peter H. 1992. No Rights on this Floor: Third Parties and the Institutionalization of Congress. *Journal of Interdisciplinary History* 22(4): 655–90.

Axelrod, Robert. 1984. *Evolution of Cooperation.* New York: Basic Books.

Bach, Stanley. 1990. Suspension of the Rules, the Order of Business, and the Development of Congressional Procedure. *Legislative Studies Quarterly* 15(1): 49–63.

Bach, Stanley, and Steven S. Smith. 1988. *Managing Uncertainty in the House of Representatives: Adaptation and Innovation in Restrictive Rules.* Washington, DC: The Brookings Institution.

Bagehot. 1993. Off With their Heads. *The Economist* 329(7842): 57.

Bailey, D. B. Shackleton. 1971. *Cicero.* London: Duckworth.

Baker, Jean. 1983. *Affairs of Party: The Political Culture of Northern Democrats in the Mid-Nineteenth Century.* Ithaca, NY: Cornell University Press.

Banks, Jeffrey S. 1991. *Signalling Games in Political Science.* Chur, Switzerland: Harwood Academic Publishers.

Baron, David P. 1993. Government Formation and Endogenous Parties. *American Political Science Review* 87(1): 34–47.

Baudelaire, Charles. 1964. *Flowers of Evil and Other Works*, ed. and trans. by Wallace Fowlie. New York: Bantam Books.

Belz, Herman. 1971. The Etheridge Conspiracy of 1863: A Projected Conservative Coup. *Journal of Southern History* 38:549–67. Reprinted in *The United States in a Partisan Era*, vol. 2, ed. Joel Silbey (1991). Brooklyn, NY: Carlson Publishing Inc.

Binder, Sarah A. 1992. A Partisan Theory of Procedural Change: Creation of Minority Rights in the House, 1789–1991. Paper presented at the American Political Science Association Annual Meeting, Chicago, IL.

Binder, Sarah A., and Steven S. Smith. 1996. *Politics or Principle? Filibustering in the United States Senate.* Washington, DC: Brookings.

Blysma, John R. 1977. Party Structure in the 1852–1877 House of Commons: A Scalogram Analysis. *Journal of Interdisciplinary History* 7(4): 617–35.

Bogue, Allan G. 1989. *The Congressman's Civil War.* New York: Cambridge University Press.

Bogue, Allan G., and Mark Paul Marlaire. 1975. Of Mess and Men: The Boardinghouse and Congressional Voting, 1821–1842. *American Journal of Political Science* 19(2): 207–30.

Boudon, Raymond. 1982. *The Unintended Consequences of Social Action.* London: MacMillan Press.

Brady, David. 1973. *Congressional Voting in a Partisan Era.* Lawrence: University Press of Kansas.

Brady, David, Richard Brody, and David Epstein. 1989. Heterogeneous Parties and Political Organization: The US Senate, 1880–1920. *Legislative Studies Quarterly* 14(2): 205–24.

Brady, David W., Joseph Cooper, and Patricia A. Hurley. 1979. The Decline of Party in the U.S. House of Representatives, 1887–1968. *Legislative Studies Quarterly* 4(3): 381–407.

Brady, David, and Bernard Grofman. 1991. Sectional Differences in Partisan Bias and Electoral Responsiveness in US House Elections, 1850–1980. *British Journal of Political Science* 21(2): 247–56.

Branch, Taylor. 1988. *Parting the Waters: America in the King Years, 1954–63.* New York: Simon and Schuster.

Bridges, Amy. 1984. *A City in the Republic.* Cambridge: Cambridge University Press.

Bryce, James. 1890. A Word as to the Speakership. *North American Review* 407:385–98.

Bulmer-Thomas, Ivor. 1965. *The Growth of the British Party System.* London: John Baker.

Burdette, Franklin L. 1940. *Filibustering in the Senate.* Princeton, NJ: Princeton University Press. Reprinted 1965. New York: Russell and Russell, Inc.

Burnham, Walter Dean. 1970. *Critical Elections and the Mainsprings of American Politics.* New York: W. W. Norton and Co., Inc.

Busbey, L. White. 1927. *Uncle Joe Cannon.* New York: Henry Holt and Company.

Buxton, Sydney. 1892. *A Handbook to Political Questions of the Day, and the Arguments on Either Side.* 8th edition. London: John Murray.

Byrd, Robert C. 1988. *The Senate, 1789–1989.* Washington, DC: U.S. Government Printing Office.

The Campaign Book of the Democratic Party. 1982. Washington, DC: R. O. Polkinhorn, Printer.

Calvert, Randall L. 1986. *Models of Imperfect Information in Politics.* Chur, Switzerland: Harwood Academic Publishers.

Carlyle, Thomas. 1837. *The French Revolution.* 2 vols. New York: Clarke, Given and Hooper.

Caro, Robert A. 1990. *Means of Ascent.* New York: Alfred Knopf.

Cicero, Marcus Tullius. [1977]. *In Catilinam, I–IV, Pro Murena, Pro Sulla, Pro Flacco,* trans. C. MacDonald. Cambridge, MA: Harvard University Press.

Clubb, J. M., W. H. Flanigan and N. H. Zingale. 1986. Realignment and Political Generations. In *Research in Micropolitics,* vol. 1, ed. S. Long, Greenwich, CT: JAI Press.

Clubb, Jerome M., and Santa A. Traugott. 1977. Partisan Cleavage and Cohesion in the House of Representatives, 1861–1974. *Journal of Interdisciplinary History* 7(3): 375–401.

Cohen, L. 1979. Cyclic Sets in Multidimensional Voting Models. *Journal of Economic Theory* 20:1–12.

Committee on Legislatures, American Political Science Association. 1954. *American State Legislatures,* ed. Belle Zeller. New York: Crowell.

Congressional Quarterly. 1982. *Congressional Quarterly's Guide to Congress, Third Edition.* Washington, DC: Congressional Quarterly, Inc.

Congressional Research Service. 1985. *Senate Cloture Rule.* Printed for Use of Committee on Rules and Administration, United States Senate, 99th Congress, 1st session. Senate Prt. 99-95. Washington, DC: Government Printing Office.

Connelly, William F., Jr., and John J. Pitney, Jr. 1994. *Congress' Permanent Minority? The Republicans in the US House.* Lanham, MD: Littlefield Adams.

Cooper, Joseph. 1962. *The Previous Question: Its Standing as a Precedent for Cloture in the United States Senate.* Senate Doc. No. 104, 87th Congress, 2d Session. Washington, DC: U.S. Government Printing Office.

Cooper, Joseph. 1977. Congress in Organizational Perspective. In *Congress Reconsidered,* ed. Lawrence C. Dodd and Bruce I. Oppenheimer, 140–59. New York: Praeger Publishers.

Cooper, Joseph, and David Brady. 1981. Institutional Context and Leadership Style. *American Political Science Review* 75:411–25.

Cooper, Joseph, and Cheryl D. Young. 1989. Bill Introduction in the Nineteenth Century: A Study of Institutional Change. *Legislative Studies Quarterly* 14(1): 67–105.

Cox, Gary W. 1987. *The Efficient Secret: The Cabinet and The Development of Political Parties in Victorian England.* New York: Cambridge University Press.

Cox, Gary W., and Mathew McCubbins. 1993. *Legislative Leviathan: Party Government in the House.* Berkeley and Los Angeles: University of California Press.

Craig, Fred W. S. 1989. *British Electoral Facts, 1832–1987,* 5th ed. Aldershot, Hants, England: Parliamentary Research Service, Dartmouth.

Crenshaw, Ollinger. 1942. The Speakership Contest of 1859–1860. *Mississippi Valley Historical Review* 29:323–38. Reprinted in *The United States in a Partisan Era,* vol. 2, ed. Joel Silbey (1991). Brooklyn, NY: Carlson Publishing Inc.

Dahl, Robert. 1956. *A Preface to Democratic Theory.* Chicago, IL: University of Chicago Press.

Damon, Richard Everett. 1971. The Standing Rules of the U.S. House of Representatives. Ph.D. diss., Columbia University.

Darnton, Robert. 1990. *The Kiss of Lamourette.* New York: Norton.

de Jouvenal, Bertrand. 1961. The Chairman's Problem. *American Political Science Review* 55(2): 368–72.

DeNardis, Lawrence Joseph. 1989. *The New Senate Filibuster: An Analysis of Filibustering and Gridlock in the U.S. Senate, 1977–1986.* Ph.D. diss., Dept. of Politics, New York University.

Denzau, Arthur, William Riker, and Kenneth Shepsle. 1985. Farquharson and Fenno: Sophisticated Voting and Home Style. *American Political Science Review* 79(4): 1117–34.

Dion, Douglas. 1991. *Removing the Obstructions.* Ph.D. diss., Dept. of Political Science, University of Michigan.

Dion, Douglas. 1992. The Robustness of the Structure-Induced Equilibrium. *American Journal of Political Science* 36(2): 462–92.

Dion, Douglas. Evidence and Inference in the Comparative Case Study. Forthcoming, *Comparative Politics.*

Dion, Douglas, and John Huber. 1996. Procedural Choice and the House Committee on Rules. *Journal of Politics* 58:25–53.

Dodd, Lawrence C., and Bruce I. Oppenheimer. 1989. The New Congress: Fluidity and Oscillation. In *Congress Reconsidered,* 4th edition, ed. Lawrence C. Dodd and Bruce I. Oppenheimer, 443–49. Washington, DC: CQ Press.

Donald, David. 1965. *The Politics of Reconstruction.* Baton Rouge: Louisiana State University Press.

Durkheim, Emile. 1897 [1951]. *Suicide.* New York: The Free Press.

Dworkin, Ronald. 1977. *Taking Rights Seriously.* Cambridge, MA: Harvard University Press.

Elster, Jon. 1983. *Explaining Technical Change.* New York: Cambridge University Press.

Engels, Friedrich. 1845 [1958]. *The Condition of the Working Class in England.* Trans. and ed. by W. O. Henderson and W. H. Chaloner. Stanford, CA: Stanford University Press.

Erasmus. 1509 [1982]. *Praise of Folly and Letter to Martin Dorp, 1515.* Trans. Betty Radic. New York: Penguin Books. (The quote introducing chapter 2 is on page 152).

Fenno, Richard. 1973. *Congressmen in Committees.* Boston, MA: Little, Brown.

Fiorina, Morris P., David W. Rohde, and Peter Wissel. 1975. Historical Change in House Turnover. In *Congress in Change*, ed. Norman J. Ornstein, 24–57. New York: Praegar Publishers.

Fiorina, Morris P., and Kenneth A. Shepsle. 1982. Equilibrium, Disequilibrium, and the General Possibility of a Science of Politics. In *Political Equilibrium*, ed. Peter C. Ordeshook and Kenneth A. Shepsle, 49–64. Boston, MA: Kluwer-Nijhoff Publishing.

Fischer, David H. 1970. *Historians' Fallacies.* New York: Harper and Row.

Follett, M. P. 1896. *The Speaker of the House of Representatives.* New York: Longmans, Green and Co.

Foner, Eric. 1970. *Free Soil, Free Labor, Free Men.* New York: Oxford University Press.

Foucault, Michel. 1979. *Discipline and Punish: The Birth of the Prison,* trans. Alan Sheridan. New York: Vintage Books.

Francis, Wayne. 1989. *The Legislative Committee Game: A Comparative Analysis of Fifty States.* Columbus: Ohio State University Press.

Freeman, Christopher. 1986. *The Economics of Industrial Innovation,* 2d ed. Cambridge, MA: The MIT Press.

Friedman, Milton. 1953. The Methodology of Positive Economics. In *Essays in Positive Economics.* Chicago, IL: University of Chicago Press.

Fudenberg, Drew and Eric Maskin. 1986. The Folk Theorem in Repeated Games with Discounting. *Econometrica* 54(3): 533–54.

Fuller, Hubert Bruce. 1909. *The Speakers of the House.* Boston: Little, Brown and Company.

Galambos, Louis. 1983. Technology, Political Economy, and Professionalization: Central Themes of the Organizational Synthesis. *Business History Review* 57:471–93.

Galloway, George. 1969. *History of the House of Representatives.* New York: Thomas Y. Crowell.

Garfield, James A. 1981. *The Diary of James A. Garfield.* Ed. H. J. Brown and H. D. Williams. East Lansing: Michigan State University Press.

Garrow, David. 1978. *Protest at Selma.* New Haven, CT: Yale University Press.

Geddes, Barbara. 1990. How the Cases You Choose Affect the Answers You Get: Selection Bias in Comparative Politics. *Political Analysis* 2:131–50.

Geertz, Clifford. 1973. *The Interpretation of Cultures.* New York: Basic Books.

Gienapp, William E. 1987. *The Origins of the Republican Party, 1852–1856.* New York: Oxford University Press.

Gilligan, Thomas W., and Keith Krehbiel. 1987. Collective Decisionmaking and Standing Committees: An Informational Rationale for Restrictive Amendment Procedures. *Journal of Law, Economics and Organization* 3:287–335.

Gilligan, Thomas W., and Keith Krehbiel. 1989a. Asymmetric Information and Legislative Rules with a Heterogeneous Committee. *American Journal of Political Science* 33(2): 459–90.

Gilligan, Thomas W., and Keith Krehbiel. 1989b. Collective Choice without Procedural Commitment. In *Models of Strategic Choice in Politics*, ed. Peter C. Ordeshook. Ann Arbor: University of Michigan Press.

Greenberg, Joseph. 1979. Consistent Majority Rule over Compact Sets of Alternatives. *Econometrica* 47(3): 627–36.

Greene, William H. 1993. *Econometric Analysis*, 2d ed. New York: MacMillan.

Guinier, Lani. 1994. *The Tyranny of the Majority*. New York: The Free Press.

Gurr, Ted. 1970. *Why Men Rebel*. Princeton, NJ: Princeton University Press.

Hammond, John Lawrence. 1938 [1964]. *Gladstone and the Irish Nation*. London: Frank Cass and Co.

Hansen, John Mark. 1991. *Gaining Access*. Chicago: University of Chicago Press.

Hardy, Ernest George. 1924. *The Catilinarian Conspiracy in its Context: A Re-Study of the Evidence*. Oxford: Basil Blackwell.

Hasbrouck, Paul DeWitt. 1927. *Party Government in the House of Representatives*. New York: The MacMillan Company.

Hatsell, John. 1818. *Precedents of Proceedings in the House of Commons*. London: Luke Hansard and Sons. (The quote from Arthur Onslow that introduces part 1 is located in volume 2, page 237.)

Haynes, George H. 1938. *The Senate of the United States*, 2 vols. Boston, MA: Houghton Mifflin Co.

Hechter, Michael. 1987. *Principles of Group Solidarity*. Berkeley and Los Angeles: University of California Press.

Hedlund, Ronald D., and Keith E. Hamm. 1976. Conflict and Perceived Group Benefits from Legislative Rules Changes. *Legislative Studies Quarterly* 1(2): 181–99.

Herzberg, Roberta. 1986. Blocking Coalitions and Policy Change. In *Congress and Policy Change*, ed. Gerald C. Wright, Jr., Leroy N. Rieselbach, and Lawrence C. Dodd, 201–22. New York: Agathon Press.

Hinckley, Barbara. 1972. Coalitions in Congress: Size and Ideological Distance. *Midwest Journal of Political Science* 16(2): 197–207.

Hinds, Asher. 1899. *Parliamentary Precedents of the House of Representatives of the United States*. Washington, DC: Government Printing Office.

Holmes, Stephen. 1988. Gag Rules or the Politics of Omission. In *Constitutionalism and Democracy*, ed. Jon Elster and Rune Slagstad, 19–58. New York: Cambridge University Press.

Holt, Michael. 1978. *The Political Crisis of the 1850s*. New York: W. W. Norton and Co.

Hoogenboom, Ari. 1988. *The Presidency of Rutherford B. Hayes*. Lawrence: University of Kansas Press.

House, Albert. 1935. The Contributions of Samuel J. Randall to the Rules of the National House of Representatives. *American Political Science Review* 29(5): 837–41.

House Committee on Rules. 1983. *A History of the Committee on Rules*. Washington, DC: U.S. Government Printing Office.

Huber, John. 1992. Restrictive Legislative Procedures in France and the United States. *American Political Science Review* 86(3): 675–87.

Hurley, Patricia, and Rick Wilson. 1989. Partisan Voting Patterns in the U.S. Senate, 1877–1986. *Legislative Studies Quarterly* 14(2): 225–50.

Hutchinson, Lester. 1966. *The Conspiracy of Catiline*. London: Anthony Blond Ltd.

Iida, Keisuke. 1993. When and How Do Domestic Constraints Matter? Two-Level Games with Uncertainty. *Journal of Conflict Resolution* 37(3): 403–26.

Ilisevich, Robert D. 1988. *Galusha A. Grow, The People's Candidate*. Pittsburgh, PA: University of Pittsburgh Press.

Illinois Commission on the Organization of the General Assembly. 1967. *Improving the State Legislature*. Urbana: University of Illinois Press.

Jacobson, Gary C., and Samuel Kernell. 1983. *Strategy and Choice in Congressional Elections*. 2d edition. New Haven, CT: Yale University Press.

James, Scott C. 1992. A Party System Perspective on the Interstate Commerce Act of 1887: The Democracy, Electoral College Competition, and the Politics of Coalition Maintenance. *Studies in American Political Development* 6(1): 163–200.

Jefferson, Thomas. 1797–1801. [1973]. *Jefferson's Manual of Parliamentary Practice*. Reproduced in *Senate Manual, 93d Congress, 1st Session*, Senate Document No. 93-1. Washington, DC: Government Printing Office.

Jellinek, Georg. 1904. Parliamentary Obstruction. *Political Science Quarterly* 19:579–88.

Jewell, Malcolm E., and Marcia Lynn Whicker. 1994. *Legislative Leadership in the American States*. Ann Arbor: University of Michigan Press.

Jones, Charles O. 1968. Joseph G. Cannon and Howard W. Smith: An Essay on the Limits of Leadership. *Journal of Politics* 30(3): 617–46.

Jones, Charles O. 1970. *The Minority Party in Congress*. Boston, MA: Little Brown.

Josephy, Alvin M., Jr. 1979. *On the Hill: A History of the American Congress*. New York: Simon and Schuster.

Joyce, James. 1916 [1974]. *Dubliners*. New York: Viking Press. (The quote in chapter 8 occurs on 132.)

Judex [A Democratic Leader]. 1890. The Speaker and His Critics. *North American Review* 405:228–36.

Kahn, Arthur D. 1986. *The Education of Julius Caesar*. New York: Schocken Books.

Kearns, Doris. 1976. *Lyndon Johnson and the American Dream*. New York: Harper and Row.

Kee, Robert. 1972a. *The Most Distressful Country*. New York: Penguin Books.

Kee, Robert. 1972b. *The Bold Fenian Men*. New York: Penguin Books.

Keller, Morton. 1977. *Affairs of State*. Cambridge, MA: Belknap Press.

Kennedy, Peter. 1985. *A Guide to Econometrics*, 2d ed. Cambridge, MA: The MIT Press.

Kernell, Samuel. 1977. Toward Understanding Nineteenth Century Congressional Careers: Ambition, Competition and Rotation. *American Journal of Political Science* 21(4): 669–93.

Kiewiet, D. Roderick, and Matthew D. McCubbins. 1991. *The Logic of Delegation*. Chicago: University of Chicago Press.

King, Gary, Robert Keohane, and Sidney Verba. 1994. *Designing Social Inquiry.* Princeton, NJ: Princeton University Press.

Kingdon, John W. 1973. *Congressmen's Voting Decisions.* New York: Harper and Row.

Knight, Jack. 1992. *Institutions and Social Conflict.* New York: Cambridge University Press.

Krehbiel, Keith. 1991. *Information and Legislative Organization.* Ann Arbor: University of Michigan Press.

Krehbiel, Keith. 1993. Where's the Party? *British Journal of Political Science* 23:235–66.

Krehbiel, Keith, and Douglas Rivers. 1988. The Analysis of Committee Power: An Application to Senate Voting on the Minimum Wage. *American Journal of Political Science* 32:1151–74.

Laitin, David. 1992. *Language Repertoires and State Construction in Africa.* New York: Cambridge University Press.

Lawson, Steven F. 1976. *Black Ballots: Voting Rights in the South, 1944–1969.* New York: Columbia University Press.

Le Breton, M. 1987. On the Core of Voting Games. *Social Choice and Welfare* 4(4): 295–305.

Loewenberg, Gerhard, and Samuel C. Patterson. 1979. *Comparing Legislatures.* Boston, MA: Little, Brown and Co.

Lowell, A. Lawrence. 1902. The Influence of Party Upon Legislation in England and America. *Annual Report of the American Historical Association for 1901.* 1:319–42.

Luce, Robert. 1922. *Legislative Procedure.* Boston, MA: Houghton Mifflin Co. (The quote that introduces part 4 is located on page 300.)

Lynn, Alvin W. 1972. *Party Formation and Operation in the House of Representatives, 1824–1837.* Ph.D. dissertation, Rutgers University.

Lyons, Francis Stewart Leland. 1977. *Charles Stewart Parnell.* New York: Oxford University Press.

Macartney, C. A. 1969. *The Habsburg Empire, 1790–1918.* New York: MacMillan Company.

MacNeil, Neil. 1963. *Forge of Democracy.* New York: David McKay Company, Inc.

Marek, George R. 1974. *The Eagles Die.* New York: Harper and Row.

Martis, Kenneth C. 1989. *The Historical Atlas of Political Parties in the United States Congress, 1789–1989.* New York: MacMillan Publishing Co.

May, Thomas Erskine. 1893. *A Treatise on the Law, Privileges, Proceedings and Usage of Parliament,* 10th ed. Ed. Reginald Palgrave and Alfred Bonham-Carter. London: William Clowes and Sons, Ltd. (The quote introducing the section on the British Parliament is taken from page 323.)

Mayhew, David R. 1974. *Congress: The Electoral Connection.* New Haven, CT: Yale University Press.

Mayhew, David R. 1991. *Divided We Govern.* New Haven, CT: Yale University Press.

McCall, Samuel W. 1914. *The Life of Thomas Brackett Reed.* Boston: Houghton Mifflin Company. (The quote from Reed occurs on page 31.)

McCormick, Richard L. 1986. *The Party Period and Public Policy.* New York: Oxford University Press.

McKelvey, Richard D. 1976. Intransitivities in Multidimensional Voting Models and Some Implications for Agenda Control. *Journal of Economic Theory* 12:472–84.

McKelvey, Richard D., 1979. General Conditions for Global Intransitivities in Formal Voting Models. *Econometrica* 47:1085–1112.

McKelvey, Richard D., and N. Schofield. 1986. Structural Instability of the Core. *Journal of Mathematical Economics* 15:179–98.

McKitrick, Eric. 1967. Party Politics and Union and Confederate War Efforts. In *The American Party Systems*, ed. William Chambers and Walter Dean Burnham. New York: Oxford University Press, 117–51.

McPherson, Edward. 1972. *Handbook of Politics*. 4 vols. New York: Da Capo Press. Reprint of 1872–94 issues.

Merton, Robert. 1957. *Social Theory and Social Structure*. Glencoe: Free Press.

Miller, William Lee. 1996. *Arguing about Slavery: The Great Battle in the United States Congress*. New York: Alfred A. Knopf.

Most, Benjamin A., and Harvey Starr. 1982. Case Selection, Conceptualization and Basic Logic in the Study of War. *American Journal of Political Science* 26:834–56.

Nichols, Roy. 1963. *Blueprints for Leviathan: American Style*. New York: Atheneum.

Niven, John. 1983. *Martin van Buren: The Romantic Age of American Politics*. New York: Oxford University Press.

Niven, John. 1988. *John C. Calhoun and the Price of Union*. Baton Rouge: Louisiana State University Press.

Nussbaum, Martha. 1986. *The Fragility of Goodness*. New York: Cambridge University Press.

Odahl, Charles Matson. 1971. *The Catilinarian Conspiracy*. New Haven, CT: College and University Press.

Olcott, Charles S. 1916. *William McKinley*. Boston: Houghton Mifflin Company.

Olson, Mancur. 1967. *The Logic of Collective Action*. New York: Schocken Books.

Oppenheimer, Bruce I. 1985. Changing Time Constraints on Congress: Historical Perspectives on the Use of Cloture. In *Congress Reconsidered*, 3rd ed., ed. Lawrence C. Dodd and Bruce I. Oppenheimer, 393–413. Washington, DC: Congressional Quarterly Press.

Ornstein, Norman J., Robert L. Peabody, and David W. Rohde. 1989. Change in the Senate: Towards the 1990s. In *Congress Reconsidered*, 4th ed., ed. Lawrence C. Dodd and Bruce I. Oppenheimer, 13–37. Washington, DC: Congressional Quarterly Press.

Pahre, Robert. 1994. Multilateral Cooperation in an Iterated Prisoners' Dilemma. *Journal of Conflict Resolution* 38(2): 326–52.

Palgrave, Reginald F. D. 1890. The Recent Crisis in Congress. *North American Review* 406:367–75.

Parnell, John Howard. 1914. *Charles Stewart Parnell: A Memoir*. New York: Henry Holt and Co.

Peters, Ronald M. 1990. *The American Speakership*. Baltimore: Johns Hopkins University Press.

Plott, Charles R. 1967. A Notion of Equilibrium and its Possibility under Majority Rule. *American Economic Review* 57(4): 787–806.

Plutarch. [1875]. *Plutarch's Lives.* Vol. IV, ed. A. H. Clough. Boston: Little Brown and Co.

Polk, James K. 1977. *The Correspondence of James K. Polk,* Vol. IV. Edited by Herbert Weaver. Nashville, TN: Vanderbilt University Press.

Polsby, Nelson. 1968. The Institutionalization of the House of Representatives. *American Political Science Review* 62:144–68.

Poole, Keith T., and Howard Rosenthal. 1991. Patterns of Congressional Voting. *American Journal of Political Science* 35(1):228–78.

Price, H. Douglas. 1971. The Congressional Career: Then and Now. In *Congressional Behavior,* ed. Nelson W. Polsby. New York: Random House.

Price, H. Douglas. 1975. Congress and the Evolution of Legislative "Professionalism." In *Congress in Change,* ed. Norman J. Ornstein, 2–23. New York: Praegar Publishers, Inc.

Proust, Marcel. 1913–1927. [1982]. *Remembrance of Things Past,* trans. C. K. Scott Moncrieff and Terence Kilmartin. New York: Vintage Books. (The quote that introduces part 3 is taken from volume 1, pages 369–70.)

Publius [Alexander Hamilton, John Jay, and James Madison]. 1787–1788. [1961]. *The Federalist Papers,* ed. Clinton Rossiter. New York: Mentor Books.

Pynchon, Thomas. 1973. *Gravity's Rainbow.* New York: Bantam Books. (The quote at the start of chapter 8 is found on page 89.)

Redlich, Josef. 1908. *The Procedure of the House of Commons: A Study of Its History and Present Form.* 3 vols. Trans. A. Ernest Steinthal. London: Constable and Co. Reprinted in 1969 by AMS Press (New York). (The quote from Sir Thomas Smith occurs in volume I, page 30.)

Reed, Thomas Brackett. 1898. *Reed's Rules: A Manual of General Parliamentary Law with Suggestions for Special Rules.* Chicago: Rand, McNally and Co.

Rice, Stuart A. 1928. *Quantitative Methods in Politics.* New York: Alfred A. Knopf.

Riker, William H. 1962. *The Theory of Political Coalitions.* New Haven, CT: Yale University Press.

Robinson, William A. 1930. *Thomas B. Reed, Parliamentarian.* New York: Dodd, Mead and Company.

Rohde, David. 1991. *Parties and Leaders in the Postreform House.* Chicago: University of Chicago Press.

Rothman, David J. 1966. *Politics and Power: The United States Senate, 1869–1901.* Cambridge, MA: Harvard University Press.

Rubinstein, Ariel. 1979. A Note about the Nowhere Denseness of Societies Having an Equilibrium under Majority Rule. *Econometrica* 47:511–14.

Rundquist, Paul S. 1990. Winning on the Left Side of the House: Minority Parliamentary Strategies in a Majoritarian Institution. Paper presented at the American Political Science Association Meetings, San Francisco, CA.

Sallust. [1921]. *Bellum Catilinae.* Trans. J. C. Rolf. Loeb Classical Library. Cambridge, MA: Harvard University Press. Rpt. 1985.

Sartori, Giovanni. 1970. Concept Misinformation in Comparative Politics. *American Political Science Review* 64:1033–53.

Schama, Simon. 1989. *Citizens: A Chronicle of the French Revolution.* New York: Alfred A. Knopf.

Schattschneider, E. E. 1942. *Party Government*. New York: Rinehart and Company, Inc.
Schofield, Norman. 1983. Generic Instability of Majority Rule. *Review of Economic Studies* 50:695–705.
Schott, Thomas E. 1988. *Alexander H. Stephens of Georgia*. Baton Rouge: Louisiana State University Press.
Scott, Joan Wallach. 1988. *Gender and the Politics of History*. New York: Columbia University Press.
Select Committee on House of Commons (Procedure). 1915. *Report from the Select Committee on House of Commons (Procedure), Together with the Proceedings of the Committee, Minutes of Evidence and Appendices*. London: Wyman and Sons, Ltd. (Ordered to be printed July 22, 1914.)
Sellers, Charles G. 1957. *James K. Polk, Jacksonian: 1795–1843*. Princeton, NJ: Princeton University Press.
Sewell, William. 1980. *Work and Revolution in France: The Language of Labor from the Old Regime to 1848*. New York: Cambridge University Press.
Sherman, John. 1968. *Recollections of Forty Years in the House, Senate and Cabinet*. New York: Greenwood Press. First published in 1895.
Shuman, Howard E. 1969. Senate Rules and the Civil Rights Bill: A Case Study. In *The Legislative Process in the U.S. Senate*, ed. Lawrence L. Pettit and Edward Keynes, 79–105. Reprinted from *American Political Science Review* (1957) 51:955–75.
Silbey, Joel H. 1967. *The Shrine of Party: Congressional Voting Behavior, 1841–1852*. Pittsburgh, PA: University of Pittsburgh Press.
Silbey, Joel H. 1977. *A Respectable Minority: The Democratic Party in the Civil War Era, 1860–1868*. New York: W. W. Norton and Co.
Sinclair, Barbara. 1989. House Majority Party Leadership in the Late 1980s. In *Congress Reconsidered*, 4th ed., ed. Lawrence C. Dodd and Bruce I. Oppenheimer, 307–29. Washington DC: CQ Press.
Sinclair, Barbara. 1993. Are Restrictive Rules Leadership Tools? House Special Rules and the Institutional Design Controversy. Paper presented at the Annual Meetings of the American Political Science Association, Washington DC. September 2–5.
Skocpol, Theda. 1979. *States and Social Revolutions*. New York: Cambridge University Press.
Skocpol, Theda. 1992. *Protecting Soldiers and Mothers*. Cambridge, MA: Harvard University Press.
Skowronek, Stephen. 1982. *Building the New American State*. New York: Cambridge University Press.
Smith, Steven S. 1989. *Call to Order*. Washington, DC: Brookings Institution.
Stealey, Orlando O. 1906. *Twenty Years in the Press Gallery*. New York: Published by the author (Publishers Printing Company, Printers).
Stewart, Charles, III. 1989. *Budget Reform Politics*. New York: Cambridge University Press.
Stinchcombe, Arthur L. 1965. Social Structure and Organizations. In *Handbook of Organizations*, ed. James March, 142–93. Chicago: Rand McNally.
Stinchcombe, Arthur. 1968. *Constructing Social Theories*. Chicago: University of Chicago Press.

Suetonius. Date Unknown [1927]. *Divvs Ivlivs by C. Svetoni Tranqvilli*, trans. and ed. H. E. Butler and M. Cary. Oxford: Clarendon.

Sullivan, Terry. 1984. *Procedural Structure*. New York: Praegar Publishers.

Sutherland, Keith Alan. 1966. *Congress and Crisis: A Study in the Legislative Process, 1860*. Ph.D. thesis, Cornell University.

Thompson, E. P. 1971. The Moral Economy of the English Crowd in the Eighteenth Century. *Past and Present* 50:76–136.

Thompson, Margaret Susan, and Joel H. Silbey. 1984. Research on Nineteenth Century Legislatures: Present Contours and Future Directions. *Legislative Studies Quarterly* 9(2): 319–50.

Tiefer, Charles. 1989. *Congressional Practice and Procedure*. New York: Greenwood Press.

Twain, Mark [Samuel Clemens]. [1898] 1963. Stirring Times in Austria. Reprinted in *The Complete Essays of Mark Twain*, ed. Charles Neider (1963). Garden City, NY: Doubleday and Co. Inc.

Uslaner, Eric. 1993. *The Decline of Comity in Congress*. Ann Arbor: University of Michigan Press.

Weingast, Barry R. 1989. Writing Scripts for the Floor: Restrictive Rules in the Post-Reform House. Working Paper in Political Science P-89-10, Domestic Studies Program, Hoover Institution, Stanford University.

Westerfield, H. Bradford. 1955. *Foreign Policy and Party Politics: Pearl Harbor to Korea*. New Haven, CT: Yale University Press.

White, H. 1980. A Heteroscedasticity-Consistent Covariance Matrix Estimator and a Direct Test for Heteroscedasticity. *Econometrica* 48:817–38.

Wilentz, Sean. 1984. *Chants Democratic*. New York: Oxford University Press.

Wilson, Woodrow. 1885 (Fifth Meridian Printing 1965). *Congressional Government*. New York: Meridian Books, Inc.

Wolfinger, Raymond E. 1971. Filibusters: Majority Rule, Presidential Leadership, and Senate Norms. In *Congressional Behavior*, ed. Nelson Polsby, 111–27. New York: Random House.

Woodward, C. Vann. 1951. *Reunion and Reaction*. Boston, MA: Little, Brown and Company.

Yeats, William Butler. 1916 [1965]. *The Autobiography of William Butler Yeats*. New York: Collier Books. (The quote in chapter 8 is on page 156.)

Young, James Sterling. 1966. *The Washington Community: 1800–1828*. Harcourt Brace Jovanovich.

Index

Printed and bound by CPI Group (UK) Ltd, Croydon, CR0 4YY

09/06/2025

14686143-0004